Truth and Truth-Making

Truth and Truth-Making

Edited by

E. J. Lowe and A. Rami

McGill-Queen's University Press
Montreal & Kingston • Ithaca

© Editorial matter and selection E. J. Lowe and A. Rami 2009.
Individual contributions, the contributors.

ISBN: 978-0-7735-3554-1 (hardcover)
ISBN: 978-0-7735-3555-8 (paperback)

Legal deposit first quarter 2009
Bibliothèque nationale du Québec

Published simultaneously outside North America by Acumen Publishing Limited

McGill-Queen's University Press acknowledges the financial support of the
Government of Canada through the Book Publishing Development Program (BPIDP)
for its activities.

Library and Archives Canada Cataloguing in Publication

     Truth and truth-making / edited by E.J. Lowe and A. Rami.

    Includes bibliographical references and index.
    ISBN 978-0-7735-3554-1 (bound).--ISBN 978-0-7735-3555-8 (pbk.)

     1. Truth. I. Lowe, E. J. (E. Jonathan) II. Rami, Adolf

BD171.T785 2009   121   C2008-907063-1

Printed and bound by Biddles Ltd., King's Lynn.

Contents

Preface   vii

Contributors   ix

1. Introduction: truth and truth-making   1
   Adolf Rami

Part I: Setting the stage

2. Truth and the truth-maker principle in 1921   39
   Kevin Mulligan

3. Truth-makers   59
   Kevin Mulligan, Peter Simons and Barry Smith

4. Truth-makers, entailment and necessity   87
   Greg Restall

5. Postscript to "Truth-makers, entailment and necessity"   98
   Greg Restall

6. Truth-making and difference-making   102
   David Lewis

7. The general theory of truth-making   115
   D. M. Armstrong

Part II: The current debate

8. Truth-making and correspondence   137
   Marian David

9. Facts and relations: the matter of ontology and of truth-making   158
    Herbert Hochberg

10. Being and truth   185
    Paul Horwich

11. An essentialist approach to truth-making   201
    E. J. Lowe

12. Are there irreducibly relational facts?   217
    Josh Parsons

13. Why truth-makers   227
    Gonzalo Rodriguez-Pereyra

14. Postscript to "Why truth-makers"   242
    Gonzalo Rodriguez-Pereyra

Bibliography   251
Index   258

Preface

In the first decades of twentieth-century philosophy *metaphysics* and *ontology* were regarded as dubious and questionable philosophical disciplines by analytic philosophers. This animosity was a consequence of the linguistic turn in philosophy at the beginning of the century and the influence of logical positivism. It also concerned the theory of truth in a substantial way. The truth-theoretic works of F. P. Ramsey and Alfred Tarski in the late 1920s and early 1930s marked the turning point to a basically linguistic way of considering the philosophical problem of truth. So-called *deflationist conceptions of truth*, which had been developed mainly under the influence of Ramsey's so-called redundancy theory of truth and Tarski's so-called semantic conception of truth, became more and more popular and dominant. Nevertheless, in the 1970s some philosophers began to cast doubt on the correctness of the linguistic turn. And at the end of the 1970s and the beginning of the 1980s metaphysical and ontological philosophical enquiries flourished again under the main influence of authors such as D. M. Armstrong, D. Lewis, M. J. Loux and P. van Inwagen. In the middle of the 1980s this metaphysical renaissance also reached the theory of truth. So-called theories of truth-making, which claim that truths have an ontological ground, attracted more and more attention. But theories of truth-making should not only interest philosophers who are concerned with the nature of truth. These theories also aim to deliver important insights concerning the relations between language, content and the world in general.

This book conveys a threefold introduction into the theory of truth-making. First, it gives an overview of the central topics and problems of the current debate concerning truth-making by means of a detailed and critical introductory essay. Secondly, it collects four of the most important classical papers in the theory of truth-making (which have not yet been collected in a single publication). Thirdly, it contains one reprinted and eight new papers written by leading researchers in the field of the theory of truth and of truth-making to provide a direct insight into the current debate concerning truth and truth-making.

It is quite common to spell the word 'truth-maker' without the hyphen. We have decided to use the spelling with the hyphen throughout the whole book and therefore to follow the European tradition of the spelling of this word that was initiated by Kevin Mulligan, Peter Simons and Barry Smith in their seminal paper "Truth-Makers".

We are grateful to the following publishers and copyright holders for permission to reproduce the following material: "Truth-Makers" by Mulligan, Simons and Smith, *Philosophy and Phenomenological Research* **44**(3) (1984), reprinted by permission of Blackwell Publishing; "Truthmakers, Entailment and Necessity" by Greg Restall, *Australasian Journal of Philosophy* **74** (1996), reprinted by permission of Taylor & Francis; "Truth Making and Difference-Making" by David Lewis, *Noûs* **35**(4) (2001), reprinted by permission of Blackwell Publishing; "The General Theory of Truthmaking", from D. M. Armstrong's *Truth and Truthmakers* (2004), reprinted by permission of Cambridge University Press; "Why Truthmakers" by Gonzalo Rodriguez-Pereyra from *Truthmakers: The Contemporary Debate*, edited by Helen Beebee and Julian Dodd (2005), reprinted by permission of Oxford University Press. Every effort has been made to contact the copyright holders of material reprinted here; however, if anyone has inadvertently been missed we will be pleased to rectify this in any future edition.

We would like to thank Tristan Palmer and Kate Williams of Acumen for their tremendous work and support.

E. J. Lowe
Adolf Rami

Contributors

D. M. Armstrong is Emeritus Professor of Philosophy at the University of Sydney. He is the author of *A Materialist Theory of the Mind* (1968), *Belief, Truth and Knowledge* (1973), *Universals and Scientific Realism* (1978), *Universals* (1989), *A Combinatorial Theory of Possibility* (1989), *What is a Law of Nature?* (1993), *A World of States of Affairs* (1997), *The Mind–Body Problem* (1999) and *Truth and Truthmakers* (2004).

Marian David is Professor of Philosophy at the University of Notre Dame, Indiana. He is the author of *Correspondence and Disquotation* (1994).

Herbert Hochberg is Professor of Philosophy at the University of Texas, Austin. He is the author of *Thought, Fact, and Reference* (1978), *Logic, Ontology and Language* (1984), *Complexes and Consciousness* (1999), *The Positivist and the Ontologist* (1999) and *Russell, Moore, and Wittgenstein* (2001).

Paul Horwich is Professor of Philosophy at New York University. He is the author of *Probability and Evidence* (1982), *Asymmetries in Time* (1987), *Truth* (1990, 2nd edn 1998), *Meaning* (1998), *From a Deflationary Point of View* (2004) and *Reflections on Meaning* (2005).

†David Lewis was Professor of Philosophy at Princeton University. He is author of *Convention* (1969), *Counterfactuals* (1973), *On the Plurality of Worlds* (1986) and *Parts of Classes* (1991).

E. J. Lowe is Professor of Philosophy at the University of Durham. He is author of *Kinds of Being* (1989), *Locke on Human Understanding* (1995), *Subjects of Experience* (1996), *The Possibility of Metaphysics* (1998), *An Introduction to the*

Philosophy of Mind (2000), *A Survey of Metaphysics* (2002), *Locke* (2005), *The Four-Category Ontology* (2006) and *Personal Agency* (2007).

Kevin Mulligan is Professor of Philosophy at the University of Geneva. He is editor of *Speech Act and Sachverhalt* (1987), *Mind, Meaning and Metaphysics* (1990) and *Language, Truth and Ontology* (1991); and he is co-editor of *Relations and Predicates* (2004).

Josh Parsons is Senior Lecturer in Philosophy at the University of Otago.

Adolf Rami is Lecturer in Philosophy at the University of Göttingen. He is the author of *Die Grenzen des Wahrheitsdeflationismus* (2009, forthcoming) and he is co-editor of *Referenz und Realität* (2007).

Greg Restall is Professor of Philosophy at the University of Melbourne. He is the author of *An Introduction to Substructural Logics* (2000) and *Logic* (2006), and he is co-author of *Logical Pluralism* (2006).

Gonzalo Rodriguez-Pereyra is Professor of Metaphysics at the University of Oxford, and Tutorial Fellow of Oriel College, Oxford. He is the author of *Resemblance Nominalism* (2002) and he is co-editor of *Real Metaphysics* (2003).

Peter Simons is Professor of Philosophy at the University of Leeds. He is the author of *Parts: A Study in Ontology* (1987) and *Philosophy and Logic in Central Europe from Bolzano to Tarski* (1992).

Barry Smith is Professor of Philosophy at the State University of New York, Buffalo. He is the author of *Austrian Philosophy: The Legacy of Franz Brentano* (1994).

CHAPTER 1

Introduction: truth and truth-making

Adolf Rami

The aim of this essay is to provide a detailed and critical overview of the main topics and problems of the current debate concerning truth-making. In §1 I give a brief outline of the history of the theory of truth-making and in §2 I identify three central goals of such a theory. In §3 I introduce the truth-maker principle and the doctrines of truth-maker maximalism and truth-maker purism. Section 4 contains a discussion and critique of several attempts to justify the truth-maker principle and §5 introduces some distinctions that concern different possible formal and ontological properties of the truth-making relation. In §6 I argue for the thesis that propositions conceived as certain kinds of abstract objects are the best candidates to fill the role of primary truth-bearers. Section 7 is about the explication of the truth-maker relation; I shall discuss and criticize a considerable number of the attempts at explication that have been made. In §8 I introduce further principles that may be combined with the truth-maker principle. It will be shown that some of these principles imply implausible consequences if they are combined with certain explications of the truth-maker principle. Section 9 is concerned with so-called supervenience principles concerning truth. I shall assess the claim that these principles are plausible replacements for the truth-maker principle. Section 10 contains four arguments against the thesis that a truth-maker theory may be conceived of as a theory of truth. It will be shown that at least two of these arguments constitute a deep challenge for a truth-maker theory of truth.

1. The history of the theory of truth-making

There is a European tradition and an Australian tradition in the theory of truth-making. The modern origins of the European tradition can be traced back to the seminal works of Ludwig Wittgenstein and Bertrand Russell on this topic. In the *Tractatus Logico-Philosophicus* (1922), Wittgenstein introduced the doctrine of logical atomism, which says that only atomic truths have truth-makers on the basis of a correspondence relation between truth-bearers and truth-makers. This doctrine marks an important difference between modern theories of truth-making and classical correspondence theories of truth. Classical correspondence theories of truth postulate for each truth a (different) corresponding truth-maker. Russell followed his former pupil and advocated his own version of logical atomism in "The Philosophy of Logical Atomism" (1918). He agreed with Wittgenstein that atomic truths have corresponding truth-makers whereas, for example, disjunctive truths do not. But unlike Wittgenstein, Russell also postulated corresponding truth-makers for general and negative truths.

Little attention was paid to logical atomism for some time after the publication of Wittgenstein's and Russell's works on this topic.[1] It was left to Kevin Mulligan, Peter Simons and Barry Smith to revive the debate concerning logical atomism and also to initiate the current debate concerning truth-making in their seminal paper "Truth-makers" (this vol., Ch. 3).

The modern Australian tradition of the theory of truth-making originates in the works of C. B. Martin and especially in his influence on his most famous pupil, D. M. Armstrong (cf. Armstrong 2004: 1), who is possibly the most important current defender of a truth-maker theory. Besides Martin and Armstrong, the Australian tradition produced a whole armada of truth-maker theorists: John Bigelow, John Fox, Frank Jackson, George Molnar and Greg Restall, to name only a few.

Current debate about theories of truth-making flourishes in Australia, Europe and the USA. The most important defenders of a theory of truth-making in Europe are E. J. Lowe, Kevin Mulligan, Peter Simons and Gonzalo Rodriguez-Pereyra. In the USA truth-maker theories are currently defended by Herbert Hochberg, Josh Parsons and Barry Smith.

2. The proposed goals of a theory of truth-making

There are at least three general goals that a truth-maker theorist typically aims to achieve. First, he may aim to vindicate the correspondence theory of truth by replacing classical versions of this theory with a more elaborate and subtle modern version of it. Classical correspondence theories presuppose a substantial external correspondence relation between truths and truth-makers. This relation is mostly conceived of as an isomorphic relation. The theory typically postulates for each truth a different truth-maker and it claims that every truth *corresponds* to a truth-maker. Modern truth-maker theorists of truth deny either some or even all of these presuppositions of a classical correspondence theory.

Secondly, truth-maker theorists may aim to use a truth-maker theory to justify a certain kind of ontology. They may use it to vindicate the postulation of certain ontological categories such as facts, states of affairs, tropes or universals. Armstrong, for example, makes use of a so-called *truth-maker argument* to argue for the recognition of states of affairs. His argument runs as follows. According to the truth-maker theory a singular predication of the logical form '*Fa*' requires a truth-maker. But neither the object *a*, nor the universal of *F*-ness, nor the sum or set consisting of these two entities can account for the truth of such a predication. Each of these four entities may exist and nevertheless '*Fa*' might be false. There is only one entity that can account for the truth of '*Fa*' according to Armstrong – namely, *a*'s being *F* – and this kind of entity is best conceived of as an obtaining state of affairs (cf. Armstrong 1997: 115–16).

Thirdly, a truth-maker theory may be used to detect so-called ontological "cheaters" (cf. Merricks 2006: 3–5). An ontological cheater typically defends a very restrictive and sparse kind of ontology. A truth-maker theorist may use the truth-maker principle to demonstrate that the cheater cannot account for certain important truths on the basis of his restrictive ontology. Martin and Armstrong, for example, made use of this strategy to argue against behaviourism and phenomenalism (cf. Armstrong 2004: 1–3).

3. The truth-maker principle: maximalism and purism

A full-blooded truth-maker theory contains as central component the following *truth-maker principle*:

(TM) For every x: x is true if and only if (iff) there is a y such that y is a truth-maker for x.[2]

Therefore, a full-blooded truth-maker theory implies the following two theses:

(MAX) For every x: if x is true, then x has a truth-maker.

(PUR) For every x: if x has a truth-maker, then x is true.

Someone who accepts (MAX) is called a *truth-maker maximalist*; someone who holds (PUR) might be called a *truth-maker purist*.

But a truth-maker theory need not contain (TM) and imply (MAX) *and* (PUR). Someone may accept (PUR), but reject (MAX); and he may therefore hold instead of (TM) any restricted version of (TM). That is, he may restrict the class of truth-bearers that require truth-makers in order to be true to a certain subclass of the class of all truth-bearers.

3

Is it also possible to reject (PUR)? There are reasons for the thesis that it is not possible for a truth-maker theorist to reject (PUR). If an entity has a truth-maker, then there is something that makes it true. So if α is a truth-maker for *T*, α *makes T* true. But then it is impossible that α makes *T* true and *T* is not true. (PUR) is an *analytic* truth concerning truth-making.[3] Someone who does not accept (PUR) does not attribute the intended content to the notion of a truth-maker. So we may claim that every truth-maker theorist is a truth-maker purist.

In this respect (TM) differs from related principles such as:

(DE) For every *x*: *x* is true iff there is a *y* such that the truth of *x* depends on *y*.

(GR) For every *x*: *x* is true iff there is a *y* such that the truth of *x* is grounded in *y*.

In the cases of (DE) and (GR) it can be reasonably denied that the conditional part from the right-hand side to the left-hand side is true. The truth of the proposition that snow is white and grass is green, for example, depends on (or is grounded in) the truth of the proposition that snow is white *and* the truth of the proposition that grass is green. This may be the case and nevertheless the proposition that snow is white and grass is green may not be true. So (DE) and (GR) may be called *siblings*, but they are at most cousins of (TM).

Our results concerning (MAX) und (PUR) can be summarized as follows. It is a minimal requirement for a truth-maker theory that it implies at least (PUR) and the following principle:

(MIN) There is at least one *x* such that *x* has a truth-maker.

On this basis a truth-maker theorist has the following options: he may choose between (MAX), (MIN) or any thesis weaker than (MAX) and stronger than (MIN) that restricts the possession of a truth-maker to a certain class of truth-bearers.

Someone who rejects (MAX) is called a *truth-maker anti-maximalist*. There are three prominent kinds of anti-maximalism that should be mentioned here: (a) logical atomism, which holds that only logically atomic sentences have truth-makers,[4] while logically complex sentences have none; (b) contingent anti-maximalism, which holds that only contingently true propositions have truth-makers, while necessary truths have none (cf. Dodd 2002: 70); and (c) synthetic anti-maximalism, which holds that only synthetically true propositions have truth-makers, while analytic truths have none.[5]

4. Motivating the truth-maker principle

(TM) (or any restricted version of it) is by no means an uncontroversial principle; so it requires justification (cf. Dodd 2002: 70–71; Beebee & Dodd 2005b: 4–5; Rodriguez-Pereyra, this vol., Ch. 13, 230; Merricks 2006: 2). There seem to be two kinds of strategy to provide such a justification. According to the first strategy, our acceptance of (TM) is justified by the explanatory resources of (TM): one can justify (TM) by pointing out the explanatory roles that (TM) can fill concerning (a) the solution of philosophical problems and (b) the vindication of certain philosophical theses. According to the second strategy our acceptance of (TM) is justified by the intuitive appeal of (TM): one can justify (TM) by pointing out that (TM) provides the best (or only adequate) explication of an important philosophical intuition (cf. Beebee & Dodd 2005b: 5).

Several attempts have been made to pursue the first strategy. It has been claimed that (TM) is required: (a) to solve the problem of universals in an adequate way; (b) to provide a more plausible and powerful alternative to W. V. Quine's famous criterion of ontological commitment; (c) to vindicate realism and reject antirealism; (d) to vindicate the correspondence theory of truth; and (e) to falsify behaviourism and phenomenalism.

But most of these attempts do not seem to be successful. If we regard the problem of universals as a serious ontological problem, we have to explain how it is possible that two different entities exemplify the same property. According to Rodriguez-Pereyra, a solution to this problem needs to invoke the existence of an entity that entails that two objects a and b are both F; and it is possible to satisfy this requirement on the basis of a certain restricted variant of (TM). Both of these claims seem to be problematic. A solution to the problem of universals seems to require more than postulating a certain entity that entails that two objects a and b are both F. If we aim to solve the problem of universals exclusively on the basis of a restricted variant of (TM) and without including further substantive principles, then we trivialize the problem. This is first because it is then a rather trivial matter to find the required entity; for example, the fact that two objects a and b are both F could fill this role. Secondly, invoking a truth-maker for a proposition is not to explain the truth of this proposition. It is therefore by no means clear that (TM) (or any variant of it) has any substantive explanatory power concerning the solution of the problem of universals (cf. MacBride 2002: 31; Beebee & Dodd 2005b: 5–6; Daly 2005: 98–102).

In fact, (TM) (or any restricted version of it) provides an *alternative* to Quine's criterion of ontological commitment. But it is by no means clear whether it is more plausible and more powerful than Quine's criterion (cf. Rodriguez-Pereyra 2002: 26–30; Beebee & Dodd 2005b: 7; Liggins 2005: 105ff.; MacBride 2005: 117–18).

If we exclusively rely on (TM) (or any restricted version of it) and do not replenish (TM) with further substantive principles, then (TM) seems neither to imply any form of realism nor to be incompatible with any form of anti-realism.

5

Any explanatory power concerning the realism/anti-realism issue seems to stem from further substantive principles that might be added to (TM), but not from (TM) itself (cf. Beebee & Dodd 2005b: 7ff.; Daly 2005: 95–8; Morris 2005: 57–60).

It is by no means clear what a correspondence theory of truth is exactly. There are conceptions of a correspondence theory of truth that are compatible with (TM) and conceptions that are incompatible with (TM). Matters do not depend only on our conception of a correspondence theory of truth, but also on certain details concerning the explication of (TM). Because of this confused situation we should not include the vindication of the correspondence theory of truth among the explanatory merits of (TM) (cf. Daly 2005: 94–7).

It is in fact true that (TM) can be used to argue against both behaviourism and phenomenalism, as Armstrong has emphasized in several of his writings (cf. Armstrong 2004: 1–3). But it is also true that it is not necessary to assume (TM) to argue effectively against behaviourism and phenomenalism. There are weaker and less controversial claims than (TM) that may also fill this role. So (TM)'s strength concerning behaviourism and phenomenalism can hardly be cited to favour (TM) over its rivals (cf. Beebee & Dodd 2005b: 15–16; Liggins 2005: 113–14).

Can we nevertheless justify (TM) because of its intuitive appeal? Is there any philosophical intuition such that (TM) can be regarded as the best explication of this intuition? The accuracy of the intuition that truth depends in some sense on reality can hardly be denied. A truth-maker theorist may in principle adopt a strategy of arguing that (TM) provides either the *best explication* or the *only adequate explication* of this plausible intuition.

Against the feasibility of the second strategy the following argument can be cited: if (TM) provides the only adequate explication of the intuition that truth depends in some sense on reality, it cannot be the case that (TM) is false while the intuition is true, but it is in fact possible that the intuition that truth depends in some sense on reality is true and (TM) is false, because there are other possible principles that might be regarded as equally plausible explanations of the intuition that truth depends in some sense on reality and these further principles are incompatible with (TM) (cf. Horwich 1998: 104–5; Künne 2003: 166). For example, any precisification of either the thesis that truth supervenes on whether things are[6] or the thesis that truth supervenes on how things are can be conceived of as a plausible explication of the intuition that truth depends in some sense on reality.[7] But both theses are incompatible with the doctrine of maximalism; namely, that *every* truth has a truth-maker.

A truth-maker theorist may respond to this kind of argument by claiming that there are restricted variants of (TM) that are perfectly compatible with the rival theses. Granted, but these variants are so restrictive that on its basis (TM) can no longer be regarded as a genuine competitor of the supervenience principles concerning an adequate explication of the intuition that truth depends on reality. (TM) is compatible with both principles only if it is restricted to the class of the positive existential propositions. But then the explanatory force of (TM) is also narrowed down to a minimum.

Rodriguez-Pereyra (this vol., Ch. 13) has tried to resist this kind of argument in another way. According to him, the intuition that truth depends in some sense on reality in fact implies the version of (TM) restricted to an important class of synthetic propositions. But his argument is not conclusive. He operates with certain variants of the intuition that truth depends on reality – namely, that truth is grounded in reality or that truth is determined by reality – and claims that it is quite obvious and undeniable that expressions such as 'depend', 'grounded' or 'determined' express relations.[8] But even if we accept this claim we do not get what he desires. Certainly, if 'depends' expresses a relation, then this relation has *relata*. And in the claim that truth depends on reality, that means that the *relata* are truths, on the one hand, and any entities, on the other. So we come to the conclusion that truths depend on entities, or on something. We can take this result for granted and nevertheless reject the thesis that those entities that truth depends on are truth-makers according to a restricted variant of (TM).[9] Even if we concede the further thesis that grounding and dependence are asymmetric relations, we can neglect (TM) or any restricted version of it. (We have already shown that there are considerable differences between (DE) and (GR) on the one hand and (TM) on the other hand. Because (PUR) is an analytic truth, (TM) is a stronger principle than (DE) or (GR). So it is impossible to justify (TM) or any restricted variant of it on the basis of (DE) or (GR) or any restricted variant of these principles.)

A further possible reaction to Rodriguez-Pereyra's argument would be to drop his assumption that it is necessary to take a sentence such as 'Truth depends in some sense on reality' at face value and interpret it as involving any kind of relation. One may claim on the contrary that truths depend on reality to the extent that something is true, because something in reality is such and such. According to this strategy the claim that truth depends in some sense on reality has a deep structure that invokes no relational expression, but only the connective 'because'. (It may be necessary to strengthen this strategy by arguing that sentences of the form 'The proposition that p is true, because p' cannot be reduced to sentences that invoke a genuine relation by means of an abstraction principle; cf. Künne 2003: 154–56, 166–7; Hornsby 2005: 34–9; Schnieder 2006b: 35–7.)

What about the best explication strategy? The prospects for this strategy seem as bad as those of the only adequate explication strategy. Compared with the supervenience principles we have mentioned, (TM) and most of its restricted variants are ontologically quite generous. They postulate many rather dubious entities to explicate an intuition. If an ontologically more parsimonious explication of the very same intuition is also possible, then it is questionable whether the thesis that (TM) provides the best explication of the intuition that truth depends on reality can be justified at all.

There is after all a problem for both strategies. The intuition that truth depends on reality is ambiguous. It has a generic and a non-generic reading. According to the generic reading it says that truth typically depends on reality: that is, certain paradigmatic truths depend on reality. According to the non-generic reading it says that all truths depend on reality. Only if we interpret it on the basis of the second reading do we have a chance to justify (TM). According to the first reading it is possible to justify only a restricted version of (TM). But it is by no means clear which reading of the intuition should be favoured and how the paradigmatic cases should be identified. So on a closer look the intuitive appeal of the claim that truth depends on reality diminishes. Justifying (TM) on the basis of an ambiguous intuition does not appear to be a good strategy.

The result of our investigations in this section can now be summarized as follows: one of the most difficult and important tasks for a truth-maker theorist is to justify (TM) in a plausible way and to give reasons for preferring it over its possible rivals.

5. Possible properties of the truth-maker relation

A truth-maker theorist may ascribe quite different formal and ontological properties to the truth-maker relation. I shall mention four such properties.

First, he may conceive of the truth-maker relation as either an internal or an external relation. There are (at least) two kinds of internal relation; we may call relations of the first kind *existential internal relations* and those of the second kind *qualitative internal relations*. A two-place relation like the truth-maker relation is either of these if it satisfies the following definitions (cf. Armstrong, this vol., Ch. 7, 119; David 2005: 144–6; Rodriguez-Pereyra 2006a: §3):

>   (EI)   For every two-place relation R: R is an existential internal relation
>   iff it is necessary that for all x and y: R obtains between x and y if x
>   exists and y exists.

>   (QI)   For every two-place relation R: R is a qualitative internal relation
>   iff it is necessary that for all x and y: R obtains between x and
> y if there are intrinsic properties u and v: x exemplifies u and y
>   exemplifies v.

The truth-maker relation is an external relation if it satisfies neither of these definitions. One guiding intuition concerning a correspondence theory of truth says that the relation that accounts for the truth of a truth-bearer is some kind of a representation relation. That is, the content of a truth-bearer, if it is in fact true, is related in a substantive way to portions of reality. According to this intuition a correspondence relation is an external relation. So a truth-maker internalist who holds that the truth-maker relation is internal should not claim to be a correspondence theorist (in the narrow sense). Most truth-maker theorists are internalists concerning the truth-maker relation.

Secondly, a truth-maker theorist may or may not take the truth-maker relation to be an isomorphic (one-to-one) relation. Someone who holds the first view can therefore be called a truth-maker isomorphist. Truth-maker anti-isomorphism typically has the form that the truth-maker relation is regarded to be a many-to-many relation. That is, different truths may have the same truth-maker and one and the same truth may have different truth-makers. Truth-maker isomorphism holds that there are no two different truths that have the same truth-maker and that no two different truth-makers make the same truth-bearer true. Truth-maker isomorphism seems to be an unwelcome position in so far as it threatens to trivialize a truth-maker theory, because it intuitively seems to be an easy and trivial matter to postulate for each truth that p an exclusive truth-maker by means of the fact that p. But the explanatory value of such a move is questionable. Therefore, most truth-maker theorists reject anti-isomorphism (cf. Armstrong 1997: 129–30; 2004: 22–5; Merricks 2006: 4).

Thirdly, the truth-maker relation may be conceived of either as a genuine relation or as a merely disjunctive relation. A so-called truth-maker universalist holds that the relation that obtains between a truth and a truth-maker is the same in all cases. According to a truth-maker disjunctivist, the truth-maker relation has to be defined not by one kind of relation, but by means of different relations that are connected to each other in some way. To my knowledge, all truth-maker theorists up to now have been truth-maker universalists, but if the truth-maker relation is some kind of internal relation, then it may be claimed that truth-maker disjunctivism is a better choice.

Lastly, one may regard the truth-maker relation as a relation that obtains between truth-bearers and truth-makers of either only one kind or various different kinds. Someone who holds the view that truth-makers are entities of only one kind may be called a truth-maker monist. We can distinguish radical forms of monism from moderate forms of monism. The most radical form of truth-maker monism claims that there is only one truth-maker of one kind for all truths. This kind of monism is a thesis that a plausible truth-maker theory should not imply, because it would trivialize the whole theory. Truth-maker anti-monism holds the view that there are truth-makers of different kinds. That is, for example, objects, facts, tropes or events can all be regarded to be truth-makers. The facts that it is most plausible to regard objects as truth-makers for at least certain existential truths and that not all truths can be made true by objects seem to favour anti-monism over any moderate monism (cf. Mulligan *et al.*, this vol., Ch. 3, §3; Armstrong 1997: 116–19; Dodd 2002: 72–3; Beebee & Dodd 2005b: 9–10; Merricks 2006: 17–22).

6. Truth-bearers and truth-makers

Among truth-maker theorists there is considerable disagreement concerning the question which kinds of entity should be accepted as truth-*makers*: some only accept states of affairs as truth-making entities;[10] some only accept individuals and states of affairs;[11] and some only accept individuals and particular properties.[12] On the other hand there is considerable agreement concerning the question which kinds of entity should be regarded as primary truth-*bearers*. Most truth-maker theorists hold that propositions are the primary truth-bearers (cf. Rodriguez-Pereyra, this vol. Ch. 13, 227; Armstrong 1997: 131; 2004: 12–16; Dodd 2002: 71; David 2005: 156–9; Lowe 2006: 177–180; Merricks 2006: 6–11).

There are many different entities that we classify as true or false, for example, thoughts, utterances, assumptions, theories, sentences, assertions and beliefs. We may call those entities to which we primarily ascribe truth in natural language 'primary truth-bearers'; but I intend to use the term for those entities that can be called true *simpliciter* and whose truth is a necessary condition of the truth of other entities. (TM) seems to be by definition a principle that quantifies over entities that can be true *simpliciter*.

Propositions are the only entities that may be conceived of as bearers of the property of truth *simpliciter*. But it is not necessary to hold the view that *every* proposition is true *simpliciter*. One may claim that some propositions are only true relative to a time, a place, a person or a standard. For example, it may be argued that the proposition that John is rich is true relative to one standard of richness and false relative to another standard. Such a conception requires a specific kind of individuation of propositions. But, in contrast to this position, we can individuate propositions in such a way that the sentence 'John is rich' expresses different propositions if it is evaluated relative to different standards. So in general, if we want to defend the claim that all propositions are true *simpliciter* we have to individuate propositions in such a way that certain sentences that are evaluated relative to different times, places, persons or standards do not express the same proposition.

There is a further important notion of relative truth that we have to take into account: world-relative truth. Some truths are only true relative to some possible worlds while others are true relative to all possible worlds. Is it possible to individuate propositions in such a way that no sentence expresses the same proposition if it is evaluated relative to different possible worlds? It is possible, but it seems to be rather counterintuitive, because if there is no proposition that can be true relative to a world w_1 and false relative to a world w_2, then we have to accept the consequence that every proposition is true or false relative to every possible world, and therefore all propositions would be necessarily true or false. There is, after all, a way to avoid this consequence. We can introduce a non-standard notion of necessary and contingent truth and falsehood; namely, a counterpart theory of necessary and contingent truth and falsehood. On this basis the necessary truth of a proposition does not depend on the truth of this proposition relative to different worlds. Rather, it depends on the fact that every counter-proposition of this proposition is true relative to every possible world. A counter-proposition p^* of a proposition p is a proposition that is not identical with p, but that is in a certain way intimately related to the proposition p. That is, the content represented by p is in a certain way partly identical with the content represented by p^*. Every counterproposition of p is in the same uniform way intimately related to the proposition p.

If someone recoils from an individuation of propositions that cannot account for the possibility that in some cases literally one and the same proposition is expressed by one and the same sentence relative to different possible worlds, there is also a further strategy that allows for the thesis that every proposition is true *simpliciter* without making use of a conception of counterpropositions. On the basis of this strategy the content of a proposition does not change from possible world to possible world. This strategy rather rejects the view that the notion of world-relative truth is treated as explanatory prior to the notion of truth *simpliciter*.

In general we can distinguish different conceptions concerning the explanatory priority of simple truth and world-relative truth. A concrete realist concerning possible worlds is forced to treat world-relative truth as explanatory prior to simple truth. Therefore, he can only accept a principle like the following (cf. Lewis 1986: 5–20):

(WR)   For every proposition x: if x is true, then there is a possible world w such that x is true relative to w.

An actual realist concerning possible worlds, on the other hand, can hold the reverse priority. He can regard simple truth to be more basic than world-relative truth if he accepts the following two principles (cf. Plantinga 1974: 46):

(AT)   For every proposition x: x is true in the actual world iff x is true.

(WT)   For every proposition x and possible world w: x is true in w iff x would have been true had w been actual.

So if we hold (AT) and (WT), every proposition can be conceived of as true *simpliciter*. Nevertheless, we can also account for the fact that every proposition can be conceived of as true relative to a possible world. Propositions can fill the role of genuine primary truth-bearers if we accept (AT) and (WT), on the one hand, and, on the other, an individuation of propositions that accounts for the fact that certain sentences express different propositions if they are evaluated relative to different times, places, persons or standards. If someone does not accept either of our two strategies concerning world-relative truth, he cannot take (TM) at face value and has to stick to a world-relative version of (TM).

11

If we introduce propositions as truth-bearers there are further properties of propositions that should be evaluated in connection with (TM). What about the existential modal status of propositions? Do propositions exist in all possible worlds? If we hold the view, as most people do, that a truth-maker necessitates the truth of a proposition, then a proposition must exist in every possible world in which its truth-maker exists. This requirement can easily be satisfied if we assume the following:

> (PN)   For every proposition x: if x exists in some possible world, then x exists in every possible world.

But (PN) can be accepted only if propositions are conceived of as purely abstract entities, that is, as simple abstract entities or complex abstract entities with only abstract constituents. But if we accept (AP), (AT) and (WT), then (TM) is a principle that concerns only truth *simpliciter* and therefore actual truths. So it is possible on this basis to restrict (PN) as follows:

> (PN*)   For every proposition x: if x exists in the actual world, then x exists in every possible world.

Although (PN*) is weaker than (PN), it forces us to treat propositions as purely abstract entities; because if we assume, for example, that propositions may have concrete constituents, then we have to assume on the basis of (PN*) that every concrete constituent of a true proposition exists in every possible world; and this is in fact not acceptable.

Alternatively, we may hold that propositions and their truth-makers always coexist:

> (PE)   For every proposition x and possible world w: x exists in w, if a truth-maker for x exists in w.

If we assume (PE), it appears to be the case that we are no longer forced to treat propositions as *purely* abstract entities; we may also treat them as abstract entities with concrete constituents. But the appearance is deceptive, because even if we accept (PE) we must concede that at least some propositions are purely abstract entities. The proposition that there is at least one cat can be true in different possible worlds because of completely different concrete entities that function as truth-makers for this proposition. So there may be no concrete entity that coexists with a true proposition in different possible worlds. Therefore we are forced to hold the view that there are at least some propositions that are purely abstract entities if we assume (PE) and that propositions are primary truth-bearers in the specified sense. Someone who wants to avoid this consequence has to reject the claim that a truth-maker necessitates the truth of a proposition. He must hold instead so-called *conditional necessitarianism*, which says that a truth-maker only then necessitates the truth of a proposition if it is necessary that if both the truth-maker and the proposition exist, then this proposition is true (cf. Merricks 2006: 7–8).

7. Explicating the truth-maker relation

There are several different ways to explicate the truth-maker relation. According to the orthodox view, truth-making can be defined as follows (cf. Restall, this vol., Ch. 4, 89; Horwich, this vol., Ch. 10, 186; Fox 1987: 189; Rodriguez-Pereyra 2006a: 186; 2006b: 959; Schnieder 2006b: 26; Caputo 2007: 278ff.):

> (TMN)   For every object x and proposition y: x is a truth-maker for y iff it is necessary that if x exists, then y is true.

On the basis of (TMN), the truth-maker relation is conceived of as an existential internal relation. The existence of a proposition and a truth-maker is sufficient for the truth of the proposition.

Quite often (TMN) is formulated in a way that makes use of semantic ascent (cf. Fox 1987: 189; Dodd 2002: 71; Beebee & Dodd 2005b: 2; Rodriguez-Pereyra 2006a: 186). According to this version, strict implication is conceived of as a relation between propositions. So if we make use of the abstraction principle:

> (ANP)   For all p and q: it is necessary that (if p then q) iff the proposition that p entails the proposition that q,

we can reformulate (TMN) as follows:

> (TME)   For every object x and proposition y: x is a truth-maker for y iff the proposition that x exists entails the proposition that y is true.

To the extent that (ANP) does not seem to be problematic, (TME) can be regarded as a purely notional variant of (TMN).

An adequate definition of the truth-maker relation must satisfy at least four conditions. It should not fall victim to any of the following problems: (i) the problem of counterintuitive truth-makers; (ii) the problem of excluded truth-makers; (iii) the problem of missing truth-makers; and (iv) the problem of unnecessary truth-makers. A definition falls victim to the first problem if it classifies as truth-makers for a certain proposition entities that are intuitively not truth-makers for this proposition. It falls victim to the second problem if it fails to classify as a truth-maker for a certain proposition an entity that intuitively is a truth-maker for this proposition. It falls victim to the third problem if it fails to account for any truth-maker for a certain proposition that intuitively has a truth-maker. Finally, it falls victim to the fourth problem if it classifies a truth-maker for a certain proposition that intuitively has no truth-maker.

Does the definition (TMN) fall victim to any of these four problems? It clearly falls victim to the first problem. First, according to (TMN), every object is a truth-maker for every necessary truth (cf. Restall, this vol., Ch. 4, 89–90; Williamson 1999: 254; Rodriguez-Pereyra 2006a: 186–7; Schnieder 2006a: 62; Caputo 2007: 279). This is a rather counterintuitive consequence. Secondly, some contingently existing entities make some contingent truths true according to (TMN), but these entities are intuitively not truth-makers for these truths. Here is a list of examples: (a) the beauty of Ann's smile makes it true that Ann smiles; (b) the singleton that Peter is a member of makes it true that Peter exists; (c) Peter's knowledge that the earth is round makes it true that the earth is round; and (d) God's willing that Peter love Ann makes it true that Peter loves Ann (cf. Smith 1999: 278; Schnieder 2006b: 62ff.; Caputo 2007: 279–80). Thirdly, if we combine (TMN) with further principles, several counterintuitive consequences concerning the truth-makers for some or all propositions can be derived.

The following principle of disjunctive distribution concerning truth-makers seems to be a rather plausible principle:

(DP)   For every x and for every P and Q: if x is a truth-maker for the proposition that P or Q, then x is a truth-maker for the proposition that P or x is a truth-maker for the proposition that Q.

But certain instances of (DP) cause trouble for (TMN). The proposition that snow is white or snow is not white is a necessary truth. As we have seen above, every entity makes a necessary truth true. According to (DP), if something is a truth-maker for the proposition that snow is white or snow is not white, then it is a truth-maker for the proposition that snow is white or it is a truth-maker for the proposition that snow is not white. Let us assume that snow is white. Then there is nothing that makes the proposition that snow is not white true. So everything makes the proposition that snow is white true. And this result can be generalized for every truth. Therefore we have the extremely implausible consequence that every truth is made true by everything (cf. Restall, this vol., Ch. 4, 90); Read 2000: 71; Rodriguez-Pereyra 2006a: 186–7).

Implausible results can also be derived from (TMN) if we combine it with Meinongianism. This doctrine says in general that there are entities that do not exist. Meinongianism also assumes that there are entities that necessarily do not exist such as the round square or a trilateral rectangle. If we add these entities to the domain of (TMN), then they make every truth true. And again, (TMN) falls victim to problem (i).[13]

What about problem (ii)? If we have the intuition – as some philosophers have – that an object can make an (inessential)[14] singular predication true, then we have reasons to claim that (TMN) falls victim to the problem of excluded truth-makers. If we assume, for example, that the proposition that this rose is red is made true by a certain red rose and nothing else, (TMN) cannot account for this fact, because the rose is not necessarily red and so there are worlds in which this rose exists, but in which the proposition that this rose is red is false (cf. Rodriguez-Pereyra, this vol., Ch. 13, 232–4; Parsons 1999: 329–30; Dodd 2002: 74). This kind of reasoning can be used to argue not only against (TMN), but also against the weaker thesis that necessitation is a necessary condition of truth-making.[15]

(TMN) falls victim to problem (iii) if it is combined with further principles. The converse Barcan formula says that for every formula φ the following schema has only true instances: $\Box \forall x \varphi \rightarrow \forall x \Box \varphi$. For example: $\Box \forall x E!x \rightarrow \forall x \Box E!x$ is a true instance of this schema. If we now assume that it is necessary that everything exists, we can derive on the basis of the converse Barcan formula that everything exists necessarily. This by itself is an extremely counterintuitive consequence.[16] But if we stick to our assumption and the converse Barcan formula, it is undeniable. And it also has the consequence that every truth-maker exists necessarily. Therefore, according to (TMN), only necessary truths can be made true by a truth-maker. So no contingent truth has a truth-maker. We have many missing truth-makers on this basis, which is an unacceptable result for a truth-maker theorist (cf. Williamson 1999: 264–5; Rodriguez-Pereyra 2006a: §2).

Problem (iv) is not a problem peculiar to (TMN), but is rather a more general problem, one that concerns truth-maker maximalism. That is, it is a problem for (TMN) if we combine it with truth-maker maximalism. There are many different propositions whose truth intuitively depends either not exclusively or not at all on the existence of an entity.

Most notoriously difficult are so-called negative propositions: basically, negative predications such as the proposition that grass is not black and negative existentials such as the proposition that there are no unicorns. Intuitively these propositions do not have truth-making entities if they are true. So it is a counterintuitive consequence if the truth-maker theorist is forced to find such truth-making entities.

Which truth-maker candidates is a truth-maker theorist able to offer to undermine our intuitions? The following candidates have been offered, none of which seems to undermine our intuitions in a reasonable way. (a) Absences or lacks are not entities we should add with seriousness to our ontology (cf. Molnar 2000: 75ff.; Dodd 2007: 387). (b) Negative facts and so-called polarities[17] cannot be regarded as a serious solution. If we postulate them to solve the problem, we are only cheating (cf. Beall 2000: 264; Priest 2000: 317ff.; Dodd 2007: 389–92). (c) So-called excluders seem to work in only some cases. The fact that grass is green, for example, is an excluder of the fact that grass is black. But not all negative propositions have excluders. The proposition that water is odourless is a negative true proposition, but there is no excluder that accounts for this truth (cf. Molnar 2000: 73–5; Dodd 2007: 387). (d) Totality states of affairs[18] are nothing but negative facts in disguise (cf. Molnar 2000: 81–2; Merricks 2006: 59–64; Dodd 2007: 387–9).

Other problematic classes of propositions include: *general propositions* such as the proposition that every table is extended; *subjunctive conditionals* such as the proposition that if I were a good tennis player I would not have studied philosophy; or any other *modal propositions* such as the proposition that it is necessary that all bachelors are unmarried. We have no clear intuitions of what a truth-maker for such propositions may look like. And so it is rather difficult for the truth-maker theorist to offer plausible truth-maker candidates in these cases (cf. Armstrong 2004: 68–111; Merricks 2006: 146–69).

There is, after all, a general solution to the problem of unnecessary truth-makers. But the costs of this solution are extremely high und unwelcome. All we need to do to justify truth-maker maximalism is to combine (TM) with two further principles. The first principle introduces the following version of truth-maker monism:

(SM)   For every x: if x is a truth-maker, then x is an obtaining state of affairs or fact.

The second principle puts forward a conception of abundant states of affairs:

(US)   For every p: the state of affairs that p obtains iff p.

On the basis of these two assumptions we can provide truth-makers for any truths and so we can vindicate maximalism. But then the truth-maker principle loses its proposed explanatory power, because it is brought down to trivialities such as the following:

(TM*)   For every p: the proposition that p is true iff there is a q such that the fact that q is a truth-maker for the proposition that p.

(TM**)   For every p: the proposition that p is true iff the fact that p is a truth-maker for the proposition that p.

These principles are trivialities in so far as the notion of a truth-maker bears no important explanatory weight: truth-makers reduce to mere shadows of true propositions (cf. Mulligan 2007: 58–63; Horwich, this vol., Ch. 10, 187–8).

It is widely held that (TMN) and (TME) are inadequate because of the vast number of objections one can cite against them. Nevertheless, most truth-maker theorists regard the necessitation of a truth by a truth-maker as a necessary condition of truth-making.[19] They therefore hold that it is a criterion of adequacy of a truth-maker theory that it implies the following principle (Bigelow 1988a:

125; Armstrong 1997: 115ff.; Smith 1999: 276; Williamson 1999: 254; Read 2000: 67; Molnar 2000: 84; Dodd 2002: 71; Beebee & Dodd 2005b: 2; Merricks 2006: 5):[20]

> (TN) For every x and y: if x is a truth-maker for y, then x necessitates the truth of y.

Apart from (TMN) and (TME), are there any plausible alternative explications of the truth-maker relation?

7.1 A first alternative to the orthodox view

Some have proposed to save (TMN) and its relative (TME) by exchanging the notion of strict entailment in (TME) for a more restrictive notion, namely relevant entailment (cf. Restall, this vol., Ch. 4, 95–6; Armstrong, this vol., Ch. 7, 121; Rodriguez-Pereyra 2006b: 969, 974–5). So the following principle is offered instead of (TME):

> (TME*) For every object x and proposition y: x is a truth-maker for y iff the proposition that x exists *relevantly* entails the proposition that y is true.

Relevant entailment is a rather technical notion, and how it has to be understood in detail depends on the logic we choose. On the one hand, there are many different logical systems that offer different notions of relevant entailment and it is (a) a difficult task to choose among them and (b) by no means clear whether there is any system that offers the results that are needed for an adequate explication of the truth-maker relation. On the other hand, (TM) is not intended to be a principle whose plausibility depends on logical issues. If (TM) is an important principle concerning truth, then it must have its importance independently of any vexed issues that concern the explication of the notion of entailment.

7.2 A second alternative to the orthodox view

What about other alternatives to (TMN)? Smith (1999: 279) has offered two explications of the truth-maker relation that are restricted variants of (TMN). The first of these variants strengthens (TMN) by exchanging the conditional with the biconditional so that we get the following:

> (TMN=) For every object x and proposition y: x is a truth-maker for y iff it is necessary that (x exists iff y is true).

How does (TMN=) improve on (TMN)? (TMN=) also falls victim to the problem of counterintuitive truth-makers, but not in such a disastrous way as (TMN) does. According to (TMN=), a necessary truth is made true by any necessarily existing object, instead of by just any object. And of the four problem cases concerning contingent truth-makers only problem (iv) pertains to (TMN=). It also has the consequence that singletons are truth-makers for existential claims such as the claim that Peter exists. Furthermore, the principle of disjunctive distribution concerning truth-makers also causes trouble. If we combine this principle with (TMN=), we can derive the result that everything is made true by every necessary existent object. Contrary to (TMN), Meinongianism is not problematic for (TMN=).

(TMN=) is also confronted with the problem of excluded truth-makers and the same problem of missing truth-makers as (TMN). Furthermore the problem of missing truth-makers can be formulated for (TMN=) without making use of any further principles. According to (TMN=), contingent *existential* generalizations have no truth-makers, because (TMN=) requires that a truth-maker for an existential claim exists in every possible world in which the existential proposition is true. But no contingent object exists relative to every possible world in which an existential proposition is true. Universal generalizations are in a similar way confronted with this problem (cf. Schnieder 2006a: 66–8; Caputo 2007: 281–2). Since (TMN=) also falls victim to the problem of unnecessary truth-makers if it is combined with maximalism, we have enough good reasons to reject (TMN=) too.

Let us now turn to Smith's second refinement of (TMN). Smith has added the further notion of the total projection of a proposition to circumvent the problem concerning existential and universal generalizations. On this basis we get the following restriction of (TMN) (cf. Smith 1999: 282; Schnieder 2006a: 64–5; Caputo 2007: 280):

(TMNS) For every object x and proposition y: x is a truth-maker for y iff it is necessary that if x exists, then y is true and x is part of the mereological sum of entities z such that it is necessary that if y is true then z exists.

But (TMNS) is no real improvement of (TMN=). (TMNS) lacks the resources to solve the problem of missing truth-makers concerning existential and general claims, because no entity that actually makes true an existential claim is part of the mereological sum of those entities that must exist if the existential claim is true. And in all other cases (TMNS) has the same problems as (TMN=).[21]

7.3 A third alternative to the orthodox view

Let us briefly discuss a further restriction of (TMN) to demonstrate that there are no good prospects to save (TMN) by means of a restriction:

(TMNK)   For every object x and proposition y: x is a truth-maker for y iff it
is necessary that if x exists, then y is true and if x did not exist then
y would not be true.

Like (TMN=), this restriction can circumvent some of the problems of (TMN). The
only improvement that (TMNK) provides for the problem of missing truth-makers
concerning existential and universal generalizations is that in the case of existential generalizations it transforms the problem into one of excluded truth-makers.
Only if there is exactly one actual object that makes an existential claim true in the
actual world can (TMNK) provide a truth-maker for the existential claim. All other
plausible truth-makers are excluded. So the prospects for a plausible restriction of
(TMN) seem to be extremely dim. The result of investigations concerning (TMN)
can therefore be formulated as follows: neither (TMN) nor any modal restriction
of (TMN) seems to provide an adequate definition of the truth-maker relation.

7.4 A fourth alternative to the orthodox view

What are the alternatives to (TMN) or any modal restriction of (TMN)? Some
truth-maker theorists have argued for the option to replace the modal notion of
strict implication by the notion of essential implication that was famously introduced by Kit Fine (1994, 1995a; cf. Lowe 1994).

Fine has noticed that although the proposition that Socrates exists is necessarily equivalent to the proposition that the singleton of Socrates exists, there is
an important difference between these two propositions. It is essentially true that
if the singleton of Socrates exists, then Socrates exists, but it is by no means essentially true that if Socrates exists, then the singleton of Socrates exists.[22] To account
for this asymmetry we need a notion that is stronger than the modal notions that
are usually used to account for essence. So Fine has postulated a new non-modal
notion of essence. Unlike the usual modal notions, this notion is object relative
and it can be expressed using the operator 'It is part of the essence of ... that ...'.
If we replace the notion of necessity in (TMN) with Fine's notion of essence, then
we have to choose between three different possible reformulations of (TMN) (cf.
Lowe 2006: 202–4; Caputo 2007: 284–5):

(TME1)   For every object x and proposition y: x is a truth-maker for y iff it
is part of the essence of x that if x exists, then y is true.

(TME2)   For every object x and proposition y: x is a truth-maker for y iff it
is part of the essence of x and y that if x exists, then y is true.

(TME3)   For every object x and proposition y: x is a truth-maker for y iff it
is part of the essence of y that if x exists, then y is true.

On the basis of a first intuitive check neither (TME1) nor (TME2) can be conceived of as plausible definitions of the truth-making relation. Both explications are disqualified right from the start because, at least for most truth-makers, it is no part of their essence that any proposition is true. Furthermore, (TME1) falls victim to a specific version of the problem of counterintuitive truth-makers. It is part of the essence of a material object that it has a colour. Therefore it is part of the essence of the state of affairs that a material object u has a colour that if it obtains then u exists. So every singular fact that says that a certain material object u has a colour becomes a truth-maker for every singular existential proposition about the material object u. But this is a rather counterintuitive result.

So only (TME3) should be considered as a possible alternative to (TMN). Does it fall victim to any of our four problems? It seems to be that (TME3) falls victim to problem (i), the problem of counterintuitive truth-makers. It is part of the essence of every essential truth that it is true. On this basis the claim that it is part of the essence of a proposition that it is true if a certain entity exists cannot be false irrespective of which entities exist. So every essential truth is made true by everything according to (TME3).[23] Furthermore, it is plausible to claim that it is part of the essence of a proposition that if it is true then its negation is not true. Therefore it would be essentially true that either a proposition or its negation is true. And if we assume that a certain proposition is true and its negation is false, and if every essential truth is made true by everything, then we can derive on the basis of (DP) that everything makes a proposition true if its negation is false. Apart from that, (TME3) can deal with all the mentioned examples of counterintuitive truth-makers concerning purely contingent truths.

(TME3) also falls victim to problem (ii), the problem of excluded truth-makers, in the same way as (TMN). But it is immune to (iii), the problem of missing truth-makers, as it was presented above. And like all conceptions we have considered up to now, it falls victim to (iv), the problem of unnecessary truth-makers, if it is combined with maximalism.

There is, finally, a more fundamental problem for (TME3). Most philosophers regard Fine's notion of essence as obscure and badly motivated. He has no formal semantics to offer for the operator 'it is part of the essence of … that …' and he gives only one intuitively reasonable example to motivate his notion. That is, someone who holds (TME3) has the obligation to clarify and justify the notion of essence in a more precise and detailed way than Fine has done.

(TMN) relies on the notion of necessity and strict implication. These notions are relatively clear and for both notions there are rich resources to provide a formal semantics. Nevertheless, an adequate explication of (TM) seems to require more, and above all a stronger notion than the familiar modal notions. Fine's notion of essence is the first alternative for a truth-maker theorist to explicate the truth-maker relation. But there are other notions that have been proposed. I want to discuss three further alternatives.

7.5 A fifth alternative to the orthodox view

Some philosophers have suggested replacing the connective '$\Box(\ldots\rightarrow\ldots)$' that represents strict implication in (TMN) by the connective 'because'. So we get the following explication instead of (TMN) (cf. Schnieder 2006b: 30; Caputo 2007: 298):

> (TMB)   For every object x and proposition y: x is a truth-maker for y iff y is true because x exists.

Intuitively (TMB) outshines any of the other approaches, because it does not fall victim to the problems of counterintuitive truth-makers, excluded truth-makers or missing truth-makers. Nevertheless, like all other approaches, (TMB) falls victim to the problem of unnecessary truth-makers if it is combined with truth-maker maximalism.[24]

But there is a more general and fundamental problem with (TMB) that concerns the connective 'because' itself. It is said that sentences of the form 'p because q' are, express or can be used to give *explanations*. And there are different kinds of explanations that can be given by means of using such sentences. The three most prominent are causal and epistemic explanations, and explanations of action. The statement that *the ship sank because it was hit by a torpedo* provides a causal explanation: the fact or event that the torpedo hit the ship caused the fact or event that the ship sank. The statement that *Peter believes that Mary loves him because Mary has kissed him intimately* provides an epistemic explanation: the fact that Mary has kissed Peter intimately is a reason for Peter to believe that Mary loves him. The statement that *Peter killed Mary because Mary was unfaithful to Peter with Paul* provides an explanation of action: the fact that Mary was unfaithful to Peter with Paul is a reason for Peter to bring it about that Mary was killed by him.

Philosophers have argued that there are even further kinds of explanations expressed by sentences of the form 'p because q'. Some hold the view that such sentences may also express conceptual explanation. The statement that *this ball is coloured because it is red* provides a conceptual explanation based on the conceptual relations that obtain between the concept COLOUR and the concept RED. Others even think that there are genuine, irreducibly metaphysical explanations. The statement that *Socrates is wise because he exemplifies the universal of wisdom* could be regarded as an example of such a metaphysical explanation.

On this basis four problems for a defender of (TMB) emerge. First, he must explain whether 'because' is an ambiguous or an indexical expression. If we compare the following possible abstraction principles concerning the four mentioned kinds of explanations, it is not at all clear which of the two options should be chosen:

> (BC)   For every p and q: p because$_c$ q iff the fact/the event that q causes the fact/the event that p.

(BJ)   For every p and q and every person x: x believes that p because$_j$ q iff the fact that q justifies x's belief that p.

(BA)   For every p and q: p because$_a$ q iff the fact that q gives an agent reasons to bring it about that p.

(BB)   For every p and q: p because$_b$ q iff the fact that q provides a conceptual explanation of the fact that p.

(BG)   For every p and q: p because$_g$ q iff the fact that p is grounded in/supervenes on the fact that q.

Secondly, he must clarify general semantic features of the connective 'because'. Only two things seem to be clear and true in general. 'Because' is a *factive connective*, because the following principle is true:

(BFA)   For every p and q: if p because q, then p and q.

And 'because' is an *irreflexive connective*; this fact can be expressed as follows:[25]

(BIR)   For every p: it is not the case that p because p.

But it is not so clear whether 'because' is an asymmetric or a non-symmetric connective and whether it is transitive or non-transitive.

Thirdly, a defender of (TMB) must explain what kind of explanation (TMB) gives. It is clear that it is not intended as causal or epistemic explanation or an explanation of action. But it is not clear at all whether it provides a conceptual or a genuine metaphysical explanation.

Fourthly, if (TMB) is supposed to provide a conceptual or a metaphysical explanation, then these notions must be clarified, because it is not clear what the exact explanatory result of such explanations is. This can be done, for example, on the basis of (BB) and (BG) and an explication of the notions contained in these principles.

7.6 A sixth alternative to the orthodox view

Other philosophers have suggested explication of the truth-maker relation by means of the notion 'is true in virtue of' so that we get the following principle instead of (TMN) (cf. Rodriguez-Pereyra, this vol., Ch. 13, 238; 2006b: 960):

(TMV)   For every object x and proposition y: x is a truth-maker for y iff y is true in virtue of x.

But it might be doubted that (TMV) provides an explication of the truth-maker relation at all. First, 'is true in virtue of' has the same logical complexity as 'is a truth-maker for'. But it is a necessary requirement of an explication that it reduces a certain notion to a more complex notion. If this is impossible, then no genuine explication of a notion can be given.[26] Secondly, 'is true in virtue of' is a mere synonym of 'is a truth-maker for' and is as much in need of explication as 'is a truth-maker for' or 'makes true' are. Thirdly, 'is true in virtue of' and 'is true because of' seem to express the same notion. And the most natural explication of 'is true because of' can be provided if we substitute 'is true because of' for 'is a truth-maker for' in (TMB), which turns (TMV) into (TMB).[27] So (TMV) neither is a plausible alternative to (TMB) nor can be regarded as an *explication* of truth-maker relation at all.[28]

7.7 A seventh alternative to the orthodox view

The last proposal of an explication of the truth-maker relation I want to discuss makes use of the notion of intrinsicality and it can be formulated as follows:

(TMI)   For every object x and every p: x is a truth-maker for the proposition that p iff x is intrinsically such that p.[29]

The property of being such that something is red is an extrinsic property. But a red rose has this property intrinsically, because it is itself red, while a blue car has this property extrinsically, because it is not itself red. In this sense a red rose is a truth-maker for the proposition that something is red, while a blue car is no truth-maker for this proposition. And in the same sense Socrates is the truth-maker for the proposition that Socrates is wise. Such examples motivate the basic idea behind (TMI). And the account seems to work for most atomic and existential propositions. But it might be doubted that it works for more complex propositions. There seems to be no entity that is intrinsically such that if Peter is tired, then he goes to bed. And there seems to be no entity that is intrinsically such that Peter is tired and Mary is lucky. There are also atomic propositions, such as the proposition that it is raining, that seem to cause trouble, because there seems to be no entity that is intrinsically such that it is raining. Therefore it might be questioned whether (TMI) is a plausible explication of the truth-maker relation.

There is one further problem. (TMI) cannot be formulated using exclusively nominal variables. The most natural variant of (TMI) that employs only nominal variables is:

(TMI*)   For every object x and proposition y: x is a truth-maker for y iff x is intrinsically such that y is true.

23

But on this basis the account does not work at all, because it implies that only a proposition can be intrinsically such that a certain proposition is true and so every proposition would be a truth-maker for itself. For someone who does not accept sentential quantification this might be a decisive objection.

Our investigations in this section have shown that the explication of the truth-maker relation is presumably the most difficult task for a truth-maker theory. In addition to the orthodox account (TMN), we have discussed several alternative accounts. All of these accounts can be confronted with several problems and are therefore in need of further justification.

8. Further important principles concerning truth-making

At least some truth-makers are entities that have parts. There are truth-makers of propositions whose parts make the very same proposition true. For example the mereological sum of all pigs on earth makes the proposition that there are pigs on earth true and so does every single pig on earth. But no proper part of a pig makes this proposition true. So some truth-maker theorists have introduced the notion of a minimal truth-maker that can be defined as follows (cf. Horwich, this vol., Ch. 10, 187; Armstrong, this vol., Ch. 7, 128–9; Rodriguez-Pereyra 2006b: 978–9):

> (MT) For every x and y: x is a minimal truth-maker for y iff x is a truth-maker for y and there is no z: z is a proper part of x and z is a truth-maker for y.

On this basis the following questions deserve to be considered: (i) does every truth have a minimal truth-maker; (ii) are there any reasons why we should claim that only minimal truth-makers are genuine truth-makers? There are certain propositions that seem to have no minimal truth-maker, for example, the proposition that there are infinitely many natural numbers. This proposition is made true by the mereological sum of all natural numbers, but it is also made true by the mereological sum of every second or every third natural number. All these are infinite sums and there are infinitely many infinite sums that the sum of all natural numbers contains. So there is no minimal truth-maker for the proposition (see Armstrong, this vol., Ch. 7, 130). And we can provide only a minimal truth-maker for this proposition if we assume an abundant conception of states of affairs. But as we saw in the previous section, such an account undercuts the explanatory power of (TM). However, it seems to be the case that only propositions that contain the notion of infinity lack minimal truth-makers. So the claim that every truth has a minimal truth-maker is not generally true, but it is true for most kinds of (true) propositions.

24

If it is true – as we have shown – that some truths do not have minimal truth-makers, then we cannot hold the view that all truth-makers are minimal truth-makers without excluding some truths from truth-making. Truths that lack minimal truth-makeres are not just necessary truths. There are also contingent truths of this sort, for example the truth that there are infinitely many electrons. So a restriction of the truth-maker principle to exclude truths without minimal truth-makers seems to be rather *ad hoc* and unsystematic. Therefore it is not a good strategy to restrict the class of truth-makers to the class of minimal truth-makers.

But there might nevertheless be reasons to restrict the class of (non-minimal) truth-makers to a certain degree. It has been argued that the following intuitively plausible and widely accepted principle of conjunctive distribution multiplies (non-minimal) truth-makers beyond plausibility (cf. Mulligan *et al.*, this vol., Ch. 3, 80; Restall, this vol., Ch. 4, 89, 95; Read 2000: 71; Rodriguez-Pereyra 2006b: 970):

(CP)   For every x and for every P and Q: if x is a truth-maker for the proposition that P and Q, then x is a truth-maker for the proposition that P and x is a truth-maker for the proposition that Q.

Intuitively, the fact that snow is white and grass is green (or the mereological sum of the fact the snow is white and the fact that grass is green) seems to be a plausible truth-maker for the proposition that snow is white and grass is green. If we apply (CP), we can derive the consequence that the fact that snow is white and grass is green (or the mereological sum of the fact the snow is white and the fact that grass is green) is a truth-maker for the proposition that grass is green and the proposition that snow is white. For someone who accepts (TM) on the basis of (TMN), these results seem to be rather unproblematic. But if we accept a more restrictive explication of the truth-maker relation, things are quite different. If we accept (TMB), we can argue as follows. The proposition that snow is white is true because snow is white or because the fact that snow is white obtains, but it is not true because snow is white and grass is green or because the fact that snow is white and grass is green obtains. So, given (TMB), (CP) seems to produce implausible (non-minimal) truth-makers. Nearly the same kind of reasoning can be put forward on the basis of (TMNK) or (TME3). Therefore there are interpretations of (TM) that are in conflict with (CP) in the sense that they produce counterintuitive (non-minimal) truth-makers when combined with (CP) (cf. Rodriguez-Pereyra 2006b: 970–73).

A further useful principle in connection with truth-making seems to be the so-called *entailment principle*, which can be stated as follows (cf. Mulligan *et al.*, this vol., Ch. 3, 80); Restall, this vol., Ch. 4, 91; Armstrong, this vol., Ch. 7, 120–21, 127); 1997: 130; Rodriguez-Pereyra 2006b: 962):

(EP)   For every x, y and z: if x is a truth-maker for y and y entails z, then x is a truth-maker for z.

This principle seems to be useful because it helps in finding truth-makers for several kinds of truths (cf. Armstrong 2004: 55, 84, 98). But this principle is not only problematic when it is combined with (TMN), but also causes trouble for any theory of truth-making when it is combined with further plausible principles.

There are two different routes to demonstrate that (EP) leads to trouble. Both routes require two further principles to derive implausible consequences from (EP). The first principle that is required in both cases is a widely accepted claim about the truth-makers of identity propositions expressed by sentences of the form '$a = a$'. This principle can be stated in the following way (cf. Simons 1992: 162ff.; Armstrong 2004: 39; Rodriguez-Pereyra 2006b: 964):

(IP)   For every object x: x is a truth-maker for the proposition that $x = x$ and there is no object y such that x is not identical with y and y is a truth-maker for the proposition that $x = x$.

If we now add one of two possible principles to (EP) and (IP), we can derive unacceptable consequences on the basis of these assumptions. The first says that there is at least one necessarily existing object. Let us assume for the sake of argument that the number zero exists in every possible world. According to (IP), the number zero is the only object that makes the claim true that zero is identical with zero. This claim is a necessary truth, because zero exists in every possible world. Now let us assume that the proposition that Peter exists is made true by Peter. The proposition that Peter exists implies the proposition that zero is identical with zero, because the latter is a necessary truth. So according to (EP), Peter is a truth-maker for the proposition that zero is identical with zero. This is by itself a rather implausible consequence, but since (IP) says that there is no object that is not identical with zero that is a truth-maker for the proposition, we have to accept on the basis of (IP) that Peter is identical with zero. But that is not all: we have to accept for any truth-maker for any proposition that it is identical with zero on the present assumptions. And this is in fact a highly implausible consequence. It forces us to consider whether (EP) or (IP) or the existential assumption is false (cf. Rodriguez-Pereyra 2006b: 964–5).

That the argument does not depend on the claim that there are necessarily existing objects can be shown by a modified version of it. Even if we reject that claim, we can derive implausible consequences from (EP) and (IP) if we combine them with an already familiar principle; namely, the principle of disjunctive distribution (DP).

Let us again assume that Peter makes the proposition that Peter exists true. The proposition that Vienna is identical with Vienna or it is not the case that Vienna is identical with Vienna is a logical truth and therefore also necessarily true. The proposition that Peter exists implies the latter proposition. And so on the basis of (EP) we have to accept that Peter is a truth-maker for that logical truth. It is an empirical fact that Vienna exists. So the proposition that Vienna is identical with Vienna is true. And because Peter is a truth-maker for the logical disjunction, he is, according to (DP), also a truth-maker for the proposition that Vienna is identical with Vienna. But (IP) says that that there is no object not identical with Vienna that is a truth-maker for the proposition that Vienna is identical with Vienna, and so we have to accept that Peter is identical with Vienna. But that is not all: if we generalize this result, we reach the conclusion that there is one and only one truth-maker for every truth. This result is not acceptable for a truth-maker theorist. Hence he has to consider whether (EP), (IP) or (DP) is false (cf. Rodriguez-Pereyra 2006b: 963–4).

There is a possible and plausible response the truth-maker theorist might make against both arguments. He may insist on intuitive grounds that neither Peter nor Vienna is identical with the number zero. These intuitive facts falsify (IP) on the basis of the given evidence. So it seems that we need only to reject (IP) to save (EP) and (CP).

But even if we reject (IP), there are reasons to doubt (EP), because (EP) confronts any theory of truth-making with the problem of counterintuitive truth-makers. According to (EP), every necessary truth is made true by every entity. And if we combine (EP) with (CP), we can derive the even more problematic conclusion that every entity is a truth-maker for every truth. So there are reasons to question (EP) independently from (IP). A truth-maker theorist, therefore, must either reject (EP) or restrict it to *purely* contingently true propositions.[30]

So far our investigations have shown that a truth-maker theorist has to (a) give a plausible justification for (TM) and (b) provide an adequate explication of the truth-maker relation; in addition he is forced to (c) give serious thought to the question which further principles he advances beside (TM).

9. Truth supervenes on being

If we accept (TM) without any restriction, we are committed to truth-maker maximalism. But we have seen that truth-maker maximalism confronts any explication of the truth-maker relation with the problem of unnecessary truth-makers. To avoid this problem, one may either restrict (TM) to a certain class of propositions or one may reject (TM) and replace it with an alternative principle that also captures the intuition that truth depends in some sense on reality.

If one chooses the first option, there seem to be different possible kinds of restriction. As a first possibility one could restrict (TM) to the class of contingently true propositions. In this case a truth-maker theorist no longer needs to provide truth-makers for modal truths; but the most problematic class of truths still remains on the agenda, namely true negative propositions. So one may try to restrict (TM) to the class of positive contingently true propositions. The problem with this strategy is that it seems to be impossible to distinguish positive from negative propositions in general (cf. Molnar 2000: 72–3). Someone who wants to establish a truth-maker theory for a formal language may restrict (TM) to the class of atomic truths, treating negative truths as not atomic. But as far as natural language is concerned, drawing a distinction between atomic and non-atomic propositions seems to be as problematic as drawing a distinction between positive and negative propositions. One could, for example, restrict (TM) to the class of positive existential propositions, because it seems undeniable that the existence of Peter is a necessary and sufficient condition for the truth of the proposition that Peter exists and that the existence of a cow is a necessary and sufficient condition for the truth of the proposition that at least one cow exists (cf. Dodd 2007: 384). But with such a radical restriction of (TM) its explanatory resources shrink to a minimum.

So the truth-maker theorist seems to face a dilemma: because of the problem of unnecessary truth-makers he is forced to restrict (TM) in some way, but there seems to be no plausible restriction that (a) circumvents the problem of unnecessary truth-makers and (b) preserves the explanatory power of (TM).

Philosophers who see no possible way to escape this dilemma have proposed to reject (TM) completely. Some have offered an alternative way to spell out the intuition that truth depends in some sense on reality. A well-known alternative employs the slogan that *truth supervenes on being*. Bigelow (1988a: 133, 135) has famously offered the following explication of this slogan (cf. Rodriguez-Pereyra, this vol., Ch. 13, 228; Dodd 2002: 73; Beebee & Dodd 2005b: 4):

(TS) For every proposition x: if x is true, then either at least one entity y exists that would not exist if x were not true or at least one entity y does not exist that would exist if x were not true.

A concrete realist about possible worlds or someone who believes in quantification over possible objects is in the position to provide the following alternative formulation of (TS) (Lewis, this vol., Ch. 6, 110; MacBride 2005: 121; Hofmann 2006: 412):

(WS) For every proposition x and every possible world w: if x is true in w, then there is a world v: x is not true in v and either something that exists in w does not exist in v or something that exists in v does not exist in w.

In both versions the supervenience principle is applicable only to contingently true propositions, hence it is more restrictive than the unrestricted (TM). But the most important advantage of (TS) and (WS) over any variant of (TM) is that they can be applied to positive and negative contingent truths without postulating any entities that are responsible for the truth of negative truths. Because of this advantage Bigelow favours (TS) and David Lewis favours (WS) over any variant of (TM).

Although (TS) and (WS) have some advantages when compared with (TM), these principles themselves face certain problems. First, (TS) and (WS) seem to offer only a necessary condition for the truth of contingent propositions, while (TM) in its restricted or unrestricted version pretends to offer necessary and sufficient conditions for truth. Is it possible to conceive of (TS) and (WS) in such a way that these principles provide necessary and sufficient conditions for contingent truths? If we grant the existence of states of affairs (or similar entities), then it seems to be the case that (TS) and (WS) can provide necessary and sufficient conditions for the truth of most contingent propositions. But there is one important exception. General states of affairs are dubious entities, and if we avoid postulating general states of affairs, then it seems to be difficult to find entities whose existence accounts for the truth of certain general propositions, such as the proposition that all electrons have a charge, on the basis of (TS) and (WS). So in the case of a certain class of (general) propositions, (TS) and (TM) seem no less problematic than (TM).

Secondly, according to (TS) and (WS) the relation of supervenience between truths and beings is a symmetric relation, but truths depend in an asymmetric way on reality: the proposition that snow is white is true because snow is white, but it is not the case that snow is white because the proposition that snow is white is true (cf. Rodriguez-Pereyra, this vol., Ch. 13, 229); Beebee & Dodd 2005b: 4; Dodd 2007: 394–5).

(TS) and (WS) are symmetric supervenience principles, but supervenience between truths and beings need not be interpreted in a symmetric way. We may, for example, make use of Fine's notion of essence to strengthen (TS) in such a way that supervenience between truth and beings is no more symmetric:

> (TS*)   For every proposition x: if x is true, then either (at least one entity y exists and it is part of the essence of x that y would not exist if x were not true) or (at least one entity y does not exist and it is part of the essence of x that y would exist if x were not true).

Such a move surely imports certain problems with the notion of essence that we have already mentioned. But it nevertheless shows that a defender of the claim that truth supervenes on being has options to react to the asymmetry objection.

Thirdly, some philosophers have argued that the thesis that truth supervenes on being is an incorrect interpretation of the undeniable Moorean fact that if a proposition is true in one world and not true in another world, then there must be some difference between these two worlds. A defender of the slogan that truth supervenes on being misinterprets this fact in so far as he claims that the difference between worlds must be a difference in being (cf. Bigelow 1988a: 126). But a difference between worlds need not be grounded in a difference in being; it needs only to be grounded in a difference in how things are. Therefore we should not hold the thesis that truth supervenes on whether things are, but rather the thesis that truth supervenes on how things are (cf. Lewis, this vol., Ch. 6, 110–12; Dodd 2002: 74ff., 78–81). And so Lewis (this vol., Ch. 6, 112), for example, has argued for replacing (WS) with the following principle (cf. MacBride 2005: 123; Hofmann 2006: 413ff.):

(WS+) For every proposition x and every possible world w: if x is true in w then there is a world v: x is not true in v and either something that exists in w does not exist in v or something that exists in v does not exist in w or either some n-tuple of things stands in some fundamental relation in w and not in v or some n-tuple of things stands in some fundamental relation in v and not in w.

This objection depends heavily on certain fundamental metaphysical assumptions. It will convince only someone who denies in principle the existence of entities such as states of affairs, or someone who grants the existence of such entities but denies their fundamental ontological status and therefore rejects the thesis that a world is the totality of certain states of affairs. So for someone like Lewis, who rejects states of affairs and any entities that offend against Hume's metaphysical principle that there are no necessary connections between different individuals and holds that a world is the totality of certain individuals, this objection is forceful, but for many others it may not be at all.

10. Truth and truth-making

(TM) undoubtedly makes use of the notion of truth. Let us now assess whether it is possible to interpret a theory of truth-making as a theory of truth. A theory of truth can be conceived of as an analysis of the concept of truth, or as an analysis of the property of truth, or as both. Which of these three options one chooses depends on two assumptions: (a) whether one makes a fundamental difference between properties and concepts; and (b) which explanatory goals one thinks should be satisfied by a theory of truth.

It is not required that one specifies the ontological kind or nature of concepts and properties to draw a distinction between them. For this purpose one needs only to provide different conditions of identity. A quite natural way to do this is to individuate concepts by means of the notion of cognitive equivalence and properties by means of the notion of necessary equivalence:

(IOC)   For every concept x and y: x is identical with y iff it is necessarily true that for every person p and every object z: p believes of z that it falls under x iff p believes of z that it falls under y.

(IOP)   For every property x and y: x is identical with y iff it is necessarily true that for every object z: z exemplifies x iff z exemplifies y.

According to the orthodox view, an analysis of the concept of truth has to provide a principle that specifies necessary and sufficient conditions for the application of the concept of truth. Such a principle must have the general form: 'For every proposition x: x is true iff … x …'. One adequacy condition such a principle must satisfy is that the predicative expression on the right-hand side of the biconditional expresses the same concept as 'is true'. If we assume (IOC), conceptual identity is constituted by cognitive equivalence. But an analysis of the concept of truth should explicate not only the application conditions of the concept of truth, but also the possession conditions of the concept of truth. If we presuppose the orthodox view concerning the application conditions that says, for example, that for every proposition x: x is true iff x is F, then the orthodox view concerning the possession conditions says that someone possesses the concept of truth iff he knows that for every proposition x: x is true iff x is F. The orthodox view concerning the analysis of the concept of truth is in many ways problematic and has been rejected by many current researchers (cf. Alston 1996; Horwich 1998; Hill 2002). Nevertheless, a theory of truth-making can only be interpreted as a theory of the concept of truth if we presuppose the orthodox view concerning the analysis of the concept.

The orthodox view concerning an analysis of the *property* of truth is in many respects similar to the orthodox view concerning the concept. According to this view, an analysis must provide necessary and sufficient conditions for the application of the property. As with the concept, this should be done by formulating a principle of the general form 'For every proposition x: x is true iff … x …'. Such a biconditional is said to be adequate only if the predicative expression on the right-hand side expresses the same property as 'is true'. The first difference between the orthodox views concerning concepts and properties becomes obvious if we presuppose (IOC) and (IOP), because then a principle that specifies application conditions of the property of truth must have a different logical strength from a principle that specifies the conditions of application of the concept. The second difference concerns an important explanatory difference between concepts and properties. Concepts have a cognitive dimension that properties do not have. Concepts can be mastered or possessed while properties lack such a cognitive status and can only be recognized indirectly by the mastery of the corresponding concepts. Therefore, unlike an analysis of the concept of truth, an analysis of the property of truth is not required to deliver any possession conditions. If we presuppose the orthodox view, the explication of the application conditions seems to exhaust the analysis of the property of truth.

31

On the basis of these preparatory remarks we can now set about answering the key question of this section: can a theory of truth-making be interpreted as an analysis of the concept or of the property of truth? There are three objections to be found in the literature that cast doubt on a positive answer to this question.

The first objection may be called the *circularity objection*. If we combine (TM) with (TMN), then we can formulate a principle that contains the truth-predicate on the left-hand side and the right-hand side of the biconditional. But then the notion of truth is partly explained by the notion of truth itself; hence the principle provides a viciously circular analysis of truth. We get the same result if we combine (TM) with nearly any other explication of the truth-maker relation we have discussed. The only exception is (TMI). Moreover, it is not necessary to combine (TM) with a fully fledged explication of the truth-maker relation; it is enough to combine it with (TN) to reach the same result. So it seems that (TM) cannot be conceived of as a principle that provides an analysis of truth, because of circularity (cf. Merricks 2006: 15).[31]

The second objection might be called the *vacuity objection*. It says that if we, for example, combine (TM) with (TMN), we get a principle from which we can eliminate the truth-predicate entirely if we make use of sentential quantification. This leads, in case of (TM) and (TMN), to the following principle:

(TMP) For every p: p iff there is a y and it is necessary that if y exists then p.

This principle, the objectors claim, has the same content as the combination of (TM) with (TMN). But (TMP) does not contain the notion of truth. Therefore we have to conclude that (TM), if it is combined with (TMN), is not a principle that concerns the notion of truth in any substantial way. So it could not be interpreted as a principle that provides an analysis of truth in any sense. The same result can be derived if we combine (TM) with most of the discussed explications of the truth-maker relation. There is only one important exception: because of the specific semantics of the essence-operator we cannot eliminate the notion of truth in the same way from (TME3) (cf. Horwich, this vol., Ch. 10, 188–9, 199; Lewis 2001: 278–9; Fox 1987: 189; Bigelow 1988a: 127; Künne 2003: 164; Smith & Simon 2007: 80).

Let us call the third objection the *generality objection*. It says that (TM) can be conceived of as a principle providing an analysis of truth in some sense only if it is combined with maximalism. But we have seen that maximalism is an extremely implausible view because of the problem of unnecessary truth-makers. So it is highly questionable whether (TM) can be conceived of as a central ingredient of a theory of truth. If we reject maximalism, we need to combine (TM) with further principles, which commits us to the view that truth has a disjunctive nature. But this consequence is not really problematic (cf. Smith & Simon 2007: 82). According to the moderate deflationist, for example, truth is an infinitely disjunctive property (cf. Horwich 1998: 143). So if a truth-maker theory could justify the view that truth need be conceived of not as an infinitely disjunctive property, but rather as a much less disjunctive and finite property, then the theory would be preferable to the deflationist theory from an ideological point of view. But the really problematic aspect of such a theory concerns the restriction of (TM). As we have seen, it is an extremely difficult task to restrict (TM) to a class of propositions in a reasonable way. So even if we reject maximalism, it is questionable how we should integrate (TM) into a theory of truth.

Could one react to these objections on the basis of the distinctions we have made concerning the analysis of truth? Let us start with the circularity objection. A circular principle seems to be in any case inadequate for explicating our understanding of the concept of truth on its basis. The property of truth is a very specific kind of extrinsic property. And if it is a relational property, its relationality is based on a very specific internal relation. So it might be necessary to make use of the truth-predicate to specify the application conditions of the concept and the property of truth if we presuppose the orthodox view. Circularity might be inevitable. In this way it could be argued that (TM) might nevertheless be regarded as a principle that offers an analysis of the property of truth.

The vacuity objection is not directed against maximalism. So let us for the sake of argument assume that maximalism is true. If maximalism is true, sentences of the form 'The proposition that p is true' are cognitively equivalent to sentences of the form 'There is something and it is necessary that if it exists then the proposition that p is true'. So in principle it would be possible that the combination of (TM) and (TMN) functions as an explication of the application conditions of the concept of truth. If (TMP) has the same content as the combination of (TM) with (TMP), then these two principles must be cognitively equivalent. These two principles are only cognitively equivalent if sentences of the form 'p' are cognitively equivalent to sentences of the form 'The proposition that p is true'. Someone who does not believe in the existence of propositions might believe that grass is green, but not that the proposition that grass is green is true. So sentences of the form 'p' and 'The proposition that p is true' are not cognitively equivalent. Moreover, someone may accept that killing is wrong, but he may hold the view that moral propositions do not have truth-values. In this case he would not accept that the proposition that killing is wrong is true. So we have again reasons to believe that cognitive equivalence does not hold in general between sentences of the form 'p' and 'The proposition that p is true'. So it might be doubted that (TMP) and the combination of (TM) and (TMN) are cognitively equivalent. What is beyond doubt is that these two principles are necessarily equivalent. But if they are only necessarily equivalent and if we assume (IOC), (IOP) and maximalism, then the combination of (TM) and (TMN) can be conceived of as an explication of the application conditions of the concept of truth independently of the fact that (TMP) is not concerned with the concept of truth at all. So there is a possibility to deflect the vacuity objection.

There is nevertheless a more powerful fourth objection that disqualifies (TM) even if we grant maximalism. Let us call this objection *the objection from explanatory order*. The proposition that grass is green, for example, is true, because grass is green. This kind of explanation works for nearly any proposition. According to (TM), it must also be the case that the proposition that grass is green is true, because it has a truth-maker. If we again grant that maximalism is true, then the truth-maker explanation must also hold generally. But now the question arises: which kind of explanation is the more fundamental one?[32] Or in other words: is grass green, because the proposition that grass is green has a truth-maker, or does the proposition that grass is green have a truth-maker, because grass is green? It is indisputable that only the latter is true. So we have reasons to reject the thesis that (TM) combined with any explication of the truth-maker relation is a correct explication of the application conditions of either the concept or the property of truth. This kind of objection seems to hold independently of whether or how we distinguish between the concept and the property of truth. And the same holds in the case of the generality objection. So there seem to be sufficient reasons to conclude that a truth-maker theory should not be conceived of as a theory of truth. That is, if the truth-maker principle has any explanatory force at all, it has nothing to do with the analysis of the nature of truth.[33]

11. Conclusion: open questions

Our investigations have shown that a truth-maker theorist has to meet at least the following five challenges. He has to (i) give a plausible justification for (TM) or at least a restricted variant of it, and (ii) provide an adequate explication of the truth-maker relation. In addition he is forced to (iii) give serious thought to the question which further principles concerning truth-making he advances beside (TM). He has to (iv) show why (TM) or at least a restricted variant of (TM) is superior to any of the supervenience principles concerning truth we have seen; and finally he is forced to (v) provide good reasons why we should accept (TM) (or a restricted variant of (TM)) although a theory of truth-making cannot be conceived of as a theory of truth. These five challenges represent open questions to a truth-maker theorist in the current debate. Several attempts are made in this volume to answer some of these open questions.

Notes

1. Exceptions who independently introduced theories of truth-making are Husserl (1900/01), Stout (1911) and Pfänder (1921).

2. Alternatively, (TM) can be formulated as follows: For every x: x is true if and only if there is a y such that y makes x true.

3. This was pointed out to me by Marian David.

4. Wittgenstein and Russell are the pioneers of logical atomism. But neither of them defended logical atomism in its pure form. In Russell (1918) the view is held that beside atomic truths, also general and negative truths have truth-makers. The conception in Wittgenstein's *Tractatus Logico-Philosophicus* (1922) may be characterized as follows: every truth has a truth-maker, but only atomic truths *correspond* with their truth-makers. Cf. Simons (1992).

5. In Rodriguez-Pereyra, this volume, Ch. 13, 228), the view is held that only *certain* synthetic truths, including inessential predications, have truth-makers.

6. The pioneer of this rather specific notion of *supervenience* concerning truth is John Bigelow. Cf. Bigelow (1988a).

7. One may argue against these alternative strategies by claiming that they interpret the mentioned intuition in an incorrect way, because dependence is asymmetric while supervenience is not. Orthodox approaches of supervenience may have this consequence, but there is no reason why supervenience has to be explicated in a symmetric way.

8. This is in an abundant sense of relation, according to David Lewis's distinction between sparse and abundant properties and relations.

9. One could argue that my argument works only if I make use of the dependence reading. If I claim that truth is *determined by* something, the existence of any object that may fill this role must provide a necessary and sufficient condition for truth. Nevertheless, we need not regard the mentioned objects as truth-makers. If I say that the truth of '$p \wedge q$' is determined by the truth of 'p' and the truth of 'q', do I really have to say that the sum of these two truths is a truth-maker for '$p \wedge q$'? I doubt it.

10. If we accept obtaining states of affairs (or facts) as entities, then these entities seem to be the most natural candidates for filling the role of truth-makers. The view that *only* states of affairs are truth-makers seems plausible then only if we conceive of states of affairs as entities that are different from propositions, but nevertheless closely related to propositions. Cf. Mulligan (2007: 51–7).

11. Someone who accepts obtaining states of affairs as entities and as truth-makers may nevertheless reject the thesis that every truth-maker is an obtaining state of affairs. D. M. Armstrong, for example, holds that an obtaining state of affairs is the instantiation of a monadic or non-monadic universal by individuals. On this basis only those propositions that are at least partly *about* universals have states of affairs as truth-makers. Existence, for example, is no universal; therefore existential propositions do not have states of affairs as truth-makers; their truth-makers are individuals. Cf. Armstrong (1997: 113–26).

12. It seems to be possible to identify true propositions and obtaining states of affairs. On this basis, obtaining states of affairs can no longer be truth-makers. But there are other entities that may fill the role of truth-makers instead; for example, particular properties (= tropes or moments). Cf. Mulligan *et al.* this vol., Ch. 3, 61–2, 65–71.

13. The truth-maker theorist is free to reject Meinongianism as a response to this argument.

14. (TMN) can account for the fact that objects are truth-makers for essential predications.

15. Another example to illustrate Parsons's point would be the following: intuitively the proposition that the second Beatle exists is made true by Paul McCartney, but the existence of Paul McCartney does not necessitate the truth of this proposition.

16. So there are good reasons for the truth-maker theorist to reject the converse Barcan formula. The converse Barcan formula fails, for example, in Kripke's famous system of modal logic.

17. Polarities are formal entities that account for the positive or negative status of facts and they may be represented by the signs '+' and '–'. If we conceive facts as ordered n-tuples of properties, relations and individuals, then <the property of redness, Peter's ball, +>, for example represents the positive fact that Peter's ball is red, while <the property of redness, Peter's ball, –> represents the negative fact that Peter's ball is not red.

18. According to Armstrong, for example, the totality state of affairs that the actual sum of animals is the totality of animals is a truth-maker for the proposition that there are no unicorns. A sum of entities of a certain kind K is only then the totality of entities of kind K if there is no entity that is an entity of K and is not part of the sum of entities of kind K. Cf. Armstrong (2004: 75–6).

19. An important exception is Parsons (1999); cf. Merricks (2006: 5).

20. Even if someone holds (TN) instead of (TMN), some of the problems for (TMN) are also problems for (TN): for example, the combination of the converse Barcan formula with (TN), and the combination of truth-maker maximalism with (TN).

21. If we have the intuition that the truth-maker relation is an asymmetric relation, then (TMN=) offends against this intuition while (TMNS) is compatible with it. Cf. Caputo (2007: 282–3).

22. A similar asymmetry concerns truth. It is necessarily true that the proposition that snow is white is true iff snow is white. And it is essentially true that if the proposition that snow is white is true, then snow is white. But it is not essentially true that if snow is white then the proposition that snow is white is true.

23. There are two possibilities for a defender of (TME3) to deflect this kind of argument. (a) He may claim that, for a certain class of essential truths only, the following schema has true instances: if the proposition that p is an essential truth, then it is part of the essence of the proposition that p that it is true. And on this basis he may then, for example, restrict the class of true instances of this schema to logical truths. Cf. Lowe (2006: 203). In this case the problem would concern only logical truths. But the defender of (TME3) has the burden of proof: he must provide reasons why it is plausible and necessary to restrict the instances of the schema in this way. (b) He may in general reject the claim that the following schema has true instances: the truth of the proposition that it is part of the essence of the proposition that p that it is true is sufficient for the truth of the proposition that it is part of the proposition that p that ($q \rightarrow$ the proposition that p is true). Nonetheless, the defender of (TME3) again has the burden of proof: he must provide good reasons to justify this move.

24. Someone who accepts that the problem of unnecessary truth-makers can only be solved by a trivialization of (TM) may hold the following principle:

    (TB)   For all propositions x: x is true iff there is a p such that x is true, because p.

25. In Rodriguez-Pereyra, this vol., Ch. 13, 232, it is claimed that there are true reflexive because-statements. The truth-teller proposition says of itself that it is true. This proposition is true, because it is true. But reflexive explanations are no explanations at all. So it might be doubted that the truth-teller case provides an example of a true because-statement that provides some kind of explanation.

26. In Rodriguez-Pereyra (2006b: 960–61) this point seems to be accepted and therefore an implicit definition of the truth-maker relation is suggested.

27. One may claim that 'in virtue of' is superior to 'because of', because only the second has causal associations. First, I doubt that there are any causal associations in the case of 'is true because of'. Secondly, 'in virtue of' seems to be as ambiguous or indexical as 'because of'. 'The ship sank because of a leak in the bow' and 'The ship sank in virtue of a leak in the bow' seem to be both meaningful descriptions of a possible state of affairs. Both sentences express causal explanations.

28. And this is also true of an explication of the truth-maker relation that contains 'is true in virtue of' only as a component. Cf. Armstrong, this vol., Ch. 7, 126.

29. Parsons himself gives the following formulation: x makes p true iff x is intrinsically such that p. But this formulation is incorrect, because 'p' must be regarded as a nominal variable relative to its first occurrence and as a sentential variable relative to its second occurrence. Cf. Parsons (2005: 166–7).

30. A purely contingent proposition is a proposition that only contains contingent propositions as constituents. This further qualification is required, because Restall has shown that a restriction only to contingent propositions that may contain non-contingent propositions as constituents fails. Cf. Restall, this vol., Ch. 4, 91; Armstrong, this vol., Ch. 7, 121.

31. This objection was also pointed out to me by E. J. Lowe in 2005.

32. Similar observations are made in Schnieder (2006b: 39–42) and Mulligan (2007: 53).

33. I am thankful for discussions, corrections and helpful comments with Christian Beyer, Erich Fries, Tim Kraft, E. J. Lowe, Felix Mühlhölzer, Günther Patzig, Peter Rami and Gonzalo Rodriguez-Pereyra. Special thanks to Marian David for his detailed comments.

PART I

Setting the stage

CHAPTER 2

Truth and the truth-maker principle in 1921[1]

Kevin Mulligan

1. Truth-makers

Friends of truth-making in the first half of the last century make up a small but select band of philosophers: G. F. Stout (1911, 1930); Ludwig Wittgenstein (1979: 15, 95); Bertrand Russell (1918: I; 1940: 227); John McTaggart (1921: bk I, chs 1–2); Alexander Pfänder (1921: 231–43, 75–89); C. D. Broad (1933: 56ff.); and J. L. Austin (1961: 91, 104ff.). The band of truth-makers thus includes many philosophers from Cambridge. If we assume that Wittgenstein's appeal to truth-making in 1913 and 1914 is still at work or on display, if not expressed, in the *Tractatus*,[2] then we may say that 1921 is the *annus mirabilis* or at least the first high-point of the theory of truth-making.[3] For it is in the third or fourth most important treatise on logic to appear in 1921 (the year in which the great Cambridge treatises of John Maynard Keynes and W. E. Johnson appear), Pfänder's *Logik*, that the truth-maker principle is first formulated and defended. And in the same year McTaggart gives an account of truth and truth-making that is closer to Pfänder's than to any other account.

According to the truth-maker principle, every truth is made true by a truth-maker. Any philosophy of truth-making and of truth has therefore to consider the following questions. Is truth a property? If so, of what? Of judgements, beliefs, judgings or propositions? Is the property of truth a mere appearance or is it ineliminable? What sort of a tie is truth-making? Is it a relation? Or is talk of x making y F merely elliptical for some sort of non-relational tie of explanation or grounding? What sort of entity is a truth-maker if every truth has one?

Pfänder gives clear answers to many of these questions. Some of the answers are to be found elsewhere in the phenomenological tradition. But the views of McTaggart in 1921 are also, as we shall see, very close to some of the views put forward in the same year by Pfänder.

Taking his cue from Gottfried Leibniz, the Munich philosopher Pfänder argued at some length in his 1921 *Logik* for the truth-maker principle. In particular, he asks and answers the important question: what, if anything, makes the truth-maker principle true? Pfänder's theory of truth is of considerable interest since, unlike many contemporary friends of truth-making, he rejects not only the view that some truths have no truth-bearers but also the view that it is just a contingent fact that all truths have truth-makers. The tie between truth and truth-making, he thinks, is a very intimate and *a priori* one. The truth-property, he argues, is a relation or, as he sometimes says, a property that rests on a relation, and that every truth has a truth-maker is a consequence of the fact that the truth-maker principle is in fact a particular principle of sufficient reason[4] (PSR). The claim that it is an *a priori* truth that every truth has a truth-maker admits of many interpretations. On Pfänder's account of the claim it is an *a priori* truth that holds in virtue of the essences of truth and of truth-bearers. The very idea that universal laws sometimes hold in virtue of the essences of the objects they deal with or in virtue of the essences of the properties they ascribe or in virtue of the concepts occurring in such laws is fundamental within the philosophy of Edmund Husserl. But Pfänder's application of the idea to truth and truth-making is an application that is all his own.

Pfänder is, with Husserl, one of the two founders of phenomenology. Until the appearance of his *Logik*, Pfänder had been known principally for very careful analyses of the will, the emotions and the distinction between causes and motives. Nor did he return to logic after 1921 in his published work. Indeed, his book seems to have had little effect, even within phenomenology. Husserl does not refer to it in his *Formal and Transcendental Logic* and seems not to have had a very high opinion of it. Nevertheless, it is in his *Logik* that Pfänder formulates a very general programme for logic that may be considered to be implicit in much previous phenomenology:

> Logic until now has *in fact* always been a systematic science of thoughts. But it has concentrated exclusively on *assertive thoughts* [*behauptenden Gedanken*] and has not taken into account questions, assumptions, conjectures and the like, nor those other thoughts we call valuings, criticisms, assessments, requests, advice, warnings, decisions, intentions, prescriptions, commandments, prohibitions, orders and laws … But there is no objective reason why logic should restrict itself for ever to the special group of *assertive* thoughts, to their elements and connections.   (Pfänder 2000: 19)

This is not quite Husserl's view. Husserl had formulated a number of theorems and axioms that would now be considered parts of axiological logic, deontic logic and the logic of action. Husserl himself, however, always argued that these principles were not a part of logic but of formal, "parallel disciplines". But it was something very like Pfänder's programme that was rapidly taken up by analytic philosophy as the different parts of philosophical logic – as opposed to discussions of the so-called "logic" of colours or of God-talk – spread their wings.[5]

After indicating the Leibnizian starting-point for Pfänder's theory, I set out Pfänder's account of truth and truth-making and then consider the main distinctions and claims he makes.

2. The Leibnizian starting-point

Many of the more interesting ideas in contributions to (philosophical) logic by the phenomenologists have their source in Husserl's reworkings of claims made originally by Bernard Bolzano (about logical consequence, explanation [*Abfolge*], logical probability, properties, essence and modality), who has been rightly called the Bohemian Leibniz. As we shall see, however, Bolzano himself clearly rejects the main plank in Pfänder's account of truth and truth-making. It is rather Leibniz himself who seems to have inspired this account.

Leibniz, Pfänder claims, was the first philosopher to set forth the following general principle of sufficient reason:

(PSR)   Everything has a sufficient reason,

and clearly take this to comprehend three further principles concerning: (a) the existence of something; (b) the occurrence of an event; and (c) the obtaining (*Bestehen*) of a truth. Leibniz "thus distinguishes the grounds of existence, of occurrences and of truth" (Pfänder 2000: 221–2).[6] Although Pfänder makes no reference to Leibniz's writings, he seems to have in mind passages such as §§31–2 of the *Monadology*:

> §31 Nos raisonnements sont fondés sur deux grands principes, celui de la contradiction en vertu duquel nous jugeons faux ce qui en enveloppe, et vrai ce qui est opposé ou contradictoire au faux. [Our reasonings are founded upon two great principles, that of contradiction, in virtue of which we judge false that which contains a contradiction, and true that which is opposed to or contradicts the false.]

> §32 Et celui de la raison suffisante, en vertu duquel nous considérons qu'aucun fait ne saurait se trouver vrai, ou existant, aucune énonciation véritable, sans qu'il y ait une raison suffisante, pourquoi il en soit ainsi et non pas autrement. Quoique ces raisons le plus souvent ne puissent point nous être connues. [And that of sufficient reason, in virtue of which we think that no fact can be true or exist, no statement true, unless there be a sufficient reason why it should be so and not otherwise. Although these reasons usually cannot be known by us.]

41

Just what Leibniz took "a fact is true (*vrai*)", "a fact exists" and "a statement is true (*véritable*)" to mean and how he took such claims to be connected are questions for the specialists. But Pfänder is clearly right to say that Leibniz thinks that there are different principles of sufficient reason, at least one of which concerns truth.[7] Pfänder's account of Leibniz as a friend of truth-making has recently received French support. Jean-Baptiste Rauzy's fascinating study, *La Doctrine Leibnizienne de la vérité* (2001), argues at some length for the view that for Leibniz the truth-predicate has no meaning outside the context of an *adequatio rei*. In particular: "Concepts and connections among concepts ... are the reasons why a particular sentence is true; ... they play the role of truth-makers" (Rauzy 2001: 47; see also Mugnai 2002; Rauzy 2002).

Within the philosophical tradition influenced by realist phenomenology, the Leibnizian version of the truth-maker principle did not go unchallenged. In 1938, in a chapter of his *Möglichkeit und Wirklichkeit* entitled "The Disappearance of the Principle of Sufficient Reason", Nicolai Hartmann rejected truth-maker maximalism: "Not every judgement has its sufficient reason" (Hartmann [1938] 1966: 275, ch. 38(a)). Against a long tradition, Hartmann argues that only in the sphere of real entities does the principle of sufficient reason always hold. It does not hold everywhere in the ideal sphere, not in mathematics and not in logic.

3. Pfänder's account

Let us, then, look at Pfänder's account. Like Wittgenstein in the same year, Pfänder thinks that truth-bearers "project" (*entwerfen*), like a magic lantern (*Projektionslampe*) (Pfänder 2000: 36; Wittgenstein 1922: 2.0212, 3.11, 3.12). They project states of affairs, he says (Pfänder 2000: 36), a picture of the world, Wittgenstein says (Wittgenstein 1922: 2.0212). Pfänder thinks truth-bearers are judgements, which he takes to be non-temporal entities, not mental acts of judging.[8] Unlike Wittgenstein, Pfänder denies that truth-bearers are pictures (*Abbilder*): "someone who makes pictures of objects obtains a picture gallery but not judgements" (Pfänder 2000: 80), he notes sardonically. Like many phenomenologists, he thinks that states of affairs may contain individual properties or general attributes, that obtaining states of affairs make judgements true and false, and that even an obtaining state of affairs containing a substance and an individual property is an ideal entity. Unlike Wittgenstein, Pfänder thinks that the logical variety of truth-bearers is matched by a corresponding formal ontological variety of states of affairs: there are negative, universal and disjunctive states of affairs. This was the view of all the early phenomenologists except for Roman Ingarden.

Like Wittgenstein, Pfänder claims that the logical constants do not represent. But he takes this claim to be compatible with the view that there are non-atomic states of affairs. Husserl had mentioned in his *Logical Investigations* the possibility that the logical constants have no "correlates" but endorsed only the weaker claim that they have no correlates in the sphere of real objects (Husserl 1970: vol. II 782 [VI §43]). In 1921 Pfänder endorses the stronger view: in the concepts of disjunction, conjunction and implication there is "no reference to an object" (*Gegenstandsmeinung*); they are "pure, functioning concepts", not "concepts of objects" (Pfänder 2000: 157).

This particular fundamental thought of Pfänder's had been published in 1916 by his pupil, Maximilian Beck (1916: 20–25), who refers to Pfänder's 1912/1913 lectures in Munich. Beck adds that the concepts of logical forms such as conjunction and implication are themselves essences that, unlike all other objects, are not known through concepts: in thinking conjunctively or hypothetically we "intuit [*erschauen*] in their effect" their content (*ibid.*: 24). This is a point that might be put more snappily, although just as obscurely, by saying that logical form is something that shows itself.

There are many principles of sufficient reason. In addition to the three already mentioned, Pfänder, following Schopenhauer, distinguishes the principle that every action is grounded in a motive, that atemporal being always has a ground and the principle that every piece of knowledge (*Erkenntnis*) has a ground, a cognitive ground (Pfänder 2000: 222–3; cf. §6 below). But only those principles that deal with "logical objects" are of interest to logic. If there is a logical PSR it must satisfy three requirements:

> The principle must, first, deal with purely logical objects; it must, secondly, assert something which is purely logical about these objects; and it must, thirdly, base what it asserts on the specifically logical essence of the objects it is about.
>
> Of the different logical objects, only judgements, not concepts nor inferences [*Schlüsse*] are suitable subjects for the [logical] PSR. This principle must therefore assert something about judgements.
>
> (*Ibid.*: 225)

What does Pfänder's truth-maker principle, his logical PSR, assert?

> The genuine sense of the PSR is that it specifies in a general way what a judgement requires in order for its claim to truth to be not mere pretence but a satisfied claim. The principle therefore says
>
> Every judgement, in order to be really true, stands necessarily in need of a sufficient reason.
>
> By the *ground* of a judgement is to be understood what can support the assertoric content of the judgement. This reason is "*sufficient*" if it alone suffices to support the complete assertoric content of the judgement, if nothing else is required to *make the judgement completely* [sic] *true*. (*Ibid.*: 227, last emphasis added)[9]

The three claims,

(i) every judgement, in order to be really true, stands necessarily in need of a sufficient reason,
(ii) the truth of a judgement necessarily stands in need of a sufficient reason, and
(iii) the obtaining (*Bestehen*) of every truth has its sufficient reason,

are equivalent (*ibid.*: 228). Each claim, Pfänder points out, satisfies the three requirements that a PSR must satisfy in order to be a logical principle: each ranges over logical objects – judgements, truths, the obtaining of truths; each makes a purely logical assertion; and finally, each version of the principle "grounds its assertion on the specific essence of its logical objects" (*ibid.*).

What is the *content* of the logical PSR?

> [I]t is not simply the sense of truth which the principle would give. For the sufficient ground is not itself the truth of the judgement but its foundation. There is, however, a reciprocal connection between the truth of a judgement and its sufficient reason. If a judgement is really true then it has a sufficient reason; and if it has a sufficient reason then it is really true. But the two thoughts: "A judgement is true" and "A judgement has a sufficient reason" do not on this account have the same meaning, they are rather only equivalent. Thus were the [logical] PSR to assert
>
> > A judgement is true – this says no more than that the judgement has a sufficient reason
>
> the principle would be false and could not possibly be a supreme logical principle. If, however, we isolate the basis on which the equivalence, which is erroneously taken to be an identity of meaning, rests in the final analysis, this points us to the true logical sense of the PSR ....The equivalence is based on the inner connection which the truth of a judgement has to the judgement, on the one hand, and to the sufficient ground, on the other hand.   (*Ibid.*: 226)

Now, "[t]he [logical] principle of sufficient reason is itself a judgement and so must, if it is to be true, itself have a sufficient ground". What, if anything, makes the principle true?

Pfänder dismisses a number of candidates. The principle is not a principle that enjoys immediate self-evidence if this means that it bears its truth on its face and requires no sufficient ground. For it is a judgement that "falls within its own domain of validity". Other, non-logical principles of sufficient reason, such as the principle that every event has a cause or the principle that every action, including that of holding a judgement to be true, has a ground, are clearly irrelevant. Nor should we say, in a vaguely neo-Kantian fashion, that reason requires that every truth have a sufficient reason. For if reason does require this it is *because* every truth requires a sufficient ground. Nor is an appeal to experience of much help. For even if experience showed that all truths hitherto examined did in fact have a sufficient reason, this would lend only a very low probability to the truth of the logical PSR (*ibid.*: 230–31). Rather, "[i]ts own sufficient ground lies ... in the *essence of judgement* and in the *essence of truth*" (*ibid.*: 232).

Pfänder summarizes the route that leads him to claim that the logical PSR is rooted in the *essences* of truth and of judgement and not, he stresses, in the *concepts* of truth and of judgement as follows:

> It lies in the essence of every judgement to make a claim to truth. Truth, as we have seen, is, according to its very essence, something which cannot attach to a judgement all by itself but only in a certain relation to something else, namely in the relation of agreement with the objects dealt with by the judgement. Only if this relation obtains can the judgement be true. But this relation requires necessarily in order to obtain two foundations, namely the judgement on the one hand and the behaviour of the objects the judgement deals with on the other hand ... Thus if a judgement is not only to lay claim to truth but also to have truth then the corresponding behaviour of the objects is absolutely necessary as a ground. The truth of a judgement, according to its essence, only obtains ... if this reason is a sufficient reason. It follows that every judgement, in order to be true, stands necessarily in need of a sufficient reason. (*Ibid.*: 231–2)

In order to better understand and evaluate Pfänder's account, I turn now to its main elements.

4. The elements of Pfänder's account

Pfänder gives an account of the essence of judgement, of states of affairs and of truth, explains – as we have seen – what the logical PSR means and then gives an account of what grounds the truth of this principle, of what makes it true. He also provides an account of the difference between the logical PSR or truth-maker principle and the principle that every piece of knowledge has a cognitive ground, that where there is knowledge a judgement has been made a piece of knowledge. I shall consider each of these elements of his account in turn.

4.1 Judgements aim at truth

What is the essence of judgement? That it claims to be true, Pfänder says. This is a claim that had been made earlier, by Husserl, Adolf Reinach and Max Scheler, although at one point Husserl also argues that it is wrong.[10] The view that belief claims to be true has in the meantime become very common. Pfänder says:

> Now this assertion-function contains in itself the *claim to truth*. Every judgement necessarily in virtue of its essence makes this claim to truth. A thought, however otherwise constituted, which does not essentially contain the claim to truth, is thus certainly no judgement. The claim is not a determination which attaches externally albeit necessarily to the judgement but is essentially internal to the judgement. It is therefore *implicitly co-asserted* in every judgement that it itself is true … The implied co-assertion of the truth of the judgement is contained in the judgement even if the judger does not innerly perform the co-assertion. The implied co-assertion can be drawn out [*herausgezogen*] and developed as a so-called truth-judgement of the form "'S is P'is true". But this developed truth-judgement is by no means identical in meaning with the original judgement "S is P".
>
> (Pfänder 2000: 69; cf. 98, 128)

It is not at all clear what Pfänder means by "implicitly co-asserted". Presumably, whatever is co-asserted, however implicitly, is also represented. But the judgement that it is raining does not contain any concept representing truth or judgement. The truth of the equivalence between 'It is raining' and 'That it is raining is true', an equivalence accepted by Pfänder (*ibid.*: 69), is compatible with it being the case that members of a community regularly judge that it is raining and do not possess the concepts of truth or of judgement. The sense in which a judging or a judgement aims at truth can perhaps be brought out better with the help of a distinction sometimes employed by Husserl. Judgings and judgements are "intentionally directed towards" truth but do not represent it. Indeed, it would be even more accurate to say that judgings and judgements are primarily directed towards the obtaining of states of affairs but do not represent these and, secondarily, towards the truth of truth-bearers. Consider, by way of analogy, propositional emotions such as regret and sadness. Sam's regret that *p* or his sadness that *p* are "directed towards" the axiological states of affairs (*Wertverhalte*),

It is regrettable that *p*,
It is sad that *p*,

but do not represent these. What does "directed towards" mean? At least this. Sam's regret and his sadness are right or appropriate only if the respective *Wertverhalte* obtain. Similarly, the judgement that it is raining is right only if the state of affairs that it is raining obtains.

Pfänder might reply to this suggestion by reminding Husserl that by "implicitly co-asserted" (*implizite mitbehauptet*) he does not mean that a judger of a judgement "innerly performs" (*innerlich vollzieht*) the co-assertion. But then it is not clear what he has in mind. It is interesting to note that in his discussion of ascents other than the ascent to mention of judgements and states of affairs or to predications of truth and of obtaining such as,

> It is raining
> _____
> The judgement that is raining is true,

for example,

> This is sulphur
> _____
> This falls under the concept of sulphur,

and

> This is sulphur
> _____
> This belongs to the class of things consisting of sulphur,

he says that in each case there is an implication but that it is a mistake to assume that what is implied is a "development of the sense" of its starting-point (*ibid.*: 82–3). But what, one would like to know, is the reason for distinguishing between the ascent to truth, on the one hand, and the ascent to concepts and classes, on the other hand?

The weakness in Pfänder's account of the "ascent" from ordinary judging or judgement to mention of judgements and predications of truth is not unrelated to a certain weakness in his account of states of affairs. Judgements, he says, implicitly co-posit states of affairs (*ibid.*: 250) that may or may not obtain.

Alexius Meinong (1977: 101) pointed out that the word "*Sachverhalt*" ordinarily carries the connotation of factuality. Similarly, in ordinary English, talk of "obtaining states of affairs" is pleonastic. Pfänder, like many phenomenologists, uses "*Sachverhalt*" to refer to what judgements are directed towards and in such a way that "obtaining *Sachverhalt*" is not pleonastic. But he says very little about the difference between *Sachverhalte* and obtaining *Sachverhalte*.

The difference is clearly marked by Ingarden, for whom every categorical judgement has a *formal object*: the intentional state of affairs meant by the content of the judgement. A true categorical judgement has also a *material object*: an objective state of affairs, that is, an obtaining state of affairs. Some of the features of the intentional state of affairs and of the objective state of affairs are identical (Ingarden 1925: 127–8; 1994: 286). Ingarden notes that there is only a trace of the distinction between intentional and objective states of affairs in Pfänder. Pfänder does indeed say in one passage that every judgement posits a formal state of affairs ("*Formalsachverhalt*"; Pfänder 2000: 250).[11] It has become common in the philosophy of emotions to call values the formal objects of emotions. And, as we have seen, the relation between emotions and their formal objects has much in common with the relation between judgements and their formal objects.

4.2 Grounds, grounding, making and because

By a "*Grund*" Pfänder normally means, like other phenomenologists, either an obtaining state of affairs or a true proposition. Grounds or reasons are propositional or state-of-affairsish (*sachverhaltlich*). In order to bring into focus Pfänder's view that obtaining states of affairs ground truths, it will be useful to consider three different views about truth and its grounds, all of which are incompatible with Pfänder's views.

In the *Tractatus* (1922: 5.101) Wittgenstein calls the truth-possibilities of the truth arguments of a proposition that "*bewahrheiten*" it (make it come true) its "truth grounds". These grounds are themselves truth-bearers. And, in a striking passage, Bolzano declares that grounds are always propositions and rules out the very idea of truth-making long before it was actually formulated by his heirs:

> [T]he sense of the question is this: Does a certain thing, X, have the property [*Beschaffenheit*] x because the proposition, X has the property x, is true; or, conversely, is this proposition true because the thing X has this property? – The right answer, in my opinion, is: neither the one nor the other. The reason [*Grund*] why a proposition is true lies, if the proposition's truth has a reason, in another truth, not in the thing with which it deals. And it is even less correct to say that the reason why X has the property x lies in the truth that X has the property x. If indeed X is an existing thing then there can be no reason why it has the property x, but there can be a cause why it has the property x, this cause lies in another thing. (Bolzano 1978: 60)

At the beginning of his *Logical Investigations*, Husserl, too, endorses the view that the logical grounds of the truth of truths are always truth-bearers in a passage that also rejects the view Pfänder was to defend some twenty years later to the effect that judgements implicitly assert that they have a ground and alludes to objections to the view that judgements claim to be true:

The fundamental distinction between a *purely logical ground of truth* and a *normatively logical ground of judgement* is not to be found in Sigwart. On the one hand, a truth (not a true judgement, but the ideally valid unity), has a ground, which is tantamount to saying that there is a theoretical proof which deduces the truth from this objective, theoretical ground. The principle of sufficient reason is to be taken in this sense, and in this alone. And on *this* acceptation of ground, it is not at all the case that every judgement has a ground, let alone that it "implicitly asserts" such a ground. Every final principle of grounding, every genuine axiom, is in this sense groundless, as in the opposite direction likewise every judgement of fact. Only the probability of a fact can be grounded, not the fact itself, or the judgement of fact. The expression "ground of judgement", on the other hand – if we ignore the psychological "grounds" i.e causes of judging and their motivating contents – means no more than our *logical right* to judge. In this sense, every judgement certainly "claims" this right (though there are objections to saying that the right is "implicitly asserted").

(Husserl 1970: vol. I, 153, Prolegomena §39; translation modified)[12]

In contrast to these three views about grounds, Pfänder thinks that obtaining states of affairs may function as grounds.

Are grounds always and only states of affairs or propositions? In a number of passages Pfänder may seem to be allowing for a third possibility.

As we have seen, the truth-maker principle itself is supposed to be grounded in the essences of truth and of judgement. Pfänder often mentions instances of "the essence of *x*" as grounds. Thus he says that "the judgement 'red is different from green'" has its "sufficient ground in the essence of the objects it deals with" (2000: 230–31).

He mentions an objection that threatens to restrict the scope of the logical PRS: that there are analytic judgements and mathematical axioms that are true "all by themselves", which require no sufficient reason to be true. (Wittgenstein, in the same year, makes the epistemological claim that it is a mark of logical propositions that one can recognize "in the symbol alone" that they are true; Wittgenstein 1922: 6.113). But this, Pfänder thinks, is wrong. Each true analytic judgement and mathematical axiom "is grounded in the behaviour of the objects it deals with. Only the behaviour of these objects can really make [it] true" (2000: 239).

Analytic judgements and mathematical axioms behave, in this respect, like the judgement that red is different from green. Another example Pfänder discusses is the category of non-informative identities, such as 'sulphur = sulphur' (*ibid.*: 185). In such a case, "the essence of an object is what grounds immediately and finally that it is self-identical" (*ibid.*: 191).

This proposition is not, he says, a logical proposition; it is a proposition that belongs to formal ontology and that "forms the last foundation of the logical proposition of identity", that is to say, "A = A" (*ibid.*). But Pfänder seems to be not entirely certain that all analytic judgements are made true by the essences of the objects they are about: "thus *at best* in the case of ... logical-analytic judgements, not in the case of synthetic judgements, could the *subject-concept* form the sufficient reason for predication" (*ibid.*: 225–6; cf. 196; emphasis added).

Are these different examples of cases where what grounds are the essences or concepts of objects or the behaviour of objects counter-examples to the claim that only true truth-bearers and obtaining states of affairs can ground? In order to answer this question we must look at Pfänder's understanding of the relation between essentiality, universality and modality.

4.3 Essence, universality and modality

> We thus see that universality and necessity can both be traced back
> one step further: In every case they are to be found if and only if the
> predicate is grounded in the essence of the subject.
>
> (Reinach 1979: 165)

When Pfänder talks of the essence of this or that he sometimes seems to be assuming that he is quantifying over ideal objects: essences. This is indeed how Husserl and his heirs usually talk of essences. But sometimes Pfänder's essence talk seems to commit him to saying only things of the form: *x* is essentially *F*. In both cases, though, he assumes that essentiality induces necessitation. Thus in his treatment of non-informative identities, as we have seen, he argues that the necessary truth of such identities is determined by the essences of objects.

Although Pfänder never says clearly what the logical form of appeals to essence is, there are two ways of reading most of the invocations of essence in the quotations from Pfänder given so far. When Pfänder says, for example, that "the judgement that every truth has a sufficient ground is true is grounded in the essences of truth and of judgement", this may be taken to be the result of ascent (cf. Pfänder 2000: 330) from "the judgement that every truth has a sufficient ground is true because each truth instantiates Truth and each judgement instantiates Judgement", or from "the judgement that every truth has a sufficient ground is true in virtue of the essential properties of truth and judgement". These two ways of understanding Pfänder's talk of truths being grounded in the essence of this or that might be called the *instantiation* and the *predicative* accounts of essential grounding. The first, unlike the second, refers to essences. They are both compatible with the view that what grounds are truths or facts.

Husserl's favoured account of essential grounding is the instantiation account. The locus of necessity, he thinks, is to be found in particular instantiations of laws that are grounded in essences (cf. Mulligan 2004). Understood in this way, the phenomenological account of essential grounding is quite clearly a continuation of ideas to be found in Plato and Aristotle (cf. Politis 2004, 2009 forthcoming). It is equally clearly a development of Bolzano's theory of essentiality and necessity in terms of general propositions that hold in virtue of the fact that an object or objects fall under a certain concept. Indeed, Husserl often talks of laws that hold in virtue of certain concepts occurring in these laws. On occasions, however, he also distinguishes between laws grounded in concepts used in the laws and laws grounded in the essences of objects over which the law quantifies. This is a distinction Pfänder observes more carefully than Husserl.

Must essential grounding be understood in one of the two ways outlined? A third possibility, recently defended by Kit Fine (1995b), takes the predicate 'x makes it true that p in virtue of the essence of x' to be unanalysable.

A fourth view, put forward by Meinong, denies that what grounds is always propositional or states-of-affairsish (cf. 'because of'). In 1907 Meinong asserts that only objectives can be grounds: "That 2 is smaller than 3 has no ground which lies outside this objective but it is all the more certain that it has a ground within the objective: this ground lies in the nature or make-up, in the being-so of the objects 2 and 3" (Meinong 1973: 260). He came to think this view was "artificial" (Meinong 1968: 583 n.1). If the "*Satz vom Grund*" is to be upheld, then, Meinong thinks, the notion of a *Grund* has to comprehend both objectives *and* objects, ideal objects:

> The objective that red is not green is not based on any objective and one can only assign as a ground or grounds for our objective the objects red and green with some degree of naturalness by suitably extending the concept of a ground so that it comprises objects where this is needed. Similarly, what must be "considered" in order to arrive at the evident knowledge that red differs from green is no sort of objective but once again the objects red and green. Thus the concept of a "ground of knowledge" also needs to be extended in a suitable way. In general: if "why" asks for an objective or a judgement, then it is wrong to say that one may ask "why" everywhere in the intellectual sphere. The requirement can only be maintained if one thinks that one may content oneself with an object or an idea. (*Ibid.*: 583–4)

4.4 Truth

What is the essence of truth? The truth-judgement, Pfänder often says, is a relational judgement. This claim goes well beyond the much less controversial equivalences noted by Pfänder (and Husserl). There is the equivalence between obtaining states of affairs and truth: "If the judgement is true, then the corresponding state of affairs obtains, and if the state of affairs, which the judgement posits, obtains, then the judgement is true. But this connection grounds no identity of sense, but only an equivalence" (Pfänder 2000: 79). If we add to this equivalence one already mentioned, we obtain:

> It is raining iff the judgement that it is raining is true iff the state of affairs that it is raining obtains.

Here is Pfänder's formulation of his claim that the truth-property is a relation:

> The truth-judgement, which expressly asserts of a judgement that it is true, is a relational judgement, which puts (posits, *setzt*) the object of its subject-term, the relevant judgement, in a definite relation to the behaviour of the other object with which the judgement judged about deals. The predicative determination of the truth-judgement is the relational determination "true".   (*Ibid.*: 82)

In order to understand this passage, answers are needed to at least two questions: what does "the behaviour of the other object with which the judgement judged about deals" refer to; and what does "put" mean? Pfänder nowhere gives clear answers to these questions. The answer to the first question *seems* to be that "the behaviour of the other object with which the judgement judged about deals" refers to a state of affairs. This in turn suggests that the truth relation, acording to Pfänder, is the relation of *being true of*, which relates a judgement that p and the state of affairs that p.

What does "put" in the passage quoted mean? In his anatomy of types of concepts Pfänder distinguishes four categories, two of which have already been mentioned: (a) formal or purely functioning concepts, such as conjunction; (b) concepts that refer to objects; and (c) concepts that refer to objective (*sachliche*) relations. Different from all of these are (d) concepts that "posit" but do not refer to objective relations (*ibid.*: 170ff.; cf. Beck 1916: 33ff.). Pfänder gives a number of examples of such concepts, in particular the concepts expressed by prepositions in nominal phrases ('the fish in the water'). The truth-concept is not one of the examples he gives. But as far as I can see he treats it as one of the "concepts which put into a relation" (*In-Beziehung-setzende Begriffe*). Similarly, he allows for a positing of properties as well as of relations. Thus he says that "The function of assertion in a judgement does not *mean* the 'obtaining by itself' of the state of affairs, but merely posits it" (Pfänder 2000: 60).

The assertive function in a judgement, we might say, does not refer to the obtaining of a state of affairs, nor does it say a state of affairs obtains; rather, it shows what would be the case were the state of affairs to obtain. But presumably to posit is to represent and so we are led back to the worry outlined above: the judgement that it is raining does not represent, either in a positing or in a referring way, or in any other way, states of affairs, judgements, propositions or truth.

At one point, Pfänder says not that truth-judgements are relational judgements but that the truth property *rests* on a relation: "Truth is a determination of a judgement which rests on its agreement with the behaviour of the objects it deals with. It does not attach to the judgement itself but only in its relation to the objects it deals with" (*ibid.*: 235).[13]

In order to understand a little better Pfänder's oscillation between the claim that truth is a property that rests on a relation and the claim that it is a relation, it will be helpful to look briefly at an exactly contemporary account of truth and truth-making.

5. McTaggart and Pfänder

At the beginning of the *The Nature of Existence* (1921), the Cambridge philosopher McTaggart sets out an account of truth that has much in common with that given by Pfänder and that considers more fully a question passed over by Pfänder: if truth is a relation, why does it look like a monadic property? Unlike Pfänder, McTaggart argues for Meinongian assumptions (*Annahmen*), beliefs and assertions as truth-bearers and takes beliefs to be "events" in the mind (1921: §10 11). Propositions are not truth-bearers, he thinks, for there are no propositions. Thus on the matter of truth-bearers McTaggart agrees with Anton Marty. He says of every belief what Pfänder says of judgements: that it "professes to be true" (*ibid.*: §20 20). McTaggart notes that his theory, although not a resemblance theory of correspondence, might "be called with some appropriateness the picture theory of truth" (*ibid.*: §13 13). Pfänder, as we have seen, rejects picture theories of truth. Like Pfänder (most of the time), McTaggart thinks that truth is a relation and a relation that involves truth-making: "If I say 'the table is square' the only thing which can make my assertion true is the fact that the table *is* square – that is, the possession by the table of the quality of squareness" (*ibid.*: §9 10).

"What is it that makes a belief false?" A false belief owes its falsity to a relation to fact: "a relation of non-correspondence to all facts" (*ibid.*: §19 19–20). McTaggart's facts are not the obtaining states of affairs of the phenomenologists such as Husserl, Reinach and Pfänder. McTaggart's facts, like those of D. M. Armstrong, are entities in which objects and properties or relations come together. He does not allow for states of affairs all of which exist necessarily and some of which obtain contingently and others non-contingently.

Truth is a relation, the relation of correspondence. Correspondence is "indefinable as is the sort of correspondence which is the relation of truth" (*ibid.*: §10 11). McTaggart then points out that truth seems to be a quality: "We say that a belief is true, without any mention of a term other than a belief" (*ibid.*: §11 11).

And there is indeed, he thinks, such a quality in addition to the relation of correspondence. Is "true", then, ambiguous? Are there two types of truth?

> There is, no doubt, a quality of being a true belief, which is possessed by true beliefs. But a belief only has that quality because it stands to some fact in that relation of correspondence of which we have been speaking. It is only a matter of convenience whether we give the name of truth to the relation in which the belief stands or to the quality which arises from the relation. It seems better to give it to the relation, because the relation is prior to the quality. The belief does not stand in the relation because it has the quality. It has the quality because it stands in the relation – indeed, its quality is just the quality of being a term in the relation.
>
> In the case of any belief whose nature is known, it is sufficient to say that it is a term which stands in this relation to something. It is not necessary to specify the other term, because there is only one term to which any belief can have that relation, and we know what that term is when we know what the belief is about. If the belief "the table is square" is true at all, it can only be by correspondence to one thing – the squareness of the table. And thus the fact that truth is a relation tends to fall into the background, since, in any particular case, it is superfluous to mention one term of the relation.
>
> (*Ibid.*: §11 12–13)

McTaggart argues that facts "determine" the truths of beliefs (*ibid.*: §16 16) but does not, as far as I can see, say what the relation between correspondence and truth-making is.[14] Correspondence, unlike truth-making, is a symmetrical relation. And a truth stands in a relation of correspondence to a fact *because* the fact makes the truth true.

McTaggart's distinction between truth as a monadic quality and truth as a relation is of great interest. In the passage just quoted he claims two things about the two types of truth. First, a belief has the quality of truth *because* it stands in the correspondence relation. Secondly, the quality of being true of a belief, he says, "is just the quality of being a term in the relation". How should the second claim be understood?

Suppose Sam stands in the relation of hitting to Mary. Then Sam exemplifies the relational property of hitting-Mary. He exemplifies the relational property because he stands in the relation. Similarly, some monadic predicates are derelativizations of relational predicates (e.g. 'tall') and if such a predicate applies to an object, this is because the relational predicate applies to more than one object. McTaggart's suggestion is perhaps best understood as claiming that the truth property behaves like a relational property and that the truth-predicate is a derelativization of a relational expression. Just as "the fact that truth is a relation tends to fall into the background, since, in any particular case, it is superfluous to mention one term of the relation", so too, when we use predicates that are the results of derelativization it is often superfluous to mention the second term.

As we have seen, Pfänder oscillates between saying that truth is a property that rests on a relation and saying that it is a relation. As far as I can see, there is no trace in Pfänder of the claim that monadic truth *is* a relational property. But it is clear that this is a claim that fits much of his account.

A view that, as far as I can see, is not considered by McTaggart or Pfänder is that truth is a relational property that "rests" not on the relation of correspondence or agreement but on the relation or tie of grounding or truth-making. The corresponding linguistic claim would then be that 'true' is a derelativization of 'makes true'.

6. *x* makes *y* true versus *x* makes *y* a piece of knowledge

Pfänder contrasts at some length the truth-maker principle and its epistemic counterpart: if *y* is a piece of knowledge (*Erkenntnis*), then there is something that makes *y* a piece of knowledge, a type of making many philosophers appeal to, even enemies of truth-making. Thus Wittgenstein is perhaps talking about knowledge-making in the following passage: "'I have compelling grounds for my certitude [*Sicherheit*]'. These grounds make the certitude objective" (1972: §270).

The theory of truth-making, Pfänder argues, is not to be confused with the theory of verification. His arguments for this elementary thesis are of some interest because of the large number of identifications, witting and unwitting, of verifiers and truth-makers and of reductions, witting and unwitting, of truth to verifiability and even to verification.

The background to Pfänder's discussion is Husserl's claim in the *Logical Investigations* that truth and verifiability are distinct but that *x* is true iff *x* is verifiable. Husserl sometimes seems to claim that verifiability is more fundamental than truth. It is often unclear whether he simply means that the experience of verification is the origin of the concept of truth (as regret is the origin of the concept of objective regrettability; cf. §4 above) or a stronger claim. Early and late, Husserl took verifiability to be "ideal verifiability":[15] verifiability in principle by someone, in some possible world. Some philosophers even identify truth and verification or reduce truth to verification. According to Schlick and Heidegger, to be true or to be true in some privileged or basic sense is just to be verified, for something to "disclose" itself.

More recently Göran Sundholm has explored in a most interesting way the possibility that "the intuitionistic view of truth as existence of proof" can be subsumed "under the general truth-maker schema". If Pfänder is right, proving is not any sort of truth-making, just as to verify is not to make true. There is nevertheless, he argues, a sense in which the principle of cognitive reason is a "special form" of the logical PSR (Pfänder 2000: 233).

Pfänder argues that a true judgement is a piece of knowledge only if its truth has been "made evident" (*ersichtlich*): "A cognitive ground is the ground which makes a judgement a piece of knowledge, which therefore makes the truth of the judgement evident" (*ibid.*: 234). What makes the knowledge-maker principle, every piece of knowledge has a sufficent ground, true? The essences of knowledge and of truth (*ibid.*: 235). The principle is independent of the particular natures of cognizing subjects, although the truth of a judgement can only be evident for someone.

Pfänder distinguishes two ways in which true judgements can be made evident. First, evidence may be direct. Then the state of affairs posited by a judgement is made evident and so the truth of the judgement is necessarily evident. "The evident state of affairs is then the sufficient ground of the judgement which is a piece of knowledge" and the judgement itself is an "immediately evident" judgement (*ibid.*: 236). Pfänder says nothing about what it is for a state of affairs to become evident. Perhaps, like Husserl, he has in mind a perception of an obtaining state of affairs. Indeed, at one point he speaks of a "direct intuition" of the behaviour of objects (*ibid.*: 230). But then it is not clear why such a perception does not itself deserve to be called a "piece of knowledge". Pfänder appears to be committed to the view that there are two types of knowledge: judgements and perceptions or intuitions (or whatever else is involved when a state of affairs becomes directly evident). But his official view is that every piece of knowledge is a judgement, qualified in certain ways. The second way in which true judgements can be made evident is via other true judgements. Then these judgements are the sufficient reasons that make a judgement mediately evident (*ibid.*: 236–7).

The logical PSR does not say "that every judgement, in order to be true, requires a proof [*Beweis*]". A proof "is the establishment [*Begründung*] of a judgement on the basis of certain other judgements the truth of which has been established"; it is a tie between judgements. It is therefore what is sometimes called an "objective proof".[16] But a judgement may be true and so have a sufficient ground "and yet be incapable of proof". Mathematical axioms and judgements such as that red is different from green are incapable of proof.

> The proposition asserting that no judgement can be true in the absence of a proof would therefore be a clearly false proposition. Such a blind desire for proof could only be made by a time which has completely lost faith in its ability to grasp the truth of certain judgements in direct intuition and is sunk in never-ending relativism. (*Ibid.*: 229–30)

7. Conclusion

Pfänder's main achievement in his work on truth and truth-making, apart from several important incidental clarifications, is to have given a clear formulation of one version of truth-maker maximalism: *essentialist,* a priori, *factualist truth-maker maximalism.* Every truth has a truth-maker, an obtaining state of affairs or fact, in virtue of the essences of truth and of truth-bearers, and that this is so is something we know *a priori.* He fails to consider whether this view is independent of his claims to the effect that truth is a relation and wobbles between the view that truth is a relation and the view that it is no relation but rests on a relation. But it seems that *a priori,* essentialist truth-maker maximalism is independent of the claim that truth is or rests on a relation (cf. Mulligan 2006a, 2007).

Notes

1. An earlier version of this paper appeared in a German translation in 2006 as part of a Festschrift for Hans Burkhardt, the eminent Leibniz scholar from Munich. Work on this revised version was supported by the Swiss FNS project on the metaphysics of properties and relations.
2. Wittgenstein was to use "*wahr machen*" throughout his later writings.
3. The verb "*wahr machen*", to make true, plays a central role in the semantics of Bernard Bolzano, where it has a very different meaning from that it enjoys below.
4. I sometimes translate "*Grund*" as "reason", sometimes as the more robust "ground".
5. Pfänder's *Nachlass* shows how he attempted to develop a logic of imperatives and a logic of values.
6. Sundholm (1994) notes a passage in Pfänder's *Logik* that may have contributed to the development of the idea that existence claims can be substantiated through general constructions and also the relation between Leibniz's PSR and the truth-maker principle.
7. Cf. *Théodicée* (Leibniz 2001: I §44); *Essais* (Leibniz 1966: IV xvii, §3); and, on the connection between PSR and truth, "Primae veritates" (Leibniz 1971).
8. Unlike Bolzano, Frege and the early Husserl, Pfänder thinks that mental acts stand in a *sui generis* relation of production to ideal thoughts (Pfänder 2000: 16, 81).
9. For an interesting objection to a PSR for states of affairs, cf. van Inwagen (1986: 202–4).
10. Husserl (1974) argues that the claim to truth does not belong to the proper essence of judgements. Cf. Mulligan (2004).
11. The subject concept in a judgement also has both a material and a formal object; cf. Pfänder (2000: 196).
12. It should, however, be noted that at this point in the *Logical Investigations*, Husserl is not yet entirely clear about the distinction between the obtaining of states of affairs and the truth of propositions.
13. If Pfänder is right and truth is relational, then it is a relational modality. Neither Pfänder nor Husserl has much to say about the very idea of relational modalities. But in 1938 Nicolai Hartmann, who in many respects was much more of a realist than any of the realist phenomenologists, published his account of the relation between absolute and relational modalities. One of the central claims of his *Möglichkeit und Wirklichkeit* is that whereas actuality and non-actuality are absolute modalities, necessity and possibility are relational modalities. All necessity is made necessary. Hartmann defends the necessity-maker principle for real or natural necessity ("real determination", "*Realdetermination*"), and for ideal necessity ("ideal determination", "*Idealdetermination*") that is to say, determination in virtue of essences, which he takes to comprehend (i) logical necessity, (ii) metaphysical necessity in the real world and (iii) metaphysical necessity for non-logical idealia. The category of determination itself, like that of dependence, he argues, is not a modal category.

14. Nevertheless Broad (1933: 67) says that McTaggart has given conclusive reasons for the correspond-ence theory of truth and falsehood, and given conclusive answers to the objections against it. Broad criticizes and modifies part of McTaggart's theory of correspondence (*ibid.*: 77–8).

15. Hartmann and Ingarden were quick to point out that the principle that every truth-bearer can be falsified or verified is unverifiable.

16. Cf. Sundholm (1994: 123 n.15), who refers to Per Martin-Löf's distinction between objective and subjective proofs. Pfänder distinguishes between the truth-connection (*Wahrheitszusammenhang*) presupposed by every inference and a connection of grounds (*Begründungszusammenhang*). Not every instance of the former is also an instance of the latter (Pfänder 2000: 248, 329). On Pfänder's distinction see Ingarden (1994: 286).

CHAPTER 3
Truth-makers[1]

Kevin Mulligan, Peter Simons and Barry Smith

> When I speak of a fact ... I mean the kind of thing that makes a prop-
> osition true or false. (Russell 1972: 36)

1. Making true

During the realist revival in the early years of this century, philosophers of various
persuasions were concerned to investigate the ontology of truth. That is, whether
or not they viewed truth as a correspondence, they were interested in the extent
to which one needed to assume the existence of entities serving some role in
accounting for the truth of sentences. Certain of these entities, such as the *Sätze
an sich* of Bolzano, the *Gedanken* of Frege, or the propositions of Russell and
Moore, were conceived as the *bearers* of the properties of truth and falsehood.
Some thinkers, however, such as Russell, Wittgenstein in the *Tractatus,* and
Husserl in the *Logische Untersuchungen*, argued that instead of, or in addition
to, truth-bearers, one must assume the existence of certain entities *in virtue of
which* sentences and/or propositions are true. Various names were used for these
entities, notably 'fact', '*Sachverhalt*', and 'state of affairs'.[2] In order not to prejudge
the suitability of these words we shall initially employ a more neutral terminology,
calling any entities which are candidates for this role *truth-makers*.[3]

The fall from favour of logical realism brought with it a corresponding decline
of interest in the ontology of truth. The notions of correspondence and indeed
of truth itself first of all came to appear obscure and 'metaphysical'. Then Tarski's
work, while rehabilitating the idea of truth, seemed to embody a rejection of a
full-blooded correspondence.[4] In the wake of Tarski, philosophers and logicians
have largely turned their attentions away from the complex and bewildering difficulties of the relations between language and the real world, turning instead to

59

the investigation of more tractable set-theoretic surrogates. Work along these lines has indeed expanded to the extent where it can deal with a large variety of modal, temporal, counterfactual, intentional, deictic, and other sentence-types. However, while yielding certain insights into the structures of language, such semantic investigations avoid the problem of providing an elucidation of the basic truth-relation itself. In place of substantive accounts of this relation, as proffered by the *Tractatus* or by chapter II of *Principia Mathematica*,[5] we are left with such bloodless pseudo-elucidations as: a monadic predication '*Pa*' is true iff *a* is a member of the set which is the extension of '*P*'. Whatever their formal advantages, approaches of this kind do nothing to explain how sentences about the real world are made true or false. For the extension of '*P*' is simply the set of objects such that, if we replace '*x*' in '*Px*' by a name of the object in question, we get a true sentence. Set-theoretic elucidations of the basic truth-relation can, it would seem, bring us no further forward.

Putnam (1978: 25ff.) has argued that Tarski's theory of truth, through its very innocuousness, its eschewal of "undesirable"' notions, fails to determine the concept it was intended to capture, since the formal characterization still fits if we re-interpret "true" to mean, for example, "warrantedly assertable" and adjust our interpretation of the logical constants accordingly. Putnam's conclusion (*ibid.*: 4) is that if we want to account for *truth*, Tarski's work needs supplementing with a philosophically non-neutral correspondence theory. This paper is about such a theory. If we are right that the Tarskian account neglects precisely the atomic sentences, then its indeterminacy is not surprising.[6] If, as we suggest, the nature of truth is underdetermined by theories like that of Tarski, then an adequate account of truth must include considerations which are other than purely semantic in the normally accepted sense. Our suggestion here – a suggestion which is formulated in a realist spirit – is that the way to such a theory lies through direct examination of the link between truth-bearers, the material of logic, and truth-makers, that in the world in virtue of which sentences or propositions are true.

The glory of logical atomism was that it showed that not every kind of sentence needs its own characteristic kind of truth-maker. Provided we can account for the truth and falsehood of atomic sentences, we can dispense with special truth-makers for, e.g. negative, conjunctive, disjunctive, and identity sentences. As Wittgenstein pregnantly put it:

> My fundamental idea is that the 'logical constants' do not represent;
> that the *logic* of facts does not allow of representation.
>
> (*Tractatus*, 4.0312)

This insight is an indispensable prerequisite for modern recursive accounts of truth. It adds further weight to the idea that our attentions should be focused on atomic sentences. We shall in fact concentrate on those which predicate something of one or more spatio-temporal objects. Whether this is a serious limitation is not something that we need here decide, for sentences of this kind must at all events be handled by a realist theory.

The neutral term 'truth-maker' enables us to separate the general question of the need for truth-makers from the more particular question as to what sort – or sorts – of entities truth-makers are. In the main part of the paper we shall consider the claims of one class of entity, which we call *moments*, to fill this role. Since moments, once common in philosophical ontologies, have been relatively neglected in modern times, we shall both explain in some detail what they are, and suggest arguments for their existence independent of their possible role as truth-makers. We shall then consider the light that is thrown by this discussion of moments on better-known theories of truth-makers – and particularly upon the theory of the *Tractatus*.

2. Moments

A moment is an existentially dependent or non-self-sufficient object, that is, an object which is of such a nature that it cannot exist alone, but requires the existence of some other object outside itself. This characterization needs sharpening, but it will be useful to provide some preliminary examples of types of moments, and some indications of the honourable pedigree of the concept in the philosophical tradition.

Consider, first of all, that sequence of objects described at the beginning of Robert Musil's novel *The Man without Qualities:*

> A depression over the Atlantic
> an area of high pressure over Russia,
> patches of pedestrian bustle,
> the pace of Vienna,
> a skidding,
> an abrupt braking,
> a traffic accident,
> the carelessness of a pedestrian,
> the gesticulations of the lorry driver,
> the greyness of his face,
> the prompt arrival of the ambulance,
> its shrill whistle,
> the cleanliness of its interior,
> the lifting of the accident victim into the ambulance.

It might at first seem strange to admit expressions like '*a*'s carelessness' or '*b*'s cleanliness' as referring expressions at all. There is an ingrained tendency amongst contemporary philosophers to regard such formations as mere *façons de parler*, properly to be eliminated from any language suitable for the purposes of philosophical analysis in favour of more robust talk involving reference only to, for example, material things. Here, however, we wish to revert to an older tradition which can readily accommodate expressions of the type illustrated as designating spatio-temporal objects, albeit objects which exhibit the peculiarity that they depend for their existence upon other objects.[7] A skidding, for example, cannot exist unless there is something that skids and a surface over which it skids. A smiling mouth smiles only in a human face.

The concept of moment makes its first appearance in the philosophical literature in the *Categories* of Aristotle, Chapter 2. Here Aristotle introduces a fourfold distinction among objects according as they are or are not said of a subject and according as they are or are not in a subject:[8]

	Not in a subject (Substantial)	In a subject (Accidental)
Said of a subject (Universal, General)	[Second Substances] man	[Non-substantial Universals] whiteness, knowledge
Not said of a subject (Particular, Individual)	[First Substances] this individual man, horse, mind, body	[Individual Accidents] this individual whiteness, this individual knowledge of grammar

An individual accident is, in our terms, one special kind of moment, being such that, to use Aristotle's words, "it cannot exist separately from what it is in" (*Cat.*, 1ª20). This "being in" is not the ordinary part–whole relation; for the parts of a substance are themselves substances (*Met.*, 1028ᵇ9–10), where the entities "in" a substance are its individual accidents. If we are prepared to follow Aristotle and many Scholastics in accepting that there are particulars standing to many non-substantial predicates as individual substances stand to substantial predicates, then we tap a rich source of moments. The particular individual redness of, say, a glass cube, which is numerically distinct from the individual redness even of a qualitatively exactly similar cube, is a moment, as is the snubbedness of Socrates' nose, and the particular individual knowledge of Greek grammar possessed by Aristotle at some given time.

Whilst accidents or particularized qualities are the kinds of moments most commonly found in the tradition, it must be pointed out that many other objects meet our definition. One group of examples not foreign to Aristotle are boundaries (the surface of Miss Anscombe's wedding ring, the edge of a piece of paper,

the Winter Solstice). And further examples are provided by all kinds of configurations and disturbances which require a medium, such as a smile on Mary's
face, a knot in a piece of string, sound waves, cyclones, etc., and more generally
all events, actions, processes, states, and conditions essentially involving material
things: the collision of two billiard balls or Imperial State carriages, the thrusts
and parries of duelling swordsmen, the explosion of a gas, the remaining glum of
Mary's face, John's having malaria, two billiard balls' being at rest relative to each
other, and countless more.

We make no attempt here to carry out the task of dividing all these examples
into mutually exclusive and exhaustive categories. It is important for our purposes
only to realize that moments may be parts of other moments, that moments, like
substances, may be divided into simple and complex. This is most clearly shown
for temporally extended moments. The first wrinkling of John's brow is a part of
his frown, the first dull throbbing a part of his headache, the final C major chord
a part of a performance of Beethoven's Fifth. More controversially, perhaps, we
would regard certain kinds of spatially extended moments as parts of others, as
the redness of one half of a glass cube is part of the redness of the whole cube.[9]

Although we have cast our net wide, we know *a priori* that not everything can
be a moment: the world is not a moment, since if it were, it would require some
thing outside itself in order to exist, in which case it would not be the world.[10]

Moments reappear in post-Scholastic philosophy as the modes of Descartes,
Locke, and Hume. For Descartes, a mode is that which is not a substance, where:

> By substance we can mean nothing other than a thing existing in such
> a manner that it has need of no other thing in order to exist.
> *(Principia philosophiae*, I, LI)

While transposed into the idiom of ideas, Locke's definition is in accord with that
of Descartes:

> Modes I shall call complex Ideas, which however compounded,
> contain not in them the supposition of subsisting by themselves, but
> are considered as Dependencies on, or Affectations of Substances;
> such are the Ideas signified by the Words Triangle, Gratitude, Murther,
> etc. *(Essay*, Book II, chap. XII, §4)

Hume, though he has less to say about modes than Locke, assumes that it is well-
known what they are, and gives a dance and beauty as examples (*Treatise*, Book
I, Part II, § VI).

It was, however, in the philosophy of the German-speaking world that the
Aristotelian ontology, and particularly Aristotle's theory of substance and accident,
was most systematically preserved.[11] Thus the doctrine of moments was fundamental to many students of Brentano, having ready application in psychology.

Carl Stumpf explicitly distinguished among the contents of mental acts between dependent ("partial") and independent contents (1873: 109), a distinction refined and generalized to all objects by his student Husserl.[12] In his early ontology Meinong took it for granted that properties and relations are particulars, not universals.[13]

In modern Anglo-Saxon philosophy commitment to entities of this kind is rarer, a notable swimmer against the tide being Stout, with his "characters". Support for the notion has been otherwise sporadic, and never enthusiastic, often coming, again, from philosophers acquainted with the Scholastic notion of accident.[14]

We have taken the term "moment" from Husserl's masterful and painstaking study of the notions of ontological dependence and independence and of associated problems in the theory of part and whole.[15] A moment is an object whose existence is dependent upon that of another object. This dependence is itself no contingent feature of the moment, but something essential to it. An adequate theory of moments must therefore involve appeal to the notion of *de re* or ontological necessity,[16] in contrast to both *de dicto* (logical) necessity and causal necessity. The objects on which a moment depends may be called its fundaments. Now an object one of whose parts is essential to it (as, say, his brain is essential to a man) is in one sense dependent on that part, dependent as a matter of necessity. Here, however, the whole contains the part it needs. Thus it is already, in relation to that part, self-sufficient, by contrast with other parts – organs other than the brain, for example – which can exist together in a whole of this kind only in so far as they are bound up with (are moments of) the brain. So we specify that the fundaments of a moment cannot be wholly contained within it as its proper or improper parts. This also excludes the undesirable consequence of having everything figure as its own fundament, and hence, trivially, as a moment of itself. Moments may accordingly be defined as follows: *a* is a moment iff *a* exists and *a* is *de re* necessarily such that either it does not exist or there exists at least one object *b*, which is *de re* possibly such that it does not exist and which is not a proper or improper part of *a*. In such a case, *b* is a fundament of *a*, and we say also that *b* founds *a* or *a* is founded on *b*. If *c* is any object containing a fundament of *a* as proper or improper part, but not containing *a* as proper or improper part, we say, following Husserl, that *a* is dependent on *c*. Moments are thus by definition dependent on their fundaments. Objects which are not moments we call independent objects or substances. There is nothing in this account which precludes fundaments from themselves being moments, nor the mutual foundation of two or more moments on each other.[17]

Clearly moments, like substances, come in kinds, including natural kinds.[18] And just as commitment to individual substances or things entails neither the acceptance nor the rejection of an ontology of universals or species which these exemplify, so we can distinguish a realist and a nominalist option with regard to kinds of moments. A strong realism, as in Aquinas and perhaps Aristotle, sees both substances and moments as exemplifying universals. On the other hand, a thoroughgoing nominalism, which is only one step – but it is an important step – removed from reism, accepts only particular substances and moments, conceiving the existence of our talk about moment-kinds as having its basis simply in relations of natural resemblance among examples of moments given in experience.

Further details about the kinds of moments and substances may be spared here. Suffice it to note that all the intuitive examples offered above clearly fit our specification, since in each case there exist objects, not part of those in question, whose existence is a prerequisite for that of the respective moments. In most of the examples it is clear that the moments are not of the right category to be even possible parts of their fundaments, which reinforces Aristotle's remark that accidents are in their substances but not as parts. At the same time his "in" is frequently inappropriate; for instance a duel is "in" neither of the duellers, not is it "in" the duelling pair or the aggregate of duellers.[19]

3. Moments as truth-makers

The idea that what we call moments could serve as truth-makers is perhaps unusual, but it is not without precedent. If we return to Russell, we find that amongst the examples of facts he gives is the death of Socrates, "a certain physiological occurrence which happened in Athens long ago" (*loc. cit.*). From this we infer that, for Russell, at least some states and events are truth-makers. This indicates that he is not conforming to the ordinary usage of 'fact', since what is normally said to be a fact is not the death of Socrates but that Socrates died.[20] Socrates' death took place in Athens, and was caused by his drinking hemlock. We do not however say that Socrates' death is true, but that he died had no cause and did not take place anywhere, at any time. This discrepancy was pointed out by Ramsey, who drew the conclusion that facts are not to be distinguished from true propositions.[21] Here then, we shall distance ourselves from Russell's usage, but not from his theory.

Support for Ramsey's distinction and, surprisingly, for a view of some moments as truth-makers comes from other quarters. Davidson, not known as a friend of facts, says of a sentence like 'Amundsen flew to the North Pole in 1926' that "if [it] is true, then there is an event that makes it true" (1980: 117) and holds that "the same event may make 'Jones apologized' and 'Jones said "I apologize"' true" (*op. cit.*: 170).

The clue that moments may serve as truth-makers comes initially from linguistic considerations. Most terms which describe moments, or under which moments fall, are in fact nouns formed by nominalization of verbs and verb-phrases. These are morphologically varied: some have separate but related forms ('birth', 'flight', 'death'), some are simply gerunds ('overturning', 'shooting'), some are homeomorphic with the corresponding verb ('hit', 'kiss', 'smile', 'jump', 'pull'), and some are formed using particular morphemes for the purpose ('generosity', 'redness', 'pregnancy', 'childhood', etc.). Of these the most neutral and universally applicable is the gerundial form ' – – ing', which, when applied not to a verb but to a noun or adjective complement, attaches to the copula to give phrases of the form 'being (a) – – '. Gerundial phrases are often equivalent to other morphological forms: there is no difference in our view (or Aristotle's) between a cube's being white and its whiteness, nor is there a difference between the collision of two objects and their colliding. All of these forms are, however, radically distinct from nominalizations constructed by means of the conjunction 'that', a fact not always appreciated in the analytic literature on propositions, states of affairs, facts, etc.

Thus, following Russell's suggestion, we shall here consider the theory obtained from the view that what makes it true that Socrates died is Socrates' death, what makes it true that Amundsen flew to the pole is his flight, what makes it true that Mary is smiling is her (present) smile, and so on. Or, in other words, that for many simple sentences about spatio-temporal objects the truth-makers for these sentences are the moments picked out by gerundials and other nominalized expressions closely related to the main verbs of the sentences in question. In place of Tarski-biconditionals of the form:

'This cube is white' is true iff this cube is white,

we thereby obtain – at least in simple cases – sentences of the form:

If 'This cube is white' is true, then it is true in virtue of the being white (the whiteness) of this cube, and if no such whiteness exists, then 'This cube is white' is false.

Because the whiteness in question here is a particular dependent on the cube, and not a universal whiteness shared by all white things, its existence does nothing to make sentences about other things being white either true or false.

If all atomic sentences contain a main verb, and all nominalizations denote moments, then it would follow, in fact, that all truth-makers are moments, that what makes it true that a is F is a's being F, what makes it true that an R's b is a's R-ing b, and so on. This simplest possible version of the theory is inadequate as it stands, however. Not only because, as we shall see, there are certain types of not obviously non-atomic sentences, for example existence and identity sentences, recalcitrant to the analysis, but also, and more importantly, because the theory which claims that by nominalizing a sentence we have thereby designated the relevant truth-maker can hardly count as a substantial elucidation of making true. It seems – like Tarski's theory – to turn on a linguistic trick.

In fact the device of nominalization gives us only the kernel of a theory. That this kernel requires considerable expansion may be gathered from certain intuitive considerations relating to the status of moments as entities in the world existing independently of our sentence-using acts. For we want to say, surely, that if a moment a makes the sentence p true, and b is any moment containing a as part, then b makes p true as well. That John's head ached between 1pm and 1.10pm is made true not just by that ten-minute segment of his headache, but by any part of it containing this segment. So p may have a minimal truth-maker without having a unique one.[22] Further, a sentence may be made true by no single truth-maker but only by several jointly, or again only by several separately. Thus we know that viral hepatitis comes in two sorts: acute infectious or A-hepatitis, and homologous serum or B-hepatitis. If the hapless Cyril has both A- and B-hepatitis simultaneously, then that he has viral hepatitis is made true both by the moment or moments which make it true that he has A-hepatitis, and by the moment or moments making it true that he has B-hepatitis, though either would have sufficed alone. So the sentence 'Cyril has viral hepatitis' has in such circumstances at least two truth-makers. In general there is no guarantee that the logical simplicity of a sentence guarantees the uniqueness or the ontological simplicity (atomicity) of its actual or possible truth-maker(s).

There is, of course, a temptation to argue that 'Cyril has viral hepatitis' is not logically simple but implicitly disjunctive, its logical form being not adequately mirrored in its grammatical form, which is that of a logically simple sentence. But we believe that the given sentence is indeed logically simple: it contains no logical constants and no expression, 'viral hepatitis' included, which is introduced into the language by definition as equivalent to an expression containing a logical constant.

In taking this view we are consciously departing from a dogma that has characterized much of analytic philosophy since its inception: the dogma of logical form. This has many manifestations. One version appears in *The Principles of Mathematics* where Russell, whilst on the one hand regarding all complexity as mind independent, nevertheless holds that this same complexity is capable of logical analysis (1903: 466). This idea of a perfect parallelism of logical and ontological complexity is the misery of logical atomism, leading Russell to a metaphysics of sense-data and Wittgenstein to supraexperiential simples.[23] Here, in contrast, we uphold the independence of ontological from logical complexity: ontologically complex objects (those having proper parts) are not for that reason also in some way logically complex, any more than there is reason to suppose that to every logically complex (true) sentence there corresponds an ontologically complex entity which makes it true.

A second and more elusive version of the dogma enjoys wider support. It includes the Russell–Wittgenstein position as a special case, but is not confined to logical atomists. Roughly speaking, it says that if a sentence has or could have more than one truth-maker, then it is logically complex. If the sentence appears nevertheless to be simple in form, this complexity is hidden and is to be uncovered by a process of analysis.

One possible argument for this view may be put in terms of truth-makers thus: since disjunctive and existential sentences may have more than one truth-maker, and conjunctive and universal sentences must, except in degenerate cases, have more than one, sentences which may or must have more than one truth-maker are implicitly disjunctive or existential, or conjunctive or universal. As it stands this argument is palpably invalid, being of the form 'All A are B, therefore all B are A'; but there are other reasons why the position has been found attractive.[24] Here, however, we shall confine ourselves to registering our dissent from the view. Although 'Cyril has viral hepatitis' may be logically equivalent to (i.e. have the same truth-conditions as) 'Cyril has A-hepatitis or Cyril has B-hepatitis', this is not something that can be established by any lexical, grammatical, or logical analysis of the meaning of the sentence, but at most by empirical research. This research does not uncover a hidden ambiguity in the term 'hepatitis'; we simply discover that the term is determinable.

Since we are realists in respect to moments, and regard their investigation as a substantial, often as an empirical matter, we hold it to be perfectly normal for us to know that a sentence is true, and yet not know completely what makes it true. Thus the characterization of that theory whereby the meaning of a sentence is given by its truth-conditions as 'realist' (Dummett 1973: ch. 13) is for us ironical. A knowledge of truth-conditions takes us at most one step towards reality: one can, surely, envisage understanding a sentence (knowing its meaning), whilst at the same time having only partial knowledge of the nature of its possible truth-makers. Those who used the term 'hepatitis' before the discovery of its varieties did not fail to understand the term; they were simply (partly) ignorant about hepatitis. That the investigation of what makes a particular sentence true is thus fundamentally an empirical, not a philosophical one, is not belied by the fact that for many sentences we can pick out the relevant truth-makers by nominalization. There is, in the general case, no cheap and easy way to determine the truth-makers even of simple descriptive sentences via linguistic transformations.

Are all truth-makers moments? For three kinds of sentences this may be questioned. The first are predications which are, as Aristotle would say, in the category of substance: predications like 'John is a man', 'Tibbles is a cat', and so on, telling us what a thing is. Since these are true atomic sentences, but logically contingent, we should expect them to have truth-makers. In virtue of the special status of such sentences, might it not be the things themselves, John and Tibbles, which play the role of making true, or are there certain moments of John and Tibbles which are essential to them as men or cats which serve to make the given sentences true? One reason for thinking the latter is that, if John makes the sentence 'John is a man' true, then he also makes 'John is an animal' true, which means that these two sentences, having the same truth-maker, have the same truth-conditions, and are logically equivalent. Only if logical equivalence and synonymy are the same, however, is this objection really telling. We conceive it as in principle possible that one and the same truth-maker may make true sentences with different meanings:

this happens anyway if we take non-atomic sentences into account, and no arguments occur to us which suggest that this cannot happen for atomic sentences as
well. A more important point is that if John makes it true both that John is a man
and that John is an animal, and Tibbles likewise makes it true both that Tibbles is
a cat and that Tibbles is an animal, then there is no non-circular way of accounting
via truth-makers for the fact that both are animals but that one is a man and the
other a cat. Such an account could be provided if there are moments characteristic
of humanity and of felinity which are both characteristic of animality.

A second group of problem sentences are singular existentials such as 'John
exists'. These are certainly logically contingent, and perhaps atomic, and so they
ought intuitively to have truth-makers, but then the question arises what these
are. We baulk, for reasons familiar from the tradition, at providing John with a
special moment of existence. The resort to the sentence '$a.a$ = John', widely held
to be equivalent to 'John' exists, is no step forward, since we are left with the question what, if anything, makes the sentence 'John = John' true, and such sentences
belong to our third problem group. A natural way out is, again, to elect John
himself truth-maker of the given sentence, which would once more lead us to a
view according to which at least some truth-makers are not moments. Indeed, a
reist who recognized the need for truth-makers would have no option but that
of taking things to do the job in every case. One the other hand, someone who
has committed to moments would in any event have the problem of providing an
account of sentences expressing their existence, and again the relevant moment
itself would seem to be the most obvious candidate truth-maker.[25]

The third kind of problem sentences are identities. One possible line is that
these too are made true by the objects in question, for instance that 'Hesperus =
Phosphorous' is made true by Venus. This has the consequence that the identity is
equivalent to 'Venus exists' as this sentence has been conceived above. A different
solution is required for the view of those logicians and metaphysicians who think
that an identity of the form '$a = a$' may be true even though there exists no object
designated by the term 'a'. One alternative here is to embrace commitment to
non-existent objects which may be taken as truth-makers for the given sentences
even in those circumstances where 'a exists' is false. Proponents of such a view
will need to embrace a new entity, such as a moment of existence, as truth-maker
for true sentences of the form 'a exists'.[26] The view is, we believe, worth pursuing,
though we do not follow it up here. But there is another view which holds that in
some cases 'a' may not designate, yet '$a = a$' be true. Here we cannot imagine what
might serve as truth-maker. And indeed this suggests the most plausible solution:
there is none. The grounds for believing that '$a = a$' is true even when 'a' is empty
are that the sentence is a logical truth, i.e. that identity is a logical constant. This
account is therefore in harmony with the logical atomist principle that no special
objects correspond to the logical constants. As in the case of singular existentials, the special status of identity sentences is reflected in their special position
in regard to truth-makers.[27]

Whether or not it is correct that things as well as moments can be truth-makers, the possibility emphasizes one merit of the present theory over rival correspondence theories of truth which invoke a special category of non-objectual entity – facts, states of affairs, or whatever – simply to serve as truth-makers. For if we are convinced for other reasons that things and moments exist, and if – as we shall argue below – we can be said unproblematically to be acquainted with them, for example perceptually, then the resultant theory of truth-makers is both more economical and stronger than rival theories whose truth-makers are less firmly tied into our ontology and epistemology.

The relation of making true is to be distinguished both from that of designation and from that between an object and a predicate or concept under which the object falls. Truth-makers cannot, on our theory, be the designata of the sentences they make true, even if we confine ourselves to atomic sentences. This is, of course, no news to those who believe (as we do) that sentences do not designate at all. But for those who incline to the contrary it only needs pointing out that sentences with more than one truth-maker would on their account have to be treated either as ambiguous or as multiply-designating. Both alternatives are implausible. We argued against the first above. As to the second, we are not against plural or multiple designation as such – quite the contrary[28] – but there is no distinction amongst multiple designating or plural terms which corresponds to that between several objects' jointly (i.e. conjunctively) making a sentence true, and their severally (i.e. disjunctively) making a sentence true.

A further difficulty faced by any view to the effect that (true) atomic sentences designate their truth-makers is that, if we are right about singular existential sentences being made true by their subjects, then both 'a' and 'a exists' have the same designatum, so one has the problem of explaining their syntactic and semantic diversity. Since the nominalizations considered above can appear as rightfully in designating phrases as any other common nouns, truth-makers can be designated. But this is not to say that they are designated by the sentences they make true. It is still more obvious that truth-makers do not fall under sentences as objects fall under predicates. The semantic relations of designating, falling under and making true are all distinct. What makes 'John's headaches' true – a moment of John – is something that falls under the predicate 'is a headache' and is designated by 'John's (present) headache'. But from the fact that sentences, terms, and predicates have different syntactic and semantic roles, it does not follow that there are three kinds of entity standing over against them. Nor however does the fact that truth-makers are designated by terms and fall under predicates imply that any of these syntactic and semantic roles collapse into one another.

Since truth-makers can be designated, they can be quantified over. From 'John's singing exists',[29] we can infer '$a.a$ is a singing and John does a' or, more idiomatically, 'John is singing', and conversely. That many normal sentences about events are equivalent to existential sentences was asserted already by Ramsey (1978: 43), and the same view has also been taken by Davidson (1980: 118). It is certainly true that 'Amundsen flew to the North Pole' does not, where 'Amundsen's flight to the North Pole took place' does, imply that only one flight took place. Both Ramsey and Davidson conclude from this that sentences like the former are existential sentences in which events are quantified over. But this is an instance of the dogma of logical form at work. The sentence is undoubtedly logically equivalent to such an existential generalization, but that tells us only that they have the same truth-conditions. Despite this, and despite their having the same event as truth-maker, the two are of quite different form. The Ramsey–Davidson view may spring in part from an echo of the false view that truth-makers are designated by their sentences. Realizing that uniqueness is not guaranteed, they move from designation to the next best thing, quantification. No doubt events make quantificational sentences true, but they make other, non-quantificational sentences true as well, including sentences equivalent to the quantificational ones.[30]

4. Moments as objects of perception

Most philosophers will acknowledge the credentials of at least some of the objects we have called moments. However, many of the sentences of the types we have considered require, on our theory, truth-makers whose existence is controversial, such as particularized qualities. So if moments are to play the role we suggest, it is incumbent on us to give a general defence of their existence, controversial cases included, which is as far as possible independent of their putative status as truth-makers. This is the more important since we have dissociated ourselves from the Ramsey–Davidson argument via logical form, which is treated by many as a principal reason for believing in events and their ilk.

A number of arguments can be offered by friends of moments against the sceptic.[31] We shall concentrate here on just one such, which turns on the fact that moments, like things, may be the objects of mental acts, in particular of acts of perception. If it is conceded that there are episodic mental acts such as seeings, hearings or smellings which have as their objects such things as Mary or a table, then, the argument goes, acts of similar kinds must be recognized which take as their objects such moments as the roughness of the table, Mary's smile, John's gait or Rupert's howling.[32] The philosopher staring hard at a picture of two swordsmen en face may be tempted to think that only independent objects are depicted – the two swordsmen, their swords. But whoever observes swordsmen in the real world sees not only them and their swords but also their particular lunges, parries and much else. These are also depicted in fencing manuals, and it is perception of them, not simply of the swordsmen, which forms the basis for our judgements of a swordsman's competence. Similarly what his mother hears is Rupert's howling, and it is this, or perhaps a particular pitch this howling suddenly takes on, which causes her to get up to feed him. This last point makes clear that, counting events

71

as moments, we accept that moments can stand in causal relations to one another. Rupert's howling causes Susan's hearing him howl, and this (given the prevalent neural conditions underlying maternal concern) causes her to get up. The episodic perceivings are themselves moments standing in causal relations to other events.

This argument has the advantage that it can claim to be neutral with respect to particular theories of perception. The proponent of moments claims merely that whatever connection a theory of perception makes between perceptions and their objects, this connection holds whether the object is a thing or a moment or a combination of the two. This includes theories which award a central role to a causal connection between object and perceptual act. Thus any account of the role of sensations in perceiving things will, we claim, have a parallel in the perception of moments. Profile and perspective problems will present themselves in precisely the same way for perceivings of things and moments. (Do I see the swordsman or just the profile presented to me? Do I see his easy parry or only the phase not obscured by his interposed shoulder?) Further, the problems posed by the interplay between cognition or background knowledge and perception, and by the intentionality (opacity) of perception are – quite reasonably – assumed to arise for both things and moments. Thus the proponent of moments as the sorts of moments they are, only that what we perceive in such cases are moments. Someone seeing a flash of lightning sees a moment: a discharge dependent on the charged air and water-molecules in which it takes place. But he may well not know that it is such a discharge, and there is, surely, a sense in which he does not see its fundaments.[33]

Many philosophers are prepared to accept truth-bearers as abstract entities, and would argue that this obviates the need for truth-makers, since predications about truth-makers can, they contend, be traded in for predications about truth-bearers, with little or no trouble. It is a distinguishing feature of the perceivability-argument for moments that it thwarts a move of this kind. For the moments we have given as examples can, but their associated abstract truth-bearers cannot, be objects of perceptual acts.[34]

The main objection to moments has always been that any job they do can be done by independent objects, together with (on a weak option) the senses of predicate expressions and the relation of falling under, or (on a strong option) universals and the relation of exemplifying. But whoever wishes to reject moments must of course give an account of those cases where we seem to see and hear them, cases we report using definite descriptions such as 'the smile that just appeared on Rupert's face'. This means that he must claim that in such circumstances we see not just independent things *per se*, but also things as falling under certain concepts or as exemplifying certain universals. On some accounts (Bergmann, Grossman) it is even claimed that we see the universal in the thing. But the friend of moments finds this counterintuitive. When we see Rupert's smile, we see something just as spatio-temporal as Rupert himself, and not something as absurd as a spatio-temporal entity that somehow contains a concept or a universal. The friend of moments may simply take the everyday descriptions at face value, which means that his account has a head-start in terms of naturalness.

Confronted with *prima facie* examples of perceivings of moments, such as John's hearing the angry edge to Mary's voice, or Tom's seeing the kick that Dick gives Harry, or Susan's seeing Rupert's smile, the opponent of moments may react in a number of different ways. One ploy is to claim that the noun-phrases apparently designating moments may be replaced *salva veritate* by expressions designating only independent things: 'Susan sees Rupert's smile' by 'Susan sees the smiling Rupert', for example. For moments of moments, as in our first example, or relational moments, as in our second, the replacements will have to be more complicated. 'John hears Mary's angrily edged voice' will not do, as a voice is itself a moment, so it must be something like 'John hears the angrily-speaking Mary', or, more implausibly still, 'John hears the with-an-angrily-edged-voice-speaking Mary', the hyphenated phrase being treated as an unanalysed predicate. For the relational example we need two perceptual acts: 'Tom sees the kicking Dick and the kicked Harry', or, since we have ostensibly only one act here, 'Tom sees the two-person complex consisting of the kicking Dick and the kicked Harry'.

Leaving aside all worries as to the precise nature of the relation between Rupert himself and the smiling Rupert,[35] and questions as to whether there are such things as person-complexes, such attempts are thwarted by opacity problems. For Susan can of course see the smiling Rupert without seeing his smile, John can hear Mary, and, we should add, her angry voice, while missing its angry edge, and Tom can see the two men and miss the kick. In saying this we are deliberately using the perceptual verb 'see' transparently. It might be thought that a way round the recognition of a separate category of moments would be to distinguish between this transparent sense, and an opaque or phenomenological sense, e.g. by subscripting the verb with 't' and 'p' respectively. But however we try to capture 'Susan sees Rupert's smile', e.g. with 'Susan sees$_p$ the smiling Rupert', or 'Susan sees$_t$ the smiling Rupert and sees$_p$ someone smiling', we always miss the mark. For instance, Susan may see$_p$ the smiling Rupert when in fact he is frowning – she mistakes his expression – or she may see$_t$ someone who is smiling, and mistake him for Rupert.

Similar problems beset attempts to use paraphrases involving propositional complements: 'Susan sees that Rupert is smiling' (she may see the smile, but fail to recognize its bearer), or complements using 'as': 'Susan sees Rupert as smiling' (so she might, but he may be frowning).

To rescue his position, the opponent of moments may resort to a series of *de re* perceptual predicates, 'sees-to-be-smiling', 'hears-to-be-angrily-speaking', etc., which allow that, e.g. Susan may see-to-be-smiling (Rupert), without recognizing that it is he, i.e. by taking the terms for the fundaments outside the scope of the intentional verb and putting them in extensional positions.[36] But this ploy cannot cope with situations like the following. Tom wrongly thinks that Dick's kicking of Harry constitutes an attack on him, where it is in fact simply their somewhat unusual way of greeting each other. The moment theorist can accept that Tom sees$_t$ Dick's kick, and since this is his greeting, Tom sees$_t$ Dick's greeting of Harry. But the opponent cannot capture this true material equivalence since he has the true 'Tom sees-to-kick (Dick, Harry)', where all the argument places are extensional, but his 'Tom sees-to-greet (Dick, Harry)' is false, since Tom does not recognize the kick for the greeting it is. There is no way for the opponent to cope with this, short of creating a new extensional position for a term designating something (i.e. some moment) which is both a kick and a greeting, and this is to concede defeat.[37]

It may be that reserves of ingenuity may turn up new ploys to keep moments at bay, but we dare to predict that they will be no more successful than these. Alternative attempts to cope with the cases we have mentioned in ways that do not involve commitment to moments will, we suggest, either fall short of adequacy or be ontologically and epistemologically more complex and more implausible.[38]

5. Truth-making and the *Tractatus*

We have argued that it is possible to establish a cast for the existence of moments, and for the role of moments as truth-makers, at least for certain large and important classes of sentences. In the present section we wish to supplement these arguments with a brief discussion of what is still almost certainly the most sophisticated account of truth-making to have appeared to date, the isomorphism theory of the *Tractatus*.

The structure of the objects which make a sentence true is not, we have argued, something that can be read off from the sentence itself by purely logical means. The determination of this structure may be at least as difficult and empirical a matter as the determination of the truth-value of the sentence in question. For Wittgenstein, by contrast, the determination of the structure of truth-makers is a task not of ontology and of the various material disciplines, but of logic, for which nothing is accidental. He could not, therefore, have included truth-makers among the objects found in everyday experience and treated of by the different sciences. He embraced instead a special category of non-objectual entities, which he called *Sachverhalte*, to do the job of making true. Yet there is much that we can learn from his theory of the *Sachverhalt*. We have indeed already taken to heart the doctrine which underlies this theory that it is a mistake to postulate special truth-makers corresponding to logically compound sentences. And we shall have occasion in §6 below to reflect upon Wittgenstein's own ingenious development of this doctrine – in his theory of the *Tatsache*.

The theory of *Sachverhalte* may be summarized briefly as follows: the simple objects which, in Wittgenstein's eyes, make up the substance of the world are configured together in various ways. An elementary sentence is true iff the simple objects designated by its constituent simple names are configurated together in a *Sachverhalt* whose constituents correspond one-to-one with the constituents of the sentence, the configuration of the objects being mirrored in the structure of the sentence. Sentence and *Sachverhalt* are then said to have the same *logische (mathematische) Mannigfaltigkeit* (4.04).

Wittgenstein tells us little as to the nature of the objects which are configurated together into *Sachverhalte*; but he does supply certain hints, as for example at 2.0131, where we are told that:

> A speck in the visual field need not be red, but it must have some colour ... A tone must have some pitch, the object of the sense of touch must have some hardness, etc.

Consider, then, a sentence like: 'This speck [here before me now] is red'. This sentence is made true, it would seem, by a *Sachverhalt* which is a combination of two objects, the speck itself and its colour. One interpretation of *Sachverhalte* sees them as involving both spatio-temporal particulars and universal properties and relations (colour, pitch, hardness, lies between, and the like).[39] Again, it is not clear how particulars and universals may both be constituents of a single entity. A more promising interpretation may be constructed on the basis of some of Wittgenstein's own remarks on the forms and natures of simple objects at the beginning of 2. It is, Wittgenstein tells us, not accidental to an object that it can occur in those *Sachverhalte* in which it does occur. Every one of its possibilities of occurrence in states of affairs must be part of the nature of the object itself, must be written into the object from the very start (2.012, 2.0121, 2.0123). Its possibility of occurring in states of affairs Wittgenstein calls the form of an object (2.0141). Distinct objects may exhibit distinct forms, may be located, so to speak, in distinct spaces of possible states of affairs (2.013).[40] Some objects are such that, in virtue of their form, they call for others as a matter of necessity; a tone must have some pitch, objects of the sense of touch must have some degree of hardness, and so on. Some objects are, that is to say, founded on other objects in the sense of our discussion above.[41]

It is, we suggest, because analytic-philosophical interpreters of the *Tractatus* have standardly lacked a theory of lateral foundation relations, relations which may bind together *individual* objects, that they have been constrained to resort to views of the kind which see *Sachverhalte* as involving both individuals and universal properties. It is open to us here, however, to develop a view of *Sachverhalte* as involving individuals alone, linked together by relations of foundation. 'This speck is red' might be made true, on such a view, by a two-object *Sachverhalt* comprising the speck and an individual moment of redness linked by a relation of mutual foundation. A sentence like 'Atom *a* strikes [at some given instant of time] atom *b*' might be made true by a three-object *Sachverhalt* comprising *a, b,* and that event or individual moment *c* which is their momentary impact, linked by relations of one-sided foundation: between *c* and *a,* and between *c* and *b.* Here the impact moment is distinct in its ontological form from the independent objects with which it is configured, but it is no less particular than these objects.[42] A realist semantics of a non-trivial sort, to be established on the basis of an investigation of the range of possible forms and kinds of (dependent and independent) objects, seems therefore not, after all, to be so completely at variance with a semantics of the kind presented in the *Tractatus.* We are driven back to one important difference, that Wittgenstein believed that an adequate semantic theory must embrace commitment to *absolutely* simple objects, where we are willing to content ourselves with the question of *relative* simplicity, for example of the simplicity that is determined by the elementary sentences of the various material sciences.[43] An investigation of the natures of dependent and independent objects treated of by these sciences then reveals itself as an investigation of objects in the light of their possible configurations into *Sachverhalte,* and a taxonomy of objects in our sense is seen to give rise to an exactly corresponding taxonomy of different kinds of *Sachverhalt* – something like the zoology of facts mentioned by Russell in his lectures on logical atomism (1972: 72ff.).[44]

As an interpretation of the *Tractatus,* however, even of a *Tractatus* modified by the admission of the possibility of our grasping the natures of (relatively) simple objects and of (relatively) simple object-configurations, an account of this kind is still so far inadequate. For it has not been made clear what these simplest kinds of object-configurations *are,* merely that, in order to exist at all, they must involve objects which manifest a distinction in form something like the distinction defended above between moments and independent objects. Wittgenstein himself, as already noted, was ever keen to emphasize that *Sachverhalte* are entities of a peculiar kind, entirely distinct from objects. And this view has acquired the status of orthodoxy amongst contemporary philosophers, despite the fact that Wittgenstein himself offered no more than loose, metaphorical indications of the difference in question. But how is a *Sachverhalt* such as, for example, that which involves the three objects *a, b,* and *r,* to be distinguished from the corresponding complex object (*a*'s-standing-in-the-relation-*r*-to-*b*)? Wittgenstein seems to have been content to regard this distinction as not further explicable, embracing mysticism of a kind which may have done much harm to the enterprise of a correspondence theory of truth. Can we do better? One course would be to develop a view of *Sachverhalte* as being distinguished from the corresponding complexes in involving, or in being in some sense dependent upon, the sentences or sentence-using acts through which they are disclosed: for example, and most naively, by treating *Sachverhalte* as ordered pairs consisting of the relevant complex object and some appropriate sentence. Such a move is however tantamount to sacrificing the conception of *Sachverhalte* as entities in the world existing independently of mind and language. To treat *Sachverhalte* in this way, or as logical fictions of any kind, is to abandon the project of a realist semantics.

Here we wish to leave open the question whether a more acceptable account of the distinction between *Sachverhalt* and complex could be developed.[45] It is one implication of our arguments above that some, at least, of the considerations which have been held to motivate the distinction are lacking in force. But are there other reasons why the logical difference between name and (elementary) sentence should be held to be reflected in a corresponding ontological difference between objects and somehow non-objectual and intrinsically unnameable *Sachverhalte*? Or is the assumption of special categories of entities to do the job of making true one more reflection of the running together of logic and ontology so characteristic of analytic philosophy?

6. Some principles of truth-making

We shall sketch one possible beginning of a formal theory of the relation of making true. Such a theory is, we shall assume, constrained by the requirements we have placed on a realist semantics, and by the principle of the heterogeneity of logic and ontology that forestalls any too ready imputation of logical structure to the objects – both dependent and independent – of the material world.[46] Thus we assume that the (ontological) relations holding among truth-makers – most importantly the relations of part and whole – are distinct from the logical relations holding among propositions or sentences. The fragments outlined here are otherwise intended to be consistent not only with the views outlined above, but also with a range of possible variants.

For the relation of truth-making we use the sign '$\vDash$', which can be read 'makes true that'. Individual truth-makers – whether moments, things, or other, more complex entities – we shall represent by letters a, b, c; sentences (or any other candidate bearers of truth) by letters p, q, r. '$\rightarrow$' in all that follows will signify a connective at least as strong as the entailment of Anderson and Belnap.

The first principle of truth-making must be that what is made true is true, i.e.

(1) $a \vDash p. \rightarrow p.$

But is the converse of (1) also valid; i.e. is it true that

(2) $p \rightarrow \exists a.a \vDash p$?

We have argued that (2) can be affirmed even of simple descriptive sentences only in certain circumstances. A simple sentence like 'Cyril has hepatitis' may be true although there is no single object that makes it true: from the point of view of its truth-makers the sentence may behave as a non-degenerate conjunction. Similarly in regard to, say, 'Jack likes Jill and Jill likes Joe' or 'There have been forty US Presidents to 1981' it is surely counterintuitive to assume that there are any single composite objects making these sentences true, a Jack's liking Jill and a Jill's liking Joe mereologically fused together, or a mereological fusion of all and only US Presidents from Washington to Reagan (in which Grover Cleveland somehow gets counted twice). Rather we should accept that the given sentences are made true by not one but several truth-makers jointly or, as we like to put it, by a manifold or plurality of truth-makers. Such a manifold is not a new, conjunctive object such as a set. There are no conjunctive objects, any more than there are disjunctive, negative, or implicative objects. A manifold is nothing other than the objects it comprehends (and thus a manifold comprehending a single object is simply that object itself).

This suggests a means of dealing formally with conjunctive sentences and related forms by introducing terms for manifolds corresponding in natural languages to singular and plural definite referring expressions like 'Jack and Jill', 'the men in this room', 'Jason and the Argonauts', and so on. Here 'Γ', 'Δ', etc., will be used to stand in for non-empty lists of such expressions. '$a \in \Gamma$' will signify that the individual a is one of Γ, that some term designating a occurs on the list Γ.[47]

We can now generalize (1) to the following axiom:

(3) $\quad \Gamma \vDash p. \rightarrow p.$

And its converse

(4) $\quad p \rightarrow \exists \Gamma . \Gamma \vDash p$

is seen to be acceptable for all simple descriptive sentences and for their conjunctive compounds.

Disjunctive sentences raise no special problems for the theory, since a disjunctive sentence is true only to the extent that one or other of its disjuncts is true – which implies that even a disjunctive sentence like 'This rabbit is male or this rabbit is female', which exhausts the usual possibilities, is made true not by nothing at all, but by whatever is the relevant actually existing condition of the rabbit. Difficult problems are however posed by compound sentences involving negation. Can it be said that all negative sentences about spatio-temporal objects are, like positive sentences, made true by some relevant object or manifold of objects, i.e. that

(5) $\quad \neg p \rightarrow \exists \Gamma . \Gamma \vDash \neg p?$

A duality of this kind can be maintained, it would seem, only for certain kinds of sentences.[48] 'This snow is not warm', for example, may reasonably be conceived as being made true by the individual moment of coldness actually inhering in the snow; 'This salt is not sweet' by the individual moment of taste inhering in the salt:

the respective moments of the coldness and taste are such that they exclude those moments whose existence is denied in the given sentences. What, however, of a sentence like 'This liquid is odourless'? Here there need be nothing in the liquid which excludes its being odorous: it may simply lack any odour.

We may be tempted in regard to this and similar examples to appeal to things themselves, rather than to moments in the things, as that which does the job of making true (to say that the liquid itself makes it true that it is not odorous); but even such a move will be inadequate to deal with other classes of negative sentences like 'Ba'al does not exist'. Here there is quite literally no thing which can do the job of making true, and whilst some might be tempted to appeal to the world as a whole to do this job, it seems more adequate to regard sentences of the given kind as true not in virtue of any truth-maker of their own, but simply in virtue of the fact that the corresponding positive sentences have no truth-maker.

The otherwise attractive principle

(6) $\quad p \leftrightarrow \exists \Gamma.\Gamma \vDash p$

must therefore be rejected in its full generality. Manageable principles having nice truth-functional properties can however be defended if we restrict our attention to those propositions satisfying (6). The stronger principle (2) picks out the propositions in this class which are atomic, but only in the sense that they can be made true by some one individual: it does not even come near to delineating the class of logically atomic propositions, since there are logically compound sentences satisfying (2), and logically atomic sentences for which (2) is false.

Clearly any whole containing a truth-maker of some proposition p which is atomic in the sense of (2) itself makes p true, i.e.

(7) $\quad \forall b: a \vDash p \wedge a \leq b. \rightarrow b \vDash p,$

where '$\leq$' signifies the relation of proper or improper part to whole.[49] The principle embodied in (7) may be extended to positive propositions in general by defining a relation $\subseteq$ of mereological containment between manifolds. Intuitively we wish '$\Gamma \subseteq \Delta$' to express the proposition that the matter of Γ is contained in the matter of Δ, such that if 'Γ' and 'Δ' are singleton-lists then '$\subseteq$' is just '$\leq$'. The definition

(8) $\quad \Gamma \subseteq \Delta: = \forall a \in \Gamma.\exists b \in \Delta.a \leq b$

will not serve, since Δ may carve up the matter of Γ in such a way that there are individuals in which Δ comprehend no single individuals in Γ. On the other hand the definition

(9) $\quad \Gamma \subseteq \Delta: = \forall a \in \Gamma.\forall c(c \leq a \rightarrow \exists b \in \Delta.\exists d.d \leq c \wedge d \leq b)$

appears acceptable.

We accordingly assert:

(10) $\Gamma \vDash p. \rightarrow \forall \Delta. \Gamma \subseteq \Delta \rightarrow \Delta \vDash p,$

which implies a principle of thinning:

(11) $\Gamma \vDash p. \rightarrow \forall \Delta. \Gamma, \Delta \vDash p.$

Two further intuitive axioms are:

(12) $\Gamma \vDash p. \wedge \Delta \vDash q: \rightarrow \Gamma, \Delta \vDash p \wedge q$

(13) $\Gamma \vDash p. \wedge p \rightarrow q: \rightarrow \exists \Delta. \Delta \subseteq \Gamma \wedge \Delta \vDash q.$[50]

And (10) and (13) in turn imply

(14) $\Gamma \vDash p. \wedge p \rightarrow q: \rightarrow \Gamma \vDash q$

whence, in particular,

(15) $\Gamma \vDash p. \rightarrow \Gamma \vDash p \vee q,$

so that

(16) $\Gamma \vDash p. \vee \Gamma \vDash q: \rightarrow \Gamma \vDash p \vee q,$

the converse of which we affirm as an axiom:

(17) $\Gamma \vDash p \vee q: \rightarrow \Gamma \vDash p. \vee \Gamma \vDash q,$

and by (14) and (12) we have also

(18) $\Gamma \vDash p \wedge q: \rightarrow \Gamma \vDash p. \wedge \Gamma \vDash q.$

Quantified sentences may be managed in a similar way as follows:

(19) $\Gamma \vDash \exists a.p: \leftrightarrow \exists a. \Gamma \vDash p$

(20) $\Gamma \vDash \forall a.p: \forall a. \Gamma \vDash p,$

which brings us back once more, within the province of truth-functional logic, to the problem of dealing with compound sentences involving negation.

It was in the face of this problem that Wittgenstein developed his theory of *Tatsachen* (facts). Wittgenstein introduces the term 'fact' as meaning "the existence and non-existence of states of affairs". The existence of states of affairs he calls a positive fact, their non-existence a negative fact (2.06).[51] Intuitively the idea seems to be that we can produce a more adequate theory of truth-makers, a theory which can cope equally with all truth-functional compounds (including – though these were perhaps not uppermost in Wittgenstein's mind – the most intractable cases of sentences asserting or denying the existence of complexes), if truth-makers are conceived not, as in the simple *Sachverhalt*-theory, as configurations of objects, but rather as new entities, formed from *Sachverhalte* by application of special functors, the existence of ... and the non-existence of ..., in a way which allows the construction of compound facts whose structure would mirror exactly the structure of logically compound propositions.

We can produce a formal approximation to what Wittgenstein might have had in mind if we introduce variables '*s*', '*t*', '*u*' to stand in for names of actual and possible *Sachverhalte*[52] (or of other candidate elementary truth-makers), writing '——*s*' as an abbreviation for 'the existence of *s*' and '——⊤*s*' as an abbreviation of 'the non-existence of *s*'. To enable us to build up recursively a vocabulary of expressions capable of designating compound facts we shall introduce

$$\text{`} \begin{array}{l} \!\!\!\!-\!\!-t \\ \vdash\!\!\!-\!\!-s \end{array} \text{'}$$

as an abbreviation for 'the exclusion of the non-existence of *t* by the existence of *s*'. If we now define **BF**, the manifold of basic candidate fact-expressions, consisting of all expressions of the forms

$$\text{`}\!\!-\!\!-s\text{', `}\!\!-\!\!\top\!\!-s\text{', `} \begin{array}{l} \!\!\!\!-\!\!-t \\ \vdash\!\!\!-\!\!-s \end{array} \text{'}$$

then the totality **F** of candidate fact-expressions may be defined as the closure of **BF** under successive applications of the functors

$$\text{`}\!\!-\!\!-(\ )\text{', `}\!\!-\!\!\top\!\!-(\ )\text{', `} \begin{array}{l} \!\!\!\!-\!\!-(\ ) \\ \vdash\!\!\!-\!\!-(\ ) \end{array} \text{'}$$

It is clear that both **F** and **BF** are in a certain sense too large: they contain expressions which do not designate facts (which do not designate anything at all). An expression '*A*' in **BF** designates a fact iff

(i) for '*A*' of the form '——*s*', *s* exists,
(ii) for '*A*' of the form '——⊤*s*', *s* does not exist (or, equivalently, '*s*' does not designate),
(iii) for '*A*' of the form '$\begin{array}{l}\!\!\!\!-\!\!-t\\\vdash\!\!\!-\!\!-s\end{array}$' , not both '*s*' and '*t*' designate facts.

An expression 'A' in **F** but not in **BF** designates a fact iff

(i) for 'A' of the form '——B', 'B' designates a fact,
(ii) for 'A' of the form '—┬—B', 'B' does not designate a fact,
(iii) for 'A' of the form '┬─C ╰─B , not both 'B' designates a fact and 'C' does not designate a fact.

Thus 'A' designates a fact iff '——A' also designates a fact. (For '"——A" designates a fact', or equivalently, 'A is a fact', we may also write '⊢A'.)

There is clearly a certain tension between this ontology of positive and negative facts and the "fundamental idea" of logical atomism expressed by Wittgenstein in the passage cited in §1 above. Yet it would contradict Wittgenstein's pronouncements at 1 and 1.1 perhaps too charitably to dismiss his talk of facts, of "the existence and non-existence of states of affairs", as a mere façon de parler. Not only Wittgenstein, but indeed almost all other philosophers who have investigated the relation of making true, have felt compelled in the face of the problems raised by negative propositions to adopt an ontology of truth-makers as special, non-objectual entities having a complexity which is essentially logical. We remain convinced nevertheless that it is possible to develop a theory of the truth-relation which appeals only to objects firmly tied into our ordinary and scientific experience. For it is in such experience, and not in the abstract models of logical semantics, that there lie the origins of knowledge of truth and falsehood.[53]

Notes

1. First published in *Philosophy and Phenomenological Research* **44**(3) (1984), 287–321.
2. Ontologies of *Sachverhalte* were defended also by Reinach (in his 1911) and Ingarden (1964/65: ch. XI; cf. the discussion in Smith 1978). Meinong preferred to use the term '*Objective*'.
3. Cf. Husserl (LU VI, §39): "At each step … one must distinguish the true-making state of affairs from the state of affairs constitutive of the self-evidence itself."
4. Aristotle's famous "To say of what is that it is not, or of what is not that it is, is false, while to say of what is that it is, or of what is not that it is not, is true" (Met. 1011ᵇ32ff.) is, as Tarski himself is anxious to claim (1944: 343), a less than full-blooded correspondence theory, but Aristotle is elsewhere (*op. cit.* 1027ᵇ22, 1051ᵇ32ff.) prepared to speak of truth reflecting "combinations" of subject and attribute in reality.
5. Cf. Also the opening sections of Weyl (1918).
6. It parallels, perhaps, the indeterminacy of a theory of the natural numbers founded on the five Peano axioms. It is not only the natural numbers as we normally conceive them which provide a model for such a theory, but also, for example, the negative integers, the even numbers, the natural numbers greater than a million, and many other progressions. Even if we add recursive axioms for addition and multiplication to eliminate the interpretations above, we cannot rule out non-standard models. We can narrow down to the natural numbers only if we take account of their application, outside the formal theory, in counting.

7. We use 'object' for all those entities which can be named, leaving open whether there are other, non-objectual entities, such as the *Sachverhalte* and *Tatsachen* of the early Wittgenstein.
8. On the provenance of such diagrams, cf. Angelelli (1967: 12).
9. Cf. Husserl (LU III, §4); Smith & Mulligan (1982: §3).
10. According to Spinoza (*Ethics,* Part I) this is the *only* non-moment and similar views can be found in Husserl. Campbell (1976: 103) suggests that Spinoza's views may be upheld on the basis of modern physics. However, as Husserl indicates, there are various possible senses of "dependent", which accordingly allow different notions of moment and substance to be defined (cf. Simons 1982a). Individual organisms, conceived by Aristotle as substances, are mere modes for Spinoza and mere aggregates for Leibniz; since all three, we may suppose, were operating with different notions of substance, these conceptions need not in fact be incompatible.
11. Cf. Smith & Mulligan (1982: §§1–3).
12. See the third Logical Investigation and also Husserl (1894), which represents a half-way stage between the early Brentanist theory and Husserl's fully developed formal ontology.
13. Findlay (1963: 129, 131); Grossman (1974: 5, 100ff.).
14. The following list is not complete, but it shows the tenacity of the idea, despite its lack of general acceptance: J. Cook Wilson (1926: II, 713), P. F. Strawson (1959: 168; 1974, 131) (particularized qualities); D. C. Williams (1953), K. Campbell (1976: ch. 14) (tropes); P. T. Geach (1969: 77–80) (individualized forms); G. Küng (1967: 166ff.) (concrete properties); D. C. Long ([1968] 1976) (quality-instances); N. Wolterstorff (1970: 130ff.) (cases or aspects); R. Grossman (1974: 5ff.) (instances); A. Kenny (1980: 35ff.) (accidents). It is interesting that none of these thinkers has recognized the possibilities of ramification among moments; e.g. that there are moments of moments, moments of parts, parts of moments, etc. Cf. Husserl (LU III, §18ff.), Smith & Mulligan (1983).
15. The interpretation and defence of Husserl's theory, the history of the concept since Brentano, and its applications in various disciplines, are all topics we have treated elsewhere: cf. the essays in Smith (1982b).
16. *De re* necessity will be understood here as a matter of the necessary structure of objects and object-configurations, not, as in many contemporary writings on essentialism and related notions, as a matter of relations between objects and concepts, or between objects and descriptions under which they fall.
17. These issues are discussed in Smith & Mulligan (1982: §6; 1983), and in Smith (1981).
18. Husserl's characterization of foundation and dependence in LU III makes indispensable use of kinds, which we have here tried to avoid: cf. Simons (1982a) and for an exposition more sympathetic to Husserl, Smith (1981).
19. When Leibniz objects to relational accidents as accidents "in two subjects, with one leg in one, and the other in the other, which is contrary to the notion of accidents" (Alexander 1956: 71), he too is misled by the connotations of "in", which applies at best to those non-relational accidents located within the space occupied by their fundaments. A better all-purpose preposition is the genitive "of".
20. See Vendler (1967: ch. 5, "Facts and Events"), who shows very clearly that: "If the correspondence theory requires a relation between empirical statements and observable entities in the world, then facts are not qualified for this latter role" (pp. 145ff.). Vendler is one of the few philosophers to have seriously studied nominalizations. Another is Husserl (in the appendix on syntactic forms and stuffs to the *Formal and Transcendental Logic*). Cf. also Strawson (1974: esp. 130 ff.).
21. Ramsey (1978: 44). Cf. Prior (1971: 5). Ramsey's arguments are anticipated by Reinach in his 1911: see esp. §8ff. of the translation.
22. We may call this minimal truth-maker *the* truth-maker for the sentence, thereby making a non-Russellian use of definite descriptions. Thus Sharvy (1980) has shown how definite descriptions may pick out maxima rather than unique objects. 'The coffee in this room', for example, picks out the total quantity of coffee in the room. That descriptions may pick out also minima is shown not only by the example mooted in the text but also by, e.g. 'the place where the accident happened', which picks out the smallest spatial extent circumcluding the accident.
23. The difference between Russell and Wittgenstein consists principally in the fact that Wittgenstein has stronger criteria for simplicity and independence: cf. Simons (1981c).

24. One attraction, which dies hard, is that of exhibiting all the entailments of a sentence as resulting from the substitution of synonyms and from the application of the inference rules for the logical constants (i.e. of exhibiting all entailments as analytic in the Fregean sense). A sentence p' *analyses* p, let us say, when p' arises from p in this manner. The two sentences are then logically equivalent, and the purely logical consequences of p' (those obtained through the rules for logical constants alone) properly include those of p. So p has some consequences which cannot be derived from it by purely logical means, but can from p'. Since p' more closely resembles the desired ideal, it is common to conceive it as exhibiting a "hidden" logical form of p. If the ideal is discredited however (cf. the attempt in Smith 1981), then this conception too loses its attraction. The ideal amounts to the disputed claim, which we reject, that necessity is analytic.

25. To regard a as truth-maker for 'a exists' is of course to cut against the grain of the established Fregean view that all meaningful existential assertions are assertions about concepts (*Grundlagen*, §53). At the same time however a reading of Kant in the light of our conception must cast doubt upon the common assumption that, with his doctrine that "existence is not a predicate", he had merely anticipated Frege. If God's existence is rejected, Kant writes, "we reject *the thing itself* with all its predicates; and no question of contradiction can arise" (A595/B623, our italics).

For Kant singular existence statements are meaningful (since synthetic), where Frege's official line (cf. e.g. his "Über den Begriff der Zahl. Auseinandersetzung mit Kerry") is that they are meaningless. Even where Frege bends over backwards to give them a meaning (in the "Dialog mit Punjer über Existenz") they come out either as necessarily true or as disguised metalinguistic statements.

26. Meinong significantly calls that which makes the difference between an object's existing and its not existing a 'modal moment' (cf. his 1915: 266ff.; Findlay 1963: ch. 4). There are other such moments, among them one marking the factuality or subsistence (*Bestehen*) of an objective or state of affairs. The doctrine of modal moments was refined and considerably extended by Ingarden in his 1964/65, esp. vol. I.

27. Not all the alternatives canvassed here are compatible with one another; the following is an inconsistent tetrad:

    (1)   '$a = a$' is true but has no truth-makers.

    (2)   If '$E!a$' is true, then a makes it true.

    (3)   '$\exists x.\Phi x$' is made true by whatever makes any instance 'Φa' true.

    (4)   '$E!a$' and '$\exists x.x = a$' are logically equivalent.

Various means of resolving this inconsistency suggest themselves. That closest to classical logic would reject (1) and make a the truth-maker for '$a = a$'; it must then regard '$a = a$' as meaningless or false if a does not exist. The solution closest to free logic is to reject (3) and replace it by:

    (3*)   '$\exists x. \Phi x$' is made true by whatever pairs a, b are such that a makes '$E!a$' true and b makes 'Φa' true.

If we introduce a non-standard particular quantifier for which there holds the equivalent of (3) with 'Σ' replacing '$\exists$', then '$\exists x.\Phi x$' and '$\Sigma x.E!x \wedge \Phi x$' are logically equivalent. Such a quantifier already exists in the work of Leśniewski (cf. Simons 1981a).

28. Simons (1982a,b).

29. Like Ramsey, we say that events exist, where it would be more idiomatic to say that they occur or happen. Similarly we use 'exist' for states of affairs, instead of the more usual 'obtain' or 'hold'.

30. *Ad hominem*, Davidson's own psycho-physical identity theory allows one single event to make true two non-synonymous sentences, one in physical, one in mental vocabulary. Davidson (1980: 214ff.).

31. A reistic ontology, in which there are only independent things standing in relations of total and partial resemblance, will be unable to account satisfactorily for the natural affinities even between these things, let alone between entities such as smiles, gaits, howls, strokes, aches, etc. The friend of moments can however point to the similarities between moments to flesh out the account, whilst however avoiding commitment to universals (cf. Simons [1983] for a sketch of an ontology of things

and moments which remains squarely within the ambit of nominalism). This is one reason for being well disposed toward moments. Other arguments turn on the fact that only a commitment to moments can enable us to render intelligible the constraints on division of material objects into smaller pieces, and that the existence of formal as well as material relations between objects makes sense only on the assumption that there are moments. Cf. Smith & Mulligan (1982, 1982).

32. This argument derives from Husserl. See e.g. LU VI, §§48–50.

33. Dependence was originally defined by the psychologist Stumpf (1873: ch. 5) in terms of the impossibility of separate perception. That is (roughly) *a* is dependent upon *b* iff *a* cannot be perceived separately from *b*. It was definitions of this sort which served as the starting point for Husserl's work on a more general, ontological theory of dependence relations and Husserl clearly believed that his work represented a natural extrapolation of that of Stumpf. It would thus be surprising if it were possible to find clear-cut examples of moments in Husserl's sense which are perceivable separately from their fundaments. Can we see a shadow or a silhouette in separation from its object, or is it not rather the case that in seeing a shadow we see also the object itself (albeit from a certain perspective)? When we perceive the warmth flowing from a source of radiant heat, do we thereby perceive also the source (again, from a certain perspective)?

34. On Locke's theory of perception we *never* perceive substances (substrata) but only their accidents (*Essay*, bk II, ch. XXIII). A less extreme and inherently more plausible position is that whenever we perceive a substance we do so by virtue of perceiving one or more of its moments. Cf. Kenny (1980: 35). If this is right, then the perception of moments, far from being peripheral, is a key issue in cognitive theory.

35. The most likely answer to this problem is that they are (if Rupert smiles) identical. (What if he does not?) But Brentano would seem to regard Rupert as a *proper part* of smiling Rupert. In his terminology, Rupert is a substance, smiling Rupert an accident. Cf. Brentano (1933: 107ff., 119ff., 151ff.); Chisholm (1978).

36. Cf. Quine (1976: ch. 17); Chisholm (1981: ch. 9).

37. While the Ramsey–Davidson account of event-sentences can in large part be replaced by a logic of predicate-modifiers – cf. Clark (1970), Parsons (1972) – this does not dispose of events, as Horgan (1978) thinks: no amount of predicate modification can account for our perception of events.

38. Even stronger arguments for the existence of moments may be formulated on the basis of their role as objects of *memory* and other acts. For here, the (normal – cf. n.33) co-presence in perception of the moment with its fundament is quite commonly confounded by the selectivity of memory. John may for many years remember, for example, the *intonation* of a particular utterance Mary once directed at him, while forgetting both Mary herself and indeed the utterance in question. Mary's smile may remind him (*de re*) of that of his nurse, whose smile captivated him at a tender age, though he has long since forgotten the nurse herself.

39. Stenius (1964: e.g. 63), and the relevant writings of G. Bergmann and E. Allaire.

40. There are two possible readings of Wittgenstein's talk of "possible states of affairs" in the *Tractatus*. On the first, Meinongian reading, we can say that there are possible states of affairs in addition to the actual states of affairs; on the second, more sober reading, we say that there are only actual states of affairs, though it is possible that others might have been actual. Here and in what follows we adopt the second reading. Terms apparently denoting possible states of affairs ought therefore to be treated in every case as syncategorematic.

41. More precisely, what we have here is generic foundation in the sense of §4 of Simons (1982a).

42. For further details cf. Simons (1981c).

43. On absolute and relative simplicity cf. Husserl (LU III§ I; *Experience and Judgment*, §§28ff.).

44. To determine which are the simplest kinds of objects constituting the subject-matter of a given material discipline is to determine also the kinds of *Sachverhalte* which make true, as a Wittgensteinian might conceive things, the elementary sentences of that discipline. Wittgenstein himself embraced something like this project with respect to the discipline of psychology in his unjustly neglected "Some Remarks on Logical Form" of 1929. It is one consequence of our arguments that Wittgenstein's idea of a directly depicting language, or of a family of such languages, may prove to be capable of being resurrected. Since, as we stressed above, there is lacking any isomorphism between the logically simple

sentences of *natural* languages and their truth-makers, a directly depicting language would need to employ mechanisms which do not closely resemble linguistic devices with which we are familiar; it may perhaps approximate to the picture-languages employed in organic chemistry. Cf. Smith (1981), Smith & Mulligan (1982: §6; 1983).

45. Such an account is attempted in Mulligan (1983); contrast Simons (1983).

46. Thus work on the formal properties of the truth-relation such as that of van Fraasen (in Anderson & Belnap 1975: §20.3), whilst having a number of methodological similarities to the account presented here, falls short of our requirements in being committed to different logical categories of truth-maker for different logical categories of sentence.

47. We spare the details of manifold theory here. It can be compared to a theory of sets truncated at the first type, without a null set and with no type difference between individuals and unit sets. Cf. Simons (1982c).

48. And we must reject also any definition of the relation of making true in terms of an existence predicate and entailment connective taken as primitive, for example of the form:

$$\Gamma \vDash p := p \,.\, E! \Gamma \vDash p.$$

This principle certainly holds from left to right: it expresses the fact that '$\vDash$' is in one sense a link between the domain of ontology and the domain of logic. But from right to left the principle fails, as can be seen, for example, by considering disjunctive values of p.

49. On the question whether p has a *minimal* truth-maker see Smith (1982a).

50. (13) may be too strong: it implies that, where pq, we can conclude that any truth-maker for p contains some truth-maker for q. Consider, however, an entailment such as: that there exists a funeral entails that there exists a death. Here a truth-maker of the antecedent, i.e. any complex event which is a funeral, need not (and typically does not) contain a death as one of its parts. Funeral and death are connected, rather precisely, by a (lateral) relation of one-sided foundation.

51. Cf. Also 2.062, 2.11, 2.201, 4.1 and compare the discussion in Dietrich (1974: §2).

52. See n.30 above.

53. Our thanks go to Roderick Chisholm, Kit Fine, Wolfgang Künne, Richard Routley and to other participants in the 1981 Wittgenstein Symposium in Kirchberg, where these ideas were first aired.

CHAPTER 4
Truth-makers, entailment and necessity[1]

Greg Restall

Australian Realists are fond of talking about *truth-makers*. Here are three examples from the recent literature

> ... suppose *a* is *F* ... What is needed is something in the world which ensures that *a* is *F*, some truth-maker or ontological ground for *a*'s being *F*. What can this be except the state of affairs of *a*'s being *F*?
>
> (Armstrong 1989a: 190)

> If *b* entails Π, what makes Φ true also makes Π true (at least when Φ and Π are contingent). (Jackson 1994: 32)

> The hallowed path from language to universals has been by way of *the correspondence theory of truth*: the doctrine that whenever something is true, there must be something in the world which makes it true. I will call this the Truthmaker axiom. The desire to find an adequate truthmaker for every truth has been one of the sustaining forces behind traditional theories of universals ... Correspondence theories of truth breed legions of recalcitrant philosophical problems. For this reason I have sometimes tried to stop believing in the Truthmaker axiom. Yet, I have never really succeeded. Without some such axiom, I find I have no adequate anchor to hold me from drifting onto the shoals of some sort of pragmatism or idealism. And this is altogether uncongenial to me; I am a congenital realist about almost everything, as long as it is compatible with some sort of naturalism or physicalism, loosely construed. (Bigelow 1988a: 122–3)

The notion of a truth-maker is a central feature of a number of philosophical programmes. We ought to have a clear understanding of what a truth-maker amounts to, of how it operates, and how it is related to other notions, such as entailment and necessity. There are hints of this in the literature but, as I will show, truth-makers are more problematic than many appear to think.

1. Dispelling myths

John Fox gives an elegant account of truth-makers in his paper "Truthmaker". He defines the "truthmaker axiom" as follows:

> By the truthmaker axiom I mean the axiom that for every truth there is a truthmaker; by a truthmaker for A, I mean something whose very existence entails A. (Fox 1987: 189)

As it stands, this axiom needs careful reading. There are a number of ways it could be misinterpreted. Firstly, think of a unicorn. Necessarily, if that unicorn exists, then the claim 'a unicorn exists' is true. So, a unicorn is something whose existence would necessitate the claim 'a unicorn exists'. This doesn't mean that the claim 'unicorns exist' is in fact true, because the truth-maker in question, the said unicorn, does not exist. For a truth-maker to be any good at making things true, it needs to exist.[2]

For a second refinement, consider a philosophical view which takes it that all things which exist, exist necessarily – for example, David Lewis' modal realism. For Lewis, existence "in the broad" is more than being an inhabitant of the actual world. In fact, for Lewis, anything which exists in this broad sense exists necessarily. However, for Lewis, actuality is a contingent matter. What is in the world I am in is a function of the world I am in. And actuality is clearly the appropriate notion for the truth-maker axiom. On this view, a truth-maker for A is some actual object (some inhabitant of the actual world) such that its actuality necessitates A.

For another refinement, consider the truth 'there have been at least three performances of Arvo Pärt's *Magnificat*'. It is hard to see what a truth-maker for this could be other than three performances of Pärt's *Magnificat*. Is there a *single object* which comprises these three performances (and whatever else in the world is needed as the truth-maker for the claim)? If there is, it is hopelessly "gerrymandered". One performance has taken place in Estonia, one in Berlin, and one in Canberra. The 'object' consisting of these performances is at least a bit strange. Some take this to be an object in its own right. Others do not. So, in deference to those of the second persuasion, let us allow a truth-maker to be an object or *objects*.

It is also important to realize what the truth-maker axiom is not. It does not posit a unique truth-maker for every claim. (There are many truth-makers for 'someone has swum across the English Channel', for example.) Similarly, the truth-maker axiom does not posit a minimal truth-maker for every claim, where a *minimal* truth-maker for a claim is a truth-maker which is a part of every truth-maker for that claim. Although people often talk of "the truth-maker" for a truth, the truth-maker axiom does not postulate any kind of uniqueness. The one truth can be made true in any of a number of different ways.

To sharpen up the truth-maker axiom, we need to take account of entailment. The classical notion of entailment in use ties entailment to necessity. On the classical account, A entails B just when it is impossible for $A \wedge \neg B$ to be true. That is, $A \Rightarrow B$ is $\neg \Diamond (A \wedge \neg B)$. This immediately gives rise to our first thesis.

The classical entailment thesis
For any A, s is a truth-maker of A if and only if s exists, and it is impossible that s exist without A.

That is, $s \vDash A$ if and only if E!$s \wedge \neg \Diamond ($E!$s \wedge \neg A)$. (Or, for more than one object, $s_1, s_2, \ldots$ are collectively truth-makers for A if and only if each s_i exists, and it is impossible for them each to exist without A. In what follows we'll ignore the case where more than one object constitutes the truth-maker, simply for convenience. Nothing of substance hangs on the distinction.)

This hypothesis has a number of pleasant consequences for truth-makers and truth-making. The first is an obvious desideratum of any account of truth-making, that if s is a truth-maker for A, that is, if s makes A true, then A is, in fact, true.

Consequence 1: If $s \vDash A$ then A

The argument is simple. If $s \vDash A$ then E!s, and $\neg \Diamond ($E!$s \wedge \neg A)$ yields A as a simple consequence.[3]

There is also a desirable result connecting truth-making and conjunction. If something makes both A and B true, then it also makes their conjunction true, and vice versa. We would hope that this would be a consequence of any account of truth-making.

Consequence 2: $s \vDash A$ and $s \vDash B$ if and only if $s \vDash A \wedge B$

It is also a simple consequence that if something makes A true, then nothing makes $\neg A$ true. As we would hope.

Consequence 3: If $s \vDash A$ then $\neg \exists t (t \vDash \neg A)$

That is enough about the desirable consequences of the strict entailment thesis. It is time to see some of its darker properties. For the first, consider the untoward properties of strict material implication as an account of entailment. It is well known that if A is necessary (so $\neg \Diamond \neg A$) then *anything* "entails" A. (For any B, $\neg \Diamond (B \wedge \neg A)$.) As a result, we have the following consequence.

Consequence 4: If *A* is true, then *any* existing *s* is a truth-maker for *A*

This follows immediately from the definition. Now, this may not be such a problem. There is something quite touching in the view that every particle in the universe (and everything else besides!) is a witness to all necessary truths.[4] If we read the classical entailment thesis contrapositively – *s* is a truth-maker for *A* if and only if were *A* to fail then *s* wouldn't exist – then you can at least see why some would be able to swallow the conclusion. After all, were 2 + 2 to not equal 4, then nothing would be quite the same.

However, polemical point scoring about relevance is not my business here.[5] The problems with the classical entailment thesis are more significant than merely conflicting with our intuitions about what counts as a truth-maker for necessary truth. They threaten collapse of the entire notion of truth-makers. To see this, we need another thesis about truth-makers.

The disjunction thesis
For any truth-maker s, $s \vDash A \vee B$ if and only if $s \vDash A$ or $s \vDash B$.

The disjunction thesis seems quite plausible. I will leave discussing the independent merits of the thesis until later. For now, let us see how the disjunction thesis and the classical entailment thesis interact.

Consequence 5: Every truth-maker makes true every truth

We assume that every instance claim of the form $A \vee \neg A$ is a necessary truth. By one fact we have already seen, every s is a truth-maker for each instance of $A \vee \neg A$. Let *A* be a truth. So, any *s* either makes *A* or $\neg A$ true, by the disjunction hypothesis. Given that *A* is true, then nothing makes $\neg A$ true. So *s* is not a truth-maker for $\neg A$. Hence, it must be a truth-maker for *A*.

The result may be called *truth-maker monism*. We end up with all truth-makers on a par, all making true every truth. This is clearly not acceptable for any philosophically discriminating account of truth-makers.

2. Jackson and necessary truths

Frank Jackson has noticed at least some of the subtleties associated with truth-makers. His approach to truth-makers (as much as we can discern from the throw-away line in Jackson 1994) denies the classical entailment thesis. We will restate Jackson's claim as follows:

Jackson's thesis
If *A* and *B* are contingent, and *A* entails *B*, then if *s* ⊨ *A*, then *s* ⊨ *B*.

So Jackson does not hold that entailment is enough for truth-making in all cases – in the cases where *A* is necessary, not everything need amount to a truth-maker for *A*. And that does seem right. Why should my refrigerator count as a truth-maker for the Goldbach conjecture[6] (or its negation)? We have already seen that assuming the classical account of entailment (*A* entails *B* if and only if it is impossible for *A* to be true and *B* to be false) and the entailment condition for truth-makers (if *s* ⊨ *A* and *A* entails *B* then *s* ⊨ *B*) is sufficient to show that every truth-maker is a truth-maker for every necessary truth.

Unfortunately, Jackson's revision will not do. The argument is simple. We need only two hypotheses. Firstly, that there is a contingent truth (say *C*) and that any truth-maker of a conjunction *A* ∧ *B* is a truth-maker for both conjuncts *A* and *B*. (This is a consequence of the classical entailment thesis, but it is very plausible in its own right.) It is very hard to see how this could fail – if anything makes *A* ∧ *B* true, it must surely make *A* true and make *B* true as well. Given these two hypotheses, then Jackson's revision still faces problems. Granted even his weaker condition, any truth-maker for a contingent truth *still* is a truth-maker for every necessary truth. The argument is as follows. Take *C*, a contingent truth; *s*, a truth-maker for *C*; and *A*, a necessary truth. Because *C* is contingent, so is *C* ∧ *A*. It is impossible for *C* to be true while *C* ∧ *A* is false (because, by hypothesis, *A* cannot be false), so on the classical account of entailment, *C* entails *C* ∧ *A*. So, by Jackson's condition, *s* ⊨ *C* ∧ *A*, and hence *s* ⊨ *A*. It follows that my refrigerator is still a truth-maker for Goldbach's conjecture (or its negation). Hence, Jackson's thesis is a useless modification. It does no work on its own. When coupled with the classical account of entailment, his proviso of *A* and *B* being contingent is irrelevant.

The problem is not restricted to the counterintuitive nature of everything being a truth-maker for necessary truths. If we grant the disjunction thesis, then even using Jackson's restricted thesis, any truth-maker for a contingent truth is still a truth-maker for every truth. The argument is as before. Since a truth-maker for any contingent claim is a truth-maker for every instance of *A* ∨ ¬*A*, that truth-maker must support either *A* or ¬*A*. Jackson's thesis does not prevent the collapse into truth-maker monism.[7]

3. Disjunction: or "or and shmor"

It is clear that the disjunction thesis is doing a lot of work in these arguments. Without it, we simply have counterintuitive results. With it, we have a dreadful collapse into monism. Granted the disjunction thesis and either the classical entailment thesis or Jackson's attempted weakening of the thesis, truth-makers cannot draw any distinctions at all other than that between truth and falsity. Perhaps the problem is with the disjunction thesis, and not with the classical entailment thesis.

Consider how the disjunction thesis could fail. Clearly if s makes A true, or it makes B true, then it will make $A \vee B$ true too. So the right-to-left part is trouble-free. The scope for dispute is the step from $s \vDash A \vee B$ to $s \vDash A$ or $s \vDash B$. Both parties in the dispute can agree that if $s \vDash A \vee B$ then there must be something which either makes A true or makes B true. The issue is whether s itself must be such a truth-maker. Suppose it is not. Then by its very existence (which entails $A \vee B$) there must be another object, a truth-maker of A or a truth-maker of B. As a result, there is a relation of necessitation between distinct objects. The mere existence of s necessitates the existence of some other object. (We must be careful here, for no particular object does it necessitate the existence of that object. Rather, it necessitates the existence of some truth-maker, of either A or of B.) But how can a relation of necessitation of this sort hold between objects? One way is for s to be an aggregate of objects, each of which must exist for s to exist. But this kind of relation of necessitation will not do the job we need to fault the disjunction thesis: if one of the parts of s is to be a truth-maker of either A or of B, then s will also be a truth-maker of A or of B (as s will necessitate anything any of its essential parts necessitate). So, this kind of necessary connection is of no help for one who wishes to fault the disjunction thesis. Anyone who wishes to fault it must explain the kinds of necessary connections between objects which ground a failure of the thesis. Another (stronger) reason to suppose that disjunction satisfies the disjunction thesis is that if it does not, it would make no difference if it did. Let me explain. Suppose that disjunction does not satisfy the disjunction property. We can define an alternative disjunction (read "shmor") by stipulating that $A \bullet B$ ("A shmor B") is made true by a truth-maker if and only if either A or B is made true by that truth-maker. Shmor is just as good a candidate for disjunction as the original variety. Clearly if A is true or if B is true, so is $A \bullet B$. Because if A is true, then it has a truth-maker, and hence $A \bullet B$ also has a truth-maker, and so is true. Conversely, if $A \bullet B$ is true, then one of A and B is true. So, necessarily $A \vee B$ is true if and only if $A \bullet B$ is true. Or and shmor are necessarily equivalent.

We can also show directly that $A \bullet \neg A$ must be true. Given that one of A and $\neg A$ is true, one has a truth-maker, and hence, $A \bullet \neg A$ is true. Since we have shown that $A \bullet \neg A$ must be true (no matter how the truth-makers decide contingent things), we have assured ourselves that $A \bullet \neg A$ is necessarily true. Yet, it need not be made true by every truth-maker. Rather, it must be made true by some truth-maker. This is a more straightforward (but obviously less reductionistic) account of the interaction between truth-making and necessity. The necessary truths are those which must be made true by some truth-maker, no matter how they are "arranged".

Given a choice between or and shmor as accounts of disjunction, how do we choose among them? $A \bullet B$ is necessarily equivalent to $A \vee B$. The disjunction property holds of $A \bullet B$, by its very construction. Who is to say that $A \bullet B$ is not the proper way to analyse the disjunction of A and B?[8]

We have seen that the classical entailment thesis collapses distinctions between truth-makers for necessary truths. We have also seen that the disjunction thesis together with the classical entailment thesis results in monism. Given that simple "fixes" such as Jackson's do not work to repair the damage, and given that there are independent arguments for the disjunction thesis, we must reject the classical entailment thesis in all its forms as an account of truth-making.

4. Truth-makers and worlds

After reading an earlier draft of this note, Frank Jackson responded with a number of arguments against the disjunction thesis. He conceded that what I have called "Jackson's thesis" is an unnecessary amendment to the classical entailment thesis. But he resisted the collapse into monism by rejecting the disjunction thesis. By examining his arguments for rejecting the disjunction thesis, we will be able to see the issues at stake in maintaining a theory of truth-makers.

Jackson's first argument goes as follows. Suppose that $s \vDash A$ for some claim A. Then $s \vDash (A \wedge B) \vee (A \wedge \neg B)$ for any B we like. But we can choose B in such a way that neither $s \vDash B$ nor $s \vDash \neg B$. In other words, we deny truth-maker monism. But with the disjunction thesis, $s \vDash A \wedge B$ or $s \vDash A \wedge \neg B$, thus contradicting our supposition that $s \vDash B$ and $s \vDash \neg B$.

It ought to be clear that this argument is a way of rephrasing our original argument proving monism from the classical entailment thesis and the disjunction thesis. If we hold to distribution (the equivalence of $s \vDash (A \wedge B) \vee (A \wedge C)$ and $\vDash A \wedge (B \vee C)$), then Jackson's argument relies essentially on the fact that any truth-maker for A is a truth-maker for $A \wedge (B \vee \neg B)$. Or equivalently, any truth-maker makes true every instance of $B \vee \neg B$. So, the argument is simply a *modus tollens* to our *modus ponens*. We have shown that the classical entailment thesis leads to trouble, given the disjunction thesis. Jackson's argument shows that, given the classical entailment thesis, the disjunction thesis leads to trouble. This, in itself, is not anything new. What Jackson's argument gives us is another example of where trouble arises. If we grant the disjunction thesis and the principle of distribution, we must deny that any truth-maker for A is also a truth-maker for $A \wedge (B \vee \neg B)$. But that is not a surprise. People have been recommending paring apart A and $A \wedge (B \vee \neg B)$ for many years.[9]

Jackson's second argument relies on what he calls a "model" of the truth-maker story. For Jackson, we can take a truth-maker for the sentence A to be the set of all worlds in which A is true. Then, $s \vDash A$ just when A is true in all worlds in s. A truth-maker is "actual" just when the actual world is a member of s. Given this model, the truth-maker for a disjunction $A \vee B$ is the union of the truth-makers for the disjuncts. So, our argument from distinct existences does not take root – the truth-maker for $A \vee B$ necessitates either the truth-maker for A or the truth-maker for *B*, since together they make up the truth-maker for $A \vee B$, and one of them (at least) must contain the actual world. The truth-makers are not disjoint objects, so that on this picture we have the (somewhat surprising) consequence that a truth-maker for all truths, the singleton set of the actual world, is a part of (a subset of) all actual truth-makers.

This picture certainly provides some kind of counter-example to the disjunction thesis. But is it a satisfying account? There seem to be reasons to think not. Firstly, the truth-makers are what we might call UCLA propositions. They are sets of possible worlds. Some, like David Lewis, take propositions to be UCLA propositions. Whether we agree with this analysis of the nature of propositions or not, it is hard to see what kind of work a UCLA proposition is doing in making a proposition true. This "model" of the theory of truth-makers is not significantly different to what I will call the simple model.

The simple model
Truth-makers are propositions.
A truth-maker is actual if and only if it is true.
A truth-maker makes a proposition true just when it entails that proposition.

Given the simple model, the disjunction thesis must fail. $A \vee B$ is a truth-maker for $A \vee B$, but not *A* nor *B*, for many choices of *A* and *B*. But the reader is entitled to wonder what has been gained by the simple model of truth-making, or Jackson's model of truth-making.

A problem with both Jackson's model and the simple model is that they stray too far from the original purpose of the truth-making account. Neither model takes seriously the view that a truth-maker for *A* is something which by its very existence ensures that *A* is true. Truth-makers, on this conception, are parts of the actual world. The way is open, on this approach, to maintain that the only way a piece of the world can ensure that $A \vee B$ is true is for it to ensure that *A* is true or for it to ensure that *B* is true. And, furthermore, we can maintain this thesis without rejecting the classical account of entailment wholesale, but rather by enriching our account to pay attention to the fine structure of worlds.

5. Bigelow and entailment

Paying attention to the fine structure of worlds can help us make sense of a passage giving Bigelow's treatment of truth-making.

> Entailment may not be all there is to truthmaking. Not every case of entailment will be a case of truthmaking. But, I claim, every case of

truthmaking will be a case of entailment. Perhaps we should formulate truthmaker more delicately, as: 'Whenever something is true, there must be something whose existence entails in an appropriate way that it is true.' This leaves much to be desired, but the main point is that unless the existence of a thing does entail a truth, that thing cannot be an adequate or complete truthmaker for that truth.

(Bigelow 1988a: 126)

We have adduced enough cases to show that classical entailment is not all there is to truth-making. Bigelow's hunch is correct.[10] But he need not look too far for his account of "appropriate entailment". Given what we have seen so far, we can model "appropriate entailment" alongside its classical cousin.

A *world* $W \langle W, \subseteq, \vDash \rangle$ is made up of a collection, W, of truth-makers, ordered by inclusion. So, if $s \subseteq s'$ then s is a part of s'. A world comes equipped with a map $\vDash$ from truth-makers to propositions,[11] which satisfies the following.

- $s \vDash A \wedge B$ if and only if $s \vDash A$ and $s \vDash B$.
- $s \vDash A \vee B$ if and only if $s \vDash A$ or $s \vDash B$.
- For every p, there is an $s \in W$ where $s \vDash p$ or $s \vDash \neg p$.
- For no s does $s \vDash p$ and $s \vDash \neg p$.[12]
- If $s \subseteq s'$ and $s \vDash A$ then $s' \vDash A$, too.[13]

We can then say that A is true in W (written '$W \vDash A$') just when for some $s \in W$, $s \vDash A$. It is simple to show that $W \vDash A \vee B$ if and only if $W \vDash A$ or $W \vDash B$, $W \vDash A \wedge B$ if and only if $W \vDash A$ and $W \vDash B$, and $W \vDash \neg A$ if and only if $W \vDash A$. So, worlds respect the truth-tabular definitions we learned at our mother's knee. We can then define classical entailment as follows: A classically entails B (written '$A \rightarrow B$') if and only if for every W, if $W \vDash A$ then $W \vDash B$. This definition parallels the classical account of entailment by defining it as truth preservation across all worlds. Similarly, A is a necessary truth just when it is true in all worlds. This notion of necessary truth is also identical to the classical dogma.

However, given the finer structure of worlds, we can define another notion of entailment. A really entails B if and only if, in every world W, every truth-maker for A is a truth-maker for B. Let us write this as $A \Rightarrow B$. Then it is simple to show that $A \Rightarrow A \vee B$, $A \wedge B \Rightarrow A$, $A \wedge (B \vee C) \Rightarrow (A \wedge B) \vee (A \wedge C)$ and that if $A \Rightarrow B$ and $B \Rightarrow C$ then $A \Rightarrow C$. However, we do not have $A \Rightarrow (A \wedge B) \vee (A \wedge \neg B)$, nor $A \Rightarrow B \vee \neg B$. Not every truth-maker need make true every necessary truth. Neither do we have that if $A \rightarrow B$, and $s \vDash A$ then $s \vDash B$. For clearly $A \rightarrow (A \wedge B) \vee (A \wedge \neg B)$, but we can find truth-makers for A which need not be truth-makers for $(A \wedge \neg B) \vee (A \wedge \neg B)$.

The entailment is nearly, but not quite, the first-degree entailment of relevant logic (see, for example, Anderson & Belnap 1975). It can be seen that we have $A \wedge \neg A \Rightarrow B$, because there are no truth-makers for $A \wedge \neg A$ in any world.

But we can get closer to first-degree entailment by setting $A \Rightarrow_2 B$ if and only if $A \Rightarrow B$ and $\neg B \Rightarrow \neg A$. Then we do not have $A \wedge \neg A \Rightarrow_2 B$, but we still have $A \wedge \neg A \Rightarrow_2 B \vee \neg B$.[14]

These models are a simple, understandable generalization of possible worlds semantics. Instead of taking possible worlds as atomic, we look inside possible worlds to see their fine structure of truth-makers. This gives us access to a more discriminating account of entailment, which can support our pre-theoretic notions of truth-making. I recommend it to all those who seek to understand contemporary work on relevant logic,[15] and for those who wish to form a robust theory of truth-making.[16]

Notes

1. First published in *Australasian Journal of Philosophy* 74(2) (June 1996), 331–40.
2. I am being a little too quick here. Given a particular unicorn, u, it may not be the case that in every world in which u exists, it is a unicorn. If this is the case, then u, by itself, is not a truth-maker for 'there is a unicorn' in any of the worlds in which it exists. However, the point that a truth-maker must exist for it to be any good as a truth-*maker* remains unscathed.
3. Using disjunctive syllogism. Relevantists will baulk at this point. But they have already baulked at the classical entailment thesis.
4. This gives logic a certain grandeur!
5. I refer the reader to Anderson & Belnap (1975), Anderson *et al.* (1992) and Routley *et al.* (1982) in which the relevant polemical points are made more forcefully than I can here.
6. The Goldbach conjecture states that every even number is the sum of two primes.
7. An anonymous referee pointed out that my "trivializing" arguments are reminiscent of Davidson's "Frege Argument", which is employed, for example, in some essays in his *Essays on Actions and Events* (1980). However, what we do with the results is obviously very different. For Davidson, the failure of intersubstitutability of logically equivalent statements is a sign that a sentential connective is not involved. On my account, on the other hand, we can construct a sentential entailment connective (see §5) for which substitutability of (classically) equivalent statements fails.
8. This argument is open to question, at the level of the definition itself. We may ask whether this is a permissible definition. An obvious question is raised by the threat of circularity. We use disjunction in the defining clause, yet we are defining disjunction. This is not a problem, because if you think that $\vee$ and • are different, then I can use $\vee$ in the defining clause. If you take • and $\vee$ to coincide, you will note that the definition is circular; but then you have no need of the argument, as you already hold its conclusion. The definition could fail for some other reason – but I cannot at present see what kind of reason this would be. I must leave it for others to show how this definition might fail.
9. For examples and more on this theme see Perry (1986). Thanks to Gary Malinas for reminding me of this paper, which has themes quite close to the topics at hand here. It will be clear to those familiar with situation semantics that this paper is recasting the ideas of situation semantics for an "Australian Realist" audience. It should also be mentioned that this approach is somewhat similar to that of van Fraassen's "Facts and Tautological Entailments" (1969). However, van Fraassen's approach takes facts to be complexes of relations and objects (he follows Russell at least that far). This present project does not follow van Fraassen or Russell down that path.
10. Bigelow also examines the problems of making truth-makers work for negative or universal claims, like 'there are fewer than $n + 1$ camels'. He proposes revising the truth-maker thesis to say that for any truth, A, either for some collection of objects their existence (appropriately) entails A, or $\neg A$ (appropriately) entails the existence of some objects which do not actually exist. This revision is orthogonal to our present purposes.

11. For the moment we consider propositions to be made up inductively from atomic propositions p_1, p_2, ... and their negations, $\neg p_1$, $\neg p_2$, ..., closing under $\wedge$ and $\vee$. We can then define $\neg(A \wedge B)$ to be $\neg A \vee \neg B$ and $\neg(A \vee B)$ to be $\neg A \wedge \neg B$. This simplifies the treatment of negation in the clauses below.

12. I have written elsewhere (1993, 1994) of the need to question the assumptions of non-contradiction and bivalence. However, the task here is to show how even those who hold staunchly to classical doctrines can understand relevant entailment, through the models of worlds made up of truth-makers.

13. This condition is not essential to the rest of the paper. You can do away with it if you like (or you can trivialize it by saying that truth-makers do not enter into part-of relations with each other, thereby making $s \subseteq s'$ only if $s = s'$). I include it only to show that it can be a part of a semantic picture of truth-makers.

14. The resulting logic is the first-degree fragment of the relevant logic, RM, as a referee pointed out to me.

15. This account of truth-makers only tells us when an entailment is true. It leaves aside the question of what it is that makes an entailment true. This is the point at which the "ternary relational" semantics for conditionals enters the theory of relevant logics. Whether or not sense can be made of these constructions in terms of truth-makers is a pressing issue. I have addressed some of the issues involved when considering connections between relevant logics and situation semantics. See Restall (1995a).

16. Thanks to Frank Jackson, Graham Priest, Daniel Nolan, Gary Malinas and Philip Pettit for encouragement, ideas and information. Thanks, too, to three anonymous referees for their helpful comments.

CHAPTER 5

Postscript to "Truth-makers, entailment and necessity"

Greg Restall

It is twelve years since the publication of "Truth-makers, entailment and necessity", and some of my views on the topics discussed have changed in that time. More recent work on truth-making (in particular, Lewis's "Truth-making and difference-making", this vol., Ch. 6) has convinced me that the idea that truth depends on ontology can be captured in a number of different ways. Which ways we take to be most appealing will depend on a whole host of views or commitments, not the least being those concerning what different kinds of things there *are*.

Elsewhere I have shown that the robust picture of truth-making in "Truth-makers, entailment and necessity" can apply in a very simple "world" in which the truth-makers are regions in which atoms are either present or not (Restall 2000). No strange "negative" or "universal" facts need to be added to that picture; regions together with their inhabitants can suffice, so worries about the queerness of "negative" or "universal" facts need not worry the friend of robust truth-making if the metaphysics is kind enough to supply everyday objects that do the job.

However, some of my views have changed more significantly, since 1996. I am now convinced by an argument of Stephen Read, in "Truthmakers and the Disjunction Thesis" (2000) that the "or and shmor" argument in §3 of "Truth-makers, Entailment and Necessity" is too swift. In the rest of this note, I will give an account of Read's concern, and then chart four possible responses to it from the perspective of one who wishes to maintain the broad outline of the position of "Truth-makers, entailment and necessity".

The crucial case, for me, is Read's example of the horse race. We are to consider a circumstance s, including a field of horses, such that *if a horse race is run, then either Valentine or Epitaph will win*. Formalize this as $<m \rightarrow (p \vee q)>$. So we grant that

$$s \vDash m \rightarrow (p \vee q)$$

The situation s makes it true that if a race is run, either Valentine is the winner, or Epitaph is the winner.

Now take a situation r in which we *start to run* that race. So

$$r \vDash m$$

The situation r makes it true that a race is run. (Let us grant that once a race is started, if it is called off before the expected conclusion, the result is *still* a race – a shorter race, but a race nonetheless.) It follows that if we consider the larger situation $(s + r)$, we have

(A) $(s + r) \vDash p \vee q$

But in addition, we have

(B) $(s + r) \vDash p$ and $(s + r) \vDash q$.

The race so far determines that one of Valentine or Epitaph is the winner, but it does not determine that Valentine is the winner, and it does not determine that Epitaph is the winner.

Here are the possible responses to such an example:

(1) *Reject the disjunction thesis.* This is Read's preferred option. Notice that this is compatible with relevantism about the notion of entailment used in expressing truth-making, but it blocks the argument of my paper to relevantism from the case of logical truths such as $<p \vee \sim p>$. I argue that we should accept a relevant entailment in the analysis of truth-making, since the disjunction thesis together with a classical entailment analysis trivializes truth-making. This argument breaks down in the absence of the disjunction thesis.

If you wish to *retain* the disjunction thesis in some form, you must respond to the dilemma of the appeal of (A) and (B). Here are the options. For the first option, we do not, in fact, modify option (1), but we *extend* it with an explanation.

(1′) *Restrictivism about truth-makers.* Yes, the existence of the race up to that point makes true the disjunction but neither disjunct, but the race up to that point is not a *genuine* truth-maker. Not every object is a genuine truth-maker. A genuine truth-maker is one that makes true each disjunct of every disjunction it makes true. A restrictivist about truth-makers does not take every object (or event or circumstance or situation) to be a truth-maker, properly so called – or at least, to be a truth-maker satisfying the disjunction thesis. The odd thing about the partially run race could be that it is a circumstance which "projects" into the future. It makes claims on what happens later, without *determining* what happens later. This overreach is what makes it a counter-example to the disjunction thesis.

But, on this view, it is not a worrying counter-example, for although $(s + r)$ makes true $<p \lor q>$, a more comprehensive circumstance (the whole race, for example) makes true one of the disjuncts, and – it is to be hoped at least – makes true a disjunct of *each* disjunction it makes true.

This kind of restrictivism (only special objects count as genuine disjunctive truth-makers) is a possible response, but as it stands, it is more of a *hope* than a response. What reassurance do we have that there are *any* truth-makers for which the disjunction thesis holds? If we are willing to grant that there are objects for which the disjunction thesis fails, why should any object be any different?

So the friend of the disjunction thesis should probably look elsewhere. Let us see what happens if we take one horn of the dilemma.

(2) *Accept (A) and reject (B)*. Despite appearances, the race thus far determines which horse will win.

This is unpalatable. It flies in the face of the examples we give that restricted parts of the world make true only limited truths. The *event* of the victory is not a part of the part of the race so far, and what makes it true that *Valentine* wins is Valentine's victory (or any other situation *including* Valentine's victory). It is a bitter pill to swallow that a half-run race determines the victor. This seems to rule out on *logical* grounds the plausible thought that the very same first half of another race can be completed in very different ways.

So, let us consider the remaining options. The most straightforward of these is the opposite of option (2).

(3) *Reject (A) and accept (B)*. Given the disjunction thesis, and given the fact that the half-run race does not make it true that Valentine wins, or that Epitaph wins, on this option, we maintain that it does not make true that either Valentine or Epitaph wins.

This also seems unpalatable. It seems that we must reject the plausible reasoning which held first that $s \vDash m \to (p \lor q)$ (that circumstances were such that *if* a race were run, then the winner would be either Valentine or Epitaph) and that $r \vDash m$, that the half-run race makes it true that a race is run. But according to option (3), we must reject one of these seemingly obvious truths. It looks as if this option is just as bad as those that have gone before, and that the dilemma is a sharp one.

In the rest of this note, I wish to explain why I think that option (3) is not so bad, and that the ideas motivating the original paper lead us to conclude that, in fact, $<m>$ (that a race is run) is *not* made true by r (the half-run race), despite appearances, and that the disjunction thesis is to be retained.

To do this, we supplement our picture slightly, with a crucial distinction.

(3′) *Pluralism about truth-making*. There is a very real sense in which a given circumstance a might make things true in *one* sense, but not in another. There are genuinely different senses of truth-making. We could say that for an object (or circumstance) a, $<p>$ is *inevitable* if and only if in any *world* in which a features, $<p>$ obtains. This is truth-making defined by *classical* entailment. In this sense, for any object a, a logical truth such as $<p \vee \neg p>$ is inevitable, since in any world in which a occurs, $p \vee \neg p$. If you like, we can say that if for a, $<p>$ is inevitable, then *a weakly makes $<p>$ true*. But we must have the understanding that there need be no connection between a and $<p>$ for this to be the case: logical necessities are weakly made true by anything and everything.

The crucial idea behind weak truth-making is a kind of supervaluation: look at *every* world in which a features. If in each of these worlds (somehow or somewhere, whether through a or elsewhere) $<p>$ is true, then $<p>$ is weakly made true by a.

(This notion of robust truth-making and weaker, supervaluationist truth-making was independently made in my "Łukasiewicz, Supervaluations and the Future" [2005] discussing two different notions of truth-at-a-time, one supervaluing over all histories, and the other staying local. The result is a logical framework synthesizing a classical supervaluation semantics with a truth-value-gap Łukasiewicz-like semantics by separating the notion of what is inevitable at a point in time from that which is *made true* by history up to that point in time.)

Now consider the horse race. Look at why we think that $<m>$ is made true by r. The fact is that *however* things turn out, whether we have a long race or a short race, whether it is stopped midstream or runs its natural course, in any world including the start-of-the-race r, we have a race. What *constitutes* the race may be different in each case, and hence, what *relevantly* or *robustly* makes $<m>$ true might differ in each case. The reasons we have for thinking that r makes $<m>$ true only support the claim that r weakly makes $<m>$ true. Acknowledging this means that we can bear the cost of denying that $r \vDash m$. We do not need to deny that there is *any* sense in which it is true, when r has obtained, that m. However, it is not *made* true (in the strong sense) by r. What makes it true that m is the *race*, and that is not yet complete.

It follows that the friend of the disjunction thesis can freely deny (A) while accepting (B). Given the half-run race, it is inevitable that either Valentine or Epitaph is the winner. We need not go further and say that the half-run race *makes* either Valentine or Epitaph a winner. What makes Valentine or Epitaph *win* is the victory at the end of the race.

This case should not be a surprise for those who take objects (such as truth-makers) to come into existence over time. If a truth-maker for $<p>$ (say, that Penny Wong is the Prime Minister of Australia, following Kevin Rudd) does not exist and neither does a truth-maker for $<\sim p>$, then the disjunction $<p \vee \sim p>$ is inevitable, and is weakly made true by anything existing. For a *strong* truth-maker for the disjunction, and for either disjunct, we must wait.

CHAPTER 6

Truth-making and difference-making[1]

David Lewis[2]

1.

The truth about truth, so far as propositions are concerned, is a long but simple story. A proposition is true iff

it is the proposition that a donkey talks, and a donkey talks; or

it is the proposition that pigs fly, and pigs fly; or

it is the proposition that cats purr, and cats purr; or

it is the proposition that servitude to the state is perfect freedom, and servitude to the state is perfect freedom; or ...

So we have the familiar biconditionals – trivial, necessary, and knowable *a priori* –

the proposition that a donkey talks is true iff a donkey talks;

the proposition that pigs fly is true iff pigs fly;

the proposition that cats purr is true iff cats purr;

and so on, for all the propositions there are.

Not for all the 'that'-clauses there are. Some 'that'-clauses fail to name propositions: for instance because of ungroundedness, or because the embedded sentence is a mere expression of feeling in the syntactic guise of a declarative sentence. Further, some propositions cannot be named by 'that'-clauses. First, because there is an uncountable infinity of propositions, whereas there are only countably many 'that'-clauses. Second, because some of the propositions, in fact most of them, cannot be named by 'that'-clauses of finite length. Third, because some propositions cannot be named at all, not even at infinite length, since we lack names for alien properties that are nowhere to be found in our actual world, and that cannot be reached by any sort of construction or extrapolation or interpolation from this-worldly properties. So the story of truth cannot be told completely. But there is no need to complete it. The untold part merely repeats the same pattern over and over, so a tiny sample tells us all we need to know.

(Compare the addition or multiplication of real numbers. Most cases involve numbers with infinite, patternless decimal expansions; we cannot express or grasp even one of these typical cases. Nevertheless we pick up the general concept easily from a tiny sample of atypically simple cases.)

This conception of truth is called "deflationary" (Horwich 1990; Soames 1999: ch. 8). The thought is that it punctures the big, interesting claims made by rival theories of truth such as the correspondence theory, the coherence theory, the pragmatic theory, or what have you. But I don't think that's right.

Suppose some grand theory of truth tells us that the true propositions are just those that satisfy some interesting condition X. Taking the deflationary conception and the grand theory together, we infer that

a donkey talks iff the proposition that a donkey talks satisfies X;

pigs fly iff the proposition that pigs fly satisfies X;

cats purr iff the proposition that cats purr satisfies X; ...

In this way, the deflationary conception and the grand theory coexist peacefully. But by taking them together, we find that the grand theory was not after all a theory about truth. It was a theory of many things. It was a theory of the talking of a donkey and the flying of pigs and the purring of cats, and much else. It told us that the talking of a donkey and the flying of pigs and the purring of cats and ... were all of them matters of correspondence to facts; or were all of them matters of the coherence of a total theory; or were all of them matters of what it's useful for us to believe; or what have you. (Or, to be more cautious, it told us that the talking of a donkey, and so on, were at least equivalent to matters of correspondence to facts, or what not. To impute a direction of conceptual priority may be a gratuitous addition.) When the grand theory was stated in terms of truth, that was just a way of abbreviating its multitude of claims by one concise slogan.

2.

To my mind the most promising, if not the most prominent, among the grand theories of truth are the theories that somehow require what's true to depend on the way the world of existing things is, or on the way some part of that world is. Such theories come in different versions, some stronger and some weaker. I myself am convinced that some version of this idea is right, though I disagree with some of my allies about which version to prefer. But I don't think these theories are theories about truth. They are theories of many things. Once again, the mention of truth is just an abbreviatory device.

Consider first the Truth-maker Principle, defended *inter alia* by C. B. Martin (1996) and D. M. Armstrong (1989b; 1997: ch. 8). The idea has turned up under different names in different philosophical traditions (Mulligan *et al.*, this vol., Ch. 3). In a slogan: every truth has a truth-maker. Spelled out at greater length: for any true proposition P, there exists something T such that T's existence strictly implies (necessitates) P.

Four preliminary comments. First, if P is a necessary proposition, then for any T whatever, T's existence strictly implies P. So the Truth-maker Principle, as I have stated it, applies only trivially to necessary truths. A non-trivial principle requiring truth-makers for necessary truths would presumably replace strict implication by some more discriminating sort of "relevant" or paraconsistent implication (Restall, this vol., Ch. 4). I will not discuss that amendment, but rather will limit my attention to contingent propositions.

Second, the Principle is meant to be more than accidentally correct. So it applies counterfactually: if proposition P is (contingently) false, then *if P were* true, it *would* have a truth-maker. Third, although the Principle applies in the first instance to true propositions, it applies derivatively to true sentences and true thoughts. If S is a true sentence of, say, Latin, then S expresses some true proposition P; and there is a second true proposition, Q, to the effect that S expresses P according to the semantic conventions of Latin; the true propositions P and Q have their truth-makers; and these truth-makers for P and Q jointly constitute a truth-maker for the sentence S. (Or, more precisely, for S as a sentence of Latin; or, more precisely still, for S as a sentence of Latin in such-and-such context.) Likewise *mutatis mutandis* for true thoughts, presumably with functional roles in place of semantic conventions.

Fourth, when we say that T's existence strictly implies P, we mean that every possible world where T exists is a world where P. Possum is a cat, and he is essentially a cat. So Possum makes true the proposition that something is a cat, because every world where Possum exists is a world where something is a cat. But what should we mean by "worlds where Possum exists"? – I myself think that worlds are big things, *cosmoi* (Lewis 1986). They do not overlap. (More precisely, they have no particular parts in common. If there are universals, presumably those are multiply located among the worlds in just the same way they are multiply located in space and time.) Possum is part of our actual world. He is part of no other world. If existing in a world means being part of that world, then Possum exists in no other world but this one; so every world where Possum exists is this world; so Possum turns out to be a truth-maker for every true proposition! That will never do – truth-making was not meant to be so easy. Of course, everyone agrees that there is some sense in which Possum can be said to exist in other, unactualized possible worlds. I myself would say that it is true in a counterpart-theoretic sense: Possum exists vicariously in another world when something that is part of that other world is Possum's counterpart, where the counterpart relation is a matter of intrinsic and extrinsic resemblance (Lewis 1986: ch. 4). But there are many rival conceptions of possible worlds, including conceptions on which worlds are not *cosmoi*, but rather are "abstract entities" which don't have such things as cats as parts of them at all. Further, some who are perfectly willing to speak as I do of unactualized possible worlds do not believe in the existence of these worlds under any conception; rather, they think that to talk of possible worlds is to engage in an innocent fiction (Armstrong 1989a; Rosen 1990). This paper is meant to be entirely neutral on all such questions; I shall take care not to presuppose my own idiosyncratic views. (What can be said from a less neutral standpoint is significantly different. See Lewis 2003, and Rosen & Lewis 2003.) My conclusions here are meant to be acceptable to anyone who agrees that talk of possible worlds is somehow legitimate, whether he takes these worlds and their inhabitants to be "concrete" or "abstract", real or fictitious. So: mean what you like by "exist in a world", provided you have some meaning in mind which does not automatically rule out that an actually existing thing, say Possum, should exist in an unactualized world. As with other grand theories, so with this one: the Truth-maker Principle coexists peacefully with the deflationary conception of truth. But when it does, the two together generate a multitude of consequences about many different things, but not particularly about truth. Thus:

> if a donkey talks, then there exists something T such that T's existence strictly implies that a donkey talks;

> if pigs fly, then there exists something T such that T's existence strictly implies that pigs fly;

> if cats purr, then there exists something T such that T's existence strictly implies that cats purr; …

Since the Truth-maker Principle is meant to apply counterfactually, it applies not only to the truths of our world but to the truths of all possible worlds. Otherworldly truths have their otherworldly truth-makers. If in some world W a donkey talks, for instance, then there exists in W something T such that T's existence strictly implies that a donkey talks.

We noted that the point of mentioning truth was that it allowed us to formulate the Truth-maker Principle concisely, rather than as an infinite list of claims about all manner of things. And when we make explicit that the Principle is supposed to apply to all worlds, we can state it thus:

for any proposition P and any world W, if P is true in W, there exists something T in world W such that T's existence strictly implies P.

The final clause means that every world where T exists is a world where P is true. So we have

(TM)　For any proposition P and any world W, if P is true in W, there exists something T in world W such that for any world V, if T exists in V, then P is true in V.

This logically implies:

for any worlds W and V, if some proposition P is true in W but not in V, then something T exists in W but not in V.

But now I say that for *any* two worlds W and V, there is some proposition true in W but not in V. For myself, I would be content to invoke the doctrine that a proposition just is a class of worlds, and any class of worlds is a proposition. But that doctrine is contentious, and I can get by with less. I need only ask you to accept that for any world W, there is the proposition that world W is actualized; this is a proposition true in W and not in any other world. Given that any two worlds are divided by some proposition, the Truth-maker Principle boils down to a Difference-Making Principle

(DM)　For any two worlds W and V, something T exists in W but not in V.

All mention of truth, and all mention of propositions, has dropped out. The Truth-maker Principle turns out to imply something about how possible worlds can and cannot differ. It says that every difference between worlds is a difference in population. And further, every difference between worlds is a *two-way* difference in population: each world has something that the other lacks. In other words, every difference between worlds requires a difference-maker. In fact, two difference-makers: one in one world and the other in the other.

I once professed agnosticism about whether there are indiscernible possible worlds (Lewis 1986: 224). The Difference-Making Principle says that there are not, since a world in which something exists could scarcely be indiscernible from a world in which it does not. (Remember that whatever existing in a world may mean, it does not just mean being part of that world.) I have no particular objection to abandoning my former agnosticism; but if neutrality were preferred, the needed amendment to what I have said would be easy and harmless. Let a *discerning* proposition be one that never has different truth values in two indiscernible worlds; understand (TM) to be restricted to discerning propositions. (I would say that discerning propositions are qualitative propositions; but those who believe in haecceitistic difference between worlds should say that haecceitistic propositions also are discerning.) It never happens that two indiscernible worlds are divided by a discerning proposition, so we get a restricted form of (DM): only when two worlds are discernible must something exist in one but not the other.

By applying the Truth-maker Principle to the proposition that world W is actualized, we derive this Principle of Distinctive Occupants

(DO)   For any world W, something exists in W and in no other world.

Call such a thing a *distinctive occupant* of world W. The principle that every world has a distinctive occupant is a special case of the Truth-maker Principle. But the general case follows from the special case: (DO) implies (TM).

> *Proof.* For any proposition P and any world W, if P is true in W and T is a distinctive occupant of W, then T is a thing that exists in W such that T's existence strictly implies P.

Hence (DO) must imply (DM). We can verify this directly.

> *Proof.* For any two worlds W and V, if T is a distinctive occupant of W, then T is something that exists in W but not in V.

Whether we have the implication from (DM) back to (TM) is a more difficult question. We can certainly get this far:

(TMP)   For any proposition P and any world W, if P is true in W, there exist some one or more things T_1, T_2, ... in world W such that for any world V, if all of the T's exist in V, then P is true in V.

(DM) implies (TMP), and conversely.

> *Proof.* Let U_1, U_2, ... be all the worlds where P is false. By (DM), we have something T_1 that exists in W but not in U_1; and we have something T_2 that exists in W but not in U_2; and so on for all the U's. Any world V where all the T's exist cannot be any one of the U's, so it must be a world where P is true.
>
> Conversely, let W and V be any two worlds. We have some proposition P true in W but not in V. All of the T's given by (TMP) exists in W; but at least one of them does not exist in V, else P would be true in V.

(TMP) is a *plural* Truth-maker Principle: it says that the T's collectively make P true. (TM) says that some one thing does the job single-handed.

One thing to do might be to rest content with (TMP), and not even try to close the gap between (TMP) and (TM). (This is suggested by Restall, this vol., Ch. 4, 88–9). That would violate the letter, but hardly the spirit, of the Truth-maker Principle as we find it defended by Martin and Armstrong. A point in favour of this course is that it gives us a very natural treatment of plural existential propositions. What makes it true that Max and Moritz exist? – Even if there is no single truth-maker, Max and Moritz can do the job together.

Or instead we might try to lump all the T's together, somehow, into a single truth-maker for P, thus getting from (TMP) to (TM). We need to find something that will exist in any world iff all the many T's exist there. Should we take the mereological fusion of the T's? That will work only under the assumption of Mereological Essentialism, but that assumption is questionable. My left hand is part of me, but it seems that I could have been without it, say because of a misadventure with thalidomide. (I myself think that some counterpart relations validate Mereological Essentialism and other equally legitimate counterpart relations do not.) Should we take the class of all the T's? That will often work, if we assume – plausibly enough, once we've decided that "in a world" needn't mean "part of that world" – that a class of things in a world is itself something in that world. But it won't work if some of the T's happen to be things – proper classes, perhaps – which are ineligible to be members of a class. (Could we really have a world so big that proper classes exist in it? For a strong case that such enormous worlds are to be taken seriously, see Nolan 1996.) If all the T's are classes, we could take their union, but that is again a special case. But the following general recipe will work, given certain plausible assumptions. Split each of the T's into its largest part which is a class and its largest part which is an individual. Take the union of (1) all the class-parts of the T's, and (2) the class of all the individual parts of the T's. In the special case where all the T's are individuals, this reduces to taking their class. In the special case where all the T's are classes, this reduces to taking their union.

It is worth noting that the Principle of Distinctive Occupants also has a plural version:

(DOP)   For any world W, some things T_1, T_2, ... exist in W and do not all exist in any other world.

Just as (TM) and (DO) are equivalent, so likewise are (TMP) and (DOP). Because (DM) is a principle of *two-way* difference-making, it has another consequence: a sort of negative mirror-image of (TMP). This will serve as an introduction to the idea of truth by lack of false-makers, our next topic.

(MI)   For any proposition P and any world W, if P is true in W, there exist some one or more possible things F_1, F_2, ... not in world W such that for any world V, if none of the F's exists in V then P is true in V.

(MI) implies (DM), and conversely.

> *Proof.* Let W and V be any two worlds. We have some proposition P true in W but not in V. None of the F's given by (MI) exists in W, but at least one of them exists in V, else P would be true in V.
>
> Conversely, let U_1, U_2, ... be all the worlds where P is false. By (DM), we have something F_1 that exists in U_1 but not in W; and we have something F_2 that exists in U_2 but not in W; ... Any world V where none of the F's exists cannot be one of the U's, so it must be a world where P is true.

Accordingly, our original Truth-maker Principle, (TM), itself implies (MI).

We have not said that the F's are false-makers for P, in other words that they are truth-makers for not-P. But that is at any rate one case that might arise. P might, for instance, be the true proposition that there are no unicorns; and the F's might be the various otherworldly unicorns. (I assume, *pace* Kripke 1980: 157–8, that 'unicorn' is a predicate that applies to some possible animals but no actual ones; and that any unicorn would be essentially a unicorn. If you like, you may imagine that genetic science has discovered a certain DNA sequence that would code for animals that exactly match the familiar stereotype; that 'unicorn' has been redefined in terms of this sequence; but that no such animals will ever be made.)

3.

The idea that we should set some sort of limits on the ways that possible worlds can differ looks clearly right. To adapt a pair of motivating examples from Martin and Armstrong, it seems preposterous to think that two possible worlds might be just alike except for a difference in counterfactual conditionals about sense-experience; or just alike except for a difference in counterfactual conditionals about how someone would behave if put to a test. To make a difference to those counterfactuals, we need some other difference: perhaps a difference in the arrangement of material objects (or else a difference in God's thoughts) in the one case, or a difference in the agent's inner states in the other. So far, so good. But I doubt that our two-way principle of difference-making is the right limit to set.

Why two-way? Certainly, one good way for two worlds to differ is for one of them to have something that the other lacks. But why must it be reciprocal? If we pass from world W to world V by removing something, why must we add something else to take its place? Why not replace it with nothing at all, and leave a gap? That is to say, why not rest content with a principle of one-way difference-making?

(DM-) For any two worlds W and V, either there is something that exists in V but not in W, or else there is something that exists in W but not in V.

Two-way difference-making is of course not ruled out. But it is no longer required. This one-way Difference-Making Principle would correspond to a weakened version of the Truth-maker Principle that has sometimes been advocated by John Bigelow: "If something is true, then it would not be possible for it to be false unless either certain things were to exist which don't, or else certain things had not existed which do" (Bigelow 1988a: 133). If we take "things" to mean "at least one thing", and if we take Bigelow's principle to apply necessarily, and if we regiment it in terms of possible worlds, it becomes:

(TM-) For any proposition P and any worlds W and V, if P is true in W but not in V, then either something exists in V but not in W or else something exists in W but not in V.

And this is equivalent to the one-way Difference-Making Principle.

Bigelow's principle (TM-) allows truths to have truth-makers, but also it allows them to be true just because they lack false-makers. The simplest case is that of a negative existential: the proposition that there are no unicorns, say. It is true in the actual world just because there are no unicorns to make it false. In any world where it is false, certain things would have to exist which in actuality do not exist, namely one or more unicorns. Those otherworldly unicorns are the one-way difference-makers between worlds like ours where the negative existential proposition that there are no unicorns is true and other worlds where it is false; and in worlds where the negative existential proposition is false, they are the truth-makers for its true negation. What more do we need?

(Two less simple cases: Take the truth that there are cats but no unicorns. Some worlds where it is false have unicorns, others lack cats. Or take the truth that either there are cats or there are no unicorns. Any world where it is false must both lack cats and have unicorns. So neither one of these compounds has a truth-maker, at least not among uncontroversial things like cats and unicorns; and neither one is true just for lack of false-makers.)

Suppose we insisted on positing some sort of truth-maker for the negative existential truth that there are no unicorns. There would have to be something in a unicorn-free world like ours to replace the missing unicorns, thereby making a two-way difference between a world without unicorns and a world with them. These unicorn-replacements would have to meet two conditions. First, none of them could possibly coexist with a unicorn; else it would make the negative existential proposition true even in a world where there was a unicorn. Second, some one of them could not possibly fail to exist in any world where there were no unicorns. (Some or other one, not necessarily the same one in every unicorn-free world.) Else there will be some worlds where the negative existential proposition is true without benefit of a truth-maker. We could call this unicorn-replacement an 'absence of unicorns', understanding that phrase as a genuinely referential term. Or we could call it 'the negative state of affairs of there being no unicorns'. Or we could call it 'the general state of affairs of everything being a non-unicorn'. Call it what you will, I think it is bad news for systematic metaphysics.

In the past, I made two different complaints (Lewis 1999a: chs 12 and 13). First, I complained that such a thing seems to be somehow constructed out of simpler things, among them the property of being a unicorn; yet this cannot be any well-understood kind of composition – mereological, or even set-theoretical – since if it were, the constructed thing would exist if its constituents did, even if unicorns existed as well. Second, I complained that in order to do its job as a truth-maker, the unicorn-replacement must be involved in necessary connections between (mereo-logically) distinct existences; and it is the Humean prohibition of necessary connec-tions that gives us our best handle on the question what possibilities there are. But now I think that the second complaint subsumes the first. For we can explain how unicorn-replacements are constructed out of their constituents, provided we define the "construction" simply in terms of the necessary connections themselves. Then indeed "unmereological composition" has been explained – but in a way that does nothing at all toward excusing or explaining the necessary connections.

To uphold the Truth-maker Principle in its original form, we need to say that if there are no unicorns, there must be a unicorn-replacement instead. Suppose there were no material objects at all; then likewise there would have to be a replace-ment for them, a truth-maker for the negative existential proposition that there are no material objects. We could call this thing an absence of material objects, or a negative state of affairs, or a general state of affairs; and again it would be objec-tionable because its *raison d'être* would require it to be involved in mysterious necessary connections.

Suppose there were no contingent things whatever. Again there would have to be a replacement. So we have a swift reason why there must be something, and not rather nothing: else the proposition that there is nothing would be a truth without a truth-maker. Altogether too swift, say I. (This is not to deny that we might find some better, less swift reason to deny the possibility of a world with no contingent things, even if that denial compromised our commitment to the combinatorial nature of possibility. See Lewis 1986: 73–4; Armstrong 1989a: 24–5, 63–4.)

Martin has noted that when I say that a negative existential truth is true for lack of false-makers, my statement that there are no false-makers is itself a nega-tive existential (Martin 1996: 61). Sometimes, in fact, as in the case of the prop-osition that there are no unicorns, it is the very same negative existential. So the proposition that there are no unicorns is true just because there are are no unicorns! What sort of explanation is that? – No explanation at all, I agree. But who says a Truth-maker Principle, whether weakened or not, must yield inform-ative explanations? I say to Martin: *Tu quoqu*! His original, full-strength Truth-maker Principle says that a positive existential, for instance the proposition that there is a cat, is true because it has a truth-maker. The statement that it has a truth-maker is itself a positive existential. In fact, it is the very same positive existential. The proposition that there is a cat is true just because there is a cat. What sort of explanation is that? – No explanation at all, and none the worse for that.

In sum, I still find *prima facie* mystery in the necessary connection whereby the truth-maker for the proposition that there are no unicorns is something that cannot possibly coexist with a unicorn. Perhaps there is a way to dispel the mystery; but not, I think, without violating the neutrality about controversial issues in the metaphysics of modality which is my policy in the present paper.

4.

Bigelow's retreat to one-sided difference-making and truth by lack of false-makers was a step in the right direction, say I. But I think we ought to consider one further step. Why shouldn't two possible worlds differ without any difference at all in their population? Why shouldn't the difference just be that something has a property – let it be a fundamental property, intrinsic and perfectly natural – in one world which it lacks in the other? Or couldn't the difference just be that two things stand in a relation – let it be a fundamental relation, intrinsic to its pairs and perfectly natural – in one world but not in the other? If we take properties seriously, why shouldn't such a difference in properties suffice to make a difference of worlds?

The strongest principle of difference-making that seems to me clearly acceptable is:

> (DM=) For any two worlds, either something exists in one of the worlds but not in the other, or else some n-tuple of things stands in some fundamental relation in one of the worlds but not in the other.

(We identify 1-tuples of things with the things themselves, so the case of a difference in fundamental monadic properties of something is covered as the case $n = 1$.) There is a corresponding version of the Truth-maker Principle (if we may still call it that):

> (TM=) For any proposition P and any worlds W and V, if P is true in W but not in V, then either something exists in one of the worlds but not in the other, or else some n-tuple of things stands in some fundamental relation in one of the worlds but not in the other.

This principle too has sometimes been advocated – somewhat hesitantly – by John Bigelow. At one point he paraphrased a demand for truth-makers as a question of "what things there must be and how they must be arranged" in order for a certain claim to be true (Bigelow 1988b: 38). It is fairly clear in context that he was not thinking only of the spatio-temporal arrangement of things; I take him to have meant something more like "what particulars and universals there must be, and how they must be arranged in a pattern of instantiation". Soon after, he offered this "attempt to re-articulate the conviction behind Truthmaker: In order for something to be true, there must not only be certain individual things, but *there must also be somehow* that these things are", where the italicized phrase is understood as a second-order quantifier (Bigelow 1988a: 159). Our first step backward from the full-strength Truth-maker Principle relieved us of the burden of finding truth-makers for negative existentials. Our second step relieves us also of the burden of finding truth-makers for predications of fundamental properties. (And again, various compound propositions are affected as well.) Suppose it is true in our actual world that something A instantiates the fundamental property F. (DM=) demands that the difference between a world like ours where A has F and another world where that is not so must either be a difference in what exists in the two worlds, or else a difference in what stands in some fundamental property or relation. If that other world is a world where A and F exist but A lacks F, then the difference is of the latter sort: F is a fundamental property; A has F in one world but not in the other.

If we had not taken this second step backward, we would need to posit a truth-maker either for the predication $F(A)$ or for its negation. A truth-maker for $F(A)$, especially if it is taken to be one single thing common to all and only the worlds where A has F, is called "the (atomic) state of affairs" or "the (atomic) fact" of A's having F. This is something that would not have existed at all if A had not had F.

(It is not something that would still have existed but would not have "obtained"; or something that would have existed but would not have deserved the name of "fact". Therefore it is nothing like a true proposition that might have been a falsehood, or a mathematical representation that might have been a misrepresentation. Not just any theory that posits something called a "state of affairs" or a "fact" is designed to meet a demand for truth-makers.)

Somehow, this state of affairs is said to be constructed – neither mereologically nor set-theoretically – from its "constituents" F and A. I used to complain that I didn't know what this unmereological composition was. But now I think I understand it well enough, because I can define it in terms of necessary connections. To say that the state of affairs is unmereologically composed of F and A (in that order) is to say nothing more or less than that, necessarily, it exists iff A has F. My only remaining complaint is that this necessary connection between seemingly distinct existences has been in no way explained or excused. Unless that mystery can be cleared up, then, despite the undeniable attraction of keeping the Truth-maker Principle as strong and simple as we can, it would be well worth taking the second step backward to get rid of it. And can that mystery be cleared

113

up? Perhaps; but, again, I think not without violating my present neutrality about controversial issues in the metaphysics of modality.

Shall there now be a third step backward? – I see no need for it. In the thesis that all contingent matters supervene on what there is, together with the pattern of instantiation of the fundamental properties and relations, I think we have reached a stable resting place. And, note well, not anything goes: worlds that supposedly differ only in their phenomenalist or behaviourist counterfactuals are still ruled out as decisively as they ever were. So likewise are worlds that differ only in their Molinist counterfactuals about the outcomes of unactualized indeterministic processes (Adams 1977; McDermott 1999). So likewise are worlds that differ only in the lawfulness of their regularities, or only in their causal relations (provided those are not fundamental). So likewise are momentary worlds that differ only in their less-than-fundamental ersatz-historical properties (Keller 2004).

Notes

1. First published in *Noûs* 35(4) (2001), 602–15.
2. Thanks are due to Robert M. Adams, D. M. Armstrong, Phillip Bricker, C. B. Martin, audiences at the Australasian Association of Philosophy conference, 1998, and the Chapel Hill Colloquium, 1999; and to the Boyce Gibson Memorial Library.

CHAPTER 7

The general theory of truth-making[1]

D. M. Armstrong

1. Introduction

We have noticed already that simply to accept the idea that truths have truth-makers by no means dictates just what these truth-makers are. The question what truth-makers are needed for particular truths (what we take to be truths!) can be, and regularly is, as difficult as the question of metaphysics, the question of ontology. To ask the truth-maker question is, I maintain, a promising way to regiment metaphysical enquiry. But it is not a royal road. No such roads are available in philosophy. In this work I will defend various particular answers to the truth-maker question, sometimes (but not invariably) defending metaphysical positions that I have advocated in earlier work, but here always putting the truth-making question at the centre. All the more reason then, to distinguish between the general theory of truth-making and particular answers that may be given to truth-making questions. The division is not all that sharp. There is, very properly, interaction between one's general theory of truth-making and the particular truth-makers one postulates for particular classes of truths. The two enterprises have to be brought into reflective equilibrium. But it does seem worthwhile to make the distinction, and this paper will be given over to the general theory with only glances at particular doctrines.

2. Historical

The notion of the truth-maker may be traced right back to Aristotle. (See, in particular, *Categories*, 14b, 14–22.) Aristotle's remarks were noted by a number of leading Scholastic philosophers, but the notion seems after this to have gone underground for some centuries, although intimations of it may be found here and there. The notion is present in Russell's thought, and in his later philosophizing he introduced a term for the notion, the somewhat unfortunate word 'verifier' (Russell 1940, 1948, 1959a).[2] Reference to truth-makers, and some development of truth-making theory, is now quite widespread among philosophers working in Australia. I think that the source is always C. B. Martin, as certainly it was for me. But the very same notion, and the very same term, were introduced quite independently by Kevin Mulligan, Peter Simons and Barry Smith in a joint article "Truth-makers" published in 1984 (this vol., Ch. 3). They provide a suggestive quotation from Husserl, and mention Russell and the *Tractatus* by Wittgenstein.

3. The truth-making relation

The idea of a truth-maker for a particular truth, then, is just some existent, some portion of reality, in virtue of which that truth is true. The relation, I think, is a cross-categorial one, one term being an entity or entities in the world, the other being a truth.[3] (I hold that truths are true *propositions*, but will leave this matter aside until §6.) To demand truth-makers for particular truths is to accept a *realist* theory for these truths. There is something that exists in reality, independent of the proposition in question, which makes the truth true. The 'making' here is, of course, not the causal sense of 'making'. The best formulation of what this making is seems to be given by the phrase 'in virtue of'. It is in virtue of that independent reality that the proposition is true. What makes the proposition a truth is how it stands to this reality.

Two questions immediately arise. First, do truth-makers actually *necessitate* their truths, or is the relation weaker than that, at least in some cases? Second, do *all* truths have truth-makers, or are there some areas of truth that are truth-maker-free, modal truths for instance? My answers to these questions are, first, that the relation is necessitation, absolute necessitation, and, second, that every truth has a truth-maker. I will call these positions respectively Truth-maker Necessitarianism and Truth-maker Maximalism.

Turning first to Necessitarianism, the first thing to notice is that the necessitation cannot be any form of entailment. Both terms of an entailment relation must be propositions, but the truth-making term of the truth-making relation is a portion of reality, and, in general at least, portions of reality are not propositions. The simplest of all truth-making relations is that which holds between any truth-maker, T, which is something in the world, and the proposition $<T$ exists$>$.[4] Here, clearly, the relation has to be cross-categorial.

It might be said, instead, that in this simple case the relation holds between T's *existence* and the proposition $<T$ exists$>$. Presumably, T's *existence* is here supposed to be a state of affairs. I think, however, that it is a mistake to recognize states of affairs having this form. To do so seems to turn existence into a *property* of T.

Although 'exists' is a perfectly good predicate, I think with Kant that it is a mistake to recognize an ontological property of existence. But if the Kantian position is wrong, *T's existence* would still be something in the world, and so the relation between it and the proposition <*T* exists> would still be a cross-categorial one.

This very simple relation between *T* and <*T* exists> may be thought to be rather trivial. Would it not be sufficient for the purposes of truth-making theory to *start* in each case from truths having the form <*T* exists> and then spell out truth-making relations in terms of entailments of propositions of this sort? The difficulty with this suggestion is that the truth-making relation seems to hold in cases where entailment is completely lacking. Suppose that it is true that there exists a certain quantity of water in a certain place at a certain time. Will not a sufficiently dense conglomeration of H_2O molecules in that space at that time be a truth-maker for this truth? It seems to me that we ought to accept such truth-makers. But if we replace this truth-maker, as we can do easily enough, with a truth of existence, this truth does not *entail* the first truth. For entailment we need an additional premise: that a quantity of water is a certain sort of conglomeration of H_2O molecules. But how is a truth-maker for this additional premise to be spelled out in terms of entailments? So I say that the conglomeration of H_2O molecules at a certain place and time (the truth-maker) necessitates that <there is water at that place and time> (the truth), but this is not entailment.

But what is the argument for saying that a truth-maker must necessitate a truth it is truth-maker for? Here is an argument by *reductio*. Suppose that a suggested truth-maker *T* for a certain truth *p* fails to necessitate that truth. There will then be at least the possibility that *T* should exist and yet the proposition *p* not be true. This strongly suggests that there ought to be some further condition that must be satisfied in order for *p* to be true. This condition must either be the existence of a further entity, *U*, or a further truth, *q*. In the first of these cases, *T* + *U* would appear to be the true and necessitating truth-maker for *p*. (If *U* does not necessitate, then the same question raised about *T* can be raised again about *U*.) In the second case, *q* either has a truth-maker, *V*, or it does not. Given that *q* has a truth-maker, then the *T* + *U* case is reproduced. Suppose *q* lacks a truth-maker, then there are truths without truth-makers. The truth *q* will "hang" ontologically in the same sort of way that Ryle left dispositional truths hanging (Ryle 1949).

Perhaps this argument gives sufficient support to Truth-maker Necessitarianism. But someone who accepted Necessitarianism for truth-makers might still hold that there can be truths that lack necessitation by a truth-maker. May there not be truths – such as *q* in the previous paragraph – that lack any truth-maker? Maximalism is needed to rule this out. What, then, is my argument for Maximalism?

I do not have any direct argument. My hope is that philosophers of realist inclinations will be immediately attracted to the idea that a truth, any truth, should depend for its truth for something "outside" it, in virtue of which it is true. What I then offer in this essay is a running through of the main categories of truths, suggesting what I hope are reasonably plausible truth-makers in each category.

I do not expect that my suggestions will all be accepted! Different metaphysicians, different proposed truth-makers. But I hope enough will be done to show that there are real prospects of providing truth-makers in all cases, and that this will encourage realists to take a favourable attitude to Maximalism. So let us treat Maximalism as a hypothesis to be tested by this whole work.

3.1 Supervenience

I have so far explicated truth-maker theory in terms of individual truth-makers for individual truths (although, as we shall see, there is no question of a one–one correlation of truth-makers and truths). But perhaps this piecemeal procedure can be bypassed. John Bigelow has introduced the very attractive slogan "Truth supervenes on being" (1988a: ch. 19). It looks rather good. Given all that there is, is one not given all truth? Truth ought to be determined by being, and that by an absolute necessity. In particular, if anything that is true had not been true, then being would have to have been different in some way.

It would seem incidentally that not only does truth supervene on being, but being supervenes on truth. For if anything that has being did not have being, then something that is true would not be true. The supervenience is symmetrical. (The word 'supervenience' suggests an asymmetry, but there seems nothing in the concept to rule out symmetry.) We will come back to this matter in the next section.

The first thing to be said here in criticism of Bigelow's suggestion is that if this is to be the sole explication of the truth-making relation, then it will rule out any serious attribution of truth-makers for modal truths, in particular for necessary truths. Suppose, or try to suppose, that some necessary truth, say <2 + 2 = 4>, is not true. How would being differ? There seems to be no coherent answer. It is true of course that many sympathizers with a truth-making programme have thought that nothing but trivial truth-makers *can* be given for modal truths. But in accordance with Maximalism, I will be attempting to do better than that in this work.

With respect to contingent truths, Bigelow's slogan seems true and valuable, and perhaps he intended no more. But to remain with it as the sole insight needed for contingent truths would still be unfortunate. It takes focus away from the piecemeal task of finding plausible truth-makers for important classes of truths, a task that ought to be undertaken by realist metaphysicians. Consider, for instance, the difficult case – difficult for truth-making theory – of contingent but universally quantified truths (with existence of the subject term presupposed). The truth <all electrons have charge *e*> may do as an example. Suppose that there are electrons, but that, contrary to the truth, some of these electrons lack charge *e*. (Perhaps the charge on these electrons is just a little bit smaller.) It is obvious that *being* would then have to be different. Supervenience holds. This, though, is not all that needs be said about truths of this sort. At least if we are Maximalists, we need to enquire just what are the particular truth-makers for these truths.[5]

3.2 Expressibility

I have suggested that the converse of the Bigelow thesis holds, at least for contingent truths. If anything had been different in any way from what there actually is, the totality of the body of truths would have had to be different in some way. But it needs to be noted that this is a further, and perhaps disputable, thesis. It is the thesis that Stephen Read (2000: 68–9) calls *Expressibility*. For all being, there is a proposition (perhaps one never formulated by any mind at any time) that truly renders the existence and nature of this being. When Wittgenstein said "Whereof one cannot speak, thereof one must be silent" he was (perhaps) suggesting that there were existences, or aspects of existence, that of necessity could not give rise to truths. At any rate, it seems that such a thesis can be held. A presumably different way in which Expressibility might fail is if there could not be infinite propositions (presumably only available, on the supposition that there are such things, to infinite minds), yet there was infinity in the world. I will leave consideration of Expressibility at this point. I have a rationalist prejudice in its favour, but no particular arguments to offer for – this prejudice.

3.3 Truth-making an internal relation

It should be noted that if, as argued, the truth-making relation is a necessitating relation, then it is an internal relation. I mean by calling a relation internal that, given just the terms of the relation, the relation between them is necessitated. Given the terms 7 and 5, in that order, then the relation of *greater in number than* must hold between them. In the same way, given a certain real object, and a certain proposition, in that order, then the truth-making relation (or the false-making relation) is automatically determined, fixed, necessitated. And although the matter requires further discussion at a later point, I suggest it is an attractive ontological hypothesis that such a relation is no addition of being. Given just the terms, we are given the ontology of the situation. The relation is not something over and above its terms (which is *not* to say that the relation does not hold, *not* to say that it does not exist).

4. False-makers

Philosophers who are introduced to the concept of a truth-maker quickly notice that there is room for the concept of a false-maker. It is the notion of a pair, some entity in the world and a proposition, such that the entity necessitates that the proposition is false. But although the notion seems a perfectly legitimate one, for a long time I could see no great use for it. Every truth-maker for a truth *p*, it would seem, is a false-maker for the proposition <not-*p*>. And if something is a false-maker for *p*, then again it is a truth-maker for the contradictory of *p*. But do we need to give much attention to the notion of a false-maker?

However, false-makers do play a more useful, or at any rate more interesting, role in some cases. Consider, in particular, one sub-class of modal truths: truths of impossibility. Suppose it is true that <it is impossible that *p* and not-*p* be both true> but necessary that one of the conjuncts be true. The truth-makers for the true conjunct will *simultaneously* be false-makers for the other conjunct. (See further Armstrong 2004: ch. 8.8.)

Again, consider the truth that a certain wall is painted green. It seems reasonable to suppose that greenness is some sort of positive property (given what we know about colour, perhaps not an ontologically high-class property, not a "sparse" one in David Lewis's terminology), and the wall's having that property is the truth-maker for that truth. Consider now the further truths that the wall is not white, is not red, is not .... One may suggest that the wall makes these truths true by being a false-maker for the corresponding positive attributions of colour. This in turn may encourage the idea that it is not necessary to postulate negative truth-makers for negative truths. Here we have the interesting, even if as I think ultimately unsatisfactory, 'Incompatibility theory' of truth-makers for negative truths.[6] (See Armstrong 2004: ch. 5.2.1 for discussion of this theory.)

5. The Entailment principle

We come to what will prove a very important thesis in truth-making theory. Suppose that *T* is a truth-maker for proposition *p*. Suppose further that *p* entails proposition *q*, with the exact force here of 'entails' subject to discussion. Then *T* will be truth-maker for *q*. This may be informally symbolized:

$$T \rightarrow p$$
$$p \text{ entails}^* q$$
$$\therefore T \rightarrow q$$

The arrow is the truth-making relation, a non-propositional necessity I have argued. The star symbol indicates that if this principle is to be applied in full generality, then the entailment here cannot be classical entailment. The problem with using classical entailment from my point of view is that if *p* is a contingent truth, then, since a contingent truth classically entails all necessary truths, any such truth can be substituted for *q*, thus making any contingent truth a truth-maker for any necessary truth. This robs truth-making theory of all interest for the case of necessary truths. Some truth-maker theorists may accept this conclusion – it accords with Wittgenstein's view of necessary truths in the *Tractatus* – but I am hoping to provide *relevant* truth-makers for all truths.

The exact limitations to be placed on entailment in the suggested Entailment principle is a technical matter, one that I am not equipped to discuss. Suggestions have been made by Restall (this vol., Ch. 3) and Read (2000), and I will simply assume that something is available. I am not arguing that classical entailment should be abandoned, but am urging that a connective that does not allow the distressing explosion of truth-makers for necessary truths should be used in this particular context. Horses for courses.

We may note, however, another strategy of some interest. This is to accept classical entailment, but to narrow the scope of the Entailment principle in some way. Restall reports (this vol., Ch. 3, §2) that one such suggestion was made by Frank Jackson. Jackson suggested that the values substituted for *p* and *q* should be restricted to contingent truths. To this Contingency restriction, as we may call it, Restall objects that, given classical entailment, contingent truth *p* entails <*p* & *N*>, where *N* is any necessary truth. But <*p* & *N*> is a *contingent* truth. So, given the Entailment principle, any truth-maker for *p* is the truth-maker for <*p* & *N*>. But it is a very plausible proposition of truth-making theory that a truth-maker for a conjunction is a truth-maker for each conjunct. So, again, the truth-maker for *p* is a truth-maker for *N*. Hence the Contingency restriction fails.

It seems to me that Jackson's suggestion can still be upheld provided we make a further restriction, which may be called the restriction to *purely* contingent truths. A purely contingent truth is one that does not contain a necessary conjunct. Nor, to ward off further cases suggested to me by Glenn Ross, whom I thank for discussion here, does it contain any necessary truth as a component in a conjunction (or disjunction or whatever) at any level of analysis. A purely contingent truth is one that is contingent *through and through*. Given such a restriction the Entailment principle seems to hold, and to be useful in truth-making theory, even if the entailment is classical. In any case, it may be noted that "impure" contingent truths of the sort that Restall points to are not ones that truth-making theory has much occasion to work with.

An important point to keep in mind about the Entailment principle is that even where *T* is a *minimal* truth-maker for the entailing proposition *p* it will not necessarily be a minimal truth-maker for the entailed *q*. The fairly straightforward notion of a minimal truth-maker will be discussed in §10.

2.6 Truths and falsehoods are propositions

Truth-maker theorists have so far paid little attention to the other term of the relation: the truths that truth-makers make true. What are the *truth-bearers*, the bearers of the predicates 'true', 'not true' and 'false'? In his very useful book *Theories of Truth* Richard Kirkham argues for a tolerant attitude (1992: 2.4). He assembles evidence that different philosophers have taken very different entities to be truth-bearers:

> Among the candidates are beliefs, propositions, judgments, assertions, statements, theories, remarks, ideas, acts of thought, utterances, sentence tokens, sentence types, sentences (unspecified), and speech acts. *(Ibid.*: 54)

This should give us all pause. I nevertheless (now!) wish to say that it is *propositions* that constitute the central case for a theory of truth-bearers. We can certainly apply the truth-predicates very widely, but I am inclined to think that all other suggested truth-bearers besides propositions are called truth-bearers on account of their relationship to certain propositions. At any rate, I am going to begin from the assumption that truths are (centrally) true propositions, and falsehoods are (centrally) false propositions. But what are propositions? What is their ontological status?

There are metaphysicians who are prepared to postulate a realm of propositions over and above the space-time world. But, presumably, we could not stand in any causal or nomic relation to such a realm. And if we cannot stand in such relations to propositions it is unclear that such a postulation is of any explanatory value. At any rate, as a naturalist, I want to look for a this-worldly account of propositions.

One view that I wish to reject is that propositions that are linguistically expressed can be identified with equivalence classes of synonymous sentences (contrary to what I said in my 1997: 10.3.1). Synonymy depends on meaning, not meaning on synonymy. Here I am taught by Marian David. He has pointed out to me that it is possible that a particular equivalence class of synonymous sentence (or word) tokens could, while remaining a synonymous class, have had a different meaning from the one it actually has. To make this vivid, consider that same class of tokens "in another possible world". Suppose that in this other world the word 'cat' is our word for a dog. The class of tokens of 'cat' in that world is still an equivalence class under the relation of synonymy. Yet those tokens in that other world pick out dogs, not cats. So, although it may be useful at times to consider such equivalence classes, it is the meaning that each individual token has that provides the semantic unity of the class.

Leaving this error behind, I begin with a suggestion that will require to be modified before being satisfactory. This preliminary suggestion is that propositions are the *intentional objects* of beliefs and certain thoughts. That is on the mental side. On the linguistic side they are the intentional objects of statements. I do not want to read too much metaphysics into the phrase 'intentional objects'. Beliefs are essentially beliefs that something is the case. Whatever is believed to be the case may then be said to be 'the intentional object of that belief', using this as a technical term only. And that is a proposition. Some thoughts that are not beliefs, mere suppositions and idle fancies for instance, also have as their intentional object that something is the case, and these objects are again propositions. Meaningful statements are statements that something is the case, and what is meant may be said to be 'the intentional object of the statement'. These objects, too, are propositions. (I will here ignore the very important distinction, and any complications that come with that distinction, between speaker's meaning and conventional meaning. I also ignore any complications introduced by indexicals.)

Propositions, on this view, are abstractions, but not in any other-worldly sense of "abstraction", from beliefs, statements and so on. They are the *content* of the belief, what makes the belief the particular belief that it is; or else the *meaning* of the statement, what makes the statement the particular statement that it is. That the content or meaning is an abstraction becomes clear when we notice that contents and meanings are types rather than tokens. Beliefs in different minds may have the very same content, numerically different statements may have the very same meaning. Content and meaning seem to be properties, though they are doubtless not purely intrinsic (non-relational) properties, of token beliefs and token statements. Furthermore, these properties will, in turn, very often be *impure* properties, in the sense that they are properties that involve essential reference to particulars, such as the property *being descended from Charlemagne*.

To go further than this here would take us, inappropriately, deep into the philosophy of mind and the philosophy of language. I would be hoping for a naturalistic theory of content and meaning, and so a naturalistic theory of the identity conditions for propositions. Our beliefs, statements and so on have certain intentional objects. There are, of course, desperately difficult problems concerning intentionality – in particular the problem how we can think and say what is not true – and some philosophers think that these problems should be addressed by metaphysics, by ontology. My own view is that these are problems, horribly difficult problems to be sure, to be addressed within the philosophy of mind, or perhaps its successor: cognitive science. But here I will simply assume that there is intentionality in the realm of the mental and, when the use of language is informed by mentality, in the linguistic realm. Indeed, I would wish to uphold a representational account of the mental. Every mental state, process and event has, or is linked to, some representational content. (This includes perception, it includes bodily sensation, which I take to be bodily perception, and it also includes introspective awareness.) If this is right, the mind is a purely intentional system. Of course, only some of these contents are contents that admit the predicates 'true' or 'not true'. Desires have content, but are neither 'true' nor 'not true'. (I think that perceptions do admit of these predicates, although it is customary among philosophers to speak more guardedly of 'veridical' and 'non-veridical' perceptions.)

We should, however, note that what follows the 'that', and so is a proposition, may not only be false but an impossibility. There is a proposition <there is a counter-instance to Fermat's last theorem>, although we now know that there can be no such counter-instance. Hobbes believed that the circle could be squared, though this is an impossibility. That <the circle can be squared> was surely the intentional object of his belief. This suggests, by the way, that an analysis of intentionality in terms of possible worlds will not succeed.

It may also be noted that an account of propositions as intentional objects (one sort of intentional object – the sort that can be true or false) will have to allow for vagueness in many propositions. Intentional objects of actual thoughts and statements can be very vague, even if there is no vagueness in reality, as I should like to think. And very vague beliefs and statements can still have truth-makers. But as one who has done no work on the topic of vagueness I will not investigate further this corner of truth-making theory. It may be hoped that nothing of first importance will be thereby omitted.

But at this point we must recognize that the account given of true propositions, in particular, is somewhat unsatisfactory. We have attached propositions to beliefs, statements and so on. Cannot there be truths which nobody has or will believe, or even formulate, much less state? Consider Newton and his image of the ocean of undiscovered truth that he said lay before him, reaching far beyond his own discoveries. We understand this well enough, and would continue to understand it even in the absence of an all-knowing creator or the ocean of truth yielding up all its secrets in the future. We may call such truths unexpressed truths. Generalizing to include falsehoods, we can speak of 'unexpressed propositions'.

True unexpressed propositions will be truths without any *concrete* truth-bearers. Some philosophers may think that we can ignore such cases. But in fact I think that this would be a mistake. They are, for me at least, conceptually very important. The reason for this is that the concept of such truths is needed to make sense of Truth-maker Necessitarianism. How can truth-makers necessitate truth-bearers if the truth-bearers are beliefs, statements and so on? How can something in the world, say the state of affairs of the dog's being on the dog-bed, *necessitate* that I have a belief that this is the case, or that somebody states that it is the case? What is necessitated can be no more than the true proposition <the dog is on the dog-bed>. That is why propositions must be the true truth-bearers, or at any rate the most fundamental truth-bearers.

This in turn requires that we now modify the suggested account of propositions as intentional objects. Actual intentional objects require actual beliefs, actual statements and suchlike, and the world cannot necessitate such actualities. So we need an account of propositions that abstracts from whether or not they are expressed.

We can, I believe, cover the cases of unexpressed propositions by treating them as possibilities, mere possibilities, of believing, or contemplating, or linguistically expressing the unexpressed proposition. If we think of the intentional object of an expressed proposition as some (hard to analyse) *property* of its vehicle, then unexpressed propositions will be *uninstantiated* properties. But I would wish to exclude uninstantiated properties from my ontology. Properties of things are, I think, *ways* that things are, and the notion of a way that nothing is seems onto-logically near unintelligible. I would find an account of unexpressed propositions in terms of uninstantiated properties acceptable only if a deflationary account of these uninstantiated properties were given. We can do this deflation, I hope, by equating these uninstantiated properties with the *mere possibility* of the instantia-tion of such a property. It will then be necessary, of course, to consider what are the truth-makers for these truths of mere possibility. That task must here be post-poned until we reach the whole great question of truth-makers for modal truths in Armstrong 2004, chapters 7 and 8. We shall find, I believe, that this-worldly truth-makers for truths of mere possibility are not all that hard to find.

Truth-makers for truths necessitate, absolutely necessitate, those truths, or so I have argued. It seems clear, however, that truth-makers cannot necessitate actual beliefs, thoughts and statements. So propositions taken as possible intentional objects are the only things that truth-makers can actually necessitate.

7. Connecting truth with reality

Propositions correspond or fail to correspond to reality. If what has been said about propositions in the previous section is correct, then it becomes pretty clear that the correspondence theory of truth can and should be upheld. Truth is a matter of the intentional object of an actual or possible belief, actual or possible statement, and so on, corresponding with some real object. (In both cases, of course, 'object' is to be taken in a broad way.)[7] What has been the bane of the correspondence theory, at least in recent philosophy, is the idea that the correspondence between true propos-itions and the reality in virtue of which they are true is a one–one correspondence. In the minimalist theory of truth, in the form put forward by Paul Horwich (1990), the theory of truth is confined to a simple (and true) principle, the equivalence schema: <*p*> is true if and only if *p*. If, under the influence of the one–one corres-pondence view, a correspondence theory is accepted, then we get a quite similar but metaphysically very extravagant theory: *p* is true if and only if it corresponds to the *fact* or *state of affairs* that *p*. Faced with a forced choice between the Horwich theory and this one–one correspondence theory, I would opt for Horwich's view.

But there is a middle way, better than either Horwich's actual view or the meta-physical version of his theory. We can accept a correspondence theory, but in a form where it is recognized that the relation between true propositions and their correspondents is regularly many–many. Indeed, even if we restrict ourselves to *minimal* truth-makers, I do not think that we ever get a one–one case. The corres-pondents in the world in virtue of which true propositions are true are our truth-makers. One thing that should recommend this more nuanced approach is the now widespread recognition that, in the theory of *properties*, it is in general a mistake to look for a one–one correlation to hold between properties and predicates. The extra space that this gives one can be used, for instance, to articulate a theory of what David Lewis called the *sparse* properties, the ones which he (and I) hold to be the ontologically significant properties of objects, those in terms of which the world's work is done. And indeed, the complex relations that predicates stand in to properties can quite naturally be thought of as part of truth-maker theory. Of course, there are philosophers who deny that we should recognize properties in our ontology. But Chapter 2 in Armstrong 2004 will argue that there is a strong case in truth-making theory for accepting the existence of properties that are independent of the mere true application of predicates.

8. A realist definition of truth?

We will work, then, with the following theory of the nature of truth:

> p (a proposition) is true if and only if there exists a T (some entity in the world) such that T necessitates that p and p is true in virtue of T.

We note that the 'only if' is particularly controversial even among those who accept some form of truth-maker theory. The necessitation, I have suggested, is a world-to-proposition necessitation, not an entailment relation.

If every truth has a truth-maker, then this formula tells us what truth in general is. But I do not wish to call it a definition, because the right-hand side of the formula may involve the notion of truth. A fundamental concept such as truth is likely to be so entwined with other fundamental notions that no total explication of it in terms of other concepts is possible. But perhaps we can use the notion of a truth-condition (to be sharply distinguished from the notion of a truth-maker – a truth-condition is no more than a proposition) and say that what we have here is a necessary and sufficient truth-condition for truth.

9. Truth-makers for p may (properly) include truth-makers for p

Suppose p to be a truth and T to be a truth-maker for p. There may well exist, often there does exist, a T' that is contained by T, and a T'' that contains T, with T' and T'' *also* truth-makers for p. We may say that truth-makers for a particular truth may be more or less *discerning*. The more embracing the truth-maker, the less discerning it is. For every truth, the least discerning of all truth-makers is the world itself, the totality of being. The world makes every truth true, or, failing that, every truth that has a truth-maker true. But this is an uninteresting truth-maker, mentioned here just for theoretical completeness.

It is necessary, though, to think carefully about these relations of inclusion among truth-makers for a particular truth. The obvious relation to identify it with is mereological inclusion, the simplest relation of whole and proper part. It will then be helpful, though perhaps not essential, to subscribe to the doctrine of Unrestricted Mereological Composition,[8] the thesis that any plurality of things, however heterogeneous, is a mereological whole. Then one can always have a single object as truth-maker. But however we settle that question, mereology may not be all that is needed. Some of us hold that there are in the world *facts* (states of affairs), entities having such forms as *a's being F* and *a's having R to b*. It is widely appreciated that these entities, if they exist, have a non-mereological form of composition (*a* and *F* might both exist, yet *a* not be *F*). Yet the state of affairs of *a's* being *F* seems to include, to have as constituents, the particular *a* and the property *F*. Furthermore, the constituents can be truth-makers on their own just as much as the states of affairs that contain them. It may be that there are other forms of composition in the world, though I myself am content with mereology and states of affairs.

This nesting of truth-makers for a particular truth may cast some light on the old idea that in a valid argument the conclusion is in some way contained in the totality of the premises. This is hard to make precise for the propositions that are linked as premises and conclusions in an argument. But if we consider truth-makers for these propositions, perhaps something more interesting emerges. Suppose that a certain valid argument is sound, having all its premises true. Next we remind ourselves of the Entailment principle (see §5):

$$T \to p$$
$$p \text{ entails}^* q$$
$$\therefore T \to q$$

The plausible Containment thesis is then that for each T, p and q, T will have a part that is a truth-maker for q. We may count T as an (improper) part of itself, so already the conclusion $T' \to q$ is a case which fits the thesis. But very often, in particular where q does not entail p, we will have cases where q has a truth-maker, T', that is a proper part of T. Instead of conclusions contained in premises we have truth-makers for the conclusion contained in truth-makers for the premises. Or so the Containment principle asserts. I do not know if the principle holds for all cases, but it certainly holds in many cases. In particular it appears to hold for the (amended) Jackson principle (§5) that links "purely" contingent premises with contingent conclusions.

Consider, for instance, the traditional syllogism: <All men are mortal>, <Socrates is a man>, so <Socrates is mortal>. The truth-maker for the first premise is, I think, the mereological sum of all the earthly lives of all men, together with the totality state of affairs that this is the totality of such lives (for totality states of affairs see Armstrong 2004: ch. 6.2). Since all of them in fact end with a death, we have here already a (non-minimal) truth-maker for the death of Socrates. This truth-maker contains as a proper part the terminating of Socrates' life by death. The containment is in this case merely mereological, because the conjunction of each life is no more than a mereological sum of the lives, and Socrates' life is one of the conjuncts. But not all containment is mereological, at any rate if there are states of affairs (facts) in the furniture of the world. States of affairs have constituents (particulars, properties and relations) that seem to be parts of states of affairs, but not to be mereological parts.

Where propositions are false, we cannot have containment of truth-makers, but may still, of course, have valid arguments. Provided, however, that the false propositions involved are not impossibilities, we can "go to possible worlds where the entailing proposition is true" and assert that, in general at least, the proposition's truth-makers in these worlds contain the truth-makers of anything it entails.

10. Minimal truth-makers

We have introduced the least discerning truth-maker of them all, W, the world. It is also the most promiscuous truth-maker, for it makes every truth, or every truth that has a truth-maker, true. More interesting, and of quite special importance for metaphysics, is the notion of a minimal truth-maker. If T is a minimal truth-maker for p, then you cannot subtract anything from T and the remainder still be a truth-maker for p. Suppose, making some quite controversial assumptions for the sake of the example, that the truth-makers include properties, that these properties are universals, that universals are contingent existences, and that having rest-mass of one kilo is one such property. It is clear that this property is a truth-maker for the truth that this property exists. What is more, it is surely a minimal truth-maker.

It is interesting to look at certain metaphysical theories from the perspective of truth-making theories, and to consider whether the account they offer of certain entities is a good candidate for a minimal truth-maker for the truth (as they take it to be) that these entities exist. David Lewis's ontology, as is well known, is exhausted by a *pluriverse* (the totality of being) consisting of all the possible worlds (Lewis 1986). He defines a 'proposition' as the class of all the worlds for which the particular proposition is true. (Notice that his system does not allow for a null world, and hence he cannot form the class of the null worlds. As a result he cannot admit impossible propositions, a weakness, I would argue, because we can and do believe and assert impossibilities.) Suppose that one thinks of each of these worlds as the truth-maker for that proposition in that world. Let the proposition be that <cats catch mice>. It will be true in our actual world – and many other worlds. This gives us the class of worlds that Lewis identifies with the proposition that cats catch mice. But it is clear that this bunch of worlds is not a minimal truth-maker for the proposition, though it may be a truth-maker.

(The mereological sum of episodes in our world involving the generality of cats catching mice when given the opportunity seems to be nearer to what is needed for a minimal truth-maker.)

Lewis, of course, is not trying to find a truth-maker for the truth of a proposition, such as the proposition <cats catch mice>. But I submit that in metaphysics we should primarily be concerned with truth-makers. And it is this, I think, that is responsible for the weird sound of Lewis's doctrine of propositions.

One might object to the idea that there are any truth-makers except minimal truth-makers. For, it may be argued, a non-minimal truth-maker involves redundancy, and the truth in question may *not* be true in virtue of the redundant material. This is a possible way to go, but I think that it is methodologically an unwise choice, for similar reasons to the logician's practice of taking 'some' not to exclude 'all'. In actual philosophical investigations it can be difficult to delineate the minimal truth-maker precisely while still being able to point to truth-makers that are non-minimal. But if someone wishes to say that what I call a non-minimal truth-maker for a certain proposition is really a portion of reality that has the real truth-maker as a proper part, then I have no metaphysical objection. It is to be noted in any case that there are certain propositions that may be true, but cannot have minimal truth-makers (see §12).

11. A truth may have many minimal truth-makers

One might think off-hand that a truth has only one minimal truth-maker. It is very important to notice that many, many truths have more than one minimal truth-maker. Consider the truth that a human being exists: <there exists an x such that x is a human being>. If we take existence omnitemporally (my own metaphysical preference, and one that will later be defended by truth-maker arguments – see Armstrong 2004: ch. 11), then every human being that has ever existed, exists now or will exist in the future is a truth-maker for this truth. Furthermore, each of these human beings seems to be, or to be very close to being, a minimal truth-maker. (My caution here is because you could quite plausibly suggest that selected portions of human beings could be omitted from these truth-makers and yet you would still have enough to be a truth-maker for this truth!) If you want a cleaner example, consider the possibility that there is a plurality of simple properties. If this possibility actually obtains, then each simple property is a minimal truth-maker for the truth <there exist simple properties>.

We may note in passing that not only are there truths that have many different truth-makers, but that every truth-maker makes many truths true. Consider the case where p has a truth-maker. Truths of the form $< p \vee \_>$ will all be true in virtue of that truth-maker. A truth-maker is, indeed, an inexhaustible fountain of truths.

12. Truths without minimal truth-makers

Is it the case that for every truth there exists at least one minimal truth-maker? It sounds very plausible, but Greg Restall (1995b) has given an ingenious counter-instance that makes it plausible that, provided the world contains at least a denumerable infinity of entities, then there are truths that have no minimal truth-maker. Suppose, for instance, that the world contains a denumerable infinity of electrons, and consider the truth <there exist an infinity of electrons>. The totality of electrons is a truth-maker for that truth. But take every third electron. That sub-totality makes the very same truth true, because the sub-totality is infinite. And so for the selection of the nth electron, where n is any finite natural number. Hence a minimal truth-maker is never reached. Any infinity in nature will make true certain truths that have no minimal truth-makers. Normally, however, a truth that has a truth-maker will have at least one minimal truth-maker.

Paul Horwich has pointed out, however, that there is a candidate for a minimal truth-maker even in the electron case (Horwich 2004). Simply postulate a fact or state of affairs: *There exist an infinity of electrons.* Horwich himself has no sympathy with the notion of truth-making, but his point is correct formally. If there is such a state of affairs, it will be a minimal truth-maker. Few upholders of the notion of truth-maker theory, though, would be likely to accept the truth-maker that Horwich offers. The state of affairs would be an extremely abstract one (in the traditional sense of the word 'abstract'). It would, for instance, sit very uneasily among the more concrete states of affairs involving particulars with their properties and the conjunctions of these states of affairs, which is a state of affairs metaphysics rather naturally deals in. It is difficult, for instance, to see any plausible causal role that could be given to a state of affairs of the sort suggested by Horwich. Nevertheless, Horwich's pointing out the formal possibility of postulating such a state of affairs serves as a useful reminder that, in passing from truths to truth-makers, no truth-maker is *automatically* picked out. No royal road to truth-makers!

I know of no other set of cases except certain truths involving infinity, such as the example given, where truths have truth-makers, but (plausibly) lack any minimal truth-maker. This result, however, does not completely stand by itself. When we come to discuss truth-makers for modal truths we shall see that it enables us to steer past a troubling, if minor, dilemma. See Armstrong 2004, chapter 7.5.

13. Unique minimal truth-makers

It seems clear, then, that many truths have many minimal truth-makers. But there are cases where truths have one *and no more than one* minimal truth-maker. For instance, if there are states of affairs, such entities as a's being F, with a a particular and F a genuine universal (or, for that matter, F a genuine trope), the truth $<a$ is $F>$ has that state of affairs as unique minimal truth-maker. The candidates for unique minimal truth-makers that a particular philosopher upholds take us into the heart of that thinker's metaphysical position. Where truth-makers are minimal but not unique, as in the case of the truth that a human being exists, it seems that the truth in question is always in some way 'abstract' (in the classical sense of this word, not Quine's "not spatiotemporal").

In one way, therefore, it is very interesting what unique minimal truth-makers a philosopher postulates. In another way, it is rather boring, because the description of the truth-maker that we would naturally give will be reproduced in the statement of the truth. Here, according to that philosopher, the truth reflects the form of reality. And whatever the truth-makers are alleged to be, the following general statement can be made: for every truth-maker T, the truth $<T$ exists$>$ has T as its unique minimal truth-maker. The metaphysician's preferred list of Ts are the sorts of thing that, as Quine would put it, "you are prepared to quantify over". But bringing Quine into the matter demands further discussion.

14. The postulation of truth-makers contrasted with "quantifying over"

To postulate certain truth-makers for certain truths is to admit those truth-makers to one's ontology. The complete range of truth-makers admitted constitutes a metaphysics, which alerts us to the important point, stressed already but bearing much repetition, that the hunt for truth-makers is as controversial and difficult as the enterprise of metaphysics. I think that proceeding by looking for truth-makers is an illuminating and useful regimentation of the metaphysical enterprise, or at least the enterprise of a realist metaphysics. But it is no easy and automatic road to the truth in such matters.

But this raises the question of Quine, and the signalling of ontological commitment by what we are prepared to "quantify over". Why should we desert Quine's procedure for some other method? The great advantage, as I see it, of the search for truth-makers is that it focuses us not merely on the metaphysical implications of the subject terms of propositions but also on their *predicates*. Quine has told us that the predicate gives us 'ideology' rather than ontology (1966: 232).[9] This saying is rather dark, but it is clear that, to some degree, he has stacked the ontological deck against predicates as opposed to subject terms. But when we look to truth-makers for truths, subject and predicate start as equals, and we can consider the ontological implications of both in an unbiased way.

The doing of ontological justice to the predicate leads us to consider whether we do not require at least selected properties and relations in our ontology. If properties and relations are admitted, we may think that some ontological connection between subjects and predicates is further required, and thus, perhaps, be led to postulate facts or states of affairs among our truth-makers. The propositional nature of truths will in any case push us in the same direction. The existence of negative truths and general truths raises the question whether negative and general facts are required as truth-makers. All these difficult metaphysical issues (which will receive discussion in Armstrong 2004, chapters 5 and 6) tend to be swept under the carpet by correlating one's ontology with the subject term only of truths (what one takes to be truths).

Some may argue that what I see here as advantages of thinking in terms of truth-makers are actually disadvantages. The world is a world of things not of facts, it may be said, and so we do not want facts, and the nightmare of such entities as negative facts, in our ontology. This is an arguable position, of course, but, conceding it true for the sake of argument, it can still be accommodated by a doctrine of truth-makers. Let the world be a world of things. The fundamental truths (those that have unique minimal truth-makers) will then have the form 'X exists' and the Xs, whatever they may be, will be truth-makers for these truths.

15. Different truths, same minimal truth-makers

Truths, we have seen, may have many minimal truth-makers. Is it the case that different truths can have the very same minimal truth-maker? (As we have noted, they all have the same maximal truth-maker, the world.) There are many examples. Trivial ones are easy to find. Just take some truth with a minimal truth-maker and add disjuncts where the additions are all false. The original minimal truth-maker will also serve for the new disjunctive truths. But there are more interesting cases. The propositions <a's surface is scarlet> and <a's surface is red> may both be true and, although the first truth necessitates the second truth, they are different truths. Yet the minimal truth-maker for both truths may well be the same: the possession by the surface of the exact shade of colour that it has.

Here is a more controversial sort of case. I will construct an artificial example because my point can then be made more clearly, but I think that there may be empirical examples: the philosophically famous case of the chicken sexers, and the ability of the old Mississippi river pilots to distinguish reefs from pseudo-reefs. (See Twain 1962: 62–3.)

Suppose, then, that a certain perceiver has the ability to spot regular pentagons, that is, decent approximations to the geometer's regular pentagons, and to distinguish them from other shapes, but has no ability to analyse the nature of the shape. This perceiver cannot count, and has quite undeveloped concepts of lines and angles. To this perceiver the shape is pretty well an unanalysed gestalt. 'Regular pentagon' would mean nothing to him, but he is still very proficient at picking the shape. Suppose he makes the true statement, or holds the belief, that a certain object has this shape that he can pick out so efficiently. He may even have his own predicate for this sort of shape. The truth that he has grasped is surely a different truth from ours when we say truly that the object is a regular pentagon. But the two truths may well have exactly the same minimal truth-maker, a unique minimal truth-maker.

It seems to be a necessary truth that the property picked out by this person is the regular pentagon shape. If we imagine that he later learns geometry, then he will rediscover this necessary truth <this shape is a regular pentagon> *a priori*.

Logical equivalences provide other, perhaps less interesting, cases of different truths with the same minimal truth-maker. Consider the truth (as we may here assume it to be) <all ravens are black>. Then consider its contrapositive: <all non-black things are non-ravens>. These truths are logically equivalent, and it is therefore very plausible to say that they have the very same minimal and all other truth-makers. But it is arguable, at least, that here we have different truths. No beginner in logic will be inclined to criticize this thesis!

So much for the "general theory of truth-making".

Notes

1. First published in D. M. Armstrong, *Truth and Truthmakers* (Cambridge: Cambridge University Press, 2004), 4–25.
2. I am indebted to the late George Molnar for pointing this out to me. Russell's later work has been amazingly neglected. Herbert Hochberg has further pointed out to me that as early as 1921, in the *Analysis of Mind*, p. 277, Russell uses the word 'verified' where he means 'made true by'.
3. Ken Barber has asked whether there are any other cases of cross-categorial relations. One could say "yes, the relation of difference", but that is rather trivial. Whether there are other important cross-categorial relations, I do not know. It will prove to be important later that the relation is an *internal* one.
4. I will use < ... > to pick out propositions, a device I was introduced to by Paul Horwich, but regularly will not bother about this in simple cases, e.g. proposition *p*. These angle brackets may be iterated for propositions about propositions.
5. Bigelow's own position about these sorts of truth is that what we have is an absence of false-makers. But since he rejects absences from his ontology, I think that here he does not advance beyond the supervenience thesis.
6. The link between Incompatibility theories and false-making was brought to my attention by Peter Simons.
7. "[D]eflationists do not connect truth with reality in the way that traditional correspondence theorists hope to do" (Williams 2002: 150).
8. Elsewhere in my argument, however, I shall actually require the truth of Unrestricted Mereological Composition. It comes, I believe, with no ontological cost.
9. Quine writes: "In science all is tentative, all admits of revision ... But ontology is, pending revision, more clearly in hand than what may be called *ideology* – the question of admissible predicates" (Quine 1966: 232).

PART II
The current debate

CHAPTER 8

Truth-making and correspondence

Marian David

The *truth-maker principle* says that for every truth there is something that makes it true, that every truth has a truth-maker. A *correspondence theory of truth* aims to account for truth in terms of correspondence with reality, or rather with appropriate chunks of reality, typically said to be facts. One feels that there is a natural kinship between the two. D. M. Armstrong puts it like this: "Anybody who is attracted to the Correspondence theory of truth should be drawn to the truth-maker. Correspondence demands a correspondent, and a correspondent for a truth is a truthmaker" (Armstrong 1997: 14).

On the other hand, it is only kinship. Armstrong also maintains (*ibid.*: ch. 8.5) that the correspondence theory is too ambitious in certain crucial respects and that the truth-maker principle improves on it by being more modest while at the same time capturing what is right about the correspondence theory. Michael Dummett, rather less sympathetic to the correspondence theory, had said earlier that "we have nowadays abandoned the correspondence theory of truth"; but he added that it nevertheless "expresses one important feature of the concept of truth…: that a statement is true only if there is something in the world in virtue of which it is true" (Dummett 1959: 14). Alex Oliver has put this more starkly: "The truth-maker principle is a sanitised version of a correspondence theory of truth" (Oliver 1996: 69).

The view seems to be that a correspondence theory of truth is committed to the truth-maker principle, but not the other way round, so that one can keep the latter while abandoning the former, as some say we must. Because of this relationship between the two, friends of the truth-maker principle maintain that it captures something (important) that is right in the correspondence theory; and those not sympathetic towards the correspondence theory would add that it captures *all* that is right in the correspondence theory, which is not very much. In this paper, I want to take a closer look at how the relationship between a correspondence theory and the truth-maker principle is to be conceived, especially considering that correspondence appears to be a symmetric relation while truth-making appears to be, or is supposed to be, an asymmetric relation.

1. From truth-making to correspondence and back

The truth-maker principle occurs in various formulations. The following three are always treated as interchangeable variants of each other. I state them assuming that the role of truth-bearers (i.e. truth-or-falsehood-bearers) is played by *propositions*; this is fairly common practice in discussions of the truth-maker principle:

> (TM)   Every true proposition is made true by something.
> For every true proposition there is something that makes it true.
> Every true proposition has a truth-maker.

The first two formulations emphasize the *truth-making relation* and remind us that we can express it in the active and the passive voice. The third formulation de-emphasizes the relation for the sake of the neat term 'truth-maker', which goes so nicely with the term 'truth-bearer'. Although this third formulation gives the truth-maker principle its name, it appears less fundamental. The term 'truth-maker' is intended merely as a label for whatever items stand in the relation of truth-making to a truth. It is the truth-making relation that is crucial. It would have been just as well to refer to the truth-*maker* principle as the truth-*making* principle.

How does this principle relate to a correspondence theory? Say one regards (TM) as expressing a basic intuition about truth. Let us see how one might arrive at a correspondence theory, taking (TM) as one's starting-point. (TM) is the most *generic* truth-maker principle. It does not say anything at all about what sorts of items are truth-makers or whether they must satisfy any further conditions. It is maximally modest on this score. It is also not very informative. One might then want to embrace a further truth-maker principle, one that is more ambitious because more specific than (TM):

> (TMF)   Every true proposition is made true by a fact.

This is a *special truth-maker principle*. Note that it does not involve a repudiation of the generic principle. On the contrary, it implies the generic principle. It is an attempt to add to the generic principle, to be more informative. Evidently, this is only one of many possible special truth-maker principles. Here is a still more special special truth-maker principle:

> (TMC)   Every true proposition is made true by a fact it corresponds with.

This principle might be what friends of truth-making have in mind when they say or imply that a correspondence theory is committed to the truth-maker principle, but not the other way round: (TMC) obviously implies (TM), but (TM) does not imply (TMC). On this way of looking at things, a correspondence theory would be a species, or rather a subspecies, of a truth-maker theory.

So far, our correspondence "theory" is a very small theory: a one-liner mini-theory. We would normally expect a bit more, some account that tells us about the nature of facts and especially about the nature of correspondence. Concerning the latter, George Pitcher (1964: 9–14) makes a helpful distinction. He points out that there are two separable aspects to the notion of correspondence. The first he calls *correspondence-as-correlation*, familiar from mathematical contexts, where one finds talk of correspondence in the sense of a correlation between the members of two sets in accordance with some rule or function. Pertaining to this aspect, our correspondence theorists might want to add further claims to (TMC), claims that commit them to one or both of the following:

Correlation:
(a) If a proposition corresponds with a fact, then there is no other fact the proposition corresponds with.
(b) If a proposition corresponds with a fact, then there is no other proposition that corresponds with that fact.

Taken together, (a) and (b) say that correspondence is a one–one relation: each true proposition corresponds with exactly one fact; and different true propositions always correspond with different facts. I said correspondence theorists *might* want to commit themselves to both parts of Correlation. In fact, it is not easy to find any who are clearly committed to part (b), which, by my lights, goes beyond what even a rather enthusiastic champion of the correspondence approach needs to maintain.[1] Explicit commitment to part (a) is equally rare. However, one does find real-life correspondence theorists moving comfortably from talk about a given true proposition to talk about *the* fact it corresponds with: a move that signals commitment to part (a) of Correlation.

The second aspect of correspondence Pitcher calls *correspondence-as-congruity*. Unlike correspondence-as-correlation, which does not imply anything about the inner nature of the corresponding items, correspondence-as-congruity involves that the corresponding items are similar in certain relevant respects, which in turn requires that they have the same or sufficiently similar *structure*. This aspect of correspondence, which is more prominent (and more notorious) than the previous one, is also much more difficult to make precise. Let us say, rather roughly, that our correspondence theorists might want to add claims to (TMC) that commit them to something like the following:

> Structure:
> If a proposition corresponds with a fact, then they have the same or
> sufficiently similar structure: the overall correspondence between a
> proposition and a fact is a matter of part-wise correspondence, of
> their having corresponding constituents in corresponding places in
> the same structure, or in sufficiently similar structures.

Take the proposition that Ludwig is hungry. Assume it is true. A correspondence theorist is likely to say that it corresponds with the fact that Ludwig is hungry; and one who is also committed to (a strong version of) Structure might add: the proposition and the fact have constituents arranged in a certain way. The constituents of the proposition are the Ludwig-concept and the hungry-concept; the constituents of the fact are Ludwig and the property of being hungry. The Ludwig-concept corresponds with Ludwig, and the hungry-concept corresponds with the property of being hungry. Proposition and fact have the same structure and have corresponding constituents in the same structure. What is this shared structure? Well, it does not have a very good name but one could say, albeit somewhat misleadingly, that it is the subject-predicate structure, meaning that it is the sort of structure that shows itself, by way of a linguistic symptom, in the grammatical subject-predicate structure of the single sentence that can be used to perspicuously describe both the proposition that Ludwig is happy and the fact that Ludwig is happy.

Correlation and Structure reflect distinct aspects of the notion of correspondence: one might want to advocate one without the other.[2] However, it is unlikely that they are entirely independent. Correlation, it seems, requires further explanation: what is the function by which true propositions are correlated with facts? It is not easy to see how an answer to this question could ultimately avoid talking about the structure and constituents of the correlated propositions and facts – especially if the correlation is supposed to be one–one. The road from Structure to Correlation is even more straightforward. The more one pushes Structure, that is, the closer the required match between true propositions and facts, the more likely that the resulting account will be committed to Correlation, although it seems to me that one might reasonably try to avoid part (b) of Correlation: different true propositions might reasonably be said to correspond to (have sufficiently similar constituent-structure as) the same fact as long as they are not too different.[3]

Here we have a model of what a correspondence theory of truth might look like. Various alternative versions could be generated from the generic truth-maker principle, (TM), by producing alternatives to the specific truth-maker principles. Our model makes it easy to see, on the one hand, why friends of truth-making who reject our sample correspondence theory nevertheless find some good in it. Its characteristic claim, (TMC), implies the generic truth-maker principle (TM): our correspondence theorists are truth-maker theorists, so they are at least in the right ballpark. One can also see why, on the other hand, our correspondence theory will meet strong resistance from many friends of truth-making. They will maintain that this attempt to fill in the generic truth-maker principle, to say something more informative than what is said by (TM), has failed; that our correspondence theorists are way too ambitious; that they end up with a whole zoo of funny facts that are not needed and are not well motivated by the basic truth-maker intuition.

This criticism should be fleshed out a bit. Friends of truth-making who reject our correspondence theory may raise objections against each of its ingredients. I shall only give a few examples, beginning with objections to Structure (the most contentious ingredient), working backwards until only the generic truth-maker principle is left standing. Many additional examples, and more argumentative support, can be found in, for example, Mulligan *et al.* (this vol., Ch. 3), Russell (1918), Fox (1987), Bigelow (1988a) and Armstrong (1989a, 1997, 2004). The objections usually rely on a methodological background principle – a truth-maker version of Ockham's razor: do not postulate a relatively more complex truth-maker for a truth where a simpler truth-maker will suffice.

- *Against Structure:* Take the disjunctive proposition that Ludwig is happy or Ludwig is hungry. There is no need for a disjunctive fact. The proposition can be made true by the fact that Ludwig is happy. Even on a very loose interpretation of Structure, this fact does not have the same complexity, does not have the same constituent-structure, as the proposition it makes true.
- *Against Correlation (b):* Take the following two disjunctive propositions: the proposition that Ludwig is happy or Ludwig is hungry, and the proposition that Ludwig is happy or Ludwig is thirsty. Again, there is no need for disjunctive facts. Both propositions can be made true by the fact that Ludwig is happy: two different propositions can have the same fact as truth-maker.[4]
- *Against Correlation (a):* Take the proposition that there are some happy dogs. There is no need to postulate an existentially generalized fact. The proposition can be made true by the fact that Ludwig is happy, and also by the fact that Lassie is happy, and also by the fact that Fido is happy, and so on. So, one proposition can be made true by many different facts.
- *Against (TMC):* Once Structure, Correlation (b) and Correlation (a) have been rejected, the claim that all true propositions are made true by *corresponding* facts has to go too, at least on any reasonably substantive interpretation of 'corresponding', one that gives some additional content to this term and does not eviscerate it to such an extent that (TMC) is nothing more than a verbose notational variant of (TMF), the claim that all true propositions are made true by facts.[5]
- *Against (TMF):* Take the proposition that Ludwig is a dog. Assuming that Ludwig is essentially a dog, Ludwig by himself suffices to make true the proposition that Ludwig is a dog. There is no need to postulate the fact that Ludwig is a dog. Also, take the proposition that Ludwig exists. It too is made true just by Ludwig himself. And the proposition that Ludwig is identical with Josef,

if true, is also made true just by Ludwig, that is, by Josef. There is no need to postulate, in addition, the fact that Ludwig exists or the fact that Ludwig is identical with Josef.

From this point on, there is considerable divergence. Some truth-maker theorists maintain that facts are not needed as truth-makers at all. For example, Kevin Mulligan *et al.* (this vol., Ch. 3) are strongly inclined to hold that facts are not even needed as truth-makers for singular contingent propositions, such as the proposition that Ludwig is happy. According to them, such propositions are made true by individual substances and/or individual accidents, also known as particularized qualities, moments, tropes or modes. Armstrong (1989a, 1997), on the other hand, maintains that facts are needed as truth-makers for propositions that attribute contingent properties (or relations) to individual substances, provided the properties (or relations) in question are genuine universals. He even holds that the most basic propositions of this sort, atomic propositions, when true, are made true by *corresponding* atomic facts – so that a version of the correspondence theory, albeit restricted to contingent atomic propositions, survives at the core of his truth-maker theory. This is why Armstrong always speaks quite favourably of the correspondence theory.[6]

Others, those who speak unfavourably of the correspondence theory, reject it not only because of its ontological dimension; they deny, in addition, the intelligibility of the idea of a proposition corresponding with a slice of reality. They hold that the very notion of correspondence, as employed by the correspondence theory, is bankrupt, and that the theory should not be allowed to survive at all, not even when restricted to atomic propositions. They would maintain, like Dummett (1959: 14), that the truth-maker principle captures *all* that is good in the correspondence theory, which is not a whole lot. This is why Alex Oliver (1996: 69) says that the truth-maker principle is "a sanitised version of the correspondence theory", although, seeing that our correspondence theory is a species of the truth-maker principle, the insult might be better put by saying that the correspondence theory is a polluted, or insane, version of the truth-maker principle.

Advocates of truth-making who are opposed to correspondence theories hold that the latter's attempts to provide more than the generic truth-maker principle, (TM), are much too ambitious. However, some do not rest content just with (TM). They too want to provide more, although they tend to be less interested in truth and the truth-making relation, and to focus more on ontological questions.[7] They want to employ the generic truth-maker principle as a guide to doing ontology, asking the question: items of what ontological categories are needed as truth-makers for the propositions we are committed to accept as true? This enterprise can be understood as trying to provide a number of special truth-maker principles of the form 'Every true proposition of type K is made true by items of ontological category C', and as aiming to eventually replace the generic truth-maker principle with one that is more informative along the ontological dimension:

(TM⁺) If y is a true proposition, then y is made true by some item from category C1 or by some item from category C2 or by some item from category C3 or by ...; and there is nothing else that makes any true proposition true.

The final version of this principle, if it can be completed, would be the ideal grand finale of truth-maker-driven ontology. One hopes that it would be fairly succinct. But even if it ends up being rather longwinded, it will still be more informative than the generic truth-maker principle, as long as there is a closure clause ('and there is nothing else that makes any true proposition true'). Moreover, one hopes that it will be accompanied by many special truth-maker principles, telling us in much more detail which types of propositions can be made true by items of which ontological categories.

2. Truth-making and a more realistic correspondence theory

In the previous section, I presented a model correspondence theory whose relation to the generic truth-maker principle, (TM), is quite perspicuous. It is easy to see why friends of truth-making might want to reject this theory on the grounds that it is overwrought along various dimensions, while at the same time applauding it, if maybe only mildly, on the grounds that it has at least a good core: its characteristic principle, (TMC), obviously implies the generic truth-maker principle, (TM). But this simple and somewhat pleasing story is not realistic. One of its main characters, the central principle of our model correspondence theory,

(TMC)   Every true proposition is made true by a fact it corresponds with

is fictitious: there is no real-life correspondence theory whose central principle takes the form of (TMC).[8] The sort of correspondence principles that one can find at the centre of some real-life correspondence theories will look much more like this (modulo variations in terminology):

(C)   A proposition is true if and only if it corresponds with a fact,

which may again be thought of as accompanied by, or embedded in, a version of Structure or Correlation or both.[9]

(C) is a (generalized) biconditional: it offers a sufficient as well as a necessary condition for a proposition's being true. (TMC), on the other hand, is only a (generalized) one-way conditional: it offers only a necessary condition. By itself, this difference would be trivial because any truth-maker principle is easily converted into a biconditional, for the simple reason that 'x makes y true' trivially implies 'y is true'. There is, however, a deeper reason for this seemingly superficial difference. Advocates of (C) want to answer the question: what is truth? They intend (C) to be understood with sufficient strength so that the biconditional can be upgraded to a property identity, telling us that truth *is* correspondence with a fact, that the property *being true* is the general relational property *corresponding with some fact*. They intend to provide a *definition* of truth, in one sense of this term.[10]

(C) does not contain the phrase 'is made true by' or the phrase 'makes true'. Its intended role as a definition also explains this second difference between (C) and (TMC): the definition provided by (C) would become circular if it did contain these phrases.

Advocates of truth-maker principles regard their favourite principle as stating an important necessary truth about truth. But they do not typically intend it as a definition, which is one reason why truth-maker principles are formulated as mere one-way conditionals even though they are trivially convertible into biconditionals: to signal that they are not intended as definitions. I take it that the fear of circularity is the main reason why truth-maker principles, although trivially convertible into biconditionals, are not typically put forth as definitions.

How serious the threat of circularity actually is at this point is somewhat less clear-cut than it might seem. It is not entirely obvious that a definition of truth using the phrase 'x makes y true' is circular. After all, the phrase does *not* decompose into 'x makes y and y is true', which would yield an explicitly and undeniably circular definition. One might suggest that 'makes true' functions like 'is a father of' and propose that a definition of truth in terms of 'makes true', or rather 'is made true by something', can be understood along the lines of a definition of fatherhood in terms of 'is a father of someone': maybe not very informative, but not entirely uninformative either – at least it tells us that what on the linguistic surface looks like an absolute property should be understood as a general relational property. On the other hand, friends of the truth-maker principle usually hold that the following states a crucial necessary condition on truth-making: if x makes y true, then, necessarily, if x exists then y is true. If this condition is intended as partly definitional of truth-making, as it seems to be, then a definition of truth in terms of 'makes true' would turn out to be (indirectly) circular after all. Although this whole issue is somewhat tricky, I will assume that the threat of circularity is serious and a major reason why truth-maker principles are typically not put forth as definitions of truth.[11]

3. Bridge-principles

Our earlier correspondence theory obviously implies the generic truth-maker principle, (TM), because the central claim of that theory, (TMC), already contains the notion of truth-making. But that theory is a fiction. Our present correspondence theory, whose central characteristic principle is (C), is not a fiction. But it does not obviously imply (TM). So what is the relation between our non-fictitious correspondence theory and (TM), the generic truth-maker principle?

Let us try a simple suggestion. They are connected by *bridge-principles*. I use this term deliberately because it is reminiscent of treatments of theory reduction in the philosophy of science. An example (no doubt vastly oversimplified) will illustrate the basic idea (cf. Hempel 1966). Say fundamental chemistry contains theoretical terms like 'H' and 'O', but does not, strictly speaking, contain common-sense terms like 'water'. One nevertheless wants to say that the theory underwrites (vindicates, is implicitly committed to) some of our ordinary beliefs about water, our *folk-theory* of water, at least the parts of it that are not false. Although the scientific theory, not containing the term 'water', does not by itself imply any principles of our folk-theory of water, one can still say that it underwrites it to the extent that laws of our folk-theory can be deduced from the conjunction of the laws of the scientific theory together with bridge-laws, such as 'Water is constituted by H_2O'. The bridge-laws themselves do not, strictly speaking, belong to the scientific theory; they serve to connect the scientific theory with our folk-theory.

Let us apply a version of this to our correspondence theory of truth (by which I do not mean to suggest that such a "theory" has anything like the sort of respectability of a serious scientific theory). Our improved model correspondence theory, whose central claim is (C), underwrites (is committed to) the generic truth-maker principle, (TM), in the sense that (TM) can be derived from the conjunction of the official theory together with at least one bridge-principle, which connects the notion of truth-making to the official terminology of the theory, but which does not, and should not, be understood as belonging to the official theory, because adding it would raise a serious threat of circularity.

The friends of truth-making, even the ones that are hostile to the correspondence theory, should take an interest in such a bridge-principle. For they will want to maintain that (TM) captures something (or everything) that is good in our improved, more realistic, (C)-based correspondence theory. It is hard to see how this claim could be upheld without a bridge-principle. Note that the overall picture fits rather well with the idea, frequently voiced by friends of truth-making, that the generic truth-maker principle, (TM), expresses a *basic intuition* about truth: the friends of truth-making, we may observe, are telling us that (TM) is part of our folk-theory of truth.

Our correspondence theorists should also take some interest in such a bridge-principle, for they will want to hold that their theory is committed to (TM). The present picture fits well with the actual practice of real-life correspondence theorists. Reading their works, one finds that they too employ the notion of truth-making – some of them quite frequently – but only, as it were, in the surrounding text. When it comes to stating the official formulation (or summary) of their theory or definition, they keep the notion of truth-making at bay so as to avoid worries about circularity. This practice suggests that they too take the notion of truth-making, and the truth-maker principle, (TM), to be parts of our folk-theory of truth, and that they conceive of their official correspondence theory as underwriting this folk-theory by way of a (typically unstated) bridge-principle.[12]

So, let us look for a bridge-principle that, in conjunction with our improved model correspondence theory whose central claim is

(C) A proposition is true if and only if it corresponds with a fact,

allows us to derive the generic truth-maker principle:

(TM) Every true proposition is made true by something.

Our correspondence theorists will aim for a strong bridge-principle, preferably a biconditional, which can be upgraded to a property identity, allowing them to say that truth-making just *is* ..., where '...' contains only vocabulary from their official theory. With such a strong principle, that is, a (real) definition of truth-making, they could maintain that their theory already contains, albeit implicitly, an account of the truth-making relation and that much of our folk-theory of truth, at least in so far as it concerns truth and truth-making, can be reduced to the correspondence theory. The simplest proposal that would support such a claim would be the biconditional: 'x makes y true if and only if y corresponds with x', which, if defensible, could be upgraded to the thesis that truth-making just is correspondence. Evidently, this is overly simplistic. For even the weaker, one-sided bridge-principle,

(B1) If y corresponds with x, then x makes y true,

which obviously would have to hold for the above proposal to be defensible, already looks quite untenable.[13]

Correspondence, it seems hard to deny, is a *symmetric* relation: necessarily, for any x and y, if y corresponds with x, then x corresponds with y. It is also a *reflexive* relation: necessarily, for any x and y, if y corresponds with x, then y corresponds with y. Truth-making, on the other hand, appears to be neither reflexive nor symmetric. (In fact, it is widely assumed, I think, that truth-making is *asymmetric*, which may well be a mistake, as we shall see below.) Assume a proposition p corresponds with a fact f. By (B1), it would follow that f makes p true. But by the symmetry of the correspondence relation, it also follows that f corresponds with p; from which it would follow, by (B1), that p makes f true. In general, according to (B1), any proposition that corresponds with a fact would not only be made true by that fact but also make it true. (B1) is not a viable bridge-principle. Hence the truth-making relation cannot just *be* the correspondence relation.

What bridge-principle could we put in place of (B1), so that (TM) is still derivable from (C) plus that principle? Leading up to another fairly simple but more tenable suggestion, let us take a closer look at the central correspondence principle, this time spelled out in slightly more formal terms. Using 'F' for 'fact', 'C' for 'corresponds with', 'P' for 'proposition', '∃' for 'there is a', and 'T' for 'true':

(C) For every y: Ty if and only if $(\exists x)$(Py & yCx & Fx)

We can observe that our correspondence theorist does not actually define truth (for propositions) just as correspondence, but by way of the complex expression 'Py & yCx & Fx'. What does this expression stand for? It stands for a relation; if the linguistic representation can be trusted, it stands for a complex, composite relation. (Admittedly, it may be somewhat unusual to refer to what is depicted by such an expression as a relation, but it is hard to see why it would not deserve that name.) Now note that, although the correspondence relation itself

$$y\mathrm{C}x$$

is symmetric, the complex, composite relation

$$\mathrm{P}y\ \&\ y\mathrm{C}x\ \&\ \mathrm{F}x$$

is asymmetric, provided the following principle – let us call it *Non-identity* – holds: necessarily, no proposition is identical with a fact; that is, necessarily, for any x and y, if Py & Fx, then $y \neq x$.

Given Non-identity, the complex relation is obviously, if somewhat boringly, asymmetric. Take any pair, p and f, such that 'Pp & pCf & Ff' holds, the result of switching 'p' and 'f' throughout the whole expression is automatically false just because nothing is both a proposition and a fact. What, then, about Non-identity? It does not contain the notion of truth-making, so our correspondence theorists can and will regard it as a fundamental metaphysical principle, belonging to the official part of their theory, together with some version of Structure and/or Correlation. Non-identity, by the way, is common ground, embraced by the friends of truth-making as well.[14]

The suggestion now is to replace the overly simplistic bridge-principle (B1) with the slightly more sophisticated

(B2) If Py & yCx & Fx, then xMTy,

where 'MT' is short for 'makes true'. The conjunction of (C) with (B2) will obviously enable us to derive the generic truth-maker principle (TM).[15]

You might complain that (B2) seems a bit shallow and that not much progress has been made. You might even suggest that an advocate of (B1) would, as it

147

were, already have intended it in the sense of (B2). Fair enough. However, there is a temptation, when thinking about correspondence theories of truth, to conceive of correspondence as somehow already "applied" to propositions and facts. Taking Non-identity for granted, "the correspondence relation" may then be conceived of as an asymmetric relation. But on reflection one will still find oneself judging that it is a symmetric relation; after all, the correspondence relation itself is symmetric. The difference between (B1) and (B2) at least sorts out this possible confusion.

The conjunction of (C) with (B2) allows our correspondence theorists to derive the generic truth-maker principle (TM); in addition, it also allows them to derive the special truth-maker principles mentioned earlier, (TMF) and (TMC):

(TM)   Every true proposition is made true by something.

(TMF)   Every true proposition is made true by a fact.

(TMC)   Every true proposition is made true by a fact it corresponds with.[16]

At this point you might find yourself worried by the following thought: how can (B2), which states after all only a sufficient condition for truth-making, yield the result that facts, even corresponding facts, must be the truth-makers of true propositions? But note that this worry reads too much into (TMF) and (TMC). They do not imply that facts, or corresponding facts, are *the*, that is, *the only*, truth-makers of true propositions. Focus for the moment just on (TMF). It says that for every true proposition there is a fact that makes it true, which allows that some, even all, true propositions are also made true by items other than facts. The inclination to read more than this into (TMF) arises, I think, because (TMF) feels redundant when taken literally, so that one naturally takes it to say something stronger than it literally says. This, in turn, has to do with another principle that has been operating in the background all along, namely the *Converse* of the generic truth-maker principle:

Converse   Every proposition that is made true by something is true.

This principle is not much discussed by friends of truth-making because it is presupposed by their use of the phrase 'makes true'. It functions as a meaning postulate for this phrase and is, consequently, even more basic than (TM) is taken to be by the friends of truth-making. One who denies Converse or, rather, one who rejects the sentence written above, next to the label 'Converse', must be using the words 'makes true' and 'is made true by' in a way that differs significantly from the way in which the friends of truth-making use them when stating the generic truth-maker principle (TM). On such a divergent (technical) use of these phrases, there would be no reason for saying that (TM), or rather, the sentence above, next to the label '(TM)', expresses a basic intuition about truth, which is of course what the friends of truth-making are saying.

Consider (TM). It is formulated as a necessary condition for truth. But, because of Converse, the condition (TM) states, *being made true by something*, is already sufficient for truth. What, then, is the point of (TMF) adding what looks like a "further" necessary condition? Is that not redundant? Well, assume x makes a proposition y true; according to (TMF), either x is already a fact or, if x is a non-fact, then x's making true y entails that there is also a fact z such that z makes true y. In other words, (TMF) tells us that a proposition is made true by a non-fact, only if it is also made true by a fact, so that such a proposition will have at least two truth-makers. Similarly for (TMC); it tells us that a proposition is made true by an item that is not a corresponding fact, only if it is also made true by a corresponding fact, so that such a proposition will have at least two truth-makers.[17] So (TMF) and (TMC) are indeed implied by the conjunction of (C) with (B2), but they are weaker than one might take them to be at first glance. (TMF) does not imply that true propositions are made true only by facts; (TMC) does not imply that true propositions are made true only by corresponding facts.

These stronger claims will be derivable from (C) in conjunction with a second bridge-principle our correspondence theorists will want to advocate. Let us turn to this now. (B2) will suggest to our correspondence theorists that the folk-notion of truth-making picks out a complex relation composed of the properties of being a proposition, being a fact, and the relation of correspondence. But (B2) is not strong enough to bear out this suggestion. This will require, in addition, a bridge-principle like (B2) but running in the opposite direction:

(B3)   If xMTy, then Py & yCx & Fx.

In conjunction with (C), this bridge-principle entails that true propositions are made true only by facts, and that true propositions are made true only by corresponding facts. One naturally expects our correspondence theorists to be committed to these stronger claims, going beyond (TMF) and (TMC), because of their advocacy of (C) as their central principle about truth, especially because they understand (C) as providing a definition of truth. It would be wrongheaded to maintain that truth *is* correspondence with a fact while allowing that some, or even all, true propositions are made true by non-facts as long as that entails that they are also made true by corresponding facts. (B3) rules out truth-makers that are non-facts and rules out truth-makers that are facts but fail to correspond with the propositions they make true.

Note also that (B3) is needed for deriving Converse. However trivial or analytic Converse might be, since it contains the notion of truth-making, it is not part of the official correspondence theory, and it cannot be derived from a bridge-principle like (B2), which has truth-making in its consequent: for deriving Converse, our correspondence theorists need a bridge-principle with truth-making in the antecedent rather than the consequent. It seems to me that the ability to derive Converse is crucial, and that it is crucial just because Converse is trivial, self-evident, analytic, platitudinous, a meaning-principle, constitutive of the very notion of truth-making (etc.). Imagine our correspondence theorists could not derive Converse. One would then have strong grounds to question whether their claim that their theory underwrites at least a significant part of our folk-theory of truth and truth-making is adequately supported. One should even worry about their derivation of (TM) from (C) & (B2). If they were not committed to Converse, why think that what our correspondence theorists call "(TM)" is the genuine article, the principle that actually involves the notion of truth-making?

Let us take stock. Our correspondence theorists advocate (C) together with some version of Structure or Correlation or both. This is their official correspondence theory. By way of connecting this theory with our folk-theory of truth and truth-making, they also advocate the bridge-principles (B3) and (B2), which together with (C) imply Converse, (TM), (TMF), (TMC), and a still stronger principle saying that true propositions are made true only by corresponding facts. Finally, since (B3) and (B2) combined make for a biconditional, they will take this to support their claim that their official theory already contains, albeit implicitly, an account of the folk-notion of truth-making in terms of the properties of being a proposition, being a fact and the relation of correspondence.

Friends of truth-making reject most of this – the friends of truth-making, that is, who reject our correspondence theory. But note that they do accept (B2); they too embrace the conditional: *if* a proposition corresponds with a fact, then it is made true by that fact. Since the conjunction (C) & (B2) implies (TM), they applaud the correspondence theory for being committed to (TM) and maintain that (TM) captures something important that is good in the correspondence theory. But the conjunction (C) & (B2) also implies (TMF) and implies (TMC). Champions of truth-making reject (TMC), hence they reject (C); contemporary champions of truth-making reject both (TMC) and (TMF); some of their ancestors, for example Russell ([1918] 1985), reject only (TMC): either way, they reject (C). Note that their attitude towards (B3) differs significantly from their attitude towards (B2). They accept (B2) but reject (B3). Obviously, (B3) cannot be an acceptable principle by their lights: correspondence with a fact, they say, is not necessary for being made true. Along with (B3), they reject the stronger versions of (TMF) and (TMC), that is, the claim that all true propositions are made true only by (corresponding) facts.[18]

Viewed from the theory/folk-theory perspective, the debate between the two parties can be understood along the following lines. Our correspondence theorists maintain that their theory underwrites, in a relatively strong sense, our folk-theory of truth, at least in so far as it involves principles (intuitions) about truth-making. The friends of truth-making who oppose our correspondence theory – I will simply call them "the Truth-makers" from now on – object that, although this theory is to be applauded for being committed to the very important folk-theory principle (TM), it nevertheless has to be rejected because its additional commitments are in conflict with our folk-theory of truth, especially with intuitions against funny facts (logically complex facts). To this our correspondence theorists will respond with a two-pronged strategy: (a) the alleged intuitions reported by their opponents are not really there or are not very strong or central; and/or (b) to the extent that they are there, they are wrong and deserve to be corrected by the correspondence theory of truth – after all, folk-theoretical principles may well be wrong and in need of correction by theory. To this the Truth-makers will respond that the relevant recalcitrant intuitions are really there and are central and strong (and, maybe, supported by considerations independent from questions about truth), so that, on the contrary, these intuitions must be seen as refuting the correspondence theory rather than deserving correction by that theory.

I will not try to enter into this debate. Instead, I want to emphasize a point that I adumbrated earlier, suggesting that the picture I have drawn here of the relationship between our correspondence theory and the truth-maker principle has some aspects to it that are a bit murky.

Let us look at the situation from the point of view of the Truth-makers. As long as we focus exclusively on the truth-maker principle, (TM), the picture seems fairly clear. The Truth-makers themselves accept (B2). By their lights, the correspondence theory is *in fact* committed to (TM) – whether its advocates believe it or not, care for (TM) or not – because (TM) follows from (B2) plus (C). The Truth-makers can reason like this: "If (B2) then, if (C) then (TM); (B2) is true; hence: if (C) then (TM), that is, (C) is committed to (TM) in the straightforward sense that (C) holds only if (TM) holds."

When Converse is added to this picture it becomes less clear. The Truth-makers do of course embrace Converse wholeheartedly. But they do not accept (B3), which is used by the correspondence theorist to derive Converse from (C). So, according to them, the correspondence theory itself is not in fact committed to Converse; remember that (B3), being a bridge-principle, is not part of the official correspondence theory. It is just that the advocates of the correspondence theory believe (B3) and so *believe* that they are in fact committed to Converse: they are subjectively committed to it but not objectively, not according to the Truth-makers.[19]

But does this consideration not tend to undermine the Truth-makers' seemingly straightforward reason for thinking that the correspondence theory is committed to (TM) via (B2)? Converse surely is very fundamental to the Truth-makers: it is a meaning-principle or – if you do not like that language – a platitude, constitutive of the very notion of truth-making. Without objective commitment to Converse, it should be at least dubious, by the lights of the Truth-makers, whether the correspondence theory can really be said to be committed to (TM), involving as it does the notion of truth-making, or merely to an impostor, labelled '(TM)', which involves some other notion labelled 'truth-making'. Of course, the correspondence theorists assent to what looks like (B2) and, consequently, to what looks like (TM). They also believe they are committed to Converse but, according to the Truth-makers, they do so based on the false (B3). Can this be enough, by the lights of the Truth-makers, to count as genuine commitment to (TM)?

4. Is truth-making asymmetric?

In this last section I want to address a point I mentioned parenthetically in the previous section. It is quite natural to think that truth-making is an asymmetric relation, and it is, I think, widely assumed that truth-making is asymmetric. Related to this, it is also quite natural to think, maybe even more so, that truth-making is irreflexive, that is, that nothing can make itself true, and this too seems to be typically taken for granted. One may note that there is a logical connection between asymmetry and irreflexivity: an asymmetric relation must be irreflexive: any case of aRa will yield a *reductio* of the assumption that R is asymmetric.[20]

The natural assumption that truth-making is asymmetric (hence irreflexive), seems to play a considerable role in people's attitudes towards the truth-maker principle *vis-à-vis* the correspondence theory. Indeed, it seems that the perceived asymmetry of the truth-making relation is part of the appeal of the truth-maker principle. The truth-maker principle, one is inclined to say, is importantly right in trying to characterize truth by way of an asymmetric relation; on this point the correspondence theory leaves something to be desired because it tries to account for truth by way of a symmetric and reflexive relation.

I have already suggested earlier that the second part of this thought, the one about the correspondence theory, may to some extent derive from a tendency to confuse the symmetric correspondence relation, yCx, on the one hand, with the complex asymmetric relation Py & yCx & Fx, on the other. Our correspondence theory says that for y to be true is for it to be related to some x by way of that complex asymmetric relation. Admittedly, this may not be quite satisfying, because the complex relation owes its asymmetry entirely to the fact that nothing can be both a proposition and a fact. One may well feel that the correspondence theory would be more satisfying if the genuinely relational component of the complex relation, yCx, were itself asymmetric; the account that is being offered of the truth-making relation by way of the complex relation Py & yCx & Fx may strike one as somewhat shallow for the same reason.

But what about the perceived asymmetry of truth-making? Is the truth-making relation really asymmetric?

Consider the proposition that Ludwig is a dog. On the face of it, it seems quite plausible to think that this proposition is made true by Ludwig himself because Ludwig is essentially a dog: Ludwig, being essentially a dog, is necessarily such that, if he exists, then the proposition that he is a dog is true – which suggests that

Ludwig is sufficient as a truth-maker for any proposition that correctly attributes one of his essential properties to him. Based on this, one will hold, accordingly, that the general existential proposition that there is at least one dog is also made true by Ludwig himself and, in addition, by each and every dog: each dog is a truth-maker for the proposition that there is a dog. Now consider the general existential proposition *that there is at least one proposition*. Assuming that every proposition is essentially a proposition, which seems plausible, it follows by the same line of reasoning that the proposition that there is at least one proposition is made true by each and every proposition, including itself: it is among its own truth-makers. So here we have a case where something makes itself true, which generates a counter-example to the natural assumption that truth-making is asymmetric, via being a counter-example to the natural assumption that truth-making is irreflexive: truth-making, it seems, is merely non-symmetric.[21]

The crucial ingredient of the reasoning leading to the counter-example is its starting-point: the assumption or intuition that Ludwig, being essentially a dog, suffices to make true the proposition that Ludwig is a dog. This assumption seems quite plausible and quite a few of the Truth-makers will think that it belongs to, or can be extracted from, our folk-theory of truth and truth-making. However, our intuitions to the effect that truth-making is asymmetric and irreflexive seem at least equally strong. They too are plausibly regarded as belonging to our folk-theory, or rather, as being extractable from our folk-theory (one would not typically expect to find them there couched in these technical terms). The reasoning above shows that there is a conflict here.[22]

How will our Truth-makers react to this? Some may want to respond that the alleged intuitions to the effect that truth-making is asymmetric and irreflexive were never really part of our folk-theory to begin with. Others may want to say the same thing about alleged intuitions to the effect that propositions correctly attributing essential properties to objects are made true just by those objects. Others may want to argue that all these intuitions do belong to our folk-theory of truth and that this theory is implicitly inconsistent, which is by no means unheard of when it comes to folk-theories (and our folk-theory of truth, in particular, is likely to be implicitly inconsistent anyway because of the intuitions that give rise to the liar paradox). This third response may then lead into a debate about which of our intuitions are mistaken and in need of correction, a debate that in many instances will be indistinguishable from the debate between advocates of the first two responses.

I will not enter into this debate. Instead, I want to end by briefly considering whether this issue bears on the relationship between our correspondence theory and the truth-maker principle, as seen from the point of view of those Truth-makers who hold that truth-making is *not* asymmetric, that is, those who accept the starting-point of the above line of reasoning and its conclusion.[23]

Based on bridge-principles (B2) and (B3), our correspondence theorists maintain that truth-making is the complex relation that holds between x and y if and only if P*y* & *y*C*x* & F*x*. According to the Truth-makers presently under consideration, this is yet another reason for rejecting this position. More specifically, it is yet another reason for rejecting bridge-principle (B3), which is the one that is directly relevant here because it says: if *x*MT*y*, then P*y* & *y*C*x* & F*x*. If truth-making is not asymmetric, this cannot be correct. The complex relation that appears in the consequent of this conditional is asymmetric, and the holding of a relation that is not asymmetric cannot be sufficient for the holding of a relation that is asymmetric.

Our correspondence theorists will not be much moved by this point. By their lights, it does not really insert a fresh consideration into the debate. The reasoning that resulted in the counter-example to the asymmetry assumption started from the Truth-makers' intuition that Ludwig himself, because he is essentially a dog, makes true the proposition that Ludwig is a dog. Our correspondence theorists are already firmly committed to the view that, since truth *is* correspondence with a fact, only facts can make true propositions true. They hold that intuitions to the contrary, if genuinely present, are in need of correction by the correspondence theory. The truth-maker relation, they say, is asymmetric.

Looking at the situation from the point of view of the Truth-makers, on the other hand, underscores the worry I raised at the end of the previous section. By their lights, the truth-making relation is neither symmetric nor asymmetric, which must surely be a fundamental fact about the nature of this relation. The Truth-makers are initially inclined to think that they and the correspondence theorists share a core insight, because it looks as if they are both committed, objectively committed, to:

> (B2)   If *y* is a proposition that corresponds with a fact *x*, then *x* makes *y* true,

which appears to build a bridge between the official correspondence theory and the generic truth-maker principle, (TM). (B2), unlike (B3), does not imply that truth-making is asymmetric. But the correspondence theorists do hold that it is; or rather, they hold that the relation expressed by the words 'makes true' is an asymmetric relation, which is quite wrong according to the Truth-makers. It seems that this should further undermine the Truth-makers' confidence in their initial view that the correspondence theorists are really committed to truth-making and not merely to "truth-making".[24]

Notes

1. G. E. Moore is the only one I am aware of who explicitly advocates both (a) and (b), although at later places in the same work he mentions only (a); cf. Moore (1953: 256, 276–7).

2. J. L. Austin ([1950] 1979) advocates correspondence with Correlation but without Structure, although he does not tell us whether he wants both parts of Correlation or only part (a).

3. Some critics find Structure an obviously ludicrous idea, but they tend to think of *truth-bearers* as *linguistic* items. Austin, for example, a prominent critic of Structure, takes the truth-bearers to be what he calls *statements*, that is, sentences as used on a certain occasion; cf. Austin ([1950] 1979: 119). It does indeed seem ludicrous to maintain that all the details of grammatical structure exhibited by our (true) sentences have their analogues in correspondingly structured facts. This is why correspondence theorists who advocate Structure will typically emphasize the gap between the sentences of ordinary language, on the one hand, and propositions, on the other hand: sentences with significantly different grammatical structures, they will say, can express the same proposition – the wider the gap one finds between sentences and expressed propositions, the closer the match one can advocate between (true) propositions and corresponding facts. This is also why correspondence theorists tend to promote *ideal languages*, designed to cut through the idiosyncrasies of ordinary language. The sentences (formulas) of an ideal language are intended to mirror perfectly the structure of the propositions they express. In this way they are supposed to provide – via the correspondence between true propositions and facts – a better representation of the real structure of facts.

4. Disjunctive facts are regarded as funny facts *par excellence* by the friends of truth-making. One of the main sources for this is Russell: "I do not suppose that there is in the world a single disjunctive fact corresponding to '*p* or *q*'. It does not look plausible that in the actual objective world there are facts going about which you could describe as '*p* or *q*'" (1956a: 209); and also: "You must not look about the real world for an object which you can call 'or', and say 'Now, look at this. This is "or"'" (*ibid*.: 209ff.). A generalized version of the second point appears in Wittgenstein's *Tractatus*, another important influence on advocates of truth-making: "My fundamental idea is that the 'logical constants' are not representatives; that there can be no representatives of the *logic* of facts" (1922: 4.0312).

5. Russell (1956a), a very important influence on contemporary advocates of truth-making, would stop at this point: he wants to keep (TMF); cf. e.g. Russell (1956a: 183).

6. This is the overall picture presented in Armstrong (1989a, 1997), and in parts of his *Truth and Truthmakers* (this vol., Ch. 7, 130–31; 2004: 48–50). However, in other parts of *Truth and Truthmakers*, Armstrong seems to take seriously an argument to the effect that particulars have all their properties necessarily. Since facts are not needed as truth-makers for propositions that attribute necessary properties to particulars, this would seem to do away with the need for facts entirely. In Russell's *The Philosophy of Logical Atomism* ([1918] 1985), a restricted version of the correspondence theory also survives at the core; but he differs significantly from Armstrong (1989a, 1997) on the range of the restriction and on the question whether facts are the only truth-makers.

7. See e.g. Mulligan *et al.* (this vol., Ch. 3), Fox (1987), Bigelow (1988a), Armstrong (1989a, 1997, 2004), and the papers in Beebee & Dodd (2005a).

8. There is an exception. My *Random House Unabridged Dictionary* (2nd edn) contains the following entry: "correspondence theory, *Philos.* the theory of truth that a statement is rendered true by the existence of a fact with corresponding elements and similar structure". This is very close to (TMC), applied to statements and enriched with a bit of Structure.

9. In the twentieth century, the formula 'truth is correspondence with a fact' came to be used as representative of the whole family of now so-called correspondence theories. Iit derives from Russell (1912: ch. 12), and Moore (1953: chs 14–15) (the latter publishes lectures given in 1910–11).

10. At least a "real definition". This does not commit them to the claim that (C) provides a definition in the sense of giving a synonym for the term 'true'. Nowadays, most correspondence theorists would consider it implausibly and unnecessarily bold to maintain that 'true' *means the same as* 'corresponds with a fact'. Interestingly, the *Oxford English Dictionary* would nevertheless seem to lend some mild support even to this bold claim, for it contains the entry: "Truth n. Conformity with fact; agreement with reality; accuracy, correctness, verity (of statement or thought)".

11. What is wrong with circular definitions? It does not seem right to respond that they are all entirely uninformative. In any case, that's a methodological or epistemological issue. What is wrong with them metaphysically speaking? With respect to definitions that are intended as real definitions, the answer must be something like this. A real definition is supposed to describe the constituent-

structure of a property or relation. A circular real definition would entail that the defined property or relation contains itself as a proper constituent: but nothing can possibly contain itself as a proper constituent.

12. In *Some Main Problems of Philosophy*, Moore employs the notion of truth-making early on (1953: 254); it then falls away and does not show up in any of his official attempts at defining truth (*ibid.*: 256, 267, and esp. 277). Russell lays out and summarizes his account of truth without the notion of truth-making; he only uses this notion afterwards to drive home the point that truths are not made true by our minds or beliefs (1912: 129). Austin says: "When a statement is true, there is, *of course*, a state of affairs which makes it true..." ([1950] 1979: 123); but again, the official formulation of his definition does not contain the notion of truth-making. Austin's definition, by the way, does not fit very neatly into the simple straitjacket of (C); cf. *ibid.*, 121–2.

13. Note that (B1), being a correspondence-to-truth-making conditional, is clearly relevant here: if it did hold, one could quickly derive (TM) from (C) plus (B1).

14. Compare this with the *identity theory of truth*, according to which a proposition is true iff it is identical with a fact; cf. Dodd (2000); David (2001). This theory is a natural enemy of both correspondence and truth-maker theorists. The identity theory, they point out, leads to the unacceptable claim that every true proposition makes itself true (via a bridge-principle saying that every proposition that is identical with a fact is made true by that fact, that is, by itself).

15. The two bolder proposals midway between (B1) and (B2),

    If Px & yCx, then xMTy,

    If yCx & Fx, then xMTy,

    are not viable. Since every proposition corresponds with itself, the first has the unacceptable consequence that every proposition makes itself true. Since every fact corresponds with itself, the second has the unacceptable consequence that every fact makes itself true.

16. (TMF) and (TMC) follow from (C) & (B2) because, if (B2) holds, then so must the conditionals that are just like (B2) except that their consequents are expanded to 'xMTy & Fx' and 'xMTy & Fx & yCx'.

17. Many friends of truth-making hold, for example, that Ludwig himself makes true the proposition that Ludwig exists. (TMF) and (TMC) allow for this, but they add the following. Necessarily, if Ludwig makes true the proposition that Ludwig exists, then there is a (corresponding) fact that makes true the proposition that Ludwig exists. Given Structure, that would be the fact that Ludwig exists. According to (TMF) and (TMC), if there were no such (corresponding) fact as the fact that Ludwig exists, making true the proposition that Ludwig exists, then Ludwig would not make the proposition true either (he would not exist).

18. Russell (1956a) is an interesting case. His overall strategy can be understood along the following lines. He wants to replace (C) with its restriction to *atomic* propositions:

    (CA) If y is atomic, then y is true iff y corresponds with a fact.

He then wants to account for the truth-values of molecular propositions by way of laws detailing the logical relations between propositions – what we would now call *recursive clauses* – such as: a disjunctive proposition is true iff at least one of its disjuncts is true. He was not, however, entirely clear about the consequences of this strategy; compare, for example, his remark that "the correspondence of a molecular proposition with facts *is of a different sort* from the correspondence of an atomic proposition with a fact" (1956a: 210, emphasis added). He should not have talked about "correspondence" here at all, for he held that there are no disjunctive facts for true disjunctive propositions to correspond with (hence, that the correspondence theory is false). He should have said instead that the truth or falsehood of every proposition can be explained in terms of (derived from) the logical relations between propositions, that is, the recursive clauses, together with (CA), that is, the correspondence or non-correspondence of atomic propositions with facts. This recursive approach to truth can be pursued with the aim to *reject* (TM) by way of the claim that not all truths have truth-makers, only atomic truths have truth-makers. But it can also be pursued – and this seems to have been Russell's intention at the time – with the aim to *secure* (TM) even though the correspondence theory has been rejected: not every truth corresponds with a fact, only atomic truths do, but every truth is made true by something (a fact, in Russell's case), where the recursive clauses are supposed to show how truth-making without correspondence, but grounded in correspondence, comes about. Unfortunately, Russell was a bit cavalier about this last part of his programme.

19. The bridge-principles, being *bridge*-principles, function somewhat like inference rules. So compare the following scenario. Say a philosopher, advocating a theory *T*, which you do not accept, derives 'There are possible worlds' from *T* by way of an inference rule that you do not accept either. Would you say that *she* is ontologically committed to possible worlds? Yes. Would you say that *her theory* is ontologically committed to possible worlds? No, she just believes, wrongly, that it is.

20. For truth-making to be an *asymmetric* relation, the following has to hold. Necessarily, for any *x* and *y*, if *x*MT*y*, then not *y*MT*x*. For truth-making to be *irreflexive*, the following has to hold. Necessarily, if *x*MT*y*, then $x \neq y$. I assume throughout that relations have such properties as being symmetric, asymmetric, reflexive (etc.) necessarily, if they have them at all. In mathematical logic one typically treats such properties as *relativized* to certain sets, so that one relation, *R*, can consistently be said to be asymmetric *in* a set *A* but not asymmetric *in* another set *B*. Both our correspondence theorists and the Truth-makers, will regard such talk as not to be taken quite literally, holding that it does not, strictly speaking, apply to *R* itself, but to different "restrictions" of *R*. For better or for worse, they want to know about the nature of the relation *R* itself, whether it is, for example, asymmetric (period).

21. Which is consistent with saying that it "typically behaves" like an asymmetric relation, meaning, roughly, that in the vast majority of cases where something *x* makes a proposition *y* true, *y* does not, and cannot possibly, make *x* true.

22. Actually, additional assumptions are involved: (a) an existential generalization is made true by anything that makes any of its instances true; (b) propositions are essentially propositions; and (c) propositions are truth-bearers. It is hard to see how a Truth-maker could object to any of them.

23. A number of contemporary Truth-makers are committed or strongly drawn to the view that propositions correctly attributing essential properties to objects are made true just by those objects (no facts need apply); cf. Mulligan *et al.* (this vol., Ch. 3, 68–9; Fox (1987: 190); Bigelow (1988a: 128); and also Armstrong (this vol., Ch. 7, 129). Armstrong's attitude towards this view in *A World of States of Affairs* is a bit complicated, because he is inclined to reject essential properties to begin with (1997: 124). His favourite argument in that book is the "truth-maker argument". Assume the proposition that *a* is *F* is true. Armstrong asks: what is its truth-maker? It cannot be *a*, because *a* can exist without the proposition being true. It cannot be the universal *being F*, for that can exist and be instantiated in the absence of *a*. It cannot be the pair of the particular and the universal, because the universal might be instantiated in some particular other than *a*. It must be the fact that *a* is *F* (cf. *ibid*.: 115). Note that this argument, which is supposed to establish the need for facts as truth-makers, does not establish such a need with respect to true propositions attributing essential properties to *a*, for which the first step of the argument fails: if *a* is essentially *F*, then *a* cannot exist without the proposition that *a* is *F* being true – nothing more than *a* seems needed in this case.

24. Thanks to Adolf Rami and Ted Warfield.

CHAPTER 9

Facts and relations: the matter of ontology and of truth-making

Herbert Hochberg

Facts, or states of affairs, were taken by Bertrand Russell to be entities that sufficed to "make true" or be the "verifiers" for atomic sentences (judgements expressed by atomic sentences, propositions). Such truth-makers were atomic facts. The recognition of atomic facts led, in turn, to questions about what other kinds, if any, of facts there were. Such questions were often raised in the context of considering what one need recognize as grounds of truth: reasons or causes for truths being true. Thus specific issues arose about purported negative facts and general facts. While Russell, like G. E. Moore, appeared to recognize that propositions or "judgement contents" were linked to the existence and nonexistence of specific facts, he did not raise a specific question about a truth-making relation. Rather, his idea, at least for atomic facts, was that a definite description of a purported fact would serve to characterize or define a truth-predicate for the atomic case along the following loose lines:

(R)   For any atomic sentence (proposition) $F^n(x_1, ..., x_n)$: $F^n(x_1, ..., x_n)$ is true if and only if there is a fact with F^n as relation and $x_1, ..., x_n$ as terms in that order.

On such a view, properly developed, there is neither a relation of truth-making that holds between a truth and a fact that "makes it true" nor a property of *truth*, as there appears to be for many of the recent advocates of "truth-making". It is also obvious that there need not be, given the recognition of facts as entities and the role they play as grounds of truth, the further recognition of propositional-style entities as so-called "truth-bearers". But these are further matters that will not be taken up here.

Many advocates of "truth-making" oppose the anti-realism of the Quinean programme for the construal of "truth" that is embodied in:

(Q) The sentence '$F^n(x_1, \ldots, x_n)$' is true if and only if the predicate 'F^n' is true of $x_1, \ldots, x_n$ (in the appropriate order, i.e. of $<x_1, \ldots, x_n>$).

(Q) purportedly lets one avoid both properties and facts as ontologically involved in an account of the truth of atomic truths, and hence as entities that need be appealed to in a viable account of truth. It thus fits with the purported nominalism that W. V. Quine, Nelson Goodman and Wilfrid Sellars brought into vogue in the second half of the twentieth century. Nominalism, in the extreme Quinean fashion, and minimalism – the rejection of facts as entities (generally in connection with issues about truth) – have gone hand in hand on the contemporary scene. Here I shall consider the issues against the historical background provided by Peter Abelard in the late-eleventh and early-twelfth centuries.

In the medieval tradition, a particular object, like a man or a statue of a man, is taken to be a substance or object that is construed as a composite of two categorially different and basic "sorts": a *substantial form* and the matter or material, or *material substance*, that the former "informs" – the resultant individual "thing" or *essential substance*, in Abelard's phrase. Abelard, now considered the major figure in the history of logic between Aristotle and the fourteenth century, developed a novel and systematic approach to basic metaphysical issues that influenced future discussion of problems stemming from the notion of substance and related issues posed by predication, individuation and universals. For a number of medieval philosophers, a form, if taken to exist at all, was not taken to exist apart or independently of some matter (or mind), while objects were taken to be of some form. Objects, or particulars, such as a piece of wax or a man, were seen as hylomorphic composites of a form present in matter. For some medievals, forms were also present *in* minds that "grasped" them in cognitive and perceptive *acts*, but not in the way that they were present *in* a particular object of that form. Just as unformed matter neither exists on its own nor is grasped by a mind, a form does not exist apart from an object or mind that it is "in", in some unspecified manner.[1] The role of forms raises perennial issues about the *connection* between an object and the attributes and relations it exemplifies – questions about the nature of *inherence* and *instantiation* (exemplification) as relations or "ties" or logical forms – as well as about the resulting composite entities. Further questions about predication and about the nature of such resulting "complexes" – taken either as facts (or states of affairs) or as particular complex objects – are familiar, as are those about purported paradoxes that arise.

1. Substance and form

Given the need for matter to be "informed" and for forms to inhere in "something", the distinctions and terminology associated with "potency" and "act" were

159

available, with matter characterized in terms of *potentiality*, meaning that "it" was capable of taking on various forms, in virtue of which there was then something of a definite *kind*.[2] This gave one aspect of the use of the phrase *'prime matter'*. Forms, by contrast, were generally spoken of as "in act" or "actual", being that in virtue of which a particular thing was of a kind and not itself something capable of becoming a thing of a kind by realizing a form. Thus a form was taken to be either simple, in that it was not a composite of a form and what the form actualized, or as composed only of other forms, as a "specific" form or species could be taken as analysable into constituent "parts" – a genus and a differentiating property.[3] Some even thought, by analogy, of a genus (animal) as the "matter" for a differentiating form (rationality) that resulted in the composite – the species – rational animal. This fit with thinking in terms of particular things, a man or a statue, and not in terms of facts, such as the fact that Socrates is a man: of "the walking Socrates" and "the sitting Plato" rather than of the facts that Socrates runs and Plato sits.

If one thinks along such lines, then a particular object is something that is a *subject* for *predications*, while forms are *predicables*: what *can be* predicated of or *inform*. In turn, forms can also be subjects of further predications, such as 'Man is rational', and thus one considers higher-order predicables that are sometimes characterized as *secondary substances*, as in Aristotle and later figures. Thus all three aspects of the hylomorphic compound – the matter, the substantial form and the compound itself – are, in one sense or another, substances. The use of the term 'substance' was further complicated by taking secondary substances, a species for example, to also be such a compound with the genus taken as the "matter" that was qualified by the *specific difference*. Thus, in various ways, one distinguished *simple* substances from *complex* substances. But the basic distinction between what was predicable and what was not was preserved through the centuries and arose in what was to become an influential dichotomy in the nineteenth century: Frege's distinction between *objects* and *functions* and Russell's taking all primitive predicates, representing universals (relations and properties), as properties of and relations between particulars, thereby forming atomic facts.

Quine transformed the Fregean pattern into a formula determining *ontological commitment*: "to be is to be the value of a variable". What one took as an entity in an ontology was an object that the quantifiers of an appropriate linguistic schema ranged over: the things that one referred to in, or that were the subjects of, true statements – what the statements were "about".[4] Being a subject and being an individual substance went hand in hand – the former indicating what the latter "is" – while the adjectival predicables became, as it were, peripheral to what existed: a matter of filling out the "significance" of the sentence or the thought it expressed, and not being a matter of what "is" in the world. Predicates, rather than seen as indicating properties and relations, were characteristically spoken of as "true of" subjects or as indicating the *way* the subjects were – the "status" of the subjects, as some medievals put it, that were the objects of the world – but not thereby indicating any *thing* or further *constituent* recognized in an "ontology".[5] This became a standard catechism of analytic philosophers in the 1950s, 1960s and 1970s. In recent years it has been resurrected in debates about "truth" and "makers of truth" brought about by the revival of interest in classical ontological problems and, particularly, issues about substance, universals, relations and facts. This is seen in the extensive recent literature dealing with trope theories, Bradley's regress and the purported analysis of particulars or individual "substances" in terms of "bundles" (whether connected with issues about time and change or simply in terms of questions about the grounds of "individuation").

It is not surprising that, in view of the appeal of analytic philosophy among English-speaking philosophers and, increasingly, in other areas of Europe, Abelard has become, in the later decades of the twentieth century, a focus of renewed attention. In his *The Philosophy of Peter Abelard* (1997), John Marenbon considers Abelard's rejection of relational accidents as "things". He takes Abelard to have argued, in *Theologia Christiana*, as follows.

If accidents are things, then the relational accident of similarity as holding between two things, say A and B, will be a further thing, the particular accident of similarity, R. But then, given two other similar things, C and D, there will be the relational accident of similarity between them, say R^*. R and R^*, however, will themselves be similar. Hence there will have to be a further thing, the relational accident of similarity that is the similarity between R and R^*. Thus an infinite series of things is generated from the original case of similarity. It supposedly is also a vicious regress since the original similarities ascribed, respectively, to A and B and C and D, are assumed to be founded on the purported *things*, R and R^*, and these, themselves, require further "such" things as grounds for their being instances that are similar. In Marenbon's words:

> The example which Abelard chooses is the relation of similarity (and its contrary, dissimilitude or oppositeness) – which in the *Dialectica* and *Logica* Abelard had treated, like other relations, in terms of particular accidents. Whereas, in these earlier works, Abelard had held that an infinite regress could be avoided so long as similarity and dissimilarity were taken as accidents in the category of relation, not that of quality, he now points out that, if the relation of similarity or dissimilarity is regarded as a thing, different from the substance which it informs, then there will be an infinite regress, since this particular similarity will be similar to that by another particular similarity, and so on. (1997: 155)[6]

What Marenbon does not mention, perhaps not noting or not caring to, is that this argument of approximately 1130 is virtually the same as the classic argument *for* the existence of universals that Russell formulated early in the twentieth century.[7] The difference between Russell's argument and Abelard's argument is as instructive as the striking similarity is of interest.[8] Abelard has an implicit premise, one that we may take to be a clearly *nominalistic* premise: what exists is a particular *thing*. Hence the argument, which presumes a distinction between particulars and universals, takes individual accidents to be either particular things or nonexistent *no-things*. In fact he assumes that relational accidents do not exist, since, as Marenbon cites him, he takes relational properties as not being "anything other than" the substances they are taken to characterize.

Abelard chooses to reinforce his point by a reference to relations in human beings: "many things in ourselves are regarded relatively, when no one of sense would accept that these relations are anything other than ourselves" (quoted in Marenbon 1997: 155). Not taking individual relational accidents as (particular) things and assuming that only particulars are existent things, he rejects relational properties quite explicitly in the above quotation and, as Marenbon sees it, goes on to reject individual qualities as well. He thus comes to hold the view that all existents (entities) are individual substances. To be is not only to be a particular thing but, more specifically, to be a particular substance.

Russell's classic argument is also based on a crucial implicit premise, but one that is diametrically opposed to Abelard's. It is that the (primitive) relational predicate of similarity (exact similarity, exact resemblance, resemblance with respect to a specific determinate – say a specific colour shade) represents a relation, and *relations are either particulars* (instances, individual accidents, tropes) *or universals*.[9] In short, Russell does not consider at all a premise, like Abelard's, that rules out universals, just as he does not consider the extreme alternative, associated in recent decades with Goodman and Quine, that predicates do not represent qualities at all but are simply "true of" particular objects: ordinary objects or *individuals* that are truly said to be of a kind or related in a specific way. This extreme treatment of predicates is not even considered by Russell, who takes the exemplification of qualities and relations by particulars to be atomic facts. The differences in their implicit premises led Russell and Abelard to use the same explicit argument – that the appeal to similarity tropes involves an unacceptable infinite regress – to arrive at diametrically opposed conclusions. Thus, at least as regards relations, Abelard, in the twelfth century, arrived at a view often attributed to his presumed teacher Roscelin and one that came to be resurrected by Quine and Goodman.[10] Russell, not considering such an extreme form of nominalism to be an alternative, and taking what is now called 'trope theory' as *the nominalist view* to be refuted, used the same pattern of argument to conclude that universals must be acknowledged, at least in the case of relations. He was thus arguing against "moderate nominalism" as opposed to "extreme" or, in D. M. Armstrong's phrase, "ostrich nominalism".

Given the recent resurgence of trope theories in contemporary metaphysics and the renewed attention that has been paid to Russell's argument and its relevance to issues about realism and "truth-makers", the shared pattern of argument employed by Abelard and Russell provides an ironic aspect of the history of the problem of universals. The irony lies in the fact that Abelard, now commonly regarded as the first systematic critic of universals as entities, employed an argument pattern against the construal of relations as particular accidents that Russell resurrected in a form that became a, if not the, basic argument for the existence of universals in the twentieth century. That argument, in turn, became a key part of the revival of realism (in more than one sense) that Russell and Moore inaugurated in England at the opening of the twentieth century with the focus on the role of facts as complex entities composed of particulars and universals. Such complexes furnished, on their correspondence accounts of truth, grounds of truth: entities that *make* truths *true*.

2. The early attempt to reduce relations to relata

One may wonder why Abelard thinks that taking similarity and dissimilarity to be relations, not qualities, avoids the purported regress. The obvious answer is that in earlier works Abelard took relations, as he does in his later work, as not being "things other than" the substances that are "regarded relatively". In short, a case of similarity does not generate an infinity of relational accidents because there are no relational accidents, as relations are not taken as "things" at all. Rather, purported relations reduce to their related particular substances: the relata of a purported relation. To take them as being in the category of *quality* would apparently involve taking them as existent particular accidents – hence as "things" – which would lead to the regressive unending series involving the "likeness" of such accidents. Thus a question arises about Abelard's construal of qualities in his earlier discussion. For if relational accidents of similarity are similar, and thus give rise to a regress, it would seem that the same problem would arise about similar non-relational qualities: this whiteness and that whiteness. An obvious purported answer would be that the similarity of particular qualities (accidents) are not further "things"; they are simply founded on the particular accidents of quality, as some hold that particular accidents of quantity found true ascriptions of relational predicates – greater than, taller than and so on. Thus while Abelard rejects relational accidents as entities, his variant of the regress argument does not imply that he had earlier rejected individual accidents of *quality* as further *things*. In the earlier argument Abelard is focused on the existence of relations: on not taking relational accidents as entities since doing so leads to the purported regress. Russell was led to deal with relations in response to the attempt to use a similarity relation to ground identity of colour, and thus avoid monadic colour universals. The question he took up was whether "sameness" of quality could be construed in terms of a similarity relation rather than understanding qualitative exact similarity to be based on identity of quality. In Abelard's later view the apparent regress is avoided by taking true relational predications to be true in virtue of the existence of the terms and not "made" true by a relation "relating" the terms. But this, in turn, raises the obvious question as to how one can take relations to be so reduced.

One familiar response has been that relational predicates, truly ascribed, are "founded" on constituent *fundaments* intrinsic to or "in" the related objects, a move found in various forms in medieval figures as well as in Meinong and in contemporary variants of trope-style accounts of predication. This response reduces relations to non-relational relata in the sense that true ascriptions of relational predicates are understood to be grounded on foundational non-relational qualities intrinsic to substances, such as purported accidents of quantity. One can then either construe those "intrinsic" qualities as constituents of substances, taken as complexes, or as "inhering", in some fundamental sense, "in" a simple substance, depending on how one considers such non-relational predications. On this reading we have a view acknowledging individual non-relational qualities of substances as foundations of relations or, better, of grounds for true ascriptions of relational predicates to substances. Such a view rejects both relational tropes and universal relations.[11] One adhering to such a view can then purportedly block the regress argument much as contemporary trope theorists reject a standard criticism, derived from Russell's original argument, that focuses on the purported need to ground the similarity of diverse but exactly similar tropes. Defenders of trope theory respond that nothing grounds the similarity but the tropes themselves, whether one speaks of the nature of a trope or not. It is simply the existence of the two individual accidents, trope x and trope y, that suffices to ground the truth that 'x is exactly similar to y', as they suffice to ground the truth of '$x \neq y$'. It is, supposedly, no more the "facts" that trope x and trope y are of kind $\emptyset$ that grounds the first than it is the fact that they are not numerically identical – that *they* are *two* and not one – that grounds the second. The tropes themselves suffice as truth grounds in both cases. For some advocates of tropes the fact that two basic sentences[12] that are logically independent have the same "truth-makers" reflects the claim that the tropes, while simple entities, are "identical" with their natures yet numerically diverse from other tropes of the same "kind". For others, that fact is due to a non-logical type of "necessitation" whereby the tropes necessitate such logically independent truths, but where the statement that they exist does not logically entail either the statement that they are exactly similar or that they are numerically diverse.

As Russell had considered the issue, the purported regress, while focused on individual relational accidents of similarity, is not directed against relations as such, but against the construal of qualities and relations as particulars or "tropes". He was arguing for the need to account for a "common" characteristic – being tropes of a specific kind – including tropes of "similarity". Abelard, however, rejected relations and his rejection of them was clearly more radical than putting relations in the category of "quality" by founding them on non-relational qualities. He declared absurd what others would come to advocate: that an intrinsic relational accident came to be in a substance, say a father, when a "related" diverse substance, a child, was born. As Marenbon quotes him: "What … could be more ridiculous than that when someone is born now to whom I am similar, something new should come to existence in me which, when he perishes, will of necessity disappear?" (Marenbon 1997: 156). Marenbon rightly goes on to note: "Abelard is still talking about similarity, but the same point could be made about many other relations, such as fatherhood and being-the-son-of" (*ibid.*). It is then understandable that the regress was earlier said to be avoided by placing them in the category of relations. To hold that they were relations was to recognize that they were not *things*. Thus, in his earlier writing, assuming he did earlier hold that individual accidents were things, he had to hold that they were not subject to the regress.

For Abelard, to ascribe a relational predicate, say 'loves', as in 'Abelard loves Heloise', is to *consider* two substances *relatively*: the substances, not a relation, are what we *regard*, but they are "regarded relatively". Thus Abelard is *regarded with respect to*, or relative to, Heloise. In holding that Abelard loves Heloise, one is not *considering* any "thing" in addition to the substances, Abelard and Heloise. True relational predications are founded on, or made true by, different ways of *apprehending* the "related" substances. The question is how to construe that. One reading involves adopting, for a substance like Abelard, the move of contemporary trope theories that ground similarities, such as the colour likeness of two tropes of the same shade, in the tropes themselves. This purportedly rebuts the charge that a trope is a complex of a universal, a shade of red, say, and an individuating particular: what Russell called a 'substratum',[13] Armstrong now calls a 'factor of particularity' and others, such as Gustav Bergmann approvingly and Bradley contemptuously, have called a 'bare particular' or Scotist 'thisness'. Applying this pattern to a substance like Abelard, his love for Heloise is not "something" that can be distinguished, as an entity, as a particular quality that is diverse from Abelard. It is simply a way we regard the individual substance, Abelard. On such a reading of his view he not only produced a twelfth-century version of Russell's classic argument pattern against construing similarity as a relational trope but also an early form of extreme nominalism that recognizes only individual substances as existents.[14] In addition, he construed relations in terms of the mental activity of the "perceiver" in the manner in which Hume treated *necessary connection* and that recent philosophers practise in focusing on the ascriptions of predicates or "concepts" to things.[15] One's *ascription* of a relational predicate to a subject is then said to be *true of* the subject, but it is not made true by the fact that the subject instantiates a relation, for there are no relations to be instantiated.

This way of taking Abelard's view about relations is connected to recent discussions by medieval scholars of the *status* of substances and of *complex significatio*.[16] Some are convinced that a number of medieval figures had a fairly clear notion of a proposition and construe references to the *status* of something to indicate the recognition of "states of affairs" or facts as what propositions purportedly signify, the obtaining of which can be said to found the truth of true propositions. Thus the status of the individual substance, *Abelard, taken as walking*, is the state of affairs or fact that *Abelard is walking*. Others, not understanding the notion to have such ontological significance, see it as simply a way of speaking of Abelard: as referring to *him* as walking. Thus for some the state of affairs is the "truth-maker", while for others it is simply the individual, Abelard, that grounds the truth "about" Abelard. Taking the notion of *status* in the latter way, one can construe Abelard's view of relational predications to fit with taking the *status* of a particular substance to be the substance itself, *as represented* in a certain way.[17] In the *Logica* Abelard writes:

> Now someone's *being a man*, which is not a thing, we call the *status* of man. We also called it the "common cause" of the imposition of a name on single men insofar as they agree with one another. We often call by the name 'cause' what are not any *thing*. For example, when we say "He was flogged *because* he does not want to go to the forum." 'He does not want to go to the forum', which occurs as a cause here, is no essence. We can likewise call the *status* of man the things themselves established in the nature of man, the common likeness of which he who imposed the word conceived. (Spade 1994: 42)

> For ... since there can be no agreement in a *thing*, if nevertheless there is some agreement among some things, it must be taken according to what is *not* any thing. Thus Socrates and Plato are alike in *being a man*, as a horse and an ass are ... alike in *not being a man*, for which reason each of them is called a "nonman." So for things to agree with one another is for each of them *to be the same* ___[18] or *not to be the same* ___ – for example, *to be a man* or *to be white* or *not to be a man* or *not to be white*. (*Ibid.*)

But we also find him saying, and not specifically about accidents:

> Furthermore, since things are granted to be entirely the same – that is, the *man* that is in Socrates and Socrates himself – there is no difference between the one and the other. For no thing is diverse from itself at one and the same time, since whatever it has in itself it has in entirely the same way. Thus Socrates, both white and literate, even though he has diverse things in himself, nevertheless is not diverse *from himself* because of them .... (*Ibid.*: 36)

This bears on Abelard's purported early acceptance of accidents as "things" in the *Logica*. Thus Spade adds a footnote emphasizing that literacy and whiteness are the "diverse things in himself". But Abelard's point is that just as the purported individual essence "the man that is in Socrates" (if there were such a "thing") is Socrates – not something other than Socrates himself – so "the white" in Socrates is not *some-thing* diverse from Socrates himself. For "whatever it has in itself it has in entirely in the same way": the man that is in Socrates, the white that is in Socrates and so on. The point is that as there is not an individual essence – the man that is in Socrates – as something different from Socrates, so there is not such "a thing" as *the individual accident in Socrates* – Socrates' whiteness – that is a *thing* diverse from Socrates yet in Socrates.[19] As the whiteness in Socrates it cannot be something other than Socrates that is like the individual accident in Plato. For the whiteness in Socrates and the whiteness in Plato are no more like than the man in Plato and the man in Socrates are. What one has are not two whitenesses but *the-whiteness-in-Plato* and *the-whiteness-in-Socrates*. To focus on each purportedly being a "whiteness" rather than a "whiteness-in-x" is simply to raise the problem all over again. What Abelard has done is recognize the basic problem faced by trope theories, a problem modern trope theorists do not seem to recognize. Michael Clanchy (1999: 83), however, takes Abelard's notorious confrontation with William of Champeaux simply to stem from Abelard's extreme Roscelinian nominalism.

The first of the three cited texts just above indicates that Abelard's considera-tion of a "common cause" for common attributions does not clearly indicate that he is inclined to realism about such a "common" feature. Likewise, it is Abelard, and not a state of affairs involving Abelard's instantiating a relation (*loving*), jointly with Heloise, or a relational quality (*loving Heloise*), that is the truth-maker or ground of truth for the assertion that Abelard loves Heloise, as it is Abelard that makes the assertion that he is walking true. Recall Donald Davidson's example declaring that it is Dolores and Dagmar (the ordered pair of?) that satisfy (satis-fies) the predicate 'x loves y'. As he later put it, he even misleadingly spoke of that kind of Tarski-style view as a "correspondence" account of truth since Dolores and Dagmar are the objects in the world that "correspond" to those names.

3. Diverse types of identity

If Abelard had held to a form of trope theory, as he apparently did in his early writings about qualities, he would have faced the question as to why his regress argument does not apply to individual accidents of quality. As noted above, some contemporary trope theorists try to answer that kind of question by holding that tropes, being what they are, that is, natured, as well as being *simple entities*, rather than complexes composed of an individuating item and a nature, suffice as grounds of exact similarity. This does not resolve the query regarding what is the truth-maker for trope x and trope y, being diverse, yet "of" the *same kind*. For we are told that that is their just being the tropes that they are or that it is *simply necessary* that two exactly similar tropes are such, given that they exist. Abelard did better in facing a related problem regarding things, identity and diversity.

Consider an object, *A*, that is *F* and *G*. Then *A*-as-having-*F*, or simply, *A*-as-*F*, is said to be *substantially identical* with *A*, as it is with *A*-as-*G*, but neither *numerically identical* with *A* nor with *A*-as-*G*. Thus Abelard distinguished, as others came to do, types of *identity* and *diversity*. Doing so is not as *ad hoc* as it first appears and can be viewed as a way of articulating the formula that declares a trope to be identical with its nature or, alternatively, of having the existence of two tropes "necessitate" their identity (diversity) of "kind". Both patterns acknowledge, in some way, a kind of "diversity in identity", as Abelard does regarding substances. It will help to recall Moore's 1901 distinction between numerical and conceptual identity in connection with his analysis of individual substances as bundles of qualities.[20]

Moore distinguished numerical from conceptual identity (likewise numerical and conceptual diversity) in a paper of 1901. In brief, conceptual identity was construed, in somewhat the familiar Russell–Leibniz manner while numerical identity (diversity) was taken as a primitive relation.[21] This allowed for two particulars to have all properties in common and yet be two.[22] This distinction, whether viable or not, is clear enough and is *prima facie* neither incoherent nor *ad hoc*. Abelard's distinction, while not the same as Moore's, is somewhat similar. Consider his use of the well-known example of the image in the wax. He argues that the image is in wax, or is made of wax, while the wax is not in wax, or made of wax. Thus one truly *predicates* 'is made of wax' of *the waxen image* but not of *the wax* the image is made of. Hence "they" must be two and not one: "they" must be diverse subjects of predication, in some sense of "diverse", even if they are the "the same" substance. In his terms, "they" *differ numerically* but, being one and the same material substance, "they" are *substantially the same*. His distinction, but not Moore's, provides an apparent way to elaborate the claim that a trope *is* its nature. The trope and its nature are the same, but, as *the one* is a trope and *the other* is a nature, they are also, in another sense, distinct, and thus the trope-as-natured differs from the trope-as-such. Hence, in virtue of being the trope-as-natured it grounds the similarity to another trope of the "same kind", while each trope being the particular trope that it is grounds their numerical diversity. The trope theorist who shirks talk of "natures", but takes exactly similar diverse tropes to necessitate their being so in virtue of their being what they are, says no more than that they are "the same" – with respect to kind – but numerically diverse. Talk of a special kind of "necessitation" simply disguises the appeal to their "conceptual identity" that Moore took to be based on a universal "concept".

Abelard's distinction helps pinpoint the problem trope theories try to avoid. It also shows that, unlike contemporary trope theorists, he recognized the kind of problem that arises and faced it, although he failed to resolve it. Contrasting his distinction with Moore's helps to see why. What Abelard does, in Moore's terms rather than his own, amounts to holding that the trope-as-natured differs from the trope-as-such in virtue of a predicate that is applied or a property that is had, but yet they are the same thing or entity. For Moore, things cannot be numerically identical – numerically one – if they are conceptually diverse, although things that are conceptually the same can be numerically diverse. Given that one thing has a property that "the other" does not, there must be two entities: that is, they must be numerically diverse. While Abelard's distinction is really designed to allow one and the same thing to be taken with and without a property, Moore's notion of numerical difference is not. Moore's distinction furnishes a way of holding that things can be different, be two and not one, while not differing in a property. This difference between the two distinctions emphasizes the basic problem of Abelard's view, which can be seen by adapting the pattern of argument that Abelard used in his well-known argument against the "realism" of William of Champeaux.

William purportedly held that Socrates and Plato were differentiated by their respective accidents. Abelard argued that since they were supposedly substantially or *materially* the same, in that they had a common nature, humanity, that furnished the "matter" for the differentiating accidents, such accidents could not differentiate them. For one and the same *specific substance*, humanity, would then have the accidents of Plato and those of Socrates. Having both sets of accidents, the common nature together with the accidents of Plato would be the same as the common nature together with the accidents of Socrates: that is, humanity with Socrates' accidents is identical to humanity with Plato's accidents, given that *the same common nature* is involved. Moreover, to hold that accidents individuate is incoherent, since some of the accidents of Plato are logically incompatible with accidents of Socrates, but the same common nature supposedly *has* all of them. In short, their *material* or *substantial identity* does not allow for their accidental (*conceptual*) *diversity*, just as, on Moore's uses of identity and diversity, being numerically one precludes being conceptually diverse.

The account of their dispute, including William's subsequent shift of view, is well known from Abelard's autobiography, whether that is historically accurate or not.[23] What is interesting is that Abelard's proclaimed refutation of William, early in Abelard's career, can be applied to his own later view. For if the wax and the image are substantially the same, then being-of-wax (or being-an-image) must apply to "both" or neither. If the accidents of Plato and Socrates cannot serve as a basis on which to hold that they are diverse particulars (given only one essence or substantial nature), as on William's purported view, then *being made of wax* and *being wax* cannot serve as a basis for holding, as Abelard apparently does, that while there is only one material substance there are numerically diverse particulars: the image that is made of wax and "the wax" that is not made of wax but "is" wax.

Abelard is arguing that we require diverse subjects, just as both Moore and Russell would later argue in criticizing attempts to ground individuation on a difference in relational properties, specifically spatial relations in their common example.[24] Given that the differing properties, which, for Abelard, cannot characterize numerically identical particulars, are instantiated, there must be numerically different particulars that instantiate the properties. The sole basis for Abelard's claim that there is numerical diversity in the case of the wax and the waxen image (and in the case of God and the Trinity, for that matter), is furnished by incompatible properties ("unmixed" in Abelard's terms). What he ends up doing is exactly what William did: claiming that there are two particulars (in one sense) that are "one" in another sense. For William, also, it would have been possible to hold that while there was one specific substance, humanity, there was numerical diversity along with such specific identity (shades of Scotus to come) in that we have diverse, but specifically identical particulars, Plato and Socrates, with diverse (incompatible) properties. He just cannot take the specific substance to "exemplify" the incompatible attributes and leave it at that. One might say that this turns William's view into Abelard's, but that points to the obvious fact that Abelard introduces distinct, additional particulars: particulars that are not *numerically identical* with the one material substance or each other but simply *materially identical* with *that substance* (whatever these phrases mean for him) and with each other. It might also be that William's later, supposedly incoherent move, claiming that Socrates and Plato, while diverse substances, were indifferently human (or indifferent with respect to humanity), was an attempt to say something along such lines.

It is interesting that Moore, in 1901, and Russell, in 1911, employed the above pattern and argued that one is incoherently forced to take the same complex object as the subject of predications, if one holds that diversity is based on qualitative or relational difference: difference of property. Hence such an account of diversity fails to distinguish the two objects. Moore concluded that we must recognize that *numerical diversity* is basic and distinct from *conceptual diversity*. He further concluded that there are numerically diverse basic particulars that cannot be construed as universals or complexes of universal properties and that simply differ numerically from other such particulars without differing conceptually (tropes). Abelard, likewise, recognizes that there are *numerically diverse* particulars that stand in a relation of *substantial identity*. Standing in the latter relation they will share certain properties; being two and not one, they also differ in other properties.

By contrast with contemporary trope theories, Abelard did not simply declare that the waxen image and the wax material are the same, yet not identical, by being what they are. He introduced purportedly distinct senses of "diversity" and "identity" to buttress his view. It is that distinction that then poses the problem, as it will later pose a similar problem for Scotus. To hold, as Marenbon does, that Abelard's view is coherent – in that distinguishing the substance-as-F from the substance-as-G, for appropriate F and G, allows for having apparently incompatible properties or predicates – will not do.[25] What one needs to do is make clear *that*, and *how*, in Abelard's terms, the particular substance A, taken as-F, is diverse from A, taken as-G. In short, one must clarify Abelard's notion of numerical diversity so that one understands just what it is that is numerically diverse from what, and that involves clarifying just what A-as-F and A-as-G are. Marenbon attempts to do so by, first, claiming that since A-as-F is not A-as-G, Abelard can hold both (i) that A-as-F is *substantially the same* as A-as-G (as the substance A is one and the same) and (ii) that they are *numerically diverse* since A-as-F is not A-as-G. Secondly, he supports this by holding that they are numerically diverse since A-as-F is not a G but A-as-G is a G. (And, thus, as applied to the interpretation of the Trinity, God as father is not God as son and, hence, is [a] father, not [a] son.) But, given that being-F is not being-G, and that they may even be incompatible, one can take the fact that-A-is-F as not being the fact that-A-is-G, if one recognizes facts. Assuming facts are acknowledged, the two facts, that-A-is-F and that-A-is-G, are obviously diverse. But that does not help. For such facts are not what either Abelard or Marenbon are talking about, nor will they serve as entities that are substantially identical with A. To identify such facts with the substance A is one way of denying that there are facts, as Abelard denies that there are relations other than the things related.[26] In terms of Marenbon's discussion, the critical question does not concern facts such as that-A-is-F, but, rather, just what A-as-F *is*, since it is talked about as an entity. It will not do to say that A-as-F *is* the substance A *in the sense of* being substantially identical with A, while *numerically diverse* from both A *and* A-as-G, which is also substantially identical with, but numerically diverse from, A. That neither explains what kind of entity A-as-F is nor clarifies the uses of 'numerically diverse' and 'substantially identical'. Finally, since it does not suffice to claim that we simply have diverse *ways* of *considering* A, the crucial problem remains: what does it mean to speak of "numerical difference" when there are not two "entities" that differ, as the entities are all the same substance? One cannot rest with: there are just two numerically diverse entities. This will no more do than the response of trope theorists who hold that the truth of a claim that numerically diverse tropes are exactly similar is grounded by their being what they are.

Marenbon's problematic defence of Abelard's discussion points to another connection between Abelard's views of substantial identity and trope theories. Some trope theorists, in effect and whether they realize it or not, distinguish x-as-a-trope from x-as-a-redness, for being-a-trope is neither being-a-red-trope nor being-this-trope. Moreover, one can distinguish x, as what is of a kind, from the kind – x as *this* redness trope from its being a redness trope – yet only one entity, the trope itself, is required.[27] In Abelard's terms, the particular substance, the trope x, is numerically distinct from the substantially identical instance of *redness*, x-as-a-redness, and, if one pardons the expression, from the substantially identical *tropiness*, x-as-a-trope.[28] This pattern comes out quite clearly in what is acknowledged in the case of the wax. In that case the difference between the properties (or between "predicates", on the extreme alternative variant that recognizes only predicates, not quality instances) that are applied to a substance and that between the properties (predicates) and the substance that they are applied to is clear. And, it leads to obvious questions about the apparently different states of affairs (assuming properties) or cases of "satisfying" predicates (considering not properties, but predicates as indicating *ways of regarding* subjects). However, the tropist, by the logic of the position, *cannot* acknowledge *any* differences of property, for that would reveal the buried complexity in the tropes.

The tropist's problem is precisely the problem Abelard faced in the case of the Trinity, given his commitment to God as a perfect unity: an absolutely simple substance, where one could not distinguish a form from what was informed or diverse forms. Thus, ultimately, he could not recognize there to be distinct properties, given his views on the Trinity, although he could recognize a distinction of "predicates" that we attribute to a substance: the substance that the predicates 'is Father' and 'is Son' are *true of*. That can be seen as one temptation leading him to suggest extreme nominalism, as he does in places, and to the two-fold explication, by Marenbon and others, of Abelard's distinction between numerical and substantial identity in terms of "predicates" as well as in terms of properties.

A longstanding criticism of trope theory argues that tropes are disguised states of affairs: disguised in that they are proclaimed to be simples, but are really complexes of a substratum and a universal quality, or several qualities. One can read Abelard as seeing and acknowledging such apparent complexity in his own view and trying to deal with it by holding that A-as-F is substantially, but not numerically, identical with the substance A. Contemporary tropists declare that a trope somehow combines being *a particular trope* with being *a kind of trope*. Doing that is supposedly not problematic, since the trope is said to be simple and yet to be of a kind by being what it is. Abelard, recognizing and acknowledging the problems such a move involved, tried to resolve them by distinguishing numerical identity from substantial identity in a way that appeared to allow for diversity in sameness. But in the end the distinction came to rest on a distinction of predicates and their use: a matter of language and its use, rather than of substance or of nature. Consistent as he was, Abelard took the path of extreme nominalism.[29] In keeping with this I have suggested that articulate tropism becomes transmuted into either extreme nominalism or a standard form of realism complete with particulars, common universals and facts. In short, the familiar tropes of todays tropists – the sneezing of Stout and the sadness of Sam – become Scotus's hylomorphic accidents.[30]

As was noted at the outset, Abelard's extreme nominalism, at places, makes it understandable why there has been a renaissance of interest in him by contemporary historians of medieval philosophy who take the modern temperament in philosophy as sympathetic to his views. That goes along with his also being considered, with Anselm, as one of the two pre-eminent figures of the early phase of the Latin medieval period, comprising the latter part of the eleventh century and the early twelfth century. He is no longer taken as a figure whose fame is primarily due to his role in one of the legendary romances of the West and to his colourful autobiographical account of his misfortunes. Rather, placed in the company of Aristotle, Ockham and Frege, Abelard is currently looked on as one of the great figures in the development of logic and a major thinker in the evolution of medieval metaphysics.

Abelard was the greatest logician between Aristotle and the Stoics in antiquity and William of Ockham and John Buridan in the fourteenth century. In many ways his achievement is much more remarkable than those of Ockham and Buridan. They had all of Aristotle's logic and built upon two centuries of intensive work by their medieval predecessors.   (Martin 2004: 158)

Abelard's philosophy is the first example in the Western tradition of the cast of mind that is now called *nominalism*. Although his view that universals are mere words [nomina] is typically thought to justify the label, Abelard's nominalism – or, better, his *irrealism* – is in fact the hallmark of his metaphysics. He is an irrealist not only about universals, but also about propositions, events, times other than the present, natural kinds, relations, wholes, absolute space, hylomorphic composites, and the like. Instead, Abelard holds that the concrete individual, in all its richness and variety, is more than enough to populate the world. .... The result is a subtle and sophisticated irrealist metaphysics, one of the most interesting and original in the history of philosophy.
                                                    (King 2004: 65–6)

In philosophy, Abelard is best known for his work in language, logic, and metaphysics, which, together with the philosophical theology of Anselm of Canterbury (1033–1109) – represents the high point of philosophical speculation in the Latin west prior to the recovery of Aristotle in the mid-twelfth century. ...
    It is not difficult to see why, of all the great philosophers of the Middle Ages, perhaps none appeals more than Abelard to the sensibilities of contemporary analytic philosophers.
                                                    (Brower & Guilfoy 2004b: 2)

Quinean nominalism dominated much of what is known as "analytic philosophy" in the third quarter of the twentieth century, serving as a counter-balance to the dominating encroachment of British ordinary-language casuism that had entrenched itself in the United States. But the basic pattern of Quine and his numerous followers of the recent past – a pattern that is currently expressed by those engaged in the revival of extreme nominalism that focuses on criticisms of the realistic theme of a "truth-maker" – was set out long ago by Abelard. Abelard had to do without Tarski's Convention-T, the twentieth-century tool for dispensing with ontological commitments to facts, properties and relations, as he had to do without most of Aristotle. Nevertheless, almost a thousand years ago he set out the now familiar pattern of those who, when faced with the problems posed by the relation of substances to attributes, take it to suffice to reiterate, in one formula or another, that all one need note is that 'A is red' *is true* if and only if *A* is red, or if and only if 'red' *is true-of A*, or if and only if being red *is the way A* is. One supposedly then need not acknowledge properties, whether as universal qualities or as particular tropes, or facts in addition to the individual substances and the predicate 'red', given the latter's linguistic "role".

4. Facts, things and being true to the facts

Abelard, not taking forms or accidents as things, avoided the problem of their connection to the substances they "inhered" in. Contemporary trope theorists, not being extreme nominalists and recognizing tropes as "things", face questions about the inherence of such accidents in objects.

One of the major attractions of the predominant line of response by trope theorists to such questions is one that is not widely discussed: the rejection of *substrata* as principles of individuation by such a theory. Construing an ordinary particular object as a bundle or composite of tropes, and thus treating "inherence" in terms of the substance being a composite of component tropes, the classical problem of individuation – a problem faced by bundle theories taking particulars as bundles or composites of universal qualities – is taken to be avoided. The tropes themselves are held to be numerically diverse while giving qualitative content to the objects (compounds) that they are constituents of.[31] Thus tropes not only resolve the problem of universals, but simultaneously dissolve the problem of the individuation of ordinary particulars. Two exactly similar objects – say two red circles – as composed of tropes are diverse in that their constituent tropes simply differ numerically from each other and from every other trope, whether exactly similar or not. This, of course, is what feeds the suspicion of tropes that are such that they resolve the problems of universals and individuation by being the kind of entity that handles both tasks.

Suppose, first, that the criticisms of trope theory are viable and, secondly, that we acknowledge the problem of individuation and take Russell, *circa* 1911, and Moore, in 1901, to have been right in arguing that one cannot construe an ordinary object as a bundle or complex of universals. Then a classic move to make holds that an ordinary object must have a unique, individuating constituent: a constituent that grounds the individuation of the object and, unlike the object's predicable attributes, is neither a predicable nor something that is common to diverse particulars, as characteristics are. One can think in terms of facts such as 'Plato is wise' having either the substantial individual Plato, or such an individuating item of Plato as the term and wisdom as the predicable. Or one can take the object Plato to be, in turn, really a complex of such an individuating item and "his" attributes. In the latter case we can, following Russell's (1940) pattern taking ordinary particulars as complexes of universal qualities,[32] construe "ordinary" particulars as facts. To simplify matters, let Plato be the name of a white circle rather than a wise philosopher, and let W and S be the respective colour and shape attributes. With β taken as the individuating *haecceitas* and C for Russell's compresence relation, we can construe the individual object Plato *as a fact*, rather than take a fact to have Plato as a term, along with some attribute. Then the object can be construed as the fact such that β and the attributes W and S are terms, T, of it. The relation C is then the relational attribute, A, of such a *thing* and $\emptyset^{\mu}(x, \Pi_1, ..., \Pi_n)$ is the logical form, F, of it (where C is a multi-grade relation that takes an individuating "item" and predicables as terms):

$$(\iota\, p)(T(\beta, p)\ \&\ T(W, p)\ \&\ T(S, p)\ \&\ A(C, p)\ \&\\ F(\emptyset^{\mu}(x, \Pi_1, ..., \Pi_n), p)).$$

Alternatively, if one seeks to work out a view more in line with the rejection of such "individuators" or if one simply rejects the problem of individuation, Plato is simply described by

$$(\iota\, p)(T(W, p)\ \&\ T(S, p)\ \&\ A(C, p)\ \&\ F(\emptyset^{\mu}(\Pi_1, ..., \Pi_n), p)).$$

This fits with recognizing that Russell's bundles of compresent qualities are really facts of compresence, if one works out his view. In view of the above description, one can say that a traditional particular ground of individuation (a *haecceitas*) and universal attributes both become terms, while C is the only predicable. With or without individuators as entities, standard predications, such as the statement that Plato is W, can now be said to be necessary in a clear and specific sense, since the property can be said to be a constituent of Plato. What that means, forgetting the complexity posed by individuators, is simply that

$$E!\ (\iota\, p)\ (A(C, p)\ \&\ T(W, p)\ \&\ T(S, p)\ \&\ F(\emptyset^{\mu}(\Pi_1, \Pi_2), p))\ \text{iff}\\ W((\iota\, p)\ (T(W, p)\ \&\ T(S, p)\ \&\ A(C, p)\ \&\ F(\emptyset^{\mu}(\Pi_1, \Pi_2), p))$$

is a logical truth. Thus it follows from "the fact" that Plato exists that Plato is W, given the use of the definite description to "denote" the object. That such a description reflects the construal of the object as a fact with certain terms is part of the story. In a crucial and clear sense, however, what is stated is clearly not a necessary truth, for standard predications have been "replaced" by existential claims. And those are not, in any sense, "necessary" or logical truths (Hochberg 2001: 128–32). This simply exhibits a feature of "bundle" analyses of objects such as Plato, whereby it is, in an imprecise sense, taken to be necessary that the bundle composed of W and S contains W.

Such an analysis of things and their connection to properties provides a way of construing ordinary particulars. A simpler pattern simply takes such particulars, or their "individuating" bare substrata, as basic particulars and terms of atomic facts. Thus we have the simpler description:

$$(\imath\, p)(T(\text{Plato}, p)\ \&\ A(W, p)\ \&\ F(\emptyset x, p))$$

or

$$(\imath\, p)(T(\beta, p)\ \&\ A(W, p)\ \&\ F(\emptyset x, p)).$$

In the latter case, some would then take the ordinary particular, Plato, to be a conjunctive fact of such atomic facts rather than a "bundle" of qualities. Such issues are of no concern here.[33]

Monadic atomic facts may then be said to be simple substances, in various senses of that phrase, while being entities that have other entities – qualities and, possibly, individuating "markers" – as *terms*. Facts are also taken to be of a specific logical form, as traditional substances were held to be "informed". But facts are not, as traditional substances were, "informed" by properties or natures, but *merely* by logical forms. It is often noted, in various contexts, that the notion of simplicity is not itself simple. With respect to facts that becomes obvious in a quite precise sense. Monadic atomic facts are simple in that: (i) they do not have other facts as constituents or as terms; (ii) they are not mereological compounds of their terms; (iii) they are terms of logical relations and are of specific forms, but are not "composed" of such terms and forms; (iv) they are supposedly not "determined" or specifiable by way of the set of items specified in their "analysis". The last point requires explanation.

It has been argued that facts must be recognized since, given a non-symmetrical relation R and terms a and b, we cannot, from the list of items R, a and b, and even adding the logical form Πxy, determine its correlate to be Rab, rather than Rba, or vice versa: distinguish a world with Rab but not Rba from one with Rba and not Rab (and no further facts, to put it somewhat exotically). But, if we recognize the need for including ordering entities in the account of what relational facts involve, we can determine, from an appropriate "list" – one that includes the account of order in the fact – whether Rab or Rba is the purported fact indicated. That issue I simply note here, without taking up the problem of order, and also note that one cannot viably argue that Rab simply differs from Rba. One must give an account of relational order "in" such purported facts. Giving such an account would then indicate a sense in which facts can be taken to be complex, and there are clearly still further senses in which they may be said to be complexes. Yet, it is one thing to take a fact to be determined or specifiable by other entities logically connected to it; it is another to hold that it is analysable or reducible to such entities, as some claim, for example, that mereological wholes are "no more" than their constituent parts. It is also another matter to claim that facts are complexes that are "composed" of such entities.

On a viable analysis of order in facts one will probably see that facts are, in an obvious way, presupposed as basic entities.[34] Much will depend on whether one construes particulars, as suggested earlier, as being facts or whether one takes there to be basic particulars. For the analysis of relational facts will differ in important ways that depend on the construal of particulars: on whether one recognizes basic particulars or takes particulars as quality bundles or relational facts of compresence that are then terms of standard relational facts. The latter views involve a more complicated construal of relational atomic facts, as standard relational facts become "complexes", in yet another sense, involving particulars, construed as facts of compresence or as quality bundles, as terms.

Facts, standing as they do in the asymmetrical logical relations T and A, can be said to have *components*: terms and attributes (relations). Moreover, the logical forms of facts differ in a significant way from the logical forms of particulars, attributes and relations. The first point is one that requires no elaboration, but the second does. Particulars and universals are of different logical kinds. Forget, for the moment, the present view construing particulars as bundles indicated by definite descriptions and take the familiar view of Russell's logical atomism period. That can be seen as employing the notion of a particular as an entity that *can* only be a term of a fact, and not what is an attribute (including relations). An attribute, by contrast, is what can be *an attribute in* a fact. If one recognizes higher-order facts, as Russell did not in the logical atomism essays,[35] then an attribute is what can also be a term of a higher-order fact. Thus, particulars and attributes differ *logically*, in their *logical forms*. On the present analysis that difference is captured by basic particulars, if such there be, being entities that can only be terms in facts. Atomic facts, as well as ordinary particulars construed as facts, on one analysis given above, can be said to be 'complex' in comparison to attributes and relations, in that the latter are terms of the former and facts of logical forms, such as ϕx and Πxy. They are also perspicuously represented by definite descriptions and not simple labels: predicates or 'names'. Yet a category of atomic fact is recognized, and the apparatus of quantification and variables is employed regarding them. In that sense one takes there to be a fact of a form standing in the logical relations A and T to terms and attributes; and hence, in that sense, facts are taken as simple substances. It is as if the traditional notion of an underlying substance returns in the case of facts, but not as that which preserves identity through change or individuation of particulars. It simply serves as the ground or basis of the unification of the terms, attribute and form into a fact. It thus reflects the basic purported difference from mereological sums, which supposedly are no more than their elements, and, like the classical substance, as a hylomorphic "compound", they can be said to be, in different senses, both simple and complex. While facts are clearly entities "over and above" their terms and forms – or "additions to being", as some say – they are completely determined (specified) by the latter. Taking facts in this way reflects Russell's 1913–14 notion that logical forms of atomic facts were not constituents of facts, as particulars, qualities and relations were taken to be, but the "way" the constituents were "put together" (Russell 1956b: 52). Thus, while using similar terminology to that of the medieval and contemporary "irrealists", he set out a clear-cut realism with the recognition of facts as irreducible "things".

5. Negation, order and truth-making

If one recognizes basic particulars, say in the form of the "markers" of an earlier section, or takes ordinary particulars as basic entities, then, along lines touched on earlier, relational facts and order can be handled much more simply. Doing so with markers as basic particulars gives such individuators a far from trivial role. For a relational fact, say that Plato is larger than Socrates, can be construed in terms of a dyadic relation holding of such individuating particulars, rather than of Socrates and Plato. Thus one might employ a pattern such as

$$(\iota\, p)(T^1(\beta, p) \ \& \ T^2(\pi, p) \ \& \ A(L, p) \ \& \ F(\emptyset xy, p)),$$

with 'T^1' for 'initial term of', 'T^2' for 'second term of'; 'L' for 'larger than', to denote the relational fact. The logical relations, *initial term of* and *second term of*, provide the ontological ground for order in a dyadic fact. Again, the role of the variable the description employs indicates the recognition of such a fact as a basic entity.

If, however, one insists that the appropriate terms of the relational fact are Plato and Socrates, taken as facts, and not as the "substrata" or "markers" involved in such facts, then the description of the appropriate relational fact becomes a far more complex matter involving a described fact as the initial term, another described fact as the second term, and a relation, L.[36] What is gained by the complexity is the representation of the radical difference between the "constituent qualities" – as terms of the facts of compresence that the objects are construed as – and the relations that *obtain between* the objects that are construed as such facts. In no reasonable sense can standard relations then be seen as "internal" to objects, while qualities, in a clear sense, can be taken as such. Moreover, one exhibits a clear sense in which objects' standing in relations requires their having non-relational qualities. Such matters also relate to the complex of issues involved in speaking of facts as 'complexes' and as simple substances.

Stephen Mumford (2007: 316–17) has recently proposed a solution to the problem of negative facts that amounts to holding that the negative proposition, $<\neg Fa>$, be replaced by $f<Fa>$, where the latter is understood in terms of

(M) $\neg$ There is a truth-maker of $<Fa>$.

In one sense it can be looked at as a form of the paraphrase Russell needs to use for a general closure fact to avoid negative facts:

(R) $(p)(p \neq$ the fact that a is $F)$,

which amounts to having to employ a basic notion of diversity and facts of diversity or negations of identity clauses. An extended disjunction, in a finite domain, along the lines of

(R*) $(p)(p =$ the fact that Gb .... $\lor p =$ the fact that $Ha \lor ... \lor p =$ the fact that $Sa)$,

hence without a negation, will still need to appeal to diversities of particulars or of properties (or negations of identities).[37] Taken in this way, what Mumford does is simply reproduce, in a disguised manner, one of the views he criticizes. Peter Simons (2007: 331–3) has taken a different tack by criticizing Mumford's abandoning negations and the standard connections between truth, falsity and negation – and, hence, the T-schema and the F-schema. What I have claimed is that he has to use a negation exactly the way Russell has to.

Looked at in another way, Mumford simply declares that while he uses a negation in (M), (M) does not state a fact or is not in need of a truth-maker. Instead of asserting 'a is not F', what we have is the assertion that '"a is F" does not have a truth maker'. So the presumption seems to be the following.

Take 'a is F' to be true. Then there is a truth-maker for it. But the statement that 'a is F' has a truth-maker does not require a further truth-maker. The truth-maker for 'a is F' will do. Where 'a is F' is false, there is not a truth-maker for 'a is F'. That absence of a truth-maker also suffices for the truth of the apparent "meta" negation (M). But "absences" or "lacks" are old stories as candidates for negation and are of no help. Moving the use of negation into a statement like (M) and declaring that a lack of a truth-maker is not an ontologically laden claim is not an argument. Mumford has truth-makers and falsehoods and the latter are what they are in virtue of "lacking" a truth-maker or there not being something. That presents the same problem that is presented by it being taken to be true that a is not F. Shifting terminology is hardly a way to avoid one's "commitments".

The whole discussion is also set in terms of an apparent relation of "truth-making", which is neither needed nor problem free. Such a relation does help to cloud what is at issue. For one immediately sees what is wrong with Mumford's pattern if it is put in terms of the kind of pattern employed earlier in this chapter. Consider a simpler version of that pattern that recognizes basic particulars, properties and relations and take monadic atomic facts as truth grounds as follows (where we ignore specifying a form since we deal with monadic, first-order facts):

'Fa' is true iff the fact having a as term and F as attribute exists.

One can then add:

'Fa' is false iff the fact having a as term and F as attribute does not exist.

Such a use of 'false' will match the specifying of '¬ Fa' as true, which is as things should be, but are not, on Mumford's form of semantic levitation to avoid negations. Whether one speaks of the world "lacking" the fact that a is F or of there

179

being a negative fact, what is said has to be probed. On the surface it appears that in the one case one recognizes *lacks* (or absences) and presences of facts, as one recognizes positive and negative facts in the other. What is of interest is how the formulation for '¬*Fa*' being true plays out. The negated existential statement, regarding the fact that *a* is *F*, is equivalent to:

> (i) Every fact is such that either *a* is not its term or *F* is not its attribute.

This is where the basic diversities mentioned earlier will play a role. For the negations employed in (i), either a primitive notion of diversity for properties and particulars or negations of identity statements of such kinds will be required and will suffice as a suitable form of Russell's closure general fact. That is, they will suffice and be required for deriving '¬*Fa*' from such a closure statement (or "list" of atomic facts).

Some have claimed that arguing for the need to ontologically ground basic truths of negation presupposes a "maximilization" principle: every truth requires a truth-maker. The idea seems to be that without such a principle one would not consider whether negative truths required a truth ground. But, surely, one can enquire whether there is an ontological ground required for a certain kind of truth without presupposing that all truths require a truth-maker. Such a query is not a premise of an argument that Russell's closure clause (or Armstrong's later variant of it) will not suffice to derive negations, which they purport to do, without appealing to fundamental "negations" – diversities – or negations of identities. Likewise, asking about the appeal to claims regarding '<*Fa*> lacking a truth ground' or 'no atomic fact is the truth ground for <*Fa*>' is hardly making a general claim. What is pointed to is the appeal to a fundamental dichotomy in responding to a request for a reason for an atomic statement (and negations of such) being true or false.

Furthermore, to require that *basic truths* have an ontological ground and that other truths be logically derivable from them (as conjunctions are from conjuncts) is not to adopt such a "maximal" principle. (For example, the question is left open as to whether "logic" itself (and hence logical truths and/or rules) must be ontologically "grounded".) One argues about particular cases. That one asks a question about a kind of truth does not mean that one presupposes a maximalizing principle.

Consider the reasoning that gives

> (M) No fact is the truth-maker for <*Fa*>

as the basis for <*Fa*> being false, and in so doing supposedly avoids negative facts or any other ontological "grounding" for true negations. If one asks why it suffices, the answer has to be that <¬*Fa*> follows from it.

Of course that answer cannot be given if one does not allow negations, in the form of <¬*Fa*>, but only in "higher level" statements like (M). Taking (M) to define *f*<*Fa*> and having the latter replace the basic negation is thus another way of not answering, for, in effect, it makes <¬*Fa*> a meta-proposition about <*Fa*>. (Russell, one might recall, did something like that with the connectives in 1940.) But suppose, unlike Mumford, one attempts to answer the question. Then one is trying to do exactly what Russell did with his general closure fact, for that is what (M) duplicates. So here we see a key difference, whether one, like Mumford, accepts a maximal principle and bars negations as truths or, like Barry Smith and Simons, rejects a maximal principle and accepts negations. For, by rejecting a maximal principle, what some appear to mean is that they do not have to show that their view suffices in the sense of deriving appropriate negations.

This is not to claim that by simply deriving appropriate statements one in all cases solves relevant ontological problems. As already suggested, that is not so in the case of logic and logical truths. We are talking about purported "matters of fact". The things and facts that there are (or "be", if one prefers) should suffice for such "matters". And that naturally leads to the view that requires one show that certain entities that purportedly suffice do so. The only obvious way of doing that, in the case of negation, is the one Russell took, whether, as earlier, he accepted negative facts or, as later, he suggested avoiding them by closure clauses. In both cases, the same kind of requirements were supposedly in effect.

Notes

1. In this vein one sometimes distinguishes between the "form–matter" dichotomy in a "physical" or "corporeal" sense and in a "metaphysical" sense. Some complications, like Aquinas's view of each "angel" being a species, are irrelevant to the philosophical issues.

2. The potency–act distinction and that of form–matter are usually taken as the basic dichotomies of Aristotle's pattern, with some suggesting the former is the "more basic" one.

3. One exception was the Hebrew neo-Platonist Solomon Ibn Gabirol (variously known as Avicebrol, Avencebrol, Avicebron; *c*.1022–*c*.1058),who took there to be both a universal matter and a universal form, with each particular form being itself composed of the universal form (the form of forms, so to speak) and a spiritual matter.

4. As Quine put matters, one's terminology was said to express one's "ideology", not reveal one's ontology. Thus the use of a first-order schema involves no ontological commitment to correlates of predicates (whether taken as properties, relations or sets) as there are no predicate quantifiers, irrespective of one's having an "ideology" involving the use of predicates as "meaningful" signs. Given the connotation of the term 'ideology', the implication is clear. The use of certain basic predicates supposedly reflects their being imposed on objects by the users of language and not the existence of properties and relations as further objects. Thus Quine virtually reiterates aspects of Abelard's views about predicates set out almost a thousand years earlier.

5. There are questions about different ways of taking the notion of the *status* of something that will be touched on below.

6. Marenbon cites the passage as (259: 2109–2122). Marenbon (1997: 46) notes that the *Logica* he refers to is what "most scholars describe" as the *Logica Ingredientibus*.

7. It is also not mentioned by Peter King in his discussion of Abelard's argument in "Metaphysics" (2004: 96). Russell's argument occurs in different places, one is in his 1911 paper "On the Relations of Universals and Particulars" (in 1956a). As Russell acknowledges, the paper derives from G. E. Moore's "Identity" (1901).

8. On Russell's argument see Hochberg (1980: 37). Whether the regress exists and, if it does, whether it is vicious have long been matters of contention between proponents and critics of trope theories.

9. Russell distinguishes universals from particulars in various ways. One is that universals, "from a logical point of view", can be predicable or attributable – the referents of (primitive) "verbs"; another involves taking universals not to be in time or space (Russell 1956a: 106–11).

10. One now commonly distinguishes Abelard from Roscelin in that the former, like Quine and Goodman, considers predicates as meaningful (significant) signs and not merely the expelled "breath" of sound or wind (or physical mark, for that matter).

11. Recent examples of such forms of trope theory are found in Campbell (1990) and Maurin (2002).

12. A basic sentence of a schema is taken to be an atomic sentence or the negation of an atomic sentence.

13. In developing his 1940 "bundle" analysis of particular objects – "substances" one might say – Russell spoke of his rejecting "bare" moments of time, "bare" points of space and "substrata". While he did not literally speak of "bare substrata", the implication that substrata are "bare" is clear.

14. For the view that Abelard is close to realism see D. E. Luscombe (1988: 291). The basic theme here is that what is the basis for the correct ascription of universals (terms, concepts) to things is the universal "idea" in the divine mind. This is a way of also reading Aquinas's "realism". The perennial problem is that there are no real diversities in God.

15. It is interesting how commonplace this pattern of idealism became in the twentieth century, encompassing the "analytic" philosophy of Quine and Goodman, on the one side, and the phenomenological existentialism of Sartre, on the other. Such are the strange fellow travellers of the last century. For all Sartre's focus on *Being* as the basis for his realism, it is only *Being* as non-characterized – without determinations – that is mind independent. Any characterization or differentiation, whether as a mountain, an obstacle or a destructive storm, is a matter of our application of our concepts. Thus we are "responsible" for even our own "births". On Sartre's pattern see Hochberg (2005).

16. For example, Nuchelmans (1973: 156–61, 219); de Rijk (1994: 203); Spade (1994: "Introduction"). On the use of the term to indicate the nature, say *man*, as it is in a particular individual, Socrates, for example, see Iwakuma (2004: 310). On this latter use, *man*, as it is in Socrates, is then a different "thing" from *man*, as it is in Plato, "although in the *status* of *man* they are *indifferently* the same as each other" (*ibid.*: 311).

17. Spade (1994: xi) takes Abelard's use of the notion of *status* in the *Glosses on Porphyry* (one of the commentaries included in the *Logica* that Marrenbon discusses) to indicate that Abelard gives some ontological "status" to the linguistic role of predicates: that the predicates are recognized as ontologically significant beyond being taken as meaningful terms having a linguistic role. But Spade gives no convincing reason for this, and the texts he refers to are quite compatible with either taking mental activity, in particular acts of "abstraction" based on *similar* particulars, as being the causal ground of predicates applying to many individual substances or even as taking the "similarity" of the many – which is not a thing or entity – as "the cause". At one place Abelard even suggests the "likeness" in the mind is a mental creation.

18. Spade uses the dash '___' as a predicate "place marker".

19. He goes on to explicitly reject individual essences – the man that is in Socrates – in the next passage (59) cited by Spade (1994: 36–7).

20. Moore had earlier (1899–1900) construed particular substances as bundles of "concepts" and, in that connection, taken such universal concepts as the "substances" of the world as the ultimate constituents of all complex entities. See Moore (1899) and Hochberg (1962).

21. This requires elaboration since Moore takes a particular redness trope to be *conceptually identical* with all other *such* tropes and with the universal concept *redness*. On some aspects of distinguishing senses of "identity" and "difference" see Bergmann & Hochberg (1957).

22. Thus Wittgenstein's oft-noted cryptic remark in the *Tractatus* was far from an original idea at Cambridge in 1911–13, let alone with respect to earlier sources.

23. Abelard is surely right in pointing to the problem of predicating incompatible accidents stemming from William's taking the species as the material substance exemplifying the accidents. It is another matter whether William is blocked from developing a view involving an appeal to some kind of complex of a specific "material substance" and some accidents that differs from another such complex with the same specific substance and different accidents. It is really an issue about the nature of the "exemplification" (or other predicative "connection") involved and the types of complexes one introduces. (Just consider diverse atomic facts with the same substratum [particular] and different properties.) Abelard even seems aware of this when he argues that particular objects, as well as universals, are not classes (collections).

24. This argument was made by Moore in the paper "Identity" (1901), and Russell in "On the Relations of Universals and Particulars" (reprinted in 1956a).

25. Marenbon contrasts two ways of construing Abelard's distinction: one, which would be in keeping with the "extreme" nominalism that rejects qualities and relations as entities, is in terms of predicates (meaningful signs) applied to things; the other, "realistic" in tone, is in terms of properties of things. Reading Abelard as indicating a form of extreme nominalism, as that phrase is used in this chapter, he thus takes Abelard's view in terms of the former while emphasizing that his distinctions regarding identity and diversity can be employed on a nominalistic or a realistic reading.

26. This is a familiar pattern in recent years. Just recall Donald Davidson's use, following Quine's lead, of Tarski's Convention-T to reject facts.

27. It would seem clear that *being a trope* characterizes things of a general ontological category of which *being a redness* is a specific kind. One distinguishes such kinds from the particular *this* that *is* of those kinds: a trope and a redness. Thus we have a pattern similar to that involved in the reading of Abelard in terms of A, A-as-F and A-as-G.

28. Gustav Bergmann, in his final book (1992), felt driven to take bare particulars (substrata) and "simple" universals to be 'Two-in-Ones'. This phrase indicated that a simple property, such as a determinate *shade of redness*, had a component individuating aspect (an *item* in virtue of which it was *that* entity) as well as a nature in virtue of which it was the universal redness and not whiteness, while a simple bare particular combined an item with its kind, *particularity*. In a way, then, he finally came to see the complexity in supposedly fundamental entities of his ontology. Abelard had tried to deal with a similar problem in the early years of the twelfth century. The phrase 'Two-in-One' was supposed to block the obvious threatening regress, as Abelard's distinguishing numerical and substantial identity supposedly allows for diversity in unity.

29. As "extreme nominalism" has been used here, it fits with Abelard's notion of universals as "words" in the sense of meaningful signs (interpreted terms that are used to "nominate" objects). It does not suggest the purely physical notion of a sign, as the *"flatus vocis"* or breath of the speaking voice, attributed to Roscelin, but which would hardly be an appropriate way to characterize the nominalism of Quine and Goodman.

30. I am obliged to F. MacBride for emphasizing the point that tropists resort to the pattern found in extreme nominalism, but in different phrasing. Trope x will do for 'Trope x is a redness', just as A will suffice, from an ontological point of view, for 'A is walking' and 'A is a man'. And, familiarly, Dolores and Dagmar (or perhaps an "ordered pair" of them) will do for 'Dolores loves Dagmar' or, more appropriately, Abelard and Heloise for 'Heloise loves Abelard'. Some then seek to close off the obvious query by the declaration that it is a matter of "necessity" that 'this redness' is a redness and 'that loving' is a loving.

31. An alternative type of trope theory, as set out by C. B. Martin (1980) takes tropes to qualify the "substance" that is, or is involved in, the analysis of the ordinary particular – as Locke is taken to have done.

32. Russell called such qualities 'particulars', although they were not particular to one ordinary object but common qualities. What he meant by so doing was that such qualities were not predicable of ordinary particulars, construed as complexes of qualities, but constituents of them. It was the ordinary particular that played the role of a predicable in that 'A is red' became 'red *is a constituent of A'*. On this view of Russell's see Hochberg (1996). In his sense, whether or not one rejects bare individuators, *universals* such as W can turn out to be "particulars", as they might only be terms in facts and not attributes, even though one can form sentences with the term 'W' as a predicate.

33. All of the present alternatives have a common way of rejecting the notorious "Bradley" problem (or "Frege" problem, if one prefers). For the details see Hochberg (2001: 123–32).

34. Basically what is involved is that one will have to introduce further logical relations, *initial term of*, and so on, that will hold of items and facts. That matter is taken up briefly below in §5.

35. He did not recognize higher-order facts in the sense of recognizing basic properties (relations) *of* properties (relations). He did, in the essays, take there to be quantified propositions with quantifiers ranging over "elementary propositions". But in the second edition of *Principia* he proposed eliminating "all second-order propositions in which the variable is an elementary proposition" (Whitehead & Russell 1950: xxx). Simply put, he took every elementary proposition to be a value of '$\phi!\ddot{u}$' and hence that '$(f).f(p)$' became equivalent to '$(\phi,x).f(\phi!x)$' and '$(\exists p).fp$' to '$(\exists\phi, x).f(\phi!x)$' (*ibid.*: xxix).

36. It could be indicated, roughly, by something like:

$$(\iota\, q)[T^1((\iota\, p)(T(\beta, p)\ \&\ T(W, p)\ \&\ T(S, p)\ \&\ A(C, p)\ \&\ F(\varnothing^\mu(x, \Pi_1, ..., \Pi_n), p)), q)\ \&$$
$$T^2\,((\iota\, p)(T(\pi, p)\ \&\ T(B, p)\ \&\ T(S, p)\ \&\ A(C, p)\ \&\ F(\varnothing^\mu(x, \Pi_1, ..., \Pi_n), p)), q)\ \&\ A\,(L, q)\ \&$$
$$F(\varnothing xy, q)].$$

(One must accommodate the obvious type differences involved that are ignored here.)

37. That argument has been made in different places; one such is Hochberg (2002).

CHAPTER 10

Being and truth

Paul Horwich

1. Introduction

Our belief that Mars is red is *true*, owing (one might think) to the *existence* of a certain bit of reality, namely, *Mars's being red*. In other words, the belief is *made true* by something like a *fact*. And presumably we can generalize: presumably *any* belief, *any* statement, and *any* proposition, if true, is made true by the presence, somewhere in the universe, of the appropriate things, or events, or states of affairs, or facts.

Such tempting thoughts are the beginnings of a branch of metaphysics known as truth-maker theory, whose primary aim is to work out, for each of the many kinds of proposition that we believe and assert, which entities would have to exist for such propositions to be true. What makes it true, for example, that either Mars is red or pigs can fly? Is it best to answer by postulating the existence of the complex fact *that either Mars is red or pigs can fly*, or should we invoke Ockham's razor and make do with Mars's being red? And what sorts of truth-makers are needed for *negative* propositions (e.g. that Mars is *not* inhabited), for *general* propositions (e.g. that every planet has an elliptical orbit), for *conditionals* (e.g. that if Mars did have inhabitants we would be able to detect them), and so on?

Those philosophers engaged in this form of enquiry believe that it promises to deliver a rich body of metaphysical knowledge – valuable, not only in itself, but because of its potential to yield a variety of important insights: into, for example, the *nature* of truth (vindicating a version of the correspondence theory), and into the viability of reductive programmes (such as phenomenalism and behaviourism).

My plan for this chapter is to investigate whether these hopes are realistic. For the sake of concreteness and ease of exposition I will often allude to D. M. Armstrong's particular execution of the project. But since my appraisal will focus on the *fundamentals* of truth-maker theorizing, it will bear equally on the many alternative forms of it that can be found in the literature.[1]

2. Truth-maker theory

A theory of truth-making is a theory of the relation '*x* makes *y* true'. It must therefore address the following questions, amongst others:

(Q1) What are the entities, *y*, that are made true?

(Q2) What are the entities, *x*, that make things true?

(Q3) Under what conditions does something of the latter kind succeed in making true something of the former kind? That is, what is the truth-making relation?

(Q4) What makes true a simple contingent claim, for example, that Mars is red? How about other logical forms such as disjunctions, negations, counterfactuals and so on?

(Q5) Does every truth have at least one truth-maker? And does every statement's set of potential truth-makers differ from every other statement's set of potential truth-makers?

(Q6) What is it for *x* to be a *minimal* truth-maker of *y*: a truth-maker of *y* such that nothing less than *x* will do? And does every truth have a minimal truth-maker?

These questions tend to be answered along the following lines:

(A1) The entities made true are *propositions* (or, for those theorists wary of propositions, sentences, utterances, states of believing, or acts of assertion).

(A2) The candidate truth-making entities are "things" in the broadest sense of the word. They may be states of affairs, events, tropes, facts, physical objects or abstract objects: anything that *exists*.

(A3) *x* makes *y* true

$\equiv$ *x* necessitates the truth of *y*

$\equiv$ *x* exists & $\Box$(*x* exists $\rightarrow$ *y* is true)

$\equiv$ *x*'s existence entails that *y* is true[2]

(A4) The *atomic* proposition, <Mars is red>, is made true by Mars being red (or by the redness of Mars, or by the fact that Mars is red, or simply by Mars itself).[3] This instance of "being" also makes true the *disjunctive* proposition <Mars is red or pigs fly>. *General* propositions, such as <All men are mortal>, are made true (arguably) by isomorphic general facts. But such facts serve also as the truth-makers for *negative* propositions: for example, <Mars is not blue> is made true by the general fact that *every* property of Mars differs from blueness.[4]

(A5) Every truth has many truth-makers. This is the case because, if a certain thing makes a given proposition true, then so does whatever *contains* that thing. And different *necessary* truths can have just the same truth-makers. For example, '(2 + 3) = 5' and '(2 × 3) > 5' are (according to Armstrong) both made true by the numbers 2, 3 and 5, and therefore by anything that includes them.

(A6) x is a *minimal* truth-maker of y

$\equiv x$ makes y true, and no part of x makes y true

$\equiv [x$ makes y true $\& -(\exists z)(z \subset x \& z$ makes y true$)]$

These points convey something of the flavour of the truth-maker research programme; but further important features of it will emerge as we proceed to consider its philosophical significance.

3. The nature of truth

Let us begin by looking at the idea that a decent theory of "*making* true" (incorporating versions of the principles just listed) might lay bare the *nature* of truth, and might support the intuition that truth is some sort of "correspondence with reality".

The *simplest* imaginable truth-maker theory (in the sense of 'the one that is easiest to formulate') states that the proposition *that Mars is red* is made true by the fact that Mars is red, the proposition *that Mars is red or green* is made true by the fact that Mars is red or green, and so on. On this account

$<p>$ is true $\leftrightarrow$ *The fact that p* makes $<p>$ true[5]

But, in addition, any truth-maker theorist worth his salt will agree that

$<p>$ is true $\leftrightarrow (\exists x)(x$ makes $<p>$ true$)$

Therefore one can arrive at the following definition of *truth*:

$<p>$ is true $\equiv (\exists x)(x =$ the fact that $p)$[6]

However, there are few advocates of the exceptionally simple truth-maker theory on which this account of truth is based. Armstrong rejects it, and so does almost everyone else in the business. For they regard it as ontologically *extravagant*: as postulating many more kinds of fact than are needed. For instance, it attributes the truth of <Mars is red or green> to the existence of a certain *disjunctive* fact: the fact that either Mars is red or Mars is green. But that is not called for, they would say. For there is an entity to which we are already committed – namely, the truth-maker for <Mars is red> – which will do a perfectly good job of making the disjunctive proposition true as well. Similarly, it is expected that there will be many other types of proposition whose truth will not require the existence of *isomorphic* facts, but for which simpler and independently needed truth-makers may be found.

For this reason, each of the truth-maker theories favoured in the literature is composed of a heterogeneous variety of complex principles. For any given type of proposition – atomic ones, negations, disjunctions, generalizations, counterfactuals, belief attributions, probability claims and so on – each theory will have its own elaborate story about which alternative aggregations of facts (or entities of other kinds) would make true propositions of that type. Consequently, the account of truth implicit in such a theory – its specification of the conditions necessary and sufficient for different propositions to be true – will be very far from simple.

But an ordinary person surely does not understand the word 'true' by means of a morass of principles such as these. His mastery of the concept does not require him to deploy a theory of that kind. It seems far more plausible and charitable to regard any such theory as taking for granted our understanding of truth, rather than attempting to supply it, and as proceeding, with the help of that notion, to articulate a body of metaphysical claims. We must first grasp what truth is, and only then can we go on to say which entities are needed to make true all the various kinds of proposition there are.

This is a liberating thought. For once we see a truth-maker theory as not aiming to articulate a concept of truth, but as already presupposing one, we are free to invoke the most plausible account of that concept that we can find, and to interpret any proposed truth-maker theory accordingly. And the most plausible account of truth is *deflationary*: it is the idea that there is nothing more to the concept than our taking '<p> is true' to be equivalent to 'p'.[7]

An important merit of this idea, besides its theoretical economy, is its capacity to fully explain how we deploy our concept of truth. It takes the primary function of this concept to be that of enabling us to formulate certain *generalizations*, and it shows us how that function will be fulfilled. Consider, for example, the sentences, 'Mars is red or it is not', 'If Einstein said that Mars is red, then Mars is red', and 'We should aim to believe that Mars is red, only if Mars is red'. These cannot be generalized in the normal way, merely by substituting a universal quantifier for a singular term. That method can be deployed only after the instances to be generalized have been transformed in light of the above equivalence schema into '<Mars is red or it is not> is true', 'If Einstein said <Mars is red>, then <Mars is red> is true', and 'We should aim to believe <Mars is red>, only if <Mars is red> is true'. For we then are able to quantify in the normal way into singular-term positions to get: 'All instances of <p or not-p> are true', 'Whatever Einstein said is true', and 'We should aim to believe only what is true'. This is what is meant by calling the concept of truth 'a device of generalization'. It follows that, appearances to the contrary, the principles at which we finally arrive are not really about *truth*. Rather, the substance, in each case, is the collection of its instances, none of which itself involves the notion of truth.

From this perspective, the real content of a truth-maker theory lies in specific claims of the form

> p in virtue of x

Truth is brought into the picture merely as an expressive device. It enables us to replace 'p' by '$<p>$ is true' to get

> $<p>$ is true in virtue of x

That is

> $<p>$ is made true by x

And we can then quantify into the position of the schematic singular terms, '$<p>$' and 'x', in order to formulate such theses as

> Every proposition is made true by something

and

> A disjunctive proposition is made true by the truth of either one of disjuncts

No theory of *truth itself* is intended here.[8]

Thus truth-maker theory is *not* a theory of truth. It relies on that notion as a device of generalization (thereby presupposing the equivalence schema) in order to articulate a theory whose real concern is with facts of the form 'p in virtue of x'.

4. Metaphysical knowledge

Even if we should not look to a truth-maker theory for accounts either of our ordinary conception of truth or of truth's underlying nature – even if I am right in supposing instead that truth is captured by the schema '$<p>$ is true $\leftrightarrow p$' – still the explanation of how all the various kinds of proposition are made true might nonetheless be expected to provide a valuable contribution to metaphysical knowledge. Thus the project of truth-maker theory might still seem to be worth pursuing. But even here there are considerable grounds for doubt.

One of the central elements of such a theory is that a simple contingent proposition of the form $<k$ is $F>$ is made true by the fact that k is F.[9] This could be extended into a general account, by supposing that *any* true proposition, $<p>$, is made true by the fact that p. But, as we have seen, truth-maker aficionados tend to reject that approach on grounds of ontological overindulgence. They tend to suppose that there is no need for such weird things as negative facts, or disjunctive facts, or counterfactual facts. And, from this point of view, interesting, non-trivial puzzles arise as to what the truth-makers could be for negations, disjunctions, counterfactuals and so on.

Now we might wonder whether intuitions about which kinds of facts are "too weird" to exist are under rational control; and, if not, whether there could be any *objective* question as to which is the correct theory of truth-makers. For example, Armstrong cites with approval Greg Restall's candidate for a truth that has no *minimal* truth-maker: namely, *that there are infinitely many things* (see Restall 1995b). Here is the argument. Suppose it is true that there are infinitely many things. No totality of these things would be a *minimal* truth-maker of that proposition; because, in order to be any sort of truth-maker for it, a totality would have to be infinite; but then some of its parts would also be infinite, and would themselves suffice as truth-makers. But this reasoning rests on the assumption that 'There being infinitely many things' cannot be a truth-making fact. (For such a truth-maker would not have any parts, so it would be minimal.) And in so far as the assumption of the non-existence of such a fact is a mere unargued-for intuition, why should we accept it?

In response, it will be said – quite reasonably – that such ontological claims are not based on bare intuition. Rather, they are constrained by our concern to provide the best possible explanation of how all the true propositions come to be true: an explanation that will not postulate entities (e.g. negative facts) unless there turns out to be some theoretical need for them.

This response is entirely adequate. However, its recognition of the crucial role of the notion of *explanation* in the foundations of truth-maker theory points us towards a serious defect in Armstrong's original approach. For the analysis of '*making* k *have property* F' that is implicit in his initial truth-maker theory is:

$$k \text{ is made } F \text{ by } x \equiv x \text{ necessitates the } F\text{-ness of } k$$
$$\equiv x \text{ exists } \& \ \Box(x \text{ exists} \to k \text{ is } F)$$
$$\equiv x\text{'s existence entails that } k \text{ is } F$$

But this cannot be what is really needed. For it fails to capture the idea (which he and the other truth-maker theorists rightly wish to capture) that when k is made F by x, then k is F *in virtue of* x; that is to say, k is F *because of* x; or in other words, there is an *asymmetric explanatory dependence* of k's being F on the existence of x.

Because of this defect, the original account of 'making' has various counter-intuitive consequences. It entails, for example, that

- Mars is made red by the fact that Mars is red;
- The state of affairs of *<Mars is red>'s being true* makes it true that Mars is red; and
- Mars is made to exist by Mars.

These absurdities stem from the supposition that *making* is a matter of mere *necessitation*. Clearly, a better definition is needed. And a natural alternative, as just indicated, is to give one in terms of the concept of *explanation*. Something along the following lines would be a reasonable start:

> k is made F by $x \equiv k$ is F *because of* x
> $\equiv k$ is F *because* x exists
> $\equiv x$ exists, and there is an *explanatory* deduction from $<x$ exists$>$ to $<k$ is F$>$[10]

In which case, substituting '$<p>$' for 'k', and 'true' for 'F', we come to:

> $<p>$ is made true by $x \equiv <p>$ is true *because of* x
> $\equiv <p>$ is true *because* x exists
> $\equiv x$ exists, and there is an *explanatory* deduction from $<x$ exists$>$ to $<<p>$ is true$>$.

5. Three objections

This improvement in our account of what truth-making *is* puts us in a better position to assess the prospects for a satisfactory truth-maker theory. Indeed, it enables us to expose some fundamental difficulties. Earlier we reviewed the reasons of ontological extravagance that are typically cited as grounds for *restricting* the general schema:

> If $<p>$ is true, then it is made true by the fact that p.

But we are now equipped to argue that *none* of its instances is correct: to argue that it is *never* possible for the fact that p to make true the proposition that p. And if this conclusion is right, the chances of there being any decent truth-maker theory begin to look rather slim.

Three interrelated considerations lead to that potentially devastating conclusion. In the first place, according to our ordinary (and scientific) practice of explanation-giving, if we want to explain, for example, why it is that $<$Mars is red$>$ is true, we first deduce *that Mars is red* from some combination of laws of physics and initial conditions: that is, we establish

> Mars is red *because* L^1 & ... & Lj & I^1 & ... & Ik

And then, invoking the biconditional

> $<$Mars is red$>$ is true $\leftrightarrow$ Mars is red

we go on to deduce that <Mars is red> is true, and hence to explain *why* it is true. Consequently

<Mars is red> is true *because* Mars is red[11]

And, in general

<p> is true *because p*[12]

Moreover, and for exactly parallel reasons, the schematic relation between p and the fact that p will be

There exists such a thing as the fact that p, because p

rather than the other way around. For we explain why *the fact that p exists*, not by deducing it directly from laws and initial conditions, but by first deducing *that p* (thereby explaining *why* it is that p), and by then invoking the biconditional, 'The fact *that p* exists $\leftrightarrow p$', to deduce that the corresponding fact exists. Thus 'the fact that p exists' is always *less* fundamental in our explanatory deductive hierarchy than 'p' is.

Therefore we have no route from the above-derived

<p> is true *because p*

to

<p> is true *because* the fact *that p* exists

Yet that is what we would need in order to be able to conclude that

<p> is made true by the fact that p.

So, even in the case of *atomic* propositions, there is no basis for such a conclusion.[13]

Proceeding to my second objection, the above problem for truth-maker theory may be deepened, as follows. We saw in §3 that one ought to construe such a theory as *not* offering an account of truth, but as deploying an independently explainable concept of truth in order to articulate certain metaphysical theses. For example, the central contention – that each truth has a truth-maker – that is

$(y)[y$ is true $\rightarrow (\exists x)(y$ is made true by $x)]$

or

$(y)[y$ is true $\rightarrow (\exists x)(y$ is true because of $x)]$

should be seen as deploying truth merely as a device of generalization in a thesis whose particular implications have the form

$$p \rightarrow (p \text{ because of } x)$$

And the idea is that, for certain basic cases of 'p', the x will be *the fact that p*. But these implications do not stand up to scrutiny. For, as we have just seen, our explanatory practice is to deduce propositions, such as <Mars is red>, from initial conditions and laws of nature, thereby explaining why, for example, Mars is red, and then to deploy the schema

$$(\exists x)(x = \text{the fact that } p) \leftrightarrow p$$

to deduce and explain why the corresponding fact exists.

This vindicates the intuition that I believe most of us have: namely, that it is *not* because of the fact that Mars is red (or the state of Mars being red) that Mars is red. On the contrary, it is because Mars is red that such a fact exists (and such a state is actual). Thus the particular metaphysical claims that truth-maker theory uses the notion of truth to generalize are even less plausible than the (above-criticized) truth-theoretic reformulations of them.[14]

A third potential nail in the coffin of truth-maker theory lies in the merits of supposing that what we mean by the word 'fact' is simply 'true proposition'. For if that is so, then it obviously can never be that

<p> is true *because* the fact *that p* exists

since this would be tantamount to supposing that

<p> is true *because* the true proposition *that p* exists

or

<p> is true *because* <p> is true!

Thus, if facts are nothing but true propositions, it cannot be that

<p> is made true by the fact that p

But what reason is there for identifying facts with true propositions? I think there are four good reasons to do so.

First, the objects of belief are propositions; but we can say, "It is a known fact that Mars is red, yet not everyone believes it"; and surely what we are talking about (that Mars is red) does not switch from one ontological category to another halfway through the sentence.

Secondly, the fact *that Mars is red* and the proposition *that Mars is red* have exactly the same structure as one another and involve exactly the same constituents; so it is hard to see what the difference between them could consist in.

Thirdly, among possible (i.e. conceivable) states of affairs, some are actual; and it is economical and plausible to identify the actual ones with *facts* and to identify the possible ones with *propositions*.

And fourthly, no compelling motive can be found for expanding our ontology by distinguishing facts (or actual states of affairs) from propositions. Arguably, we need to countenance propositions as the objects of belief, assertion and so on; but why facts in addition? Only, it would seem, if we feel that something is needed to make the propositions true; but this is precisely what is in dispute.

Thus there is ample justification for supposing that 'fact' means 'true proposition', and if this is so then the fact that p can *never* make true the proposition that p.[15]

It may be objected that I have managed to overlook the obvious difference between, for example,

(FR)   the fact that Mars is red

and

(RU)   the state (or event) of Mars being red

and that, although facts of type (FR) may be the same as true propositions (and hence incapable of making those propositions true), the (RU)-'facts' – better called events or states – are *concrete* entities (quite distinct from propositions, which are *abstract*), and therefore perfectly suitable as truth-makers.

But I have not overlooked this distinction. Rather, the above considerations suggest a more illuminating way of articulating it: a way that reveals its inability to aid the cause of truth-maker theory.

The fundamental distinction alluded to here is between Fregean propositions and Russellian propositions. On the one hand, we can deploy identity conditions according to which sentences express the same proposition as one another just in case they have the same sense (i.e. meaning). Propositions identified in this Fregean way are the objects of *de dicto* belief (e.g. the ancient belief that the Morning Star, but not the Evening Star, is visible at dawn). Alternatively, and with equal legitimacy, we can deploy Russellian identity conditions according to which two sentences express the same proposition just in case one may be transformed into the other by substitution of co-referential terms. Such propositions are the objects of *de re* belief (e.g. the ancient belief, regarding what is in fact the Evening Star, that it is visible at dawn).

Corresponding to each of these kinds of proposition, there is a kind of fact (state, event, condition, etc.). The Fregean facts are the *true* Fregean propositions (= the *actual* Fregean states = the *occurring* Fregean events = the *obtaining*

Fregean conditions). And the Russellian facts are the *true* Russellian propositions (= the *actual* Russellian states = the *occurring* Russellian events = the *obtaining* Russellian conditions).[16]

But does this not concede to the truth-maker theorist all he needs? Can his view not be that Fregean propositions are made true by Russellian facts? No, it cannot. For (i) no account would be available of what makes *Russellian* propositions true; (ii) there is no reason to accept the presupposition of this view, that Russellian facts are more fundamental than Fregean facts; and (iii), as argued above, neither of these kinds of entity is really at the foundation of things; rather, it is because Mars is red that both of the propositions, <Mars is red>$_{(FR)}$ and <Mars is red>$_{(RU)}$, are true.[17]

Thus in so far as truth-maker theory aims to get to the metaphysical rock-bottom of what is true, it is doomed to failure. For the real foundation is expressed by sentences rather than nominals.[18]

6. What might be salvaged from truth-maker theory?

Most of the hard work within truth-maker theory has been occasioned by the desire to invoke the schema

$$<p> \text{ is made true by the fact that } p$$

as little as possible. The struggle has been to account for all truths by showing how they are determined by the truth of the (hopefully) few propositions for which the schema *does* need to be invoked. Therefore if, as just suggested, *no* instances of that schema are correct (and, for parallel reasons, no instances of analogous schemata concerning, states, events, tropes, etc.), then one might well conclude that the foundations of truth-maker theory are so radically defective that the ingenious efforts towards erecting the rest of the structure on those foundations are all in vain.

But it would be an overreaction to simply throw that work away. For we would be neglecting the possibility of a *sanitized* version of truth-maker theory: a version that is not focused on truth *per se*, and that does not attempt to explain everything in terms of *what exists*, but that is concerned simply with the ways in which various kinds of phenomena are to be explained (i.e. constitutively grounded), and with which of them must (or may, or may not) be regarded as explanatorily basic. Indeed, many of truth-maker theory's characteristic concerns and claims seem quite reasonable if they are understood as part of such an enquiry. Consider, for example, the idea that there are no negative facts and that the truth-makers of negative propositions are certain *non*-negative facts: facts that will make true isomorphic propositions whose truth will then entail negative propositions. We

195

have seen that this formulation is unacceptable as it stands. But it can be regarded as a distorted rendering of something much less implausible, namely, that no explanatorily fundamental claim can take the form, 'k is *not F*'; that if k is *not F* then this must be because k *is G* (or, more generally, because p, where 'p' does not express a negative proposition).

Such intuitions issue from our *concept* of 'constitutive explanation'. Thus there would appear to be a worthwhile project of elucidating that concept (by articulating our practices of explanation giving), and of drawing conclusions about how facts of various logical types are engendered and about which of them might be fundamental.[19] Such conclusions would provide the core of truth within a truth-maker theory.

7. Philosophical import

Armstrong maintains that progress throughout philosophy can be fostered if we keep in mind that each truth must have a truth-maker. And he offers a couple of examples (2004: 1–3). The first concerns phenomenalism: the doctrine that each object consists in how it is experienced – that is, in the existence of certain sense-data. Against the objection that we may correctly speak of unperceived objects, the phenomenalist tends to reply that such remarks can be analysed in terms of *counterfactuals* – statements of which sense-data *would* exist in various hypothetical circumstances. But, according to Armstrong, the truth-making intuition gives us a way of articulating what is wrong with this move. For we can raise the question of what could possibly make such counterfactual propositions true; and we can see that no satisfactory answer is available. For, against the *strict* phenomenalist (who will countenance nothing more than *actual* sense-data), we can point out that he does not have the resources to provide his counterfactual conditionals with truth-makers. And against the more *liberal* phenomenalist (who is prepared to expand the universe to include *counterfactual facts*), we can argue that "surely" no such brute facts can exist.

But it is doubtful whether the characteristic apparatus of truth-maker theory plays any substantial role in this critique. The real objection to the strict phenomenalist is simply that, since his counterfactual propositions are not reducible to what he takes to exhaust the basic elements of reality, no such facts can exist. And the real objection to the liberal phenomenalist is that (allegedly) counterfactuals are never explanatorily fundamental; therefore deeper elements of reality must be postulated. But this objection stems, not from truth-maker theory properly so called, but rather from the above-mentioned "sanitized" investigation into our notion of "explanation". As suggested in §6, we might think of truth-maker theory as what emerges when one begins with such an entirely legitimate investigation, but then articulates it in light of certain misguided assumptions about truth and existence.

A similar dialectic characterizes the discussion of *behaviourism* (the doctrine that facts about people's mental states are reducible to facts about their behaviour). In response to the objection that someone may be in a certain mental state without revealing it in his behaviour, the behaviourist tends to reply by saying that the reducing behavioural propositions may concern mere *dispositions* to behave in one way or another. But, according to Armstrong, the truth-making intuition puts us in a position to rebut this response. For what could make true such dispositional propositions? Against the strict behaviourist one can object that *actual* behaviour cannot do that job. And against the liberal behaviourist one might maintain that the postulation of brute dispositional facts is metaphysically bizarre.

But again it is perfectly possible to formulate these criticisms without any truth-making rhetoric. To the hard-line behaviourist one can point out that his hard line has been crossed. In response to the liberal, one can claim that dispositional facts cannot be explanatorily fundamental. As before, it's not so clear that this is right; but what is clear is that, if it is right, it stems from our view of constitutive explanation. Truth-maker theory merely offers a dressed-up way of putting the point.

8. Conclusions

Let me end with a summary of my main objections to truth-maker theorizing:

(1) '<*p*> is made true by *x*' is most illuminatingly analysed, *not* as '*x* necessitates that <*p*> is true', but rather as '*x* explains (constitutively) why <*p*> is true' or '<*p*> is true in virtue of *x*'.
(2) The theory of truth supplied by a non-trivial truth-maker theory (of the sort endorsed by Armstrong and other truth-maker enthusiasts) is too long, too complex, too theoretical and too heterogeneous to be plausibly regarded as an account either of what we mean by 'true' or of the nature of truth itself.
(3) Truth-maker theories are better seen as deploying an independently grasped concept of truth in order to help formulate a body of metaphysical doctrine. More specifically (and bearing in mind the standard role of truth as a device of generalization), we should appreciate that the basic content of a truth-maker theory is formulated by propositions of the form '*p* because of *x*' or '*p* because *x* exists' – in which the notion of truth plays no role at all.
(4) Thus, claims about which kinds of entity (if any) serve as truth-makers boil down to theses about which existential theses are explanatorily fundamental. But it turns out on reflection that fundamental explanatory premises *never* take the forms '$(\exists x)(x = $ the fact that k is $F)$' or '$(\exists x)(x = $ the state of affairs of k being $F)$' or '$(\exists x)(x = $ the F-ness of $k)$'. For such entities exist *because* k is F.

Therefore the truth of $<k$ is $F>$ is not fundamentally explained by the existence of a fact (or state, or event, etc.). Rather, it is true because k is F.

(5) So it is a fallacy to presuppose that *being* is basic – or, in other words, that the world is the totality of "things", captured by means of singular terms rather than sentences.[20]

(6) The grains of truth in a truth-maker theory are: (i) schematic constitutive theses of the form 'p because q_1, q_2, ... and qn' – where 'p' ranges over the propositions of a given logical type (e.g. disjunctions, counterfactuals, etc.); and (ii) conclusions to the effect that only certain types of proposition can ever appear in any of the q-positions – that is, can achieve the status of *basic facts*. The mistakes to beware of are: first, to presuppose that only *existential* propositions may be given that foundational status; and, secondly, to think – just because the "samitized" theses (especially, generalizations of them) are most naturally articulated with the help of our concept of truth – that they *concern* truth.[21]

Notes

1. There are too many truth-maker theories for me to consider them all (or even mention them). But some influential contributions to the enterprise have been: Ludwig Wittgenstein's *Tractatus Logico-Philosophicus* (1922); Bertrand Russell's *The Philosophy of Logical Atomism*, reprinted in *Russell's Logical Atomism* (1972); Kevin Mulligan, Peter Simons & Barry Smith's "Truth-Makers" (this vol., Ch. 3); John Fox's "Truthmaker" (1987); John Bigelow's *The Reality of Numbers* (1988a); Charles Martin's "How It Is: Entities, Absences and Voids" (1996); D. M. Armstrong's *A World of States of Affairs* (1997) and *Truth and Truthmakers* (2004). (Armstrong thanks Martin for introducing him to the basic idea at some point in the 1950s.)

2. This gets across Armstrong's initial suggestion. But, as we shall see (note 10), he saw subsequently that modifications are needed in order to avoid counterintuitive consequences (e.g. that Mars makes it true that $1 + 2 = 3$).

3. I use '$<p>$' as an abbreviation of 'The proposition that p'.

4. This is one of Armstrong's ideas about how to deal with universally quantified propositions and negative propositions. But there are several alternative proposals in the literature.

5. For expository purposes I focus here and later on the idea that *propositions* are made true by *facts*. But the points apply equally well (except where explicitly indicated) to theories that focus on different truth-bearers (e.g. utterances) and different truth-makers (e.g. states of affairs).

6. One might complain that an adequate theory ought surely to capture such fundamental features of truth as that

$$<\text{Mars is red}> \text{ is true} \leftrightarrow \text{Mars is red}$$

But this demand could be accommodated by adding the following principle concerning facts:

$$(\exists x)(x = \text{the fact that } p) \leftrightarrow p$$

7. It might be thought that even if the deflationary equivalence schema provides the best account of our *concept* of truth, still, truth-maker theory might supply the best account of the *property* of truth. It might articulate the fundamental facts about that property: the facts from which all the other facts about truth should be explained. But the same simplicity considerations that favour deflationism with respect to our concept will also favour a deflationary view of the property. Arguably, all facts about

truth are satisfactorily explained by a combination of instances of the equivalence schema and facts that do not explicitly concern truth. For elaboration and defence of this point of view, see my *Truth* (1998: 50–51).

8. As noted by Wolfgang Künne (2003: 164), the above point was emphasized by one of the early Australian truth-maker theorists; namely, John Bigelow (1988a). The point is also made by David Lewis in his "Forget about 'The Correspondence Theory of Truth'" (2001).

9. See note 5. My focus on *propositions* being made true by *facts* is just for ease of formulation. The points obviously generalize to other bearers and makers of truth.

10. Armstrong has come to appreciate that the familiar notion of necessitation is too weak for his purposes. As mentioned above (note 2), reliance on that notion yields obviously incorrect results; so he proposes (2004: 10–12) to invoke restricted notions of 'necessitation*' and 'entailment*', for which, by definition, those difficulties (and others) do not arise. But of course this is simply to acknowledge the problem; it does not constitute even the beginnings of a solution to it.

   My suggestion is that the solution is to define 'making' in terms of explanation. Notice however that the needed notion is not that of "*causal* explanation", but rather that of "*constitutive* explanation". Our concern is with the x that *underlies* or *grounds* k's being F: the x in virtue of which k is F.

   Notice, also, that in order for x to *make k* have F-ness it is not enough that k's being F *supervene* on the existence of x. For the latter relation (which is a matter of *counterfactual dependence*) is compatible with x's existence supervening on k's being F. Thus the explanatory asymmetry conveyed by 'making' is not captured by considerations of supervenience.

11. This paragraph repeats a line of thought from the first edition of my *Truth* (1990: 110–12). Crispin Wright (1992: 27) has objected that the argument shows merely that what explains why Mars is red also explains why it is true that Mars is red, which does not suffice for my conclusion. But the structure of the latter explanation is, first, to deduce that Mars is red (from initial conditions and laws), and only then, in light of that result, to deduce the truth of the proposition <Mars is red>. And it is this "order of deduction" that is the basis of my conclusion regarding explanatory order.

12. Note that 'true' is *defined*, by the equivalence schema, on the basis of ordinary object-level terms that are already understood. Therefore, even when there is *no* explanation of why it is that p (e.g. when 'p' is '$1 + 1 = 2$'), it is plausible to suppose <p> is true *because p*, rather than the other way around.

13. Note that the above objection to truth-maker theory is independent of which entities are taken to be the primary bearers of truth and which entities are taken to be their truth-makers. My explicit target in the text is the idea that, in the simplest cases, the *fact* that p makes true the *proposition* that p. But instead of propositions one could focus on sentences or believings; and instead of facts one could take the truth-makers to be states, or events, or tropes. The objection, with obvious adjustments, will be no less telling.

14. The present objection (like the previous one) generalizes to all candidate bearers of truth and to all candidate truth-makers.

15. Let me acknowledge a couple of considerations (brought to my attention by Adolf Rami) that might seem to tend against the identification of facts with true propositions. (i) The subject of the sentence 'What Peter believes is disgraceful' – namely, the expression 'What Peter believes' – surely does not refer to a *proposition*. Granted. But nor does it refer to the fact of which Peter is aware. It refers, in *that* context, to Peter's state of mind, his state of believing what he does. *That* is the alleged disgrace. (ii) Galileo surely did not discover the *proposition* that the earth is round, but rather the *fact*. Certainly that is the way we talk. But we are often unable to coherently insert 'the proposition' before 'that'-clauses, even when they cannot be construed as referring to facts. For example: 'I hope that p', 'He conjectured that p', 'You are claiming that p'. This prohibition is admittedly puzzling, but it does not support a distinction between fact and true propositions.

16. Granted, the various nominal constructions:

   (i)   the proposition that k is F
   (ii) the state of k being F
   (iii) the fact that k is F
   (iv) the condition of k being F
   (v)   the event of k being F

exhibit certain syntactic differences and certain differences in meaning. In particular, there is variation as to which of the following predicates are appropriately deployed to single out which instances of (i)–(v) entail that k is F. That is:

(i*)   is true
(ii*)   is actual, obtains
(iii*) exists, is real
(iv*)   is satisfied, holds
(v*)   occurs, takes place

However, we need not conclude that the alternative sentence nominals denote different kinds of thing. Such a multiplication of entities would have to be justified in light of explanatory advantages. But it is by no means clear what those would be.

Admittedly, events and states stand in *causal* relations to one another, and that might be thought to distinguish them from propositions, which, as *abstract* entities, may seem incapable of being so related. However, one might respond that *true* propositions (= *actual* states of affairs) should not be characterized as 'abstract'. Alternatively, one might allow that characterization, but say that such abstracta may indeed cause one another. For the condition for x to cause y would include the condition that x and y be actual (*real* or *true*).

17. The present (third) objection – based on the thesis that facts are true propositions – will not count against those theories in which *sentences*, or *believings*, are taken to be the fundamental truth-bearers. However, as stressed in notes 13 and 14, the other two objections apply no matter what the bearers and makers of truth are assumed to be.

18. Why are we prone to confusion on this point? The answer, presumably, is that a natural way of specifying what is fundamental is by saying something of the form, '… are the basic elements of reality'. But that sort of claim forces us to supply a subject that will refer to a kind of thing (or to various kinds of thing); the slot must be filled by an expression of the form, 'Such-and-such entities'; a list of *sentences* (those that we take to articulate our most basic commitments) will not do. So we end up with nominalizations of those sentences, referring to facts (states, events, etc.). This result is innocuous if it is taken – as it would ordinarily be taken in non-philosophical contexts – as nothing more than a loose way of affirming those sentences, a useful approximation to what strictly speaking should be said. The trouble arises when that convenient inaccuracy is not recognized as such, so we wrongly infer that 'Such-and-such facts (states, etc.) exist' is the correct form of the most fundamental characterizations of reality.

19. Such a project appears to be close to what Kit Fine has in mind by an investigation of the *grounding* relations among propositions. See his "The Question of Realism" (2001).

20. This is an observation from the *Tractatus*. But we should not be overly surprised that a basic objection to truth-maker theory should emanate from the very work that inspired it. For a fundamental contention of that work is that, like all philosophy, it is itself flawed by the attempt to say what can only be shown. In particular, Wittgenstein's remark that the world consists of facts rather than things (para. 1.1) should not be construed as the proposal of a new sort of world-constituting *entity*, but precisely the opposite.

21. This chapter is an expanded and heavily revised descendant of "Une Critique de la théorie des vérificateurs" (2004). That paper was the translation of a talk I gave at a conference on truth-maker theory at the University of Grenoble in December 1999. I was responding to Armstrong's "Truths and Truthmakers", which he had delivered a few days beforehand at Le Collège de France. I am grateful to those who raised questions on that occasion, especially D. M. Armstrong and Kevin Mulligan; and also to Kit Fine, Adolf Rami and Jonathan Simon, with whom I have had more recent discussions of the topic.

CHAPTER 11
An essentialist approach to truth-making

E. J. Lowe

Definitions of the truth-making relation that appeal to the notion of metaphysical necessity are notoriously prone to problems, because they seem to be incapable of discriminating sufficiently finely between the truth-makers of different propositions, thus threatening to undermine or trivialize the very notion of a "truth-maker". In this chapter, another approach is developed that appeals instead to a primitive notion of *essence* and explicates the truth-making relation in terms of a relationship of *essential dependence* between a proposition and its truth-maker(s). An advantage of this approach is that it draws on a theory of essence that is, very arguably, needed in any case in order to provide a satisfactory general account of modal truth and modal knowledge. As such, it is arguably superior to an account of truth-making that appeals merely to the unanalysed notion of a true proposition's being true "in virtue of" its truth-maker(s).

The idea that all truths need to be *made* true is an appealing one. This is so whatever one may think the "primary" truth-bearers to be: sentences, statements, beliefs or propositions. To avoid undue complexity, I shall assume that *propositions* are the primary truth-bearers in what follows, but I do not think that this assumption is crucial to the general thrust of the arguments that I shall be advancing.

So, why should I say that it is an appealing idea that all true propositions need to be *made* true? Well, there is plainly a difference between a proposition's being true and that same proposition's being false, and this is a difference that we obviously want to be able to explain. It does not follow immediately that this difference is a difference between a proposition's possessing one property, *the property of being true*, and its possessing another property, *the property of being false*. For we cannot assume without argument that the predicates 'is true' and 'is false' express genuine properties of the entities to which they are applied. Indeed, although I am no nominalist and believe in the existence of properties – both conceived as universals and conceived as particulars that are instances of those universals – I do not consider that truth and falsity are properties in that sense. More precisely,

I do not consider that a true proposition is one that exemplifies the universal *truth*, nor that it possesses a truth *trope* or *mode*, whether or not conceived as a particular instance of such a universal.

If a proposition's being true were indeed a matter of its exemplifying truth or possessing a truth trope, then I think it would not, after all, be so clear why a true proposition would need to be *made* true in the sense in which it intuitively needs to be. For its being true would then just be a matter of how that proposition was "in itself", assuming, at least, that truth so conceived would be a non-relational property, as the syntax of truth-predication suggests. That is to say, a proposition's being true would, on this way of conceiving the matter, be analogous to an apple's being red, or its being round. If an apple is round, it is so because it exemplifies roundness, or possesses a roundness trope. But it does not need to be *made* round, in anything like the sense in which, intuitively, a true proposition needs to be *made* true. Of course, there will need to be a *cause* of the apple's roundness and so it will need to be "made round" in *that* sense. But it is surely no part of the intuitive idea of truth-making that making true is a kind of causing. Rather, when we say that a true proposition needs to be "made" true, we mean that it has to be true "in virtue of" something, where 'in virtue of' expresses what I would call a relationship of metaphysical explanation. In other words, a true proposition must have truth conferred on it in some way that explains how it gets to be true.

The truth-predicate, I consider, is best seen as belonging in the same category of expressions as such predicates as 'exists' and 'is identical with'. They are *formal ontological predicates* and we can say, if we like, that they express formal ontological properties and relations – truth, existence and identity – provided that we do not make the mistake of supposing that such "properties and relations" are *elements of being*, that is, existing entities in either of the ontological categories of *universal* or *trope*. Formal ontological properties and relations are not elements of being, to be included among the overall inventory of "what there is"; rather, they contribute to the nature of reality as a whole solely by helping to constitute *how* reality is. In might be thought, of course, that this was precisely the role of universals and tropes, but that would be wrong, for, according to the sort of realist position that I am defending, these *are* elements of being to be included in the overall inventory of what there is, along with other categories of entity, such as so-called concrete particulars or, to use an older terminology, *individual substances*. The nominalist will no doubt want to take issue with me here and contend that we no more need to regard roundness and redness as "elements of being", whether as universals or as "abstract" particulars, than I am saying that we need to regard truth, existence and identity in this light. The nominalist will urge that, since I have acknowledged this in the case of what I am calling formal ontological properties and relations, it is gratuitous of me to refuse to acknowledge it in the case of more mundane "properties and relations", such as redness, roundness and betweenness. I will be accused of drawing an arbitrary line and of having started out on a slippery slope down which I cannot, in any principled way, help sliding into full-blown nominalism.

Well, I reject the charge. I believe that a principled and non-arbitrary line *can* be drawn between those predicates that are candidates for expressing real universals and those that are not. Note that I am not implying here that every predicate that *is* a candidate for expressing a real universal must be taken actually to express one. I am perfectly happy with the contention, favoured by philosophers such as D. M. Armstrong, that it is a largely or perhaps even wholly empirical matter which of these predicates we should regard as actually expressing real universals and, indeed, a largely or perhaps even wholly empirical matter what real universals we should suppose reality as a whole to include. All that I am saying is that it is not an empirical matter, but rather an *a priori* one, that certain predicates, such as 'is true', 'exists' and 'is identical with', are *not* candidates for expressing real universals. That is to say, I hold that we can know, purely by reflecting on the matter, that someone could not have grasped properly the meaning of such predicates if he or she thought that their semantic role was to express certain real universals, conceived as elements of being. No doubt the nominalist will want to reply that a similar thing could be said about *all* predicates: that, in effect, a realist construal of their semantic role, if taken seriously, could only be taken to reflect an imperfect grasp of their meaning. But I believe that any such charge is certainly open to rebuttal, because I believe that a perfectly coherent account of predication can be supplied by the realist. I do not, of course, believe that *all* predication can be understood on this model, because I do not believe that all meaningful predicates should be taken to express real universals.

So why do I "draw the line" in the place I claim to, in distinguishing between those predicates that are candidates for expressing real universals and those that are not? Briefly, my guiding thought on this matter is as follows. Reality as a whole must contain what I am calling 'elements of being'. Moreover, I think that it must contain a *plurality* of such elements. Although reality is one, it is a one that embraces many. Some mystic philosophers have denied this, of course, holding that reality is one in an absolutely simple and undifferentiated way, but I can make no sense of this. I am, thus, an ontological *pluralist*, but not an ontological *relativist*: I hold that there is just one reality, but that it embraces a multiplicity of elements of being. One of the tasks of ontology, then, is to provide an inventory of those elements of being. However, such an inventory could not intelligibly be nothing more than a gigantic "washing list". It would miss the point of ontology altogether to suppose that its task were simply to enumerate all the entities that there putatively are: shoes and ships and sealing wax, cabbages and kings, and so on. Many nominalists, it seems to me, implicitly suppose that, in the last analysis, this *is* all that we may hope to do by way of characterizing the elements of being. They fundamentally agree with W. V. Quine (1961), when he said that the basic question of ontology is "What is there?", but that it could be answered by the one-word English sentence

"Everything". He meant, I think – and meant seriously – that this is the best *general* answer that we can give to that question.

To this it may be replied that Quine in fact held that the best answer to the question of what there is may be found by determining what it is that the bound variables of our best-supported scientific theories can be taken to quantify over. And it may be added that it seems that he himself thought that the answer might well turn out to be that all that exists are *numbers and sets*, since all of our best-supported scientific theories can be interpreted most economically as quantifying only over such entities, rather than, say, over spatio-temporally located material objects or materially filled regions of space-time (see Quine 1981). However, it would not be consistent with the spirit of Quine's philosophy more generally to suppose that he was seriously committed to *Pythagoreanism*: the view that, in reality, all that exists are mathematical objects. For Quine espoused the doctrine of *ontological relativity*, which excludes the idea that there is any privileged way of specifying the contents of reality that is wholly independent of one's means of representing it in language (see Quine 1968a). And what language we use is a contingent matter, determined by cultural and psychological factors. This applies quite as much to the language of science as to any other language. It may perhaps be that the language of fundamental physics and the theories expressed in that language can be interpreted, without affecting their empirical content or predictive utility, as quantifying solely over numbers and sets, and so as incurring an ontological commitment only to mathematical objects. But for a Quinean naturalist this fact should not be construed as providing support for any serious endorsement of Pythagoreanism as a contribution to fundamental metaphysics, that is, as a putative account of what the real elements of being are.

I think that Quine ultimately has nothing intelligible to say about ontology – as I conceive of it – and would happily accept that charge, on the grounds that ontology, thus conceived, is an impossible enterprise. Moreover, the reason why Quine has nothing intelligible to say about ontology as I conceive of it is that he really does believe that the only perfectly general answer that can be given to the question "What is there?" is the one-word reply "Everything". On Quine's view, the most that the doctrine of ontological relativity will allow us to say about the nature of reality "as it is in itself" is that *there are things*, where the term 'thing' is perfectly neutral, denoting no more than a possible value of a variable of quantification. Anything whatever could, of course, be such a value. There is no room, in Quine's view, for *categorial* differentiations among 'things' in any ontologically serious sense. At most he allows that different predicates may be true of different things: perhaps some things are 'cabbages', for instance, while others are 'kings'. But if we were to say that some things are 'universals', say, while others are 'particulars', he would take this as conveying no more than just another putative difference between the predicates true of different things.

It is instructive to compare Quine's minimalist ontology with various so-called 'one-category' ontologies. One such ontology is the pure trope ontology, according to which the only elements of being are tropes or property instances (see Campbell 1990). Another is the ontology of classical resemblance nominalism, according to which the only elements of being are concrete particulars, or individual substances (see Rodriguez-Pereyra 2002).[1] Ontologists espousing these views certainly do not think – or ought not to think – that belonging to an ontological category is *just* a matter of being describable by a predicate: that 'is a trope' or 'is a concrete particular' is just on a par with 'is a cabbage' or 'is a king', the former predicates differing from the latter merely in that they are universally applicable. If they thought that, it would simply be unintelligible that there was any dispute between them as to which view was correct. Neither of them thinks that telling whether something is a trope as opposed to a concrete particular is remotely like telling whether something is a cabbage as opposed to a king. The trope theorist holds that what we call cabbages are in fact "bundles" of tropes, whereas the classical resemblance nominalist holds that they are entities – concrete particulars as he or she conceives of them – which admit of no decomposition into anything other than further concrete particulars. Their difference is a difference concerning the ontological status of the entities to which *all* of our descriptive predicates apply. Two such ontologists could agree perfectly about how to *describe* the world – agree, for instance, that it includes shoes and ships and sealing wax, cabbages and kings, along with anything else that one could expect to find on a gigantic "washing list". They differ only over the *nature* of the entities to which these descriptions apply, whether or not cabbages, for instance, are "bundles of tropes". But Quine has no serious interest in any such dispute. His is most aptly characterized not as a *one*-category ontology – the one category being 'thing' in the broadest possible sense, or 'entity' – but rather as a *no*-category ontology. On Quine's view, all that we can ever do is to disagree about how to describe what there is, not over the nature of what there is to be described.

But a no-category ontology is an incoherent ontology, I believe. For either it maintains that what there is is *many*, or that what there is is *one*, or that what there is is *neither many nor one*. As I have already explained, my own view is that the only coherent position is that although reality is one, it contains multiplicity, so that what there is is *many*. Quine himself *seems* to suppose so too, for he holds that "to be is to be the value of a variable" and seems to be committed to the multiplicity of such values. Pythagoreanism would certainly respect the principle that what there is is *many*: many mathematical objects, including all the numbers. But Quine also espouses the dictum "No entity without identity" (see e.g. Quine 1968b) and in some sense that must be correct too. For how can there be multiplicity where there is neither identity nor distinctness? There can only be many if each of the many is a one that is identical only with itself and distinct from each of the rest. However, a no-category ontology leaves no scope for any real difference between one and many nor between identity and distinctness. Given his no-category ontology, Quine's one-word answer to the question "What is there?" – "Everything" – is misleading to the extent that it suggests that *what there is* is determinately and objectively either one or many. For the Quinean, all questions concerning "how many" things there are and which things are identical with or distinct from one another have to do with how we describe reality, not with what reality contains prior to or independently of our attempts to describe it. Thus Quine is implicitly quite as committed to the "amorphous lump" conception of reality as Michael Dummett is explicitly committed to it (see Dummett 1981: 563ff.). Both of them are anti-realist metaphysicians in the fullest sense of the term, because the distinction between an utterly formless 'something' and nothing at all is a distinction without a meaningful difference. Indeed, in the end they are both *nihilist* metaphysicians, because there is no coherent way for them to exempt *us* and our *descriptions* of or *thoughts* about reality from the annihilating acid of their anti-realism.

The preceding discussion may seem to have taken us far from the topic of truth-making, but the digression has not been an irrelevant one. Its purpose was to defend the view that formal ontological predicates need to be understood in a different way from ordinary, empirical or descriptive predicates. These formal ontological predicates include those used to assign entities to certain ontological categories, such as the predicates 'is a trope' and 'is a concrete particular'. They also include, I maintain, such predicates as 'is true', 'exists' and 'is identical with'. We should not expect the basis on which these predicates are correctly applied to entities to be at all similar to the basis on which empirical or descriptive predicates are correctly applied to them. It is part of the task of metaphysics to explain how empirical or descriptive predicates may be correctly applied to entities by appealing to formal ontological features of and relationships between those entities. For example, a trope theorist may explain how the descriptive predicate 'is red' is correctly applicable to an entity by saying that the entity in question is a bundle of tropes that includes a trope belonging to a certain resemblance class of tropes. A classical resemblance nominalist may explain the same thing by saying that the entity in question is a concrete particular that itself belongs to a certain resemblance class of concrete particulars. Neither of them, of course, would – or coherently could – apply the same explanatory strategy to explain how the predicates 'is a trope' or 'is a concrete particular' are correctly applicable to entities.

How, then, *are* we to explain how formal ontological predicates are correctly applicable to entities? Quite generally, I want to say, such a predicate applies to an entity *in virtue of its identity*, that is, in virtue of *what that entity is* – or, to use an older but still useful terminology, in virtue of its *essence*. It is for this reason that the predicate 'is a trope' or the predicate 'is a universal' applies to any entity. The same reason obtains in the case of the identity predicate itself, 'is identical with'. This predicate is correctly applicable to an entity x and an entity y in virtue of the identity of x and the identity of y, and, of course, if it is correctly applicable to 'them', then 'they' are one and the same entity, with the same identity. But, equally, the distinctness predicate, 'is distinct from', is correctly applicable to entities in virtue of their identities. However, at least some entities, I want to say, *depend* for their identities on the identities of other entities. What this means, as I understand it, is that it may be *part of the essence* of an entity that it is *that* entity, as opposed to any other, in virtue of a unique relationship in which it stands to one or more other entities. I use the term 'essence' here in precisely the way that Locke recommended, to denote 'the very being of any thing, whereby it is, what it is', which, he says, is the "proper original signification" of the word (Locke 1975: bk III, ch. III, §15). This is my own view about, for instance, tropes or, as I prefer to call them, *modes*. I hold that if *m* is a mode or trope – suppose, for example, that *m* is a certain *roundness* mode – then it depends for its identity on the identity of the concrete particular or individual substance that possesses it: a certain apple, say. This is because, in my view, it is part of the essence of *m* that it is *the very entity that it is* – *this* roundness mode as opposed to any other exactly resembling roundness mode – in virtue of being the roundness mode that is possessed by *this* apple. Pure trope theorists, of course, cannot take the same view of what *they* call 'tropes', since they do not believe in the existence of either universals or individual substances. So although both my 'modes' and the pure trope theorist's 'tropes' may loosely be termed 'property instances', they are in fact entities belonging to rival and quite distinct ontological categories, because the entities belonging to those putative categories are quite different in respect of 'what they are', that is, in respect of their 'identities'. The pure trope theorist must apparently hold that each trope has its identity underivatively, not that it *depends for it on* or *owes it to* other entities of any sort.

Identity dependence in the foregoing sense is a species of *essential dependence*.[2] But there are other species as well. Very plausibly, an entity can, for example, depend essentially for its *existence* on one or more other entities, without necessarily depending for its *identity* on those other entities. So-called 'immanent' universals seem to provide a case in point. Observe that, very plausibly, it is *not* part of the essence of the universal *roundness* that it has the roundness mode of a certain apple as one of its instances, for the simple reason that the universal could have lacked that particular instance. This is because the apple is a contingent being and, moreover, exemplifies roundness only contingently; it could have lacked the roundness mode that it actually possesses. Consequently, it seems, the universal does not depend for its *identity* on this or indeed, I should say, any other mode that is an instance of it. Even so, if the universal *roundness* is an *immanent* universal – as I myself hold it and all other universals to be – then it seems that it does, in a perfectly good sense, *depend essentially for its existence* on the roundness modes that instantiate it. For, on the immanent conception of such a universal, it is part of the essence of the universal that it exists only if it is exemplified by some individual substances, in virtue of those substances possessing modes that are particular instances of the universal.

It is important to recognize that relations of essential dependence do not constitute the only species of metaphysical dependence relation. Sometimes, for instance, an entity can, in a perfectly good sense, depend metaphysically for its existence on another entity, even though it does not depend *essentially* for its existence on that entity. Suppose, for example, that mathematical objects such as the natural numbers exist and are necessary beings; that is to say, that they are beings 'whose essence includes their existence'. What this means is that it is, supposedly, part of the essence of a number, such as the number 7, that it exists. One might suppose, indeed, that the number 7 does not depend essentially for its existence on anything else, not even God or other numbers, although in fact it is, I think, plausible to say that it depends essentially for its existence at least on other numbers, for it is plausibly part of the essence of the number 7 that it stands in various arithmetical relations to other numbers. Be that as it may, consider now a contingent being, such as a certain apple. This apple plausibly depends essentially for its existence on certain other contingent entities. For instance, it is plausibly part of the essence of this apple that it exists only if it has various suitable *material parts* that exist, such as its pulp, its pips and its skin. However, it is *not* plausibly part of the essence of this apple that it exists only if the number 7 exists. For it is surely no part of *what this apple is* that is related to an abstract mathematical object like the number 7 in any way. Nonetheless, it is clearly the case that this apple *could not have existed* without the number 7 existing, simply because, or so we are assuming, the number 7 is a necessary being. But this is just to say that this apple stands in a certain relation of metaphysical dependence to the number 7: the relation in which one thing stands to another when it is metaphysically necessary that the first thing exists only if the second thing does. We could call this species of metaphysical dependence *mere necessary dependence*, to distinguish it from what we have been calling 'essential dependence'.

We are now in a position to apply some of these considerations to the case of *truth*. I said at the outset that it is an appealing idea that all truths need to be *made* true. We can now try to cash out this idea in terms of the notion that the truth of any proposition is a metaphysically dependent feature of it, remembering that by a 'feature' here I do not mean a *property*, either in the sense of a universal or in the sense of a mode or trope. The idea, then, is that any true proposition depends metaphysically for its truth on something. Now, conceivably, a proposition might depend metaphysically for its truth simply on *itself*. This might be the case, for instance, with logically necessary truths. But most propositions are surely not like that. In any case, in order to proceed further, we need to consider what *species* of metaphysical dependence is most plausibly involved in truth-making. I think it is most plausibly *essential dependence* that is involved, rather than *mere necessary dependence*. We can begin to see why by noting that, analogously with the case of existence, we should say that a proposition depends necessarily for its *truth* on a certain entity just in case it is metaphysically necessary that the proposition is true only if the entity in question exists. However, this means, for instance, that the proposition that this apple is round depends necessarily for its truth on *the number 7*, for it is, clearly, metaphysically necessary that the proposition that this apple is round is true only if the number 7 exists, simply because (as we are supposing) the number 7 is a necessary being. But it would surely be quite inappropriate to say that the number 7 is a 'truth-maker' of the proposition that this apple is round.

However, it may be suggested that what is wrong with the foregoing proposal is not that it invokes the notion of metaphysical necessity, but just that it invokes it in the wrong way. The reason why the number 7 cannot be a truth-maker of the proposition that this apple is round, it may be said, is just that that proposition could have been *false* despite the existence of the number 7 and a truth-maker is not (or at least not merely) something whose existence is necessary for the truth of a proposition but, rather, something whose *non*-existence is necessary for its *falsehood*; in other words, it is something whose existence *metaphysically necessitates* the truth of the proposition. In the language of possible worlds, it is something that exists not (or at least not merely) in every possible world in which the proposition in question is true but, rather, in no possible world in which that proposition is false. However, this view of truth-making presents some serious difficulties. First, it is now being implied that if an entity, *e*, is a truth-maker of a certain proposition, *p*, then it is metaphysically necessary that *e* exists only if *p* is true, and hence that the existence of a truth-maker is, in that sense, metaphysically dependent on the truth of any proposition that it supposedly "makes true". But this seems to reverse the proper direction of dependence between truth-makers and truth. Secondly, a difficulty arises regarding the truth-makers of necessary truths. For, because any necessary being exists in every possible world and any necessary truth is false in no possible world, it turns out, according to the proposal now under consideration, that any necessary being is a truth-maker of any necessary truth, so that the truth-making relation becomes utterly indiscriminate where necessary truths are concerned.

What we should say, I believe, in order to avoid these difficulties, is that truth-making involves a variety of *essential dependence*. A truth-maker of a proposition, I am inclined to say, at least to a first approximation, is something such that *it is part of the essence of that proposition that it is true if that thing exists*. This account of truth-making enables us to say, as was suggested earlier, that any proposition that is a logically necessary truth is *its own* truth-maker: for, plausibly, it is indeed part of the essence of, say, the proposition that *nothing both is and is not the case* – the law of non-contradiction – that it is true if it exists. And since, plausibly, this proposition is also a necessary being, in whose essence it is to exist, it follows that it is part of the essence of the proposition in question that it is *unconditionally* true, as befits a law of logic. So, perhaps the chief difference between purely logical truths and other propositions is that, while it is part of the essence of *any* proposition that it is *either true or false*, only in the case of a proposition that is a purely logical truth is it part of the essence of that proposition that it is *true*. Metaphysically necessary truths that are *not* logically necessary should not be seen in the same light: they are *not* their own truth-makers. Consider, for example, the mathematically necessary truth that *7 plus 5 equals 12*. In this case, it seems that the proper thing to say is that it is part of the essence of this proposition that it is true if the natural numbers exist – or, at least, if the numbers 5, 7 and 12 exist. *These numbers* are truth-makers of the proposition in question. For it is on these numbers that the truth of that proposition essentially depends, since it is part of the essence of these numbers that they stand in the relevant arithmetical relation. So we can already see that by appealing to the notion of essential dependence to explain the idea of truth-making, we can avoid the unwanted implication that the truth-making relation is utterly indiscriminate where necessary truths are concerned, for we have already been able to discriminate between the truth-makers of logically and arithmetically necessary truths.

To illustrate this point further, suppose that it is a metaphysically necessary truth that *God is omniscient*, on the grounds that it is part of God's essence that he is omniscient. Then we can say that it is, equally, part of the essence of the proposition that God is omniscient that it is true if God exists, and hence that God himself is a truth-maker of this proposition. However, it would seem that he is not its only truth-maker, *God's omniscience* being another, where by 'God's omniscience' I mean the particular omniscience of God, which is a mode (and, perhaps, necessarily the *only* mode) of the universal *omniscience*. And it would certainly seem to be part of the essence of the proposition that God is omniscient not only that it is true if God himself exists, but also that it is true if God's omniscience exists. For, after all, it is surely part of the essence of God that he exists if and only if his omniscience exists and, equally, part of the essence of God's omniscience that it exists if and only if God exists.

It will be noticed that I have not so far invoked *facts* as truth-makers of propositions; nor do I desire to do so. It suffices, I believe, to invoke only entities in the ontological categories of *universal*, *individual substance* and *mode* for these purposes. Facts are typically invoked as truth-makers by those philosophers who believe in the existence of universals and individual substances (or "concrete particulars"), but not in the existence of modes or tropes (see esp. Armstrong 1997). They need them for this purpose because in the case of a contingently true predicative proposition of the form '*a* is *F*', where '*a*' denotes an individual substance and '*F*' expresses a universal, *F*-ness, neither *a* nor *F*-ness nor the pair of them can be a truth-maker of the proposition in question, on any remotely acceptable account of truth-making.[3] Consequently, these philosophers invoke a new kind of entity, *a*'s being *F*, or *a*'s exemplifying *F*-ness, which supposedly has both *a* and *F*-ness as 'constituents' but is in some way more than just the conjunction or sum of *a* and *F*-ness, and take *this* to be the truth-maker of the proposition that *a* is *F*. But, to my way of thinking, this manner of proceeding is mystery-mongering to no good purpose, brought about simply because the philosophers in question have tried to do without one of the fundamental categories of being.

The mysterious element in their account emerges when we ask about the nature of the supposedly contingent 'connection' between the constituents of a supposedly contingent fact. Notoriously, it will not do to regard this as being a further 'constituent' of the fact, on pain of falling into F. H. Bradley's famous regress. To label the connection a 'non-relational tie' is just to give a name to the mystery without solving it. It seems that the only tenable way of proceeding is to abandon any idea that facts are somehow 'composed' of their alleged 'constituents' and hold instead that the 'constituents' of facts are mere *abstractions from*, or *invariants across*, the totality of facts, identifying that totality with what Wittgenstein in the *Tractatus* called 'the world'. However, then it is obscure how any fact can really be contingent, because if the constituents of facts are just abstractions from the facts containing them, it would seem that the very identity of any such constituent must be determined by its overall pattern of recurrence in the totality of facts. That is to say, it becomes impossible to see how any given constituent could have been a constituent in a possible totality of facts different from the actual totality. But in that case, the very point of invoking facts in the first place has been undercut, since they were invoked to provide truth-makers of supposedly *contingent* predicative propositions – and yet now it seems that there can be no such propositions. All true predicative propositions turn out to be *necessary* truths, because the identity of any individual substance is now taken to be determined, in quasi-Leibnizian fashion, by the totality of predicative truths concerning it.[4]

How, then, can the possibility of contingent predicative truths be preserved according to an ontology that eschews facts as their supposed truth-makers? Very simply, in the following manner. Consider again the proposition that this apple is round, which would seem to be a contingent one if any proposition is. According to an ontology that includes not only individual substances (such as this apple) and universals (such as the universal *roundness*) but also *modes* (such as this apple's roundness), any *roundness mode of this apple* would clearly be a truth-maker of the proposition that this apple is round.[5] What we have found, in effect, is the sort of thing that can provide the "contingent link" between an individual substance, such as this apple, and a universal, such as the universal *roundness*, which has to exist in order for the proposition that this apple is round to be true. Any roundness mode of this apple can provide such a link, since any such mode is a contingent being whose existence suffices to guarantee that this apple exemplifies the universal *roundness*. It does so because it is part of the essence of any such roundness mode that it is an instance of the universal *roundness*, and also part of the essence of any such roundness mode that it is possessed by this apple. Consequently, if such a mode exists, the apple must possess it and it – the mode – must be an instance of the universal *roundness*, whence it follows that the apple exemplifies the universal: it does so simply in virtue of possessing a mode that is an instance of that universal.

Some philosophers who do not countenance the existence of modes make the mistake of trying to let the relationship of exemplification *itself* provide the "contingent link" between an individual substance, *a*, and a universal, *F*-ness, which has to exist (in addition to *a* and *F*-ness) in order for the proposition that *a* is *F* to be true. But this strategy is bound to fail, because the exemplification "relation" is only a formal ontological relation, not a genuine "element of being". Consequently, it is not something that can be said to *exist* at all. Other philosophers, acknowledging this point, nonetheless assume that the "relation" of exemplification is a *direct* formal ontological relation between the substance *a* and the universal *F*-ness. But then the problem is to see how this relationship can obtain merely *contingently*. For, given that *a* and *F*-ness do not *need* to stand in this relationship to one another – given, that is, that it is not part of the essence of either of them that they do so – what could possibly explain whether or not they *actually* do so? Notice that a *causal* explanation is not what is being sought at this point, but a *metaphysical* one.

Modes provide the answer to the problem. Modes are real beings that stand in non-contingent formal ontological relations *both* to individual substances *and* to immanent universals. When an individual substance possesses a certain mode, it is part of the essence of that mode that it is possessed by that substance, although not part of the essence of that substance that it possesses that mode: they stand in a relationship of asymmetrical essential dependence to one another. Similarly, it is part of the essence of any mode that it is an instance of a certain universal, although not part of the essence of that universal that it has that mode as an instance: they too stand in a relationship of asymmetrical essential dependence to one another. An individual substance *exemplifies* a given universal just in case a mode exists that stands in two such relationships of asymmetrical essential dependence, one to the substance and one to the universal. Thus exemplification is an *indirect* formal ontological relationship between individual substances and universals, and one that can be *contingent* because it can be a contingent matter whether an appropriate mediating mode actually exists.

I have been contending that the intuitively attractive idea of truth-making is best cashed out in terms of the notion of essential dependence. More specifically, I have suggested that a *truth-maker* of any given proposition is something such that it is part of the essence of that proposition that it is true if that thing exists (although, as we shall shortly see, this suggestion, as it stands, may be an oversimplification and need some adjustment). And by the "essence" of any entity I just mean that in virtue of which it is the very entity that it is. So, for example, it is part of the essence of any entity that it belongs to a certain ontological category and also part of its essence that it is *that* member of the category in question as opposed to any other. Thus, assuming that there are such entities as propositions and that they form an ontological category – even if only a sub-category of some more fundamental category – it will be part of the essence of any given proposition that it is a *proposition* and also that it is *that* proposition, as opposed to any other. However, at least some propositions depend for their identities on entities belonging to other ontological categories. More specifically, any proposition that is, as we say, "about" certain other entities depends for its identity *on those entities*. Thus the proposition that a certain individual substance, *a*, exemplifies a certain universal, *F*-ness, depends for its identity on both *a* and *F*-ness: for the proposition is *essentially* about those other entities and so would not be the very proposition that it is without being about *them*. It follows from this that it is part of the essence of the proposition that *a* is *F* that it exists only if *a* and *F*-ness themselves both exist. At least, this follows if, as I myself firmly believe, an entity cannot exist while depending for its identity on other entities that do not exist.

What we now need to notice about truth-making is this. A truth-maker of a proposition need not always be something on which the identity of that proposition depends. Thus, for example, I argued earlier that the proposition that *a* is *F* has as a truth-maker any mode of *F*-ness possessed by *a*. On the view of truth-making that I have proposed, this commits me to saying that such a mode is an entity such that it is part of the essence of the proposition in question that it is true if that entity exists. This raises a difficulty that I shall discuss shortly, but let us go along with the suggestion at least for the time being. So, suppose that *m* is a certain mode of *F*-ness possessed by *a*. Then, I want to say, *m* is a truth-maker of the proposition that *a* is *F*, and yet the proposition that *a* is *F* by no means depends for its identity on *m*. For the proposition is not "about" *m* at all: it is only about *a* and *F*-ness. So this serves to illustrate my point that a truth-maker of a proposition need not always be something on which the identity of that proposition depends.

We can now see clearly why it was important to say that a truth-maker of a proposition is something such that it is part of the essence of that proposition that it is true *if* – not if *and only if* – that thing exists. For it simply is not the case, for instance, that the proposition that *a* is *F* is true only if *m* exists: it could have been true in virtue of the existence of *another* mode of *F*-ness possessed by *a*. (After all, an apple may be round at one time, then lose its roundness and later become round again: such an apple plausibly has numerically distinct roundness modes at the two different times, and it could have lacked either one of them.) At the same time, it is worth emphasizing once again why we need to characterize truth-making in terms of *essential dependence* rather than merely in terms of what I earlier called *mere necessary dependence*: that is, why we should *not* say that a truth-maker of a proposition is merely something such that it is *metaphysically necessary* that that proposition is true if that thing exists. For, as we noted earlier, this would make any necessary being a truth-maker of any necessary truth, quite indiscriminately.

Now, however, I need to confront the difficulty that I alluded to a moment ago. I said that if *m* is a certain mode of *F*-ness possessed by *a*, then *m* is a truth-maker of the proposition that *a* is *F*, and I certainly do not want to give up that claim. But I have also suggested that a truth-maker of a proposition is something such that *it is part of the essence of that proposition that it is true if that thing exists*. This means that I must claim that it is part of the essence of the proposition that *a* is *F* that it is true if *m* exists. But this is problematic if one thinks, as I am inclined to, that no entity can be directly essentially dependent on any entity that could fail to exist in circumstances in which that entity itself did exist: that is, include in its essence a relation to such an entity. It was this thought that motivated my conviction, mentioned earlier, that an entity cannot depend for its *identity* on

213

something nonexistent. Now, clearly, we must be able to say that the proposition that a is F could be true in circumstances in which m itself failed to exist: but then the constraint on essential dependence that is now being proposed would rule out our saying that it is part of the essence of the proposition in question that it is true if *that* mode of F-ness, m, exists. Perhaps the most that we can say about the essence of the proposition that a is F is that it is part of the essence of that proposition that it is true if *some* mode of F-ness exists. But then how do we define the truth-making relation in terms of essential dependence, given the constraint being proposed, on the assumption that it is to be defined as a relation between entities, or, more precisely, as a relation between an entity and a proposition?

One possibility might be to say that an entity e is a truth-maker of a proposition p if and only if it is part of the essence of p that p is true if some entity *relevantly similar* to e exists: for example, a mode of F-ness possessed by a, in the case in which e is such an entity. But the notion of "relevant similarity" invoked here seems too vague for our current purposes and, in any case, we have still not avoided reference to e itself within the scope of the essence-operator, 'it is part of the essence of p that'. An alternative possibility might be to appeal to the essence of e rather than to the essence of p and say that an entity e is a truth-maker of a proposition p if and only if it is part of the essence of e that p is true if e exists. But this, I think, would be implausible, because it seems to me implausible to say, for example, that it is part of the essence of a certain mode of F-ness possessed by a, m, that a certain proposition about a and F-ness is true if m exists. For it is implausible – or so it seems to me – to say that a non-propositional entity such as m has it as part of its essence that it is related in any way to some *proposition*, least of all some proposition that is not even about m.

What we are looking for is a satisfactory way of completing the following biconditional statement, intended as a definition of the truth-making relation: 'An entity e is a truth-maker of the proposition p if and only if ...'. And the problem that has just been raised is a problem for our original proposal that this should be completed by the clause 'it is part of the essence of p that p is true if e exists'. But it is more specifically only a problem for the *right-to-left* reading of the biconditional. There is no problem in saying that *if* it is part of the essence of a proposition p that p is true if e exists, *then* e is a truth-maker of p. The problem only arises for the claim that if e is a truth-maker of the proposition p, then it is part of the essence of p that p is true if e exists, the problem being that this seems to require us to allow that it can be part of the essence of a proposition that it be related to an entity that might fail to exist in circumstances in which that proposition itself did exist. It is obvious that we shall be required to allow this if we hold that all propositions are necessary beings but that some of their truth-makers are not. But, as we have seen, we shall still be required to allow it if, for example, we hold that a proposition exists only in circumstances in which all of the entities that it is *about* exist: if, for instance, we hold that the proposition that a is F exists only in circumstances in which both a and F exist. For then a certain mode of F-ness possessed by a, m, need not exist in every circumstance in which that proposition exists, let alone in every circumstance in which that proposition is *true*.

I suspect that there is no simple and straightforward way to deal this problem, if indeed it is seen to be a problem. But rather than leave the issue entirely unresolved, I shall instead suggest an alternative approach, which is still in the spirit of my original suggestion. It may be that rather than simply trying to find a way to complete the foregoing biconditional statement in order to specify the relation of truth-making, we should proceed in a more roundabout manner, allowing a specification of the class of truth-makers to emerge from a *theory* of truth-making. The axioms of the theory might be taken to include something like the following.

(1) For any proposition, p, there are one or more types of entity, E_1, E_2, ..., E_n, such that, for any i between 1 and n, it is part of the essence of p that p is true if some entity of type E_i exists.

(2) An entity, e, is a *truth-maker* of the proposition p if and only if e belongs to one of the entity-types, E_i, which, according to axiom (1), is involved in the essence of p.

Thus, for example, a mode, m, of the universal F-ness that is possessed by the individual substance a would by this account qualify as a truth-maker of the proposition that a is F, for the following reason. Axiom (1) is satisfied in this case by the entity-type *mode of F-ness possessed by a*, because that is an entity-type such that it is part of the essence of the proposition that a is F that that proposition is true if some entity of that type exists. And m is an entity of that type. Hence, by axiom (2), m is a truth-maker of the proposition that a is F. In effect, this is a way of cashing out more rigorously the notion of "relevant similarity" that was toyed with earlier.

One final word: it will be noted that nowhere throughout the preceding discussion have I attempted to define *truth itself*, as opposed to the relation of *truth-making*. This is because I take the notion of truth to be primitive and indefinable, alongside the notions of existence and identity. Only some of the family of formal ontological notions are definable and truth-making plausibly ought to be one of them. But truth itself, I believe, is too fundamental a notion to admit of non-circular definition.

Notes

1. Such a theorist may also speak of *sets* or *classes*, but take a "deflationary" view of their ontological status. The same applies to the pure trope ontologist.

2. For more discussion and a definition of identity dependence, see my *The Possibility of Metaphysics: Substance, Identity, and Time* (1998: ch. 6). For a similar approach, see Fine (1995a).

3. It may be gathered from this that I do *not* regard as acceptable the account of truth-making offered by David Lewis in his "Things qua Truthmakers" (2003). For some comments on that paper, see my review of this book in the *European Journal of Philosophy* 16 (2008), 134–8.

4. This seems to be the view towards which D. M. Armstrong himself gravitates in his more recent book, *Truth and Truthmakers* (2004).

5. I defend precisely such an ontology in my *The Four-Category Ontology* (2006).

CHAPTER 12

Are there irreducibly relational facts?

Josh Parsons

1. The question

Supposing that truths require truth-makers, that true propositions are those that correspond to facts, is there a distinctive domain of facts that make true the relational truths? Or is it rather that, if we had collected the facts required to make true the other truths, the non-relational ones, we would then have enough facts to make all truths true?

If the former is the case, let us say that anti-reductionism about relational facts is true; if the latter, that reductionism about relational facts is true. Let us say that a fact is relational if it makes true some relational proposition (a proposition that asserts that a relation holds between some objects[1]), that it is irreducibly relational if, in addition, it does not make true any non-relational propositions, and that it is monadic if it is not irreducibly relational (if it makes true some proposition that does not assert that a relation holds between some objects).

Anti-reductionism (as we will say for short) holds that there are irreducibly relational facts; reductionism (as we will say for short) that while there may be relational facts, there are no irreducibly relational ones.

This is a very fine definition, but is it an interesting issue? Yes, for three reasons:

1. *Reasons internal to truth-maker theory.* If you are one of those metaphysicians who believes the antecedent of the first sentence of this chapter, that truths require truth-makers, you will naturally be interested in what manner of things you are thereby committed to. Different truth-maker theorists offer different ontologies of facts. These ontologies deal with relational facts in different ways, so independent arguments for one or other view of relational facts give us some grip on which truth-maker ontology is likely to be the right one. In particular, irreducibly relational facts could seem nominalistically unrespectable (Campbell 1990: 97–9).

217

2. *Reasons of general ontology.* If you are not a truth-maker theorist, perhaps you are not because you did not think that your favoured ontology could accommodate irreducibly relational facts. If there are independent arguments for reductionism, though, you need not worry. On the other hand, if there are independent arguments for anti-reductionism, you are thereby furnished with an argument against truth-maker theory.

3. *Reasons of historical interest.* One of the founding moments of analytic philosophy was the throwing off of Hegelian idealism by Bertrand Russell and G. E. Moore around the beginning of the twentieth century. In Russell's case, in so far as he himself reports it, this was owing to his realization of the truth of anti-reductionism about relations. According to the early Russell, most of the evils of British idealism were due to an uncritical acceptance of reductionism (Russell 1910: 162–9). But perhaps it was Russell who was uncritical?

Before we move on to the arguments for and against reductionism, I shall fill in some necessary background.

A *fact*, as I shall be using that term, is whatever it is that makes a proposition true. I do not take the use of 'fact' to imply that facts constitute some *sui generis* ontological category. Facts could be identified with tropes (Mulligan *et al.*, this vol., Ch. 3; Fox 1987), or with "states of affairs" (Armstrong 1997): complex entities constructed out of particulars and properties. It is the job of a truth-maker theory to offer and make plausible these kinds of ontological accounts of facts. Nor should facts, in this sense, be regarded as true propositions, for, unless some extreme linguistic idealism is true, synthetic propositions do not make themselves true. 'Fact' and 'making true' here are technical terms of speculative metaphysics, and are not intended as analyses of our ordinary language use of 'fact'.

For purposes of clarity, I shall sometimes speak of a fact ascribing a property or relation to an object or objects. This should be understood as shorthand for a fact that makes true some proposition that ascribes that property to that object or objects. In this chapter I shall be completely neutral on the ontological nature of facts (on whether, for example, they have properties and objects as constituents).

It is because I want to be neutral between the various truth-maker ontologies that I have defined 'relational' and 'irreducibly relational' in terms of the propositions that a given fact makes true. It would be tempting to define them in terms of the underlying structure of the fact, but since the issue is partly what requirements there are on a theory of that structure, it would be question-begging to presuppose such a structure in defining 'relational fact'.

Also note that it is possible for a single proposition to be made true by multiple facts. This will regularly be the case for any proposition made true by something smaller than the whole universe, owing to a plausible monotonicity principle: "If X makes p true and X is included in Y, then Y makes p true" (Simons 1992: 165).

Since everything is included in the universe, the universe makes every proposition true. Only some of the facts (hopefully, only one, and hopefully not the universe) that make a proposition true will be such that they have no proper parts that make the proposition true. Facts of this kind are called 'minimal truth-makers' (Mulligan *et al.*, this vol., Ch. 3, 67–8; Langtry 1975: 9). Where I speak of '*the* fact that *p*', the single fact I am referring to is the minimal truth-maker of *p*.

Making true is a slightly more contentious concept to pin down. I have argued elsewhere (Parsons 1999: 326–7) that *X* makes *p* true iff *X* is intrinsically such that *p*; to put this another way, a duplicate of *X* cannot exist without *p* being true; in yet a third way, *p* cannot become false without a non-Cambridge change in *X*. Many truth-maker theorists hold, however, that every fact *essentially* makes true all and only those truths that it makes true, a doctrine I call truth-maker essentialism. This leads them to define 'making true' thus: *X* makes *p* true iff *X* is essentially such that *p*; to put this another way, a counterpart of *X* cannot exist without *p* being true; in yet a third way, *p* cannot become false without the destruction of *X*.[2]

It would go beyond the scope of this chapter to discuss this debate further. I shall continue to use the term 'making true' by the lights of my own definition, but I shall flag those points at which a truth-maker essentialist must diverge.

2. The views

The anti-reductionists about relations include, influentially, Russell (1900: 10; 1910; 1937: 212–16; 1959b: 54–61) and, in more recent times, Reinhardt Grossman (1983: ch. 3) and D. M. Armstrong (1997: 4, 90–91, 120–22).

An anti-reductionist need not believe that *every* relational proposition is made true by an irreducibly relational fact. On the contrary, some relations seem to be systematically reducible: that is, propositions that express them are always made true by some monadic fact. These are the so-called "internal" relations, of which resemblance and the various kinds of resemblance-in-a-respect are the paradigms: if my banana bears the same-colour relation to your lemon, it is in virtue of the fact that my banana is yellow and your lemon is yellow. This latter fact is monadic: it makes true the non-relational proposition that my banana is yellow and your lemon is yellow.

Another common example of internal relations is comparative relations: the proposition that Plato was taller than Socrates can be made true by the same fact that makes true the non-relational proposition that Plato had whatever height he actually had, and Socrates had whatever height he actually had.

To use what Keith Campbell calls "the intuitive picture of divine creation: if God makes an island A with so much rock, soil, etc. as to amount to 20 hectares, and subsequently, an island B of 15 hectares extent, there is *nothing more* needing to be done to make A larger than B" (Campbell 1990: 103). In bringing about the purely monadic facts about the amounts of rock and soil, God has thereby brought it about that A is larger than B. There is no further fact that God must bring about.

Intuitively, though, not all relations are like this: some are "external". Here the classic examples are the spatio-temporal relations. You could know all the monadic facts about Sydney and all the monadic facts about Canberra, it seems, (and thus the monadic conjunctive facts about Canberra and Sydney) without knowing that Canberra is south of Sydney. God could create each city, filling each with the requisite number of persons, cafes and so on until every monadic fact concerning Sydney and Canberra was made true, but he would still not have brought it about that Canberra is south of Sydney.

It is these relations that the anti-reductionists hold to be made true only by irreducibly relational facts. Since their arguments are essentially reactive – they are objections to any attempt to show that a proposition ascribing an external relation can be made true by a monadic fact – we shall first have to describe the reductionist attempts to reduce the relational facts that ascribe external relations.

The most traditional such attempt tried to assimilate the external relations to the internal ones, comparison and resemblance. Famously, this was the strategy of Leibniz (Mates 1986: 209–18). More recently, it has been revived by Campbell (1990: 126–30). Campbell's approach requires that space-time is both "real" and "absolute", which unfortunately leaves his view open to empirical refutation (as Campbell himself points out).

Even if the problems with the Campbell view can be resolved, there is something unsatisfying about it. Even if, as a matter of fact, physics is as our metaphysical theory would like it to be, there remains the perfectly good metaphysical question of what the world would be like if this were not the case. The distinction between external and internal relations runs so deep that it seems a cheap trick to simply deny that there are any external relations. If we could be convinced of this, we would still like to know what it would be for there to be an external relation, and Campbell has no answer.

In any case, there is another way to be a reductionist about relations that allows the reconstruction of a distinction between internal and external relations. This is the "monistic theory of relations" that Russell (1937: §212) ascribes to F. H. Bradley.[3] On this view the fact that makes propositions ascribing external relations true is a monadic fact ascribing some property to the whole composed of the *relata*.

This account has the advantage of some intuitive appeal: when God has created only Sydney and Canberra, he has not yet brought about the fact that Canberra is south of Sydney; but he must have brought about that fact by the time he has finished making Australia, for he has not finished making Australia until he brings about the fact that Australia is such that Canberra is south of Sydney.

We can also now afford a distinction between internal and external relations. Some relations are such that relational propositions asserting them are made true by monadic facts ascribing properties to the relata in the relational proposition. These are the internal relations: resemblance, comparative height and so on. Other relations are *not* like this; rather, propositions asserting them are made true only by facts ascribing properties to the whole of the *relata*. Following Timothy Sprigge (1979: 164), let us call these 'holistic relations'. If the reductionist is right, all the external relations – spatio-temporal relations, causation, perhaps, and whatever other external relations we may discover – are holistic. The task facing the anti-reductionist about relations is to show that they cannot be.

3. Arguments for anti-reductionism

What are the wholes that the theory of holistic relations refers to? Are they mereological? If so, what mereological principles are assumed?

I see no reason not to say that the "whole" of some objects is the mereological fusion of those objects: that object which, to put it sloppily, has just those objects as parts.[4] On classical mereological theories[5] any arbitrary non-empty collection of objects has such a fusion. But this is not uncontentious; many metaphysicians reject this part of classical mereology (Simons 1987: 108–12). Can advocates of such restricted mereologies accept the account of relations being offered here?

Yes: recall our earlier discussion of the "monotonicity of truth-making". If the fusion of two things will do as a truth-maker for a relational proposition, so too will anything that has that object as a part. In the framework of classical mereology we can say that *any* whole that has the relata of a relational proposition as parts can make that proposition true. If you remove some of those wholes from your mereological ontology, the others can still do the work. Where a believer in "restricted composition" may have to differ from me is in what she takes to be the minimal truth-makers for propositions that ascribe an external relation.

At this point we can state the classic argument for anti-reductionism and against holistic relations as it is used by Russell, Grossman and Armstrong. External relations can be non-symmetrical, or even asymmetrical: 'is south of' is a case in point – it is true that Canberra is south of Sydney, and false that Sydney is south of Canberra. But the fusion of Canberra and Sydney is symmetrical with regard to the two cities: the fusion of Canberra and Sydney *just is* the fusion of Sydney and Canberra. It seems that the holistic account has left something out: it leaves out the "direction" or "sense" of a relational fact.

As Russell put it:

> In order to distinguish a whole (*ab*) from a whole (*ba*), as we must do if we are to explain asymmetry, we shall be forced back from the whole to the parts and their relation. For (*ab*) and (*ba*) consist of precisely the same parts, and differ in no respect whatever save the sense of the relation between *a* and *b*. (1937: 215)

221

This argument is mistaken, as can be seen once we apply it to the definition of making true given above. Consider all the parts of Australia put together in such a way that Canberra is to the south of Sydney, and then all the same things put together in such a way that Sydney is to the south of Canberra. These are certainly two possible ways of putting together those parts. As Russell says, the whole that one gets by putting them together is in either case the same thing, Australia.

But it is wrong to say that the two ways of putting Australia together do not differ! They do differ: one is the way that Australia actually *is* put together, and the other is not. The way that Australia actually is is a property of Australia, and there is a proposition that ascribes this property to Australia. Were Canberra not to the south of Sydney, this proposition would not be true; and the fact that makes it true would have to be intrinsically different. This fact, by the definition of making true given above, would then make it true that Canberra is to the south of Sydney.

It might be objected that the two ways of putting the parts of Australia together cannot really produce the same object, Australia. This is because the two ways produce qualitatively different things, while one and the same thing cannot be qualitatively different from itself. If this is right, of course, Russell's argument does not work, because we are now forced to distinguish different wholes of the same parts. But I do not think it is right. Australia cannot be put together in two different ways at the same time, in the same possible world. The kind of identity that holds between the two Australias – one with Sydney to the south, one with Canberra – is identity over time or between possible worlds. Everyone who believes in change or contingency needs to make some sense of the same thing being qualitatively different at other times or other worlds. The reader is invited to plug in her favourite account of these matters.[6]

Another problem points to a different way that Australia could be put together, in which Sydney is placed to the south of Canberra, and, *in addition*, Sydney is given all of Canberra's properties, and vice versa. All Australians would call Sydney 'Canberra' and Canberra 'Sydney'. If Australia were put together like this, would it be true that Canberra was south of Sydney? If not, there is trouble in identifying the fact that Canberra is south of Sydney with a fact about an intrinsic property of Australia, for put together this way, Australia would be intrinsically just the way it actually is, yet the relationship between Canberra and Sydney would be different.

There is a problem for truth-maker theory here, but it is not any problem to do with relations; it is, rather, the problem posed by haecceitism. Haecceitists hold that which actual individual a given possible individual represents does not supervene on any qualitative (even extrinsic) properties of that possible individual. So, for example, they can hold that it would be possible for Canberra and Sydney[7] to swap all their properties but retain their "identities", in the way described above.

Some philosophers have been tempted to reject haecceitism for reasons of difficulty in fitting it into a systematic metaphysics of modality (Lewis 1986:

220–48). If we take that route, this is no problem for us. We can simply deny that it makes sense to swap all of the properties of Canberra and Sydney without thereby swapping Canberra and Sydney themselves. Suppose, on the other hand, we do not do that, but instead embrace haecceitism. In that case, we need an account of truth-makers that reflects our views of the way the world might be different. Consider the fact that Canberra is small. If we accept haecceitism, we think that it is possible that Canberra should have all its properties swapped with Sydney. It would no longer be true that Canberra is small. It appears, however, that the world would be *intrinsically* just the way it actually is. The world, it will seem, does not make it true that Canberra is small, because the world might be just as it is and Canberra not be small. Because of the monotonicity of truth-making, it follows that the world does not include a truth-maker for 'Canberra is small'. To fully resolve these kinds of problems would take us beyond the scope of this chapter;[8] the point to note is that the problem is nothing to do with relations, but rather to do with the possibility of haecceitistic differences between duplicates.

The foregoing arguments assume my definition of making true: that the truth of a proposition is intrinsic to the fact that makes it true. Does it still work on the "truth-maker essentialist" definition: that the truth of a proposition is essential to the fact that makes it true? Yes: we just need it to be the case that the fact that Australia is such that Canberra is south of Sydney is distinct from Australia itself. Australia could exist even if Canberra were not south of Sydney, so it is not a plausible candidate for this fact, on the assumption of truth-maker essentialism. This is generally the case with truth-maker essentialism: it makes it hard to identify facts with concrete particulars.

If we abandon the nominalistic project of identifying facts with things, there is no problem in affirming truth-maker essentialism. Suppose, for example, we have an Armstrong-style ontology of states of affairs, having objects and properties as constituents. One state of affairs we might have is the state of affairs that brings together Australia with the property of being such that Canberra is south of Sydney. If we want to hang on to truth-maker essentialism, we can hold that this state of affairs cannot co-exist, even as some other state of affairs, with an Australia in which Canberra is not to the south of Sydney.

4. Arguments for reductionism

What an anti-reductionist wants to say is that the irreducibly relational facts are constituted in a different way to the monadic ones. For example, in Armstrong (1997: 121–2), the relational states of affairs bring together two or more objects with one property (a relation), where, if the relation is non-symmetric, the objects fit into different "relation places" in the state of affairs. Compare this with the reductionist account in terms of states of affairs that I described above: there a relational state of affairs would bring together a property with just one object, the whole composed of the two objects that are directly constituted into the state of affairs in Armstrong's actual anti-reductionist account.

It seems to me that an anti-reductionist account of relational facts like Armstrong's cannot really be fully described without falling back into a version of reductionism. The reason is that the vocabulary of the anti-reductionist metaphysics itself gives us non-relational propositions that describe the structure of the supposedly irreducible relational facts. For example, Armstrong writes of "the *internal* difference of organisation that exists between *a*'s loving *b*, and *b*'s loving *a*" (1997: 121).

If there is such an internal difference of organization, we can introduce non-relational properties that apply to states of affairs in virtue of their internal organization, in the same way that I introduced non-relational properties that apply to Australia in virtue of its internal organization.

Suppose there is such a thing as the state of affairs of Canberra's being south of Sydney, and that it is organized in the way in which Armstrong holds that irreducible states of affairs are, complete with "relation places" and "internal differences of organization". For convenient reference, let us call this state of affairs 'Kim', and its internal organization 'kimity'. There is a perfectly good proposition that Kim has kimity, which, in fact, Armstrong would assert, were we to ask him to explain his metaphysics of irreducibly relational facts.

Moreover, it is Kim that makes this proposition true. For kimity is an intrinsic (and, if you believe truth-maker essentialism, essential) feature of Kim. So, in fact, Kim is not an irreducibly relational fact, as it makes true the non-relational proposition that Kim has kimity. If truth-maker essentialism is affirmed, there is an even more powerful argument here. In that case, Kim could not exist without having kimity. So Kim is simply the fact that Kim exists, which is very clearly a monadic fact.

There is nothing special about the Armstrongian framework that I have assumed here. Any anti-reductionist will sooner or later have to tell us what she believes about the internal organization of irreducibly relational facts, and then an analogous argument will become available.

Perhaps I have made things too difficult for anti-reductionism in defining an irreducibly relational fact as one that makes no non-relational propositions true. In the light of the argument above, the anti-reductionist might reasonably be allowed to revise this definition.

Recall from the first section that it would be question-begging to appeal to a difference in ontological structure between irreducibly relational and monadic facts (for example, by saying that a irreducibly relational fact is one that involves a two-place universal, or contains more than one particular). The existence of irreducibly relational facts is supposed to give us a reason for believing in those differences of structure.

We might accept the following amendment, though: perhaps some propositions are truer pictures of the facts that make them true than others. 'I do this for your sake' and 'The taxi stopped with a lurch', for example, might be less ontologically perspicuous pictures of the facts that make them true than paraphrases of those propositions that eliminate the seeming ontological commitment to sakes and lurches. Similarly, 'Australia is organized the way it is' might be a less ontologically perspicuous way of describing Australia than 'Canberra is south of Sydney', because it does not mention the south-of relation between some of Australia's parts. Let us say that an irreducibly relational fact is one that does not make true any fully ontologically perspicuous non-relational proposition.

This seems reasonable, but it does not affect my argument. I do not see any way that 'Kim has kimity' falls short of full ontological perspicuity (once it is explained what Kim and kimity are). The non-relational propositions to which I am appealing are those of the metaphysics believed by the anti-reductionists themselves; what could be more ontologically perspicuous (by their lights) than that?

5. Conclusion

It is embarrassing to be in the position of presenting one's own view as a truism, but there it is: I cannot see how anti-reductionism about relational facts can be made coherent. Perhaps the appeal of anti-reductionism can be explained sociologically – with enemies like F. H. Bradley you do not need friends – but it seems hard to find metaphysical merit in it.

This result will, of course, be of intrinsic interest to the truth-maker theorists, who still mostly, like Armstrong, hang on to anti-reductionism or, like Campbell, part with it only with difficulty.

Finally, some light has been shed on the origins of analytic philosophy. Russell's argument against Bradley was mistaken. This tends to undercut the widespread view that Russell's rejection of Bradley's views about relations was the decisive break that issued in analytic philosophy as we know it. Rather, if we apply my argument against anti-reductionism to Russell himself, we see that it is hard to distinguish the most coherent form that his theory of relational facts could take[9] from the theory he ascribes to Bradley.

It is no coincidence, I think, that it is an argument of Bradley's – the regress of relations – that is best used to motivate an ontology of facts, as against a substance-attribute metaphysics (Fox 1987: 195–6;[10] Olson 1987: 51–2). Analytic metaphysics has much to learn from its roots in Hegelian idealism.

Notes

1. "Some objects", here, is the logicians' plural: a proposition can be relational if it asserts that a relation holds between some object and itself.

2. An intermediate definition is suggested in unpublished work by David Lewis. On Lewis's account of truth-making, when we refer to something as a fact, we suggest different counterpart relations to those that we suggest when we refer to something in some other way. The former relations satisfy truth-maker essentialism, while the latter do not. In this way, Lewis is able to endorse truth-maker essentialism and hold that, for example, 'This rose is red' is made true by the rose, without being drawn into the view that roses are essentially red.

3. Actually, Russell's Bradley is a considerable simplification of the original. Bradley himself seems to hold both the "monistic" view now under consideration and the Leibnizian view previously described. He goes to some length to distinguish them, and to endorse both, in the Appendix to *Appearance and Reality*: "are terms altered necessarily by the relations into which they enter? ... by this I do not mean to ask if there can be relations outside of and independent of some whole, for that question I regard as answered in the negative. I am asking whether, within the whole, and subject to that, terms can enter into further relations and not be affected by them .... And this question I am compelled to answer negatively" (1897: 514). For more discussion of Bradley's views on this issue, see Sprigge (1979). For the purposes of this chapter I am interested in the position Russell ascribes to Bradley, rather than whatever views Bradley may actually have held.

4. This is sloppy because parthood is transitive, so that the fusion of A and B must have not only A and B as parts, but also the parts of A and B, and any other fusions of those parts. A less sloppy definition of fusion says that two things overlap iff they have a common part, and that the fusion of A and B is that thing that overlaps all and only those things that overlap A or B.

5. For full expositions of "classical" mereology, see Goodman (1951: 42–51) and Simons (1987: 37–41).

6. On identity over time and across worlds, see Lewis (1986: ch. 4).

7. For a defence of this kind of property swapping, see Chisholm (1967).

8. One way to deal with the problem posed for truth-maker theory by haecceitism is to extend the concept of 'duplication' that was used in the definition of truth-making. We should say that X makes p true iff a superduplicate of X cannot exist without p being true; where a superduplicate of X is a duplicate of X that is also not haecceitistically different to X (for example, by being Canberra rather than Sydney, or by having Canberra rather than Sydney as its largest city).

9. A fully worked-out Russellian account of relational facts would presumably be similar to Armstrong's; at any rate, Armstrong (1997: 3, 90–91) takes his cue from Russell.

10. Fox says "Sometimes here, people have started on a regress" (1987: 195). 'People' are obviously Bradley here: compare Bradley's version of the regress (Bradley 1897: 18).

CHAPTER 13

Why truth-makers[1]

Gonzalo Rodriguez-Pereyra

1. Introduction

Consider a certain red rose. The proposition that the rose is red is true because
the rose is red. One might say as well that the proposition that the rose is red is
made true by the rose's being red. This, it has been thought, does not commit one
to a truth-maker of the proposition that the rose is red. For there is no entity that
makes the proposition true. What makes it true is how the rose is, and how the
rose is is not an entity over and above the rose.

Although expressed in other terms, this view has been held by various authors,
like David Lewis (1992, 2001) and Julian Dodd (2002). It is against this view that I
shall argue in this paper. I shall argue that a significant class of true propositions,
including inessential predications like the proposition that the rose is red, are
made true by entities.

No *truth-making without truth-makers* is my slogan. Although I have my view
about what kinds of entities are truth-makers, I shall not argue for or presuppose that view here.[2] All I shall argue for here is that if a proposition is made true
by something, it is made true by some *thing*, but my argument will leave it open
what kind of thing that thing is: it could be a fact or state of affairs, a trope, or any
other sort of entity.[3]

I shall presuppose that truth-bearers are propositions. The arguments for
taking propositions as truth-bearers are well known, as well as their strengths and
weaknesses. But I am not begging any question by adopting this presupposition,
since it is a presupposition that seems to be shared by the opposition.

2. The truth-maker principle

A truth-maker is an entity that makes true a proposition. That is, a truth-maker is an entity in virtue of which a certain proposition is true. By the *truth-maker principle* I shall understand the claim that necessarily the members of an important class of synthetic true propositions, including inessential predications, have truth-makers.[4] So what I shall argue for is the truth-maker principle (TM):

> (TM) Necessarily, if $<p>$ is true, then there is some entity in virtue of which it is true.[5]

Since my thesis is not that all truths, but that a class of synthetic true propositions including inessential predications have truth-makers, in (TM) '$<p>$' should be considered to stand for such truths, not for any truth whatsoever. But for the sake of simplicity and ease of exposition I shall usually speak of propositions in general – the reader should understand that I am referring to this class of synthetic propositions that includes inessential predications.

In virtue of is a primitive notion, not reducible to notions like entailment. Yet that it is primitive does not mean that it is unclear. One can clarify what it means by specifying which propositions are true in virtue of which entities.[6] And although *in virtue of* is not reducible to entailment, there are connections between the two notions. In particular, if $<p>$ is true in virtue of entity e, then $<e$ exists$>$ entails $<p>$. If so e necessitates $<p>$ in the sense that there is no possible world where e exists but in which $<p>$ is not true. Thus, according to (TM), necessarily, if a proposition is true, there is some entity that necessitates it.

But before arguing for (TM), I shall consider two other principles that have been thought to capture the idea that truths have truth-makers. Problems with finding truth-makers for negative existentials led John Bigelow (1988a: 133) to replace (TM) by the following supervenience principle:

> (ST) Necessarily if $<p>$ is true, then either at least one entity exists which would not exist, were $<p>$ false, or at least one entity does not exist which would exist, were $<p>$ false.[7]

Assuming possible worlds, (ST) can be expressed as follows:

> (ST*) For every possible world w, w^*, and every proposition $<p>$, if w and w^* contain exactly the same entities, then $<p>$ is true in w if and only if $<p>$ is true in w^*.

(ST) and (ST*) are supervenience principles for they make truth supervene upon being. In particular they make truth supervene upon what entities exist: once you fix what entities exist in a certain world, you have thereby fixed what propositions are true in that world.

Although less controversial than (TM), (ST) and (ST*) also have met resistance. Dodd (2002) argues that (ST) lacks motivation and that there is no good reason to believe in it. And Lewis (2001) also has proposed to abandon (ST).

I do not propose to abandon (ST) and (ST*). Nevertheless I do reject the idea, presupposed by both proponents and opponents of (ST) and (ST*), that these principles capture the idea that truths have truth-makers. For implicit in the idea of truth-makers there is an important asymmetry, namely that while entities make propositions true, true propositions do not make entities exist.

But the supervenience between truth and being goes both ways: truth and being supervene upon each other. Thus, in the case of (ST*), the following also holds: there are no two possible worlds in which exactly the same propositions are true but which differ as to the entities that exist in them: once you fix what propositions are true in a certain world, you have thereby fixed what entities exist in that world.

Similarly for (ST): necessarily if a certain entity e exists, then there is some true proposition, namely that e exists, that would be false were e not to exist (and some false proposition, namely that e does not exist, that would be true were e not to exist).

Thus principles (ST) and (ST*) do not capture the idea that truths have truth-makers. There is more to truth-making than the idea that truth supervenes upon being. So (ST) and (ST*) are not what the friends of truth-makers should propose or defend.

But although truth-making is more than the supervenience of truth upon being, the supervenience principles follow from (TM). If there can't be a truth without a truth-maker, then there can't be two worlds with the same entities but in which different propositions are true. Thus (ST*) follows from (TM). Similarly, if there can't be a truth without a truth-maker, if a proposition is true there must be an entity that would not have existed if the proposition in question had been false. Thus (ST) follows from (TM).

3. Dodd against the truth-maker principle

As I said, Dodd argues that (ST) lacks sound motivation. But even if (ST) does not capture the idea that truths have truth-makers, I have to meet Dodd's challenge. For if (ST) is wrong, then so is (TM), which entails it.

Dodd challenges (ST) with a simple counter-example. Imagine a world w_1 in which a certain rose is red. In that world the proposition that the rose is red is true. Now imagine a possible world w_2, where exactly the same entities as in w_1 exist, but in which the rose in question is white. In w_2 the proposition that the rose is red is false. These worlds, if possible, are a counter-example to (ST), for they are ontologically equivalent – exactly the same entities, other than propositions, exist in them – but the proposition that the rose is red is true in w_1 and false in w_2.

Dodd's counter-example is not based on a nominalistic stance. One may be a full realist about properties and so believe in the existence of properties over and above particular things like roses. If so, the proposition that the rose is red is true just in case the rose instantiates the property of being red, or the universal redness. One may even believe in the relation of instantiation as an entity over and above the particulars and the properties they instantiate. But, Dodd argues, it does not follow from the fact that the rose instantiates the property of being red that there is a further entity, over and above the rose, the property of being red, and the relation of instantiation, namely the fact or state of affairs that the rose is red.

So even if the properties of being red and being white, and the relation of instantiation exist both in w_1 and w_2, these two worlds constitute a counter-example to (ST). For they contain the same entities but different propositions are true in them. So what the worlds show is that truth does not supervene upon what entities exist or, what is the same, that truth does not supervene upon whether things are. And so (TM) must go, for (TM) makes truth depend on, and supervene upon, what entities exist.

Yet the counter-example is consistent with a weaker supervenience of truth upon being: the supervenience of truth upon how things are. For there is no possible world wn in which things are as they are in w_1 but which differs from w_1 as to what is true in it. In effect, although Dodd rejects that truth supervenes upon whether things are, he accepts that truth supervenes upon how things are. A similar conclusion is reached by Lewis (1992: 204–6; 2001: 612–14).

4. Truth is grounded

This shows that (TM) is in need of justification. How can we justify it? One way would be to derive it from a plausible and compelling idea. And this is what I shall do.

For the root of the idea of truth-makers is the very plausible and compelling idea that the truth of a proposition is a function of, or is determined by, reality. Thus suppose that the proposition that the rose is red, which makes reference to a particular rose, is true. Then the truth of this proposition is a function of reality in the sense that the truth of the proposition is determined by reality or a portion of it. Indeed, it is a relevant portion of reality, namely the rose, or perhaps that the rose is red, that determines the truth of the proposition.

Thus the insight behind the idea of truth-makers is that truth is grounded. In other words, truth is not primitive. If a certain proposition is true, then it owes its truth to something else: its truth is not a primitive, brute, ultimate fact. The truth of a proposition thus depends on what reality, and in particular its subject matter, is like. What reality is like is anterior to the truth of the proposition; it gives rise to the truth of the proposition and thereby accounts for it.[8]

Thus the idea that truth is determined by reality sounds grand, but in itself it is a very minimal idea: it is simply the idea that the truth of a truth-bearer is determined by its subject matter, or some feature of it, no matter what the nature of the subject matter may be.

That truth is determined by reality is a compelling idea, especially when one notes that it does not commit to any kind of substantive realism. For idealists can accept that truth is determined by reality – they will simply add that this reality is not mind-independent or language-independent.

There is an asymmetry implicit in the idea that truth is grounded, namely that while the truth of a proposition is grounded in reality, reality is not grounded in the truth of propositions. Thus although the truth of the proposition that the rose is red is determined by the rose's being red, the rose's being red is not determined by the truth of the proposition that the rose is red. One explains the truth of the proposition that the rose is red in terms of the rose's being red but not vice versa.

The idea that truth is grounded in reality can be expressed in many different ways. One can say, as I have now been doing it, that the truth of a proposition is determined by reality. But one can also say that a proposition is true in virtue of reality, or in virtue of what reality is like, or because of reality. For instance, the proposition that the rose is red is true in virtue of what reality is like, namely that the rose is red or the rose's being red, and it is true because the rose is red. I take all these locutions to express the idea that the truth of the proposition that the rose is red is grounded, but from now on I shall use mainly the formulation in terms of 'because'.

5. Against the primitiveness of truth

The idea that truth is grounded is so compelling that it has seemed acceptable to philosophers like W. V. Quine, Paul Horwich, and Crispin Wright, who cannot be suspected of trying to advance the cause of truth-makers.[9]

The plausibility of truth's being grounded in reality is better appreciated when one compares it with the alternatives. For suppose truth was primitive. If so, the following are different possibilities: (a) the truth of the proposition that the rose is red and the rose's being red have nothing to do with each other, and (b) the rose is red because the proposition that the rose is red is true.

(a) is not good. Surely, the rose's being red and the truth of the proposition that the rose is red are connected in some way. The proposition that the rose is red is about the colour of the rose, and so if it is true, it must have to do with the rose's being red.

231

But (b) is not better than (a). The idea that the colour of the rose depends on the truth of a certain proposition about the rose, duly generalized, commits us to a radical semantic idealism in which reality depends on truth. Propositions, on this account, would be reality-makers and to make the rose red one should just try to make the proposition that the rose is red true. There is no support for either (a) or (b), and there is a lot of evidence against them.

There is a third alternative that consists in the idea that truth is grounded in reality and vice versa. There are a few cases in which the truth of a proposition depends on its subject matter *and* vice versa. One such case is the proposition <this proposition is true>. If true, it is true because of what its subject matter is like, i.e. because <this proposition is true> is true. But if its subject matter is true, it is what it is like, namely true, because the proposition <this proposition is true> is true.

But putting this and similar cases aside, in the vast majority of cases the truth of a proposition determines in no way its subject matter. All truths about our rose and all flowers, as well as all truths about non-truth-bearers, are like that: their truth depends on what their subject matter is like without their subject matter depending in any way on whether they are true or not.[10]

6. Why truth-makers, I

Yet it seems that the idea that truth is grounded in and determined by reality is insufficient to ground (TM). For while what (TM) requires is that truth is determined by whether things are, that truth is grounded in and determined by reality is compatible with truth's being grounded in *how* things are, not in *whether* things are. Thus, it seems, Dodd's counter-example undermines the controversial (TM) but leaves untouched the uncontroversial idea that truth is a function of reality. But I shall argue that the idea that truth is grounded commits us to the idea that truths are made true by entities.

So, can one really maintain that truth is determined by reality without maintaining that there are truth-makers? In other words, can one really maintain that the proposition that the rose is red is made true by how things are but not by whether things are?

Suppose the proposition that the rose is red is made true by how the rose is. But the rose is not only red: it is also light, soft, fragrant, long, thin, etc. This is how the rose is. But if being how it is is what makes the proposition that the rose is red true, being how it is is also what makes the proposition that the rose is light true, the proposition that the rose is fragrant true, and so on.

But this is wrong. For what makes true that the rose is red is not what makes true that the rose is light. What makes true that the rose is red is that it is red, while what makes true that the rose is light is that it is light. The idea that truth is determined by reality is the idea that different truths are determined by different portions of reality, or by different features of reality, and so different truths about the same subject matter are determined by different features of the subject matter in question.

So the rose is many ways. One way the rose is is to be red; another way the rose is, is to be light, and so on. Once we have distinguished different ways the rose is, we can say that the proposition that the rose is red is true in virtue of the rose's being a certain way, namely being red, while the proposition that the rose is light is true in virtue of the rose's being a different way, namely being light. If so, what makes true a certain predication of the rose is a certain way the rose is.

But to distinguish ways presupposes that we can identify them, count them, and quantify over them. But if one can identify, count, and quantify over ways, then ways exist. That is, ways, which are truth-makers, are entities. So we are back to (TM), which claims that true propositions are made true by entities, and which entails that truth supervenes upon whether things are.[11]

But perhaps one can account for what makes the proposition that the rose is red true without reifying ways? It might be thought that one could say that the proposition that the rose is red is true because the rose instantiates the property of being red, while the proposition that the rose is light is true because the rose instantiates the property of being light. And one could insist that this does not mean that there is an entity over and above the rose, the properties of *being red* and of *being light*, and the *instantiation* relation. If so, the rose can be said to be many different ways because it instantiates many different properties, but ways are not a kind of entity, and there are no entities that make any propositions true.

But this only helps if for the rose to instantiate the property of being red is not for it to instantiate the property of *being light*. And this should not mean that there is an entity, *the-rose-instantiating-being-red*, distinct from another entity, *the-rose-instantiating-being-light*. For that means reifying how things are. And reifying how things are is admitting truth-makers.

But if it does not mean that, what does it mean? It might simply mean that the rose could have been red without being light and vice versa. If so, how the rose is could have made true that the rose is red without making true that the rose is light, and vice versa. But this is irrelevant, for the problem is not to account for the fact that what makes true the propositions that the rose is red and that the rose is light could have made true either but not both of them. The problem is to account for the fact that the propositions that the rose is red and that the rose is light are, in the actual world, made true by different features of reality without reifying those features.

Some might suggest that, since there are possible worlds in which the proposition that the rose is red is true and the proposition that the rose is light is false and vice versa, the rose's being red consists simply in that the actual world is one of the worlds where the rose is red, and the rose's being light consists simply in that the actual world is one of the worlds where the rose is light. If so, that truths are made true by how things are means, in the case of the rose, that both the proposition that the rose is red and the proposition that the rose is light are made true by how the world is, since it is both one of the worlds where the rose is red and one of the worlds where the rose is light. This amounts to saying that the truth about the rose, and the truth about everything, is determined by how the *world* is. But this is not satisfactory, for it does not account for the idea that truth is determined by subject matter since according to it all truths, whatever their subject matter, are determined by how the world is.

It may be said that this position still makes room for the idea that truth is determined by subject matter. For the truth of the proposition that the rose is red is determined by how the world is, namely by the world's being one of the worlds where the rose is red, and this in turn is determined by how the rose is. But how the rose is also determines that the world is one where the rose is light, the rose is fragrant, etc. Thus this does not avoid the false idea that the propositions that the rose is red, that the rose is light, that the rose is fragrant, etc., are all true in virtue of the same, namely how the rose is.

7. Why truth-makers, II

Thus I cannot see how one could maintain that the propositions that the rose is red and that the rose is light are true in virtue of different features of reality without reifying those features and thereby introducing truth-makers. But perhaps some are willing to insist that all inessential predications about the rose are made true by, or merely supervene upon, how the rose is. Still, a commitment to truth-makers is unavoidable, provided one accepts that truth is grounded in reality, as the following argument shows:

(1) Truth is grounded.
(2) Grounding is a relation.
(3) Relations link entities.
(4) Therefore, truth is grounded in entities.

I have stated the argument in a slogan-like fashion to facilitate discussion of the key premises. But a brief gloss will suffice to make clear exactly how the argument must be taken. The import of the second premise is that to be grounded is to be a *relatum* (of the grounding relation). Since the import of the first premise is that every true proposition is grounded, it follows that for every true proposition to be grounded is for it to be a relatum of the relation of grounding. The import of the third premise is that all relata of a given relation are entities. It follows that the grounding relation links some entities to true propositions. The entities linked by the grounding relation to true propositions are their grounds.[12]

Therefore true propositions are grounded in entities, i.e. truth is grounded in entities.

The argument is valid and I have already argued for the first premise of the argument. And as I have said, even people like Quine and Horwich are prepared to accept the first premise. This is surely because they believe they can accept it without accepting truth-makers. But given this argument, anyone who wants to maintain premise (1) while denying the conclusion (4) will have to find fault with either premise (2), or premise (3), or both.

Premise (3) is undeniable. It says about relations what the following claim says about properties: properties are had or instantiated by entities. Even Platonists, who believe properties can exist uninstantiated, will agree that if a property is instantiated, it is instantiated by an entity. Surely if a relation is instantiated, if it links anything to anything, then there are some things that it links, and so it links entities. This point is generally recognized. Mellor (1995: 156), for instance, says that for '*Obd*' to be a relational statement, *b* and *d* must exist, "since nothing relates anything to nothing".

This leaves premise (2), which I take to be the favourite target of the foes of truth-makers. But I shall now argue that premise (2) is also true.

As we saw, the proposition that the rose is red is true because the rose is red, but it is not the case that the rose is red because the proposition that the rose is red is true. In general, <*p*> is true because *p* but it is not the case that *p* because <*p*> is true. Thus if grounding is a relation, then it is an asymmetrical relation. This asymmetrical relation, which we report when we say that the proposition that the rose is red is true because the rose is red, holds between a true proposition and a thing in the world, e.g. the fact that the rose is red, in virtue of which the proposition is true. The relation in question, which holds between certain entities in the world and propositions, is no other than that of *making true*, or that of *being true in virtue of*.

If grounding is a relation, then truth is a relational property of propositions.[13] Relational properties are those that are had in virtue of an entity's bearing a certain relation to some thing or things. Thus Diego Maradona has the relational property of being famous in virtue of a relation that links him to the millions who have heard of him. Likewise, truth is a relational property that is had by a proposition in virtue of bearing a certain relation to a certain entity, its truth-maker. This does not mean that being a relation is part of the meaning of the truth-predicate. All it means is that it applies in virtue of a relation obtaining between that to which it applies and something else. But if grounding is not a relation – what is it? That is, how can the truth of the proposition that the rose is red be grounded in the rose's being red if grounding is not a relation? What is it, then, for the proposition that the rose is red to be true because the rose is red?

One thing that could be said is that for the truth of the proposition that the rose is red to be grounded in the rose's being red is for that proposition to be true if and only if the rose is red. But this is wrong, for it does not respect the asymmetry of grounding. Indeed, if all it takes for the proposition that the rose is red to be grounded in the rose's being red is that it is true if and only if the rose is red, then we should conclude that the rose's being red is no less grounded in the truth of the proposition than the truth of the proposition is grounded in the rose's being red.

Another thing that could be said is that for the truth of a proposition to be grounded is for the truth of the proposition to be deducible from, and therefore explainable by, premises including the truth-condition of the proposition. For instance, from a premise stating that the rose is red, by using the *T*-biconditionals, we deduce, and thereby explain, that the proposition that the rose is red is true. This is the line taken by Paul Horwich (1998: 105).

But this is wrong. For deducibility does not amount to explanation. Indeed, using the *T*-biconditionals we can also deduce from a premise stating that the proposition that the rose is red is true that the rose is red. But neither is the rose's being red grounded in the proposition's being true, nor do we explain that the rose is red in terms of the truth of the proposition that the rose is red.

It might be suggested that the rose's being red explains the truth of the proposition that the rose is red because certain counterfactuals hold: if the rose had not been red then the proposition that the rose is red would not have been true.

But this is wrong. First, that the relevant counterfactuals hold is simply that they are true. And so this approach attempts to explain truth by truth, which is not very illuminating. Second, that if the proposition that the rose is red had not been true then the rose would not have been red is no less true than that if the rose had not been red the proposition that the rose is red would not have been true. So that the rose's being red explains that the proposition that the rose is red is true cannot be a mere matter of certain counterfactuals holding. For the relevant counterfactuals hold in both directions.

But perhaps saying that the proposition that the rose is red is true because the rose is red simply means that we explain the truth of the proposition in terms of the rose's being red rather than the other way round? According to this, the proposition that the rose is red is true because the rose is red because we explain the former in terms of the latter. But this is wrong. We explain the truth of the proposition that the rose is red in terms of the rose's being red because the proposition that the rose is red is true because the rose is red. Explanation is not and does not account for grounding – on the contrary, grounding is what makes possible and "grounds" explanation.

Not only that. As David-Hillel Ruben says, what makes explanation possible is the presence of certain determinative relations between entities (Ruben 1990: 210). He puts it like this: "explanations work only because things make things happen or make things have some feature" (Ruben 1990: 232). So invoking explanation of the truth of the proposition that the rose is red will not save us from postulating a relation (namely grounding) between some entity and the proposition.

236

But, one might say, all there is behind the fact that the proposition that the rose is red is true because the rose is red is a move of semantic descent. Consider, for instance, the view that the truth-predicate is simply a disquotational device. Here the function of the truth-predicate is not to ascribe a property to something but simply to cancel linguistic reference so that reference to objects like the rose is restored. So to say that 'The rose is red' is true is simply to say that the rose is red.

In the same pages where he was putting forward the disquotational view, Quine admitted that truth is grounded: "No sentence is true but reality makes it so" (Quine 1970: 10). Can Quine account for the groundedness of truth without making grounding a relation? It might be thought he can: all it takes for 'The rose is red' to be true because the rose is red is that given that the rose is red we can legitimately apply the disquotational device to 'The rose is red'.

Quine's view is meant to apply to sentences rather than propositions, which I assumed as truth-bearers at the beginning of this paper. But something like it could be modelled for propositions. One could simply say that the function of the truth-predicate is to cancel propositional reference in order to restore reference to non-propositional objects or entities. So to say that the proposition that the rose is red is true is simply to say that the rose is red. The truth-predicate thus functions as a mere device of semantic descent. And, it might be thought, the proponent of this view will say that all it takes for the proposition that the rose is red to be true because the rose is red is that given that the rose is red we can legitimately apply the device of semantic descent to the proposition that the rose is red.

Maybe that is the point of the truth-predicate. The predicate is useful because it allows us to indirectly speak about the world even in cases when, due to certain technicalities, we must perform semantic ascent. Paraphrasing Quine (1970: 12), by calling the proposition true, we call the rose red. Perhaps that is what we do and what we need the truth-predicate for.

But that this view accounts for the idea that the proposition that the rose is red is true because the rose is red is illusory. This view gets the order of explanation wrong: that the proposition that the rose is red is true because the rose is red accounts for the fact that given that the rose is red we can legitimately apply the device of semantic descent to the proposition that the rose is red – not the other way around.

But, it might be said, the importance of semantic descent lies in that it allows us to speak about what we really want to talk about: the world of roses, snow, and cats. As Quine said, the truth-predicate "serves as a reminder that though [propositions] are mentioned, reality is still the whole point" (1970: 11).[14] This is surely true, but one should avoid trying to explain that the proposition that the rose is red is true because the rose is red in terms of our interests in roses rather than propositions. That we are interested in roses rather than propositions about them does not explain why propositions about roses are grounded in roses. The more likely thing is that the fact that the rose's being red grounds the truth of the proposition that the rose is red plays some part, even if a modest one, in an explanation of why we are more interested in roses than in propositions about them.

One might try to reject the idea that grounding is a relation from the identity theory of truth, according to which true propositions *are* facts. One could argue thus: (a) what grounds the true proposition that the rose is red is the fact that the rose is red; (b) the true proposition that the rose is red = the fact that the rose is red; (c) if a relation, grounding is an irreflexive relation (at least in the case of propositions about non-truth-bearers like roses); therefore, (d) grounding is not a relation (at least in the case of propositions about non-truth-bearers like roses).[15]

The problem with this argument lies in the conjunction of (a) and (b), which leads to the abandonment of premise (1) of my argument, i.e. to the abandonment of the idea that truth is grounded. For (a) and (b) entail that the proposition that the rose is red is true because it is a fact that the rose is red, and that it is a fact that the rose is red because the proposition that the rose is red is true. This, as we saw in §5, is absurd and represents an abandonment of the idea that truth is grounded.

It might be replied that this *sounds* absurd because one is implicitly presupposing that the proposition and the fact that the rose is red are not the same entity. But, the objector will say, given that the fact and the proposition are one and the same, there is no absurdity in claiming that the proposition that the rose is red is true because it is a fact that the rose is red, and that it is a fact that the rose is red because the proposition that the rose is red is true. For given the identity between proposition and fact one is not thereby claiming of two entities that they are mutually grounded. So, the objector will continue, all (a) and (b) entail is that a true proposition is grounded *in itself*.

But this *is* abandoning the idea that truth is grounded, for it amounts to taking truth as primitive. The proposition that the rose is red is true because it is a fact that the rose is red, but given the identity theory of truth this amounts to saying that it is true because it is true. That it is true is then a primitive fact about the proposition that the rose is red. Saying that the proposition that the rose is red is grounded in itself, and saying that it is not grounded, are one and the same thing.

We can see more clearly the errors that an identity theorist incurs in conjoining (a) and (b). There are two versions of the identity theory, a modest one and a robust one (Dodd 1999: 227). A robust identity theory takes facts to be entities from the realm of reference whose totality makes up the world. If the world is the totality of facts, they must have things, and perhaps also properties, as their constituents. But if so, given the identity between proposition and fact, what makes the rose red is that the proposition that the rose is red is true, which is absurd.[16]

A modest identity theory takes facts to be entities in the Fregean realm of sense. We do not encounter facts in the world of roses, atoms, houses, and people – facts are not made up of these things. On this version of the identity theory to say that the true proposition that the rose is red is grounded in the fact that the rose is red, i.e. to say that the proposition is grounded in itself means to deny that the proposition is grounded in anything about the rose. The modest identity theory, when coupled with the idea that true propositions are grounded in facts, leads to the view that the truth of the proposition about the rose is independent from the rose's being red. This is also clearly wrong.

Thus it is difficult to see what grounding could be if not a relation. But it is easy to see that it is a relation. For consider again the proposition that the rose is red. If the truth-predicate applies to it, then it applies in virtue of, or is grounded in, something. Either it is grounded in an intrinsic feature of the proposition, or it is grounded in something else. If it is grounded in an intrinsic feature of the proposition then we lose the connection between truth and the world and we are left with some version of primitive truth – something I have already rejected. So it is grounded in something else. So the proposition and that something else that grounds it are related – if they were not related, how could one be true in virtue of the other? And the way in which they are related is that one grounds the other. Therefore grounding is a relation.

8. Conclusion

As I have said, analytic truths, and some other truths, are not grounded. But the idea that most synthetic truths, including inessential predications about things like roses, cats, planets, and molecules, are grounded is a very plausible idea that most philosophers want to retain. But there is no escape from truth-makers once the groundedness of truth has been admitted. It is not possible to maintain that truth is grounded in how things are without maintaining that truth is grounded in whether things are. Thus (TM) and the idea that truths have truth-makers have been vindicated.

The idea that truths have truth-makers has important and problematic onto-logical consequences. Not only does one have to admit an extra entity, over and above the rose, to account for what makes true that the rose is red – one also has to find a truth-maker, for instance, for negative existential truths, like the truth that there are no penguins at the North Pole. What that truth-maker is, I don't claim to know. All I claim is that there must be one.[17]

Notes

1. First published in *Truthmakers: The Contemporary Debate*, H. Beebee & J. Dodd (eds), 17–31 (Oxford: Oxford University Press, 2005).
2. Succinctly, my view is that truth-makers of propositions like that *a* is *F* are facts (or states of affairs), whose all and only constituents are resembling particulars. See my *Resemblance Nominalism* (2002: 53–4, 85–7, 113–21). (Note that there I took sentences rather than propositions to be truth-bearers.)

3. I am using the words 'entity' and 'thing' interchangeably. I shall use them so throughout the paper.

4. Remarking that I take inessential predications to have truth-makers is important because some foes of truth-makers like Dodd (2002: 72) accept that essential predications and existential propositions have entities as truth-makers.

5. I follow the usual custom of letting '<p>' stand for 'the proposition that p'.

6. I explained the notion of truth-makers in that way in *Resemblance Nominalism* (2002: 35–40).

7. This is not exactly the way Bigelow formulates his principle, but the differences are irrelevant.

8. This is not true of all propositions. The truth of the proposition that bachelors are not married does not depend on what reality is like – whatever reality is like, bachelors are not married. In general, analytic propositions are not grounded in reality. And there may be some non-analytic truths that are not grounded in reality. Nevertheless a vast number of synthetic truths, like the truth that the rose is red, are grounded in reality. But since, as I have said, my aim here is not to defend the idea that all truths have truth-makers, but only that a significant class of them, including inessential predications, have, that some truths are not grounded in reality will not affect my thesis.

9. Quine (1970: 10), Horwich (1998: 105), and Wright (1992: 26) accept that 'snow is white', or the proposition that snow is white, is true because snow is white and try to explain this in terms of their respective theories of truth.

10. The case of <this proposition is true> shows that strictly speaking grounding is a non-symmetrical relation rather than an asymmetrical one. But since I am not interested in cases like these I shall continue to speak as if grounding were asymmetrical.

11. This argument may remind one of an argument for possible worlds once advanced by Lewis. Lewis argued roughly like this: it is uncontroversially true that things could have been different in many ways; ordinary language permits the existentially quantified paraphrase: there are many ways things could have been besides the way they actually are; permissible paraphrases of truths are true; there-fore, there are many ways things could have been, i.e. there are many possible worlds (Lewis 1973: 84). But my argument is not like this. Firstly, I do not appeal to permissible paraphrases. Secondly, I argue for the claim that the rose is many ways: for unless the rose is many different ways we get the result that what makes true that the rose is red is the same as what makes true that the rose is light, which is wrong.

   One might think that although strictly different from Lewis's argument, mine fails for the same reasons as his. For, it will be said, what besets Lewis's argument is that it does not follow from the fact that things could have been different ways that there are possible worlds. But what does not follow is that there are possible worlds *understood à la Lewis*, i.e. sums of concrete entities. It does follow, however, that there are ways things could have been. These ways could be uninstantiated abstract properties, sets of propositions, etc. In each case these ways are entities. And all I need for my argument to go through is that the ways the rose is, which make propositions about the rose true, are entities. This follows from the fact that the rose is many ways. Thus my argument does not fail in the way Lewis's does. But what kind of entities (facts, tropes, etc.) ways are is something I shall not discuss here.

12. Nothing in the slogan-like argument corresponds to this claim. This is because the claim that what the grounding relation links to true propositions are their grounds is controversial only to the extent that the claims that grounding is a relation and that relations link entities are controversial. Once these claims, which I shall discuss and defend below, have been granted, the claim that what the grounding relation links to true propositions are their grounds is obvious.

13. This is why the truth-maker principle is often associated with the correspondence theory of truth. For the correspondence theory of truth makes truth a relational property based on the relation of correspondence between a truth-bearer and a worldly item – normally a fact.

14. The bracketed word 'propositions' replaces Quine's word 'sentences'.

15. I am not claiming that the identity theory of truth is committed *per se* to claims (a) and (c) in the argument. An identity theorist could maintain that grounding is a reflexive relation, or that truth is not grounded, or that truth is not grounded in facts (e.g. that truths about the rose are grounded in tropes of the rose, or in how the rose is. The latter is very close to Dodd's view that truths about the rose supervene upon how the rose is, and Dodd is an identity theorist of truth [see his 2000]). The

only premise of this argument the identity theory is committed to *per se* is (b). All I am doing here is devising an argument against the idea that grounding is a relation that is based on the identity theory of truth.

16. This absurdity is a manifestation of a more basic absurdity of robust identity theories, namely their identification of facts, understood as having things (and perhaps properties) as constituents, and propositions, understood as thinkables, which are entities of different ontological categories. This absurdity is also at the root of the difficulties robust identity theories find in accounting for falsehood. Dodd (1999: 227) sees a robust identity theory in Hornsby (1997), but Hornsby (1999: 242) rejects the charge.

17. Versions of this paper were read at a conference in the University of Manchester in 2002, a seminar in Universidad Torcuato Di Tella, a seminar in Oxford, and a colloquium at Bariloche, Argentina. I thank those audiences. I thank the Leverhulme Trust, whose generous Philip Leverhulme Prize made it possible to complete this paper. Finally, I also thank the Philosophy Department at CUNY, where I started writing this paper in 2001, and Universidad Torcuato Di Tella, where I finished it in 2002.

CHAPTER 14

Postscript to "Why truth-makers"

Gonzalo Rodriguez-Pereyra

In this chapter I shall reply to a pair of articles in which the main contention of my "Why truth-makers" – namely, that an important class of synthetic true propositions have entities as truth-makers – is rejected. In §§1–5 I reply to Jennifer Hornsby's "Truth without Truthmaking Entities" (2005) and in §§6–7 I reply to Julian Dodd's "Negative Truths and Truthmaker Principles" (2007).

1.

In §1 of her paper Hornsby writes that I express my premise that truth is grounded in various ways. One of these, which she calls '(G_2)', is this:

> (G_2) The truth of <the rose is red> is explained [/determined] by the rose's being red.

When she later on refers to (G_2), she refers mainly to the formulation in terms of 'explained by'. In a footnote Hornsby writes that she is quoting almost *verbatim* as far as possible (2005: 34 n.3). Now although I said that one explains the truth of <the rose is red> in terms of the rose's being red, I did not mean this to be a way of expressing the idea that truth is grounded. Indeed I made this claim about explanation in the paragraph preceding the one where I say there are many ways of expressing the idea that truth is grounded (this vol., Ch. 13, 231). What I had in mind is that this fact about explanation is a *consequence* of the fact that the truth of <the rose is red> is determined by the rose's being red. But the idea that truth is grounded does not consist in, nor is it constituted by, the fact about explanation. But I acknowledge that I was not explicit on this, and that even if I made my statement about explanation in a different paragraph from the one where I

242

introduce several ways of expressing the idea that truth is grounded, this may not have been enough to prevent confusion.

Anyway, Hornsby contrasts (G2) with what she calls '(G1)':

(G1)   <the rose is red> is true because the rose is red.

And then she makes some curious remarks. For instance, she writes that (G2) would seem to be what I need, given that my target is the claim that truth is grounded in entities. For she writes that in my view 'the rose's being red' denotes a truth-maker and the "nice thing about (G2)" from my point of view, she writes, is that it appears explicitly to mention such an entity. But (G1) does not mention any entity, at least after the 'because' (2005: 35).

If my project had been to show that language commits us to certain entities, then perhaps I would have needed (G2). Then I could have argued that the reference to an entity by 'the rose's being red' is ineliminable and so that (G2) commits us to certain entities, the truth-makers. But that was not my project. My project was not to reach ontological conclusions by exposing a fragment of language that reveals ontology. My project was to reach ontological conclusions through a different kind of argument. In particular, I wanted to give an argument that if truth is grounded, then it is grounded in entities. And (G1) expresses the idea that truth is grounded as well as (G2). This is why I used (G1). And as Hornsby recognizes, I used mainly (G1). And the reason why I used *mainly* (G1) was precisely that 'the rose is red' does not *mention* any entity and therefore no one should think that I am arguing for the existence of truth-makers from the fact that there is a phrase that appears to mention them!

Hornsby writes that (G2) exhibits ontology if I am right, that my opponent holds that (G1) "gives the lie" to the idea that ontology is exhibited, and that a question that separates me from my opponents is which of these approximately equivalent formulations to put one's money on (*ibid.*: 36). But this is not the right diagnosis of the dialectical situation. The issue is not one about choosing between two formulations of one idea, one that exhibits ontology and the other that does not. As I just said, I worked mainly with the formulation that Hornsby says my opponents claim not to exhibit ontology, namely (G1). So the issue between my opponents and me is not one about which one of those formulations we should prefer. The issue is whether one can account for what makes true that, say, the rose is red, in terms of how the rose is or whether one must postulate some entities to account for that.

In §1.2 Hornsby writes that 'the truth of <the rose is red>' might be thought to denote a state of affairs additional to any to which someone who says that the rose is red is committed, or it might be thought simply to denote the same state of affairs as 'the rose's being red' does (*ibid.*: 36). Hornsby is right to say that I do not endorse the second alternative. But on the first alternative, Hornsby writes, a proposition's truth is an entity different from that which makes the proposition true. One then appears to be committed to "an unending hierarchy of truth-makers in respect of each proposition: the truth of $<p>$, the truth of $<<p>$ is true$>$, the truth of $<<<p>$ is true$>$ is true$>$, and so on" (*ibid.*).

Hornsby thinks there are ways out of this unending hierarchy. She thinks that by simply denying that 'the truth of $<$the rose is red$>$' denotes I could accord unequal treatment to 'the truth of $<$the rose is red$>$' and 'the rose's being red'. Then she writes that I would "acknowledge that finding a nominalization in an approximate equivalent of a sentence doesn't *in general* reveal an ontology to which one would be committed by affirming the corresponding proposition" and that I would probably acknowledge also that "no *general* support for [the claim that truth is grounded in entities] can be made with the claim [truth is grounded]" (*ibid.*). Yes, I would happily acknowledge the things Hornsby says I would. But I never said or thought that a nominalization would in general reveal the ontological commitments of the propositions, so I never thought that that truth is grounded could give support to the idea that truth is grounded in entities in that way. Only in the context of an argument, like the one I presented in §7 of "Why truth-makers", can the claim that truth is grounded give support to the idea that truth is grounded in entities.

Anyway, in a footnote, Hornsby considers something very close to what is indeed my line with respect to the problem of the unending hierarchy. She writes that I might say that even if the terms 'the truth of $<p>$', 'the truth of $<<p>$ is true$>$' and so on do not denote states of affairs, nonetheless $<<p>$ is true$>$, $<<<p>$ is true$>$ is true$>$ and so on are all grounded in an entity – namely the entity that is $<p>$'s truth-maker (*ibid.*: 37 n.7). I would indeed say that all those nested propositions are made true by $<p>$'s truth-maker. But note that in order to say this it is not necessary, as Hornsby suggests, to deny that 'the truth of $<p>$', 'the truth of $<<p>$ is true$>$' and so on denote states of affairs. One could accept that they denote states of affairs yet maintain that these states of affairs are not the truth-makers of the nested propositions. This could be maintained for many different reasons. One could maintain that the entity that makes $<p>$ and all the nested propositions true is not a state of affairs, but a trope, say, and that only tropes are truth-makers. Or one could maintain that, although some propositions like $<p>$ have states of affairs as truth-makers, not all states of affairs act as truth-makers. So one could maintain that it is the state of affairs that p that makes $<p>$ and the nested propositions true and that the states of affairs referred to by 'the truth of $<p>$', 'the truth of $<<p>$ is true$>$' and so on are the truth-makers of no propositions at all.

As I said, I think that the truth-maker of the nested propositions $<<p>$ is true$>$, $<<<p>$ is true$>$ is true$>$ and so on is the truth-maker of $<p>$. But Hornsby says that if this is the line, then in order to determine how terms like 'the truth of $<p>$' behave, one will need to decide whether or not $<p>$ has a truth-maker in some instance. And, she writes, what we need to be persuaded of in any particular case is precisely that $<p>$ has a truth-maker (*ibid.*: 37 n.7). But I gave an argument that $<p>$, when it is a synthetic proposition like $<$the rose is red$>$, has a truth-maker. Hornsby is not convinced by this argument, but we shall see below that her criticisms do not go through.

In §1.3 Hornsby writes that we need to consider whether we are apt to accept the existence of truth-makers wherever such claims apply. She wonders whether nominalized phrases such as 'the rose's not being blue', 'the rose's being red or yellow' and others are all equally good candidates for denoting truth-makers. She remembers that there are friends of states of affairs who doubt the existence of negative or disjunctive ones, and so, she writes, they will deny that things such as 'The truth of <the rose is not blue> is determined by the rose's not being blue' and 'The truth of <the rose is red or yellow> is determined by the rose's being red or yellow' (*ibid.*: 38).

First, as for negative and disjunctive facts, nothing in "Why truth-makers" commits me to their existence, or to the thesis that if they exist, they are the truth-makers of disjunctive or negative propositions. All my paper commits me to is that disjunctive and negative propositions such as <the rose is red or yellow> and <the rose is not blue> have some truth-maker: but that truth-maker might be, say, the non-disjunctive and non-negative fact that the rose is red. Note that I am not now claiming that the fact that the rose is red is the truth-maker of <the rose is red or yellow> and <the rose is not blue>. What I am saying is that this view is consistent with the thesis argued for and defended in "Why truth-makers". My thesis was that all the propositions in a certain class of synthetic propositions have truth-makers, not that each one of those propositions has its own distinctive truth-maker.

Let me now make a more general point. Hornsby's method in these passages consists in seeing whether we are disposed to assent to instances like 'The truth of <the rose is not blue> is determined by the rose's not being blue' and 'The truth of <the rose is red or yellow> is determined by the rose's being red or yellow'. I reject this method from the very beginning. What if we are not disposed to assent to some or all of these instances? What if we are disposed to assent to some or all of these instances? Nothing of ontological interest follows from this. Our dispositions to assent or dissent tell us nothing about whether the world really contains entities that act as truth-makers. Thus such dispositions are not ontologically revealing. Such dispositions can only tell us about our *intuitions* and so they can only tell us about *us*. And of course my method in "Why truth-makers" was not to prove that there are truth-makers via establishing that we would assent to linguistic instances of *any* sort.

2.

In §6 of "Why truth-makers" I put forward an argument for truth-makers based on the claim that truth is grounded. The argument, very roughly put, consists in showing that since there are many ways the rose is, one cannot account for what makes true that the rose is red without reifying those ways the rose is. At one point in the course of that argument I challenged my opponents to explain what it means, or what it consists in, that for the rose to instantiate the property of *being red* is not for it to instantiate the property of *being light*. The challenge consists in explaining that without reifying ways things are.

Hornsby writes that it is obvious that for the rose to instantiate the property of *being red* is not for it to instantiate the property of *being light*, and that it is also obvious what this means. She says that given a conception of properties we know that for any object to instantiate the property of *being red* is for that object to be red, and that for it to instantiate the property of *being light* is for it to be light; and we know that what it is for an object to be red is not what it is for it to be light (2005: 41).

First, a preliminary comment. Hornsby says that given a conception of properties we know that for any object to instantiate the property of *being red* is for it to be red. But it is the other way around. For a conception of properties is supposed to explain what it is for an object to be red. So, in any case, what one should say is that given a conception of properties one knows that for any object to be red is for it to instantiate the property of *being red*.

Secondly, but more importantly, the challenge consisted in explaining what it means, or what it consists in, that for the rose to instantiate the property of *being red* is not for it to instantiate the property of *being light without* reifying the rose's instantiation of the properties of *being red* and *being light*. Nothing in what Hornsby writes meets this challenge.

Saying that it is obvious that what it is for an object to be red is not for it to be light clearly does not meet the challenge. Could saying that being red and being light consists, respectively, in instantiating different properties meet the challenge? Not on the face of it. One has to explain how having the property of *being red* is not having the property of *being light* without reifying the having of properties. I considered certain ways of doing this in the context of trying to account for what makes true that the rose is red and I argued they were not satisfactory. But Hornsby provides no way of doing that. So far, the challenge remains unmet.

3.

In §3 of her reply Hornsby turns to my main argument for truth-makers, namely:

(1) Truth is grounded.
(2) Grounding is a relation.
(3) Relations link entities.
(4) Therefore, truth is grounded in entities.

She writes that one is entitled to (2) only if a relation is employed in the proper explication of (1). And she says that in §1 of her reply she gave reasons for doubting whether any relations are introduced in the spellings out of (1) I offered (2005: 41).

No reasons were needed to show that I did not introduce any relations when I spelled out (1), for introducing relations at that stage was never my intention. I argued for (2) in §7 of my paper.

Anyway, Hornsby does not explain why one is entitled to (2) only if a relation is employed in the proper explication of (1). But surely this is not true. Imagine someone arguing like this: (A) Hector is a Trojan; (B) Being a Trojan consists in having a property; (C) Therefore, Hector has a property. And now imagine someone objecting to this argument on the basis that one is entitled to (B) only if a property is employed or introduced in the proper explication of (A). Surely the objector would be missing the nature of this argument. Hornsby is missing the nature of my argument in the same way.

Perhaps by 'proper explication' Hornsby understands 'complete explication' and by completely explicating that truth is grounded Hornsby understands something that includes explaining or at least mentioning everything about grounding. Then one would be entitled to (2) only if a relation appeared in the proper explication of (1). But if this is what 'proper explication' means I did not need to 'properly explicate' the claim that truth is grounded in order to establish it. So, once established, I could go on to establish (2), which is what I did.

4.

In §4.1 Hornsby writes that it is true of *any* proposition <*p*> that while <*p*> is true because *p*, it is not that *p* because <*p*> is true (2005: 42). I disagree. This is not true of *any* propositions since the truth-teller is an exception, as I pointed out in §5 of "Why truth-makers". But what Hornsby says is true of any proposition is instead true of a significant class of synthetic propositions about things like roses and non-truth-bearers in general.

Hornsby writes that I do not think that this asymmetry can be explained by the fact that instances of '<*p*> is true because *p*' involve us in semantic descent, whereas instances of '*p* because <*p*> is true' do not. This is true: I do not believe that.

Hornsby suggests that whatever explanation I give of why <*p*> is true because *p*, while it is not the case that *p* because <*p*> is true, should work along the same lines of the explanation of why {*a*} has an *F*-member because *a* is *F* while it is not the case that *a* is *F* because {*a*} has an *F*-member.

Note that this assumes that the 'because' is the same in the case of the truth of <*p*> as in the case of the *F*-ness of the member of {*a*}. This assumption deserves serious discussion, but for reasons of space I shall assume it without proper discussion.

Now if the 'because' is the same then of course I take it to be a relation, and then {*a*} has an *F*-member because of a certain entity. This entity cannot be *a*, at least if F is a contingent property of a. It must be either the fact that a is F, or some other entity apt to fit the role in question. (And, although it does not follow, it is plausible to suppose that that entity is as well the truth-maker of $<a$ is $F>$.) So (assuming the 'because' is the same in both cases) Hornsby's natural idea that the explanations should work along the same lines is satisfied: they do.

In §4.2 Hornsby gives her own explanation of why $<p>$ is true because p but not vice versa. She writes:

> sometimes it is no good answering the question *Why s?* by saying *because t* unless s's being the case requires something more than t's being the case. To take the example of concern here – its being the case that $<p>$ is true requires more (in the sense elicited) than that p should be the case; and it is no good answering the question *Why p?* by saying *because $<p>$ is true*, even though one may answer the question *Why is $<p>$ true?* by saying *because p*. (2005: 44)

First, although Hornsby writes that in some cases ("sometimes") one should not answer *Why s?* by saying *because t* unless s's being the case requires something more than t's being the case, she does not say why saying that *p because $<p>$ is true* is one of those cases.

Furthermore Hornsby assumes but does not explain why that $<p>$ is true requires more than what that p requires. She says that for the rose to be red it is not required that there should be anything meaningful to say or to think, and that it is not required that the proposition that the rose is red should be propounded (*ibid*.: 43). True, for the rose to be red it is not required that the proposition that the rose is red should be propounded. But that the rose is red requires that there be something meaningful that can be said or thought, namely the proposition that the rose is red. For if the rose is red, then the proposition that the rose is red is true, and therefore the proposition exists. So, necessarily the rose is red if and only if the proposition that the rose is red is true. And so, that the rose is red requires that the proposition be true no less than that that the proposition is true requires that the rose be red.

5.

Hornsby sees a tension in my thought about truth-makers. For, she writes, on the one hand, I call them entities, I speak of our need of reifying some features of reality and I shrink from saying that any old sentence nominalization denotes such a thing. On the other hand, Hornsby says, my main argument for the existence of truth-makers "can seem to show that every proposition has a truthmaker". For, Hornsby says, I believe the existence of truth-makers is required to explain the correctness of the schema '<p> is true because p' and "in any instance of this schema, one might simply nominalize the sentence that expresses <p> to say what <p>'s truthmaker is" (2005: 45). Hornsby proposes to relieve this tension by using nominalizations but refusing to claim that their denotations exist (*ibid.*: 46).

But there is no need to relieve a tension that does not exist. For, as I have already said, I reject the idea that any nominalization of the sentence that expresses <p> gives us the truth-maker of <p>. Nothing in the argument of "Why truth-makers" suggests or implies that any sentence nominalization gives us the truth-maker of the propositions expressed by the sentence. All the argument claims is that if certain true propositions are grounded, then given that grounding is a relation and that relations link entities, those grounded propositions are grounded in entities. All this is consistent with the nominalization 'the rose's not being blue' not giving us the truth-maker of <the rose is not blue>. As I said before, this could be the fact that the rose is not blue, but it could also be the fact that the rose is red, or the red trope of the rose, or the rose itself if it is necessarily red, or whatever entity metaphysicians might discover play the role of truth-makers. The nominalization 'the rose's not being blue' does not settle the issue of what the truth-maker of <the rose is not blue> is – nor did I ever suggest it did.

6.

Dodd (2007) thinks the idea that grounding is a relation can be accommodated without thereby admitting truth-makers. Taking inspiration from Russell's theory of judgement, Dodd claims that it may well be correct to think of grounding as a relation, but it does not follow that it is a relation between a true proposition and a truth-maker, since it could be a relation of a true proposition to several objects (*ibid.*: 398). Thus, according to Dodd, for the true proposition <a is F> to be grounded is not for a binary relation to obtain between it and its truth-maker but for <a> to refer to a, <F> to express F, and for a to instantiate F. "The obtaining of any grounding relation consists in the obtaining of sub-sentential thought/world relations and the fact that the object instantiates the property" (*ibid.*).

But this is not very clear. Dodd starts by saying that although grounding is a relation it may well be a relation between a proposition and several objects: but what are those objects? He does not say. He singles out a and F as *relata* of certain relations but they are not singled out as *relata* of a relation linking them to the proposition <a is F> but of two different relations linking them to <a> and <F>. True, he says that the grounding relation, one of whose *relata* is the proposition <a is F>, consists in these other relations obtaining. Perhaps he means that <a is F> is grounded by being related to a and F. But this cannot be true since the groundedness of a proposition <p> consists in that <p> is true because p, but it makes no sense to say that <a is F> is true because a and F. This is, perhaps, why Dodd writes that for <*a* is *F*> to be grounded is for <*a*> to refer to *a*, <*F*> to express *F*, and for *a to instantiate F*. But this still does not tell us to which objects <*a* is *F*> is related by the grounding relation; unless, of course, he means that there are three such objects: *a*, *F* and *a*'s instantiating *F*. But this would be to posit a truth-maker, and it would make it unnecessary to include the non-truth-makers *a* and *F* among the *relata* of the grounding relation. Clearly, this is not what Dodd wanted to mean. But it is not easy to see what else what he writes could mean.

7.

Dodd argues that the asymmetry of the dependence between truth and reality (namely that, in general, while truth depends on reality, reality does not depend on truth) is a conceptual rather than a modal-existential asymmetry. This means, according to Dodd, that '<*a* is *F*> is true because *a* is *F*' is true because 'because' signals that what follows it is claimed to be conceptually more basic than what precedes it, and this is indeed the case (2007: 398–9). Similarly, according to this explanation, what explains why '*a* is *F* because <*a* is *F*> is true' is false is that what follows the 'because' is not conceptually more basic than what precedes it. According to Dodd, that *a* is *F* is conceptually more basic than that <*a* is *F*> is true because the identity of <*a* is *F*> is partially determined by the items to which its constituents refer, and so one can understand what is required for <*a* is *F*> to be true, namely that *a* be *F*, by engaging in semantic descent and ceasing to talk of propositions, while semantic ascent from '*a* is *F*' to '<*a* is *F*> is true' introduces a concept, namely that of a proposition, which was not in use before the ascent took place (*ibid.*: 399–400).

Provided '*F*' can be understood without understanding the concept of proposition (and truth, let us add), then there seems to be the asymmetry mentioned by Dodd.[1] But I fail to see what such an asymmetry has to do with the asymmetry that consists in that *a*'s being *F* determines that <*a* is *F*> is true but that <*a* is *F*> is true does not determine that *a* is *F*. Dodd may have accounted for an asymmetry concerning truth but he has not shown that he has accounted for the asymmetry that needed accounting for. And it is difficult to see how he could do that, since the fact that to understand the concept of the proposition that *a* is *F* one needs to understand what *a* and *F* are, but to understand that *a* is *F* one does not need to understand the concept of the proposition that *a* is *F* is perfectly compatible with (the falsity) that while *a* is *F* because <*a* is *F*> is true, it is not the case that <*a* is *F*> is true because *a* is *F*.[2]

Notes

1. I owe the important proviso in the antecedent to David Liggins.
2. Thanks to David Liggins for discussion.

Bibliography

Adams, R. 1977. "Middle Knowledge and the Problem of Evil". *American Philosophical Quarterly* **14**: 109–17.

Alexander, H. G. (ed.) 1956. *The Leibniz–Clarke Correspondence*. Manchester: Manchester University Press.

Alston, W. P. 1996. *A Realist Conception of Truth*. Ithaca, NY: Cornell University Press.

Anderson, A. R. & N. D. Belnap 1975. *Entailment*, vol. I. Princeton, NJ: Princeton University Press.

Anderson, A. R., N. D. Belnap & J. M. Dunn (eds) 1992. *Entailment: The Logic of Relevance and Necessity*, vol. 2. Princeton, NJ: Princeton University Press.

Angelelli, I. 1967. *Studies on Gottlob Frege and Traditional Philosophy*. Dordrecht: Reidel.

Anscombe, G. E. M. & P. T. Geach 1961. *Three Philosophers*. Oxford: Blackwell.

Armstrong, D. M. 1989a. *A Combinatorial Theory of Possibility*. Cambridge: Cambridge University Press.

Armstrong, D. M. 1989b. "C. B. Martin, Counterfactuals, Causality, and Conditionals". In *Cause, Mind, and Reality: Essays Honoring C. B. Martin*, J. Heil (ed.), 7–15. Dordrecht: Kluwer.

Armstrong, D. M. 1991. "Classes are States of Affairs". *Mind* **100**: 189–200.

Armstrong, D. M. 1997. *A World of States of Affairs*. Cambridge: Cambridge University Press.

Armstrong, D. M. 2004. *Truth and Truthmakers*. Cambridge: Cambridge University Press.

Austin, J. L. [1950] 1979. "Truth". Reprinted in his *Philosophical Papers*, 3rd edn, J. O. Urmson & G. J. Warnock (eds), 117–33. Oxford: Oxford University Press.

Austin, J. L. 1961. "Unfair to Facts". In his *Philosophical Papers*, 102–22. Oxford: Clarendon Press.

Beall, J. C. 2000. "On Truthmakers for Negative Truths". *Australasian Journal of Philosophy* **78**: 271–6.

Beck, M. 1916. *Inwiefern können in einem Urteil andere Urteile impliziert sein?* Dissertation, University of Munich. Borna: Robert Noske.

Beebee, H. & J. Dodd (eds) 2005a. *Truthmakers: The Contemporary Debate*. Oxford: Clarendon Press.

Beebee, H. & J. Dodd 2005b. "Introduction". See Beebee & Dodd (2005a), 1–16.

Bergmann, G. 1992. *New Foundations of Ontology*, Madison, WI: University of Wisconsin Press.

Bergmann, G. & H. Hochberg 1957. "Concepts". *Philosophical Studies* 7 (January–February): 19–27.

Bigelow, J. 1988a. *The Reality of Numbers*. Oxford: Clarendon Press.

Bigelow, J. 1988b. "Real Possibilities". *Philosophical Studies* 3: 37–64.

Bolzano, B. 1978. *Vermischte philosophische und physikalische Schriften 1832–1848*, Bernard Bolzano Works, Series II, A, vol. 12, pt. 2, J. Berg (ed.). Stuttgart: Frommann.

Bradley, F. H. 1897. *Appearance and Reality*, 2nd edn. Oxford: Oxford University Press.

Brentano, F. 1924. *Psychologie vom empirischen Standpukkt*, 2nd edn. Leipzig: Meiner. [Published in English as *Psychology from an Empirical Standpoint*, A. C. Rancurello, D. B. Terrell & L. McAlister (trans.) (London: Routledge, 1973).]

Brentano, F. 1933. *Kategorienlehre*. Leipzig: Meiner. [Published in English as *The Theory of Categories*, R. Chisholm & N. Guterman (trans.) (The Hague: Nijhoff, 1981).]

Broad, C. D. 1933. *Examination of McTaggart's Philosophy*, vol. I. Cambridge: Cambridge University Press.

Brower, J. E. & K. Guilfoy (eds) 2004a. *The Cambridge Companion to Abelard*. Cambridge: Cambridge University Press.

Brower, J. E. & K. Guilfoy 2004b. "Introduction". See Brower & Guilfoy (2004a), 1–12.

Campbell, K. 1976. *Metaphysics: An Introduction*. Encino, CA: Dickenson.

Campbell, K. 1990. *Abstract Particulars*. Oxford: Blackwell.

Caputo, S. 2007. "Truth-making: What it is Not and What it Could be". See Monnoyer (2007), 275–311.

Chisholm, R. M. 1967. "Identity Through Possible Worlds: Some Questions". *Noûs* 1: 1–8.

Chisholm, R. M. 1978. "Brentano's Conception of Substance and Accident". *Grazer Philosophische Studien* 5: 197–210.

Chisholm, R. M. 1981. *The First Person*. Brighton: Harvester.

Clanchy, M. T. 1999. *Abelard: A Medieval Life*. Oxford: Blackwell.

Clark, R. 1970. "Concerning the Logic of Predicate Modifiers". *Noûs* 4: 311–35.

Daly, C. 2005. "So Where's the Explanation?". See Beebee & Dodd (2005a), 85–103.

David, M. 2001. "Truth as Identity and Truth as Correspondence". In *The Nature of Truth*, M. Lynch (ed.), 683–704. Cambridge, MA: MIT Press.

David, M. 2005. "Armstrong on Truthmaking". See Beebee & Dodd (2005a), 141–59.

Davidson, D. 1967. "Causal Relations". *Journal of Philosophy* 64: 691–703.

Davidson, D. 1980. *Essays on Actions and Events*. Oxford: Clarendon Press.

de Rijk, L. M. 1994. *Nicholas of Autrecourt: His Correspondence with Master Giles & Bernard of Aresso, A Critical Edition and English Translation*. Leiden: Brill.

Descartes, R. 1983. *Oeuvres de Descartes*, 11 vols, C. Adams & P. Tannery (eds). Paris: Vrin.

Dietrich, R.-A. 1974. *Sprache und Wirklichkeit in Wittgensteins Tractatus*. Tübingen: Niemeyer.

Dodd, J. 1999. "Hornsby on the Identity Theory of Truth". *Proceedings of the Aristotelian Society* **XCI**: 225–32.

Dodd, J. 2000. *An Identity Theory of Truth*. New York: St Martin's Press.

Dodd, J. 2002. "Is Truth Supervenient on Being?". *Proceedings of the Aristotelian Society* 102: 69–86.

Dodd, J. 2007. "Negative Truths and Truthmaker Principles". *Synthese* 156: 383–401.

Dronke, P. (ed.) 1988. *Twelfth-Century Western Philosophy*. Cambridge: Cambridge University Press.

Dummett, M. 1959. "Truth". Reprinted in his *Truth and Other Enigmas*, 1–28. Cambridge, MA: Harvard University Press.

Dummett, M. 1973. *Frege: Philosophy of Language*. London: Duckworth.

Dummett, M. 1981. *Frege: Philosophy of Language*, 2nd edn. London: Duckworth.

Findlay, J. N. 1963. *Meinong's Theory of Objects and Values*, 2nd edn. Oxford: Clarendon Press.

Fine, K. 1994. "Essence and Modality". *Philosophical Perspectives* 8: 1–16.

Fine, K. 1995a. "Ontological Dependence". *Proceedings of the Aristotelian Society* 95: 269–90.

Fine, K. 1995b. "The Logic of Essence". *Journal of Philosophical Logic* 24: 241–73.

Fine, K. 2001. "The Question of Realism". *Philosophers' Imprint* 1(2): 1–30 (www.philosophersimprint.org/images/3521354.0001.002.pdf).

Fox, J. 1987. "Truthmaker". *Australasian Journal of Philosophy* 65: 188–207.

Frege, G. 1884. *Die Grundlage der Arithmetik: eine logisch-mathematische Untersuchung über den Begriff der Zahl*. Breslau: W. Koebner. Translated as *The Foundations of Arithmetic: A Logico-mathematical Enquiry into the Concept of Number*, J. L. Austin (trans.), 2nd rev. edn (Oxford: Blackwell, 1974).

Frege, G. 1969. *Nachgelassene Schriften*, H. Hermes, F. Kambartel & F. Kaulbach (eds). Hamburg: Meiner.

Geach, P. T. 1969. "Nominalism". In his *God and the Soul*. London: Routledge & Kegan Paul.

Goodman, N. 1951. *The Structure of Appearance*. Cambridge, MA: Harvard University Press.

Grossman, R. 1974. *Meinong*. London: Routledge.

Grossman, R. 1983. *The Categorial Structure of the World*. Bloomington, IN: Indiana University Press.

Hartmann, N. [1938] 1966. *Möglichkeit und Wirklichkeit*. Berlin: de Gruyter.

Hempel, C. G. 1965. "Aspects of Scientific Explanation". In his *Aspects of Scientific Explanation and Other Essays in the Philosophy of Science*, 331–496. New York: Free Press.

Hempel, C. G. 1966. *Philosophy of Natural Science*. Englewood Cliffs, NJ: Prentice Hall.

Hill, C. S. 2002. *Thought and World*. Cambridge: Cambridge University Press.

Hochberg, H. 1962. "Moore's Ontology and Non-Natural Properties". *Review of Metaphysics* 15: 365–95.

Hochberg, H. 1980. "Russell's Proof of Realism Reproved". *Philosophical Studies* 37: 37–44.

Hochberg, H. 1996. "Particulars, Universals and Russell's Late Ontology". *Journal of Philosophical Research* xxi: 129–38.

Hochberg, H. 2001. *The Positivist and the Ontologist: Bergmann, Carnap and Logical Realism*. Amsterdam: Rodopi.

Hochberg, H. 2002. "From Logic to Ontology: Some Problems of Existence, Predication and Modality". In *A Companion to Philosophical Logic*, D. Jacquette (ed.), 281–92. London: Routledge.

Hochberg, H. 2005. "Meinongian Reflections in Sartre and Russell". *Meinong Studies* 1: 199–231.

Hofmann, F. 2006. "Truthmaking, Recombination, and Facts Ontology". *Philosophical Studies* **128**: 409–40.

Horgan, T. 1978. "The Case against Events". *Philosophical Review* 87: 28–47.

Hornsby, J. 1997. "Truth: The Identity Theory". *Proceedings of the Aristotelian Society* XCVII: 1–24.

Hornsby, J. 1999. "The Facts in Question: A Response to Dodd and Candlish". *Proceedings of the Aristotelian Society* XCIX: 241–5.

Hornsby, J. 2005. "Truth without Truthmaking Entities". See Beebee & Dodd (2005a), 33–47.

Horwich, P. 1990. *Truth*. Oxford: Blackwell.

Horwich, P. 1998 *Truth*, 2nd edn. Oxford: Clarendon Press.

Horwich, P. 2004. "Une Critique de la théorie de vérifacteurs". In *La Structure du Monde: Objets, Propriétés, État de Choses*, J.-M. Monnoyer (ed.), 115–27. Paris: Vrin.

Hume, D. 1975. *A Treatise of Human Nature*, L. A. Selby-Bigge (ed.), 2nd edn, P. H. Nidditch (rev.). Oxford: Clarendon Press.

Husserl, E. 1894. "Psychologische Studien zur elementaren Logik". *Philosophische Monatschefte* 30: 159–91. [Reprinted in E. Husserl, *Aufsätze und Rezensionen (1890–1910)*, 92–123 (The Hague: Nijhoff, 1979); published in English as "Psychological Studies in the Elements of Logic", D. Willard (trans.), *The Personalist* 58 (1977): 295–320.]

Husserl, E. 1900/1901. *Logische Untersuchungen* [LU]. Halle: Niemeyer.

Husserl, E. 1969. *Formal and Transcendental Logic*, D. Cairns (trans.). The Hague: Nijhoff. [Originally published in German as *Formale und transzendentale Logik* (Halle: Niemeyer, 1929).]

Husserl, E. 1970. *Logical Investigations*, J. N. Findlay (trans.). London: Routledge. [Originally published in German as *Logische Untersuchungen* (Halle: Niemeyer 1900/1901, 2nd rev. edn 1913/21).]

Husserl, E. 1973. *Experience and Judgement*, J. S. Churchill & K. Ameriks (trans.). London: Routledge. [Originally published in German as *Erfahrung und Urteil: Untersuchungen zur Genealogie der Logik* (Prague: Academia, 1939).]

Husserl, E. 1974. *Formale und Transzendentale Logik*. The Hague: Martinus Nijhoff.

Ibn Gabirol, S. 1962. *The Fountain of Life*, H. Wedeck (trans.). New York: Philosophical Library.

Ingarden, R. 1925. "Essentiale Fragen: Ein Beitrag zum Wesensproblem". *Jahrbuch für Philosophie und Phänomenologische Forschung* VII: 125–304.

Ingarden, R. 1964/65. *Der Streit um die Existenz der Welt*, 2 vols. Tübingen: Niemeyer.

Ingarden, R. 1994. "Über die Stellung der Erkenntnistheorie im System der Philosophie". In his *Frühe Schriften zur Erkenntnistheorie*, collected works, vol. 6, W. Galewicz (ed.), 277–310. Tübingen: Niemeyer.

Iwakuma, Y. 2004. "Influence". See Brower & Guilfoy (2004a), 305–35.

Jackson, F. 1994. "Armchair Metaphysics". In *Philosophy in Mind: The Place of Philosophy in the Study of Mind*, M. Michael & J. O'Leary-Hawthorne (eds), 23–42. Dordrecht: Kluwer.

Kant, I. 1997. *Critique of Pure Reason*, P. Guyer & A. Wood (ed. & trans.). Cambridge: Cambridge University Press.

Keller, S. 2004. "Presentism and Truthmaking". In *Oxford Studies in Metaphysics*, vol. I, D. Zimmerman (ed.), 83–104. Oxford: Oxford University Press.

Kenny, A. J. P. 1980. *Aquinas*. Oxford: Oxford University Press.

King, P. 2004. "Metaphysics". See Brower & Guilfoy (2004a), 65–125.

Kretzmann, N., A. Kenny & J. Pinborg (eds) 1988. *The Cambridge History of Later Medieval Philosophy*. Cambridge: Cambridge University Press.

Kirkham, R. 1992. *Theories of Truth: A Critical Introduction*. Cambridge, MA: MIT Press.

Kripke, S. 1980. *Naming and Necessity*. Cambridge, MA: Harvard University Press.

Küng, G. 1967. *Ontology and the Logistic Analysis of Language*. Dordrecht: Reidel.

Künne, W. 2003. *Conceptions of Truth*. Oxford: Clarendon Press.

Langtry, B. 1975. "Similarity, Continuity, and Survival". *Australasian Journal of Philosophy* 53: 3–18.

Leibniz, G. W. 1966. *Nouveaux Essais sur l'entendement humain*. Paris: Flammarion.

Leibniz, G. W. 1971. "Primae veritates". In *Opuscules et fragments inédits de Leibniz*, L. Couturat (ed.), 518–23. Hildesheim: Georg Olms.

Leibniz, G. W. 2001. *Essais de Théodicée: sur la bonté de Dieu, la liberté de l'homme et l'origine du mal*. Paris: Flammarion.

Lewis, D. 1973. *Counterfactuals*. Oxford: Blackwell.

Lewis, D. 1986. *On the Plurality of Worlds*. Oxford: Blackwell.

Lewis, D. 1992. "Armstrong on Combinatorial Possibility". *Australasian Journal of Philosophy* 70: 211–24.

Lewis, D. 1999a. *Papers in Metaphysics and Epistemology*. Cambridge: Cambridge University Press.

Lewis, D. 1999b. "Armstrong on Combinatorial Possibility". In his *Papers in Metaphysics and Epistemology*, 196–214. Cambridge: Cambridge University Press.

Lewis, D. 2001. "Forget About the 'Correspondence Theory of Truth'". *Analysis* 61: 275–80.

Lewis, D. 2003. "Things qua Truthmakers". In *Real Metaphysics*, H. Lillehammer & G. Rodriguez-Pereyra (eds), 25–38. London: Routledge.

Liggins, D. 2005. "Truthmakers and Explanation". See Beebee & Dodd (2005a), 105–15.

Locke, J. 1975. *An Essay Concerning Human Understanding* [*Essay*], P. H. Nidditch (ed.). Oxford: Clarendon Press.

Long, D. C. [1968] 1976. "Particulars and their Qualities". Reprinted in *Universals and Particulars*, M. J. Loux (ed.), 310–30. Notre Dame, IN: University of Notre Dame Press.

Lowe, E. J. 1994. "Ontological Dependence". *Philosophical Papers* 23: 31–48.

Lowe, E. J. 1998. *The Possibility of Metaphysics: Substance, Identity, and Time*. Oxford: Clarendon Press.

Lowe, E. J. 2006. *The Four-Category Ontology: A Metaphysical Foundation for Natural Science*. Oxford: Clarendon Press.

Luscombe, D. E. 1988. "Peter Abelard". In *Twelfth-Century Western Philosophy*, P. Dronke (ed.), 279–307. Cambridge: Cambridge University Press.

MacBride, F. 2002. "The Problem of Universals and the Limits of Truthmaking". *Philosophical Papers* 31: 27–37.

MacBride, F. 2005. "Lewis' Animadversions on the Truthmaker Principle". See Beebee & Dodd (2005a), 117–40.

Marenbon, J. 1997. *The Philosophy of Peter Abelard*. Cambridge: Cambridge University Press.

Martin, C. B. 1980. "Substance Substantiated". *Australasian Journal of Philosophy* 58: 3–20.

Martin, C. B. 1996. "How It Is: Entities, Absences and Voids". *Australasian Journal of Philosophy* 74: 57–65.

Martin, C. J. 2004. "Logic". See Brower & Guilfoy (2004a), 158–99.

Mates, B. 1986. *The Philosophy of Leibniz*. Oxford: Oxford University Press.

Maurin, A. S. 2002. *If Tropes*. Amsterdam: Kluwer.

McDermott, M. 1999. "Counterfactuals and Access Points". *Mind* 108: 291–334.

McTaggart, J. 1921. *The Nature of Existence*, 2 vols. Cambridge: Cambridge University Press.

Meinong, A. 1915. *Über Möglichkeit und Wahrscheinlichkeit*. Leipzig: Barth.

Meinong, A. 1968. *Abhandlungen zur Werttheorie*, Gesamtausgabe III. Graz: Akademische Druck- u. Verlagsanstalt.

Meinong, A. 1973. "Über die Stellung der Gegenstandstheorie im System der Wissenschaften". In *Über philosophische Wissenschaft ... und andere Werke*, Gesamtausgabe V, 197–365. Graz: Akademische Druck- u. Verlagsanstalt.

Meinong, A. 1977. *Über Annahmen*, Gesamtausgabe IV. Graz: Akademische Druck- u. Verlagsanstalt.

Mellor, D. H. 1995. *The Facts of Causation*. London: Routledge.

Merricks, T. 2006. *Truth and Ontology*. Oxford: Clarendon Press.

Molnar, G. 2000. "Truthmakers and Negative Truths". *Australasian Journal of Philosophy* 78: 72–86.

Monnoyer, J. M. (ed.) 2007. *Metaphysics and Truthmakers*. Frankfurt: Ontos.

Moore, G. E. 1899. "The Nature of Judgment". *Mind* 8: 276–93.

Moore, G. E. 1901. "Identity". *Proceedings of the Aristotelian Society*: 103–27.

Moore, G. E. 1953. *Some Main Problems of Philosophy*. London: Allen & Unwin.

Morris, M. 2005. "Realism beyond Correspondence". See Beebee & Dodd (2005a), 49–65.

Mugnai, M. 2002. "Review of 'La Doctrine leibnizienne de la vérité'". *The Leibniz Review* 12: 53–63.

Mulligan, K. 1983. "Wie die Sachen sich zueinander verhalten inside and outside the Tractatus". *Teoria* 5: 145–74.

Mulligan, K. 2004. "Essence and Modality: The Quintessence of Husserl's Theory". In *Semantik und Ontologie: Beiträge zur philosophischen Forschung*, M. Siebel & M. Textor (eds), 387–418. Frankfurt: Ontos.

Mulligan, K. 2006a. "Ascent, Propositions and other Formal Objects". *Grazer Philosophische Studien* 72: 29–48.

Mulligan, K. 2006b. "Wahrheit und das Wahrmacher-Prinzip im Jahr 1921". In *Untersuchungen zur Ontologie*, G. Imaguire & C. Schneider (eds), 55–78. Munich: Philosophia.

Mulligan, K. 2007. "Two Dogmas of Truthmaking". See Monnoyer (2007), 51–65.

Mumford, S. 2007. "A New Solution for the Problem of Negative Truth". See Monnoyer (2007), 313–29.

Nolan, D. 1996. "Recombination Unbound". *Philosophical Studies* 8: 239–62.

Nuchelmans, G. 1973. *Theories of the Proposition: Ancient and Medieval Conceptions of the Bearers of Truth and Falsity*. Amsterdam: North-Holland.

Nuchelmans, G. 1988. "The Semantics of Propositions". In *The Cambridge History of Later Medieval Philosophy*, N. Kretzmann, A. Kenny & J. Pinborg (eds), 197–210. Cambridge: Cambridge University Press.

Oliver, A. 1996. "The Metaphysics of Properties". *Mind* 105: 1–80.

Olson, K. 1987. *An Essay on Facts*. Stanford, CA: CSLI.

Parsons, J. 1999. "There is no "Truthmaker" Argument against Nominalism". *Australasian Journal of Philosophy* 77: 325–34.

Parsons, J. 2005. "Truthmakers, the Past, and the Future". See Beebee & Dodd (2005a), 161–74.

Parsons, T. 1972. "Some Problems Concerning the Logic of Predicate Modifiers". In *Semantics of Natural Languages*, D. Davidson & G. Harman (eds), 127–41. Dordrecht: Reidel.

Perry, J. 1986. "From Worlds to Situations". *Journal of Philosophical Logic* 15: 83–107.

Pfänder, A. 1921. *Logik*, Jahrbuch für Philosophie und phänomenologische Forschung, vol. IV.

Pfänder, A. 2000. *Logik*, M. Crespo (ed.). Heidelberg: Universitätsverlag C. Winter. [Reprint of Pfänder 1921.]

Pitcher, G. 1964. "Introduction". In *Truth*, G. Pitcher (ed.), 1–15. Englewood Cliffs, NJ: Prentice Hall.

Plantinga, A. 1974. *The Nature of Necessity*. Oxford: Clarendon Press.

Politis, V. 2004. *Aristotle and the Metaphysics*. London: Routledge.

Politis, V. 2009 forthcoming. "Explanation and Essence in Plato's Phaedo". In *Definition in Greek Philosophy*, D. Charles (ed.). Oxford: Oxford University Press.

Priest, G. 2000. "Truth and Contradiction". *Philosophical Quarterly* 50: 305–19.

Prior, A. N. 1971. *Objects of Thought*, P. T. Geach & A. J. P. Kenny (eds). Oxford: Clarendon Press.

Putnam, H. 1978. *Meaning and the Moral Sciences*. London: Routledge.

Quine, W. V. 1961. "On What There Is". In his *From a Logical Point of View*, 2nd edn, 1–19. Cambridge, MA: Harvard University Press.

Quine, W. V. 1966. *The Ways of Paradox and Other Essays*. New York: Random House.

Quine, W. V. 1968a. "Ontological Relativity". In his *Ontological Relativity and Other Essays*, 26–68. New York: Columbia University Press.

Quine, W. V. 1968b. "Speaking of Objects". In his *Ontological Relativity and Other Essays*, 1–25. New York: Columbia University Press.

Quine, W. V. 1970. *Philosophy of Logic*. Englewood Cliffs, NJ: Prentice Hall.

Quine, W. V. 1976. *The Ways of Paradox and other Essays*, rev. edn. Cambridge, MA: Harvard University Press.

Quine, W. V. 1981. "Things and Their Place in Theories". In his *Theories and Things*, 1–23. Cambridge, MA: Harvard University Press.

Ramsey, F. P. 1978. *Foundations*, D. H. Mellor (ed.). London: Routledge.

Rauzy, J.-B. 2001. *La Doctrine Leibnizienne de la vérité*. Paris: Vrin.

Rauzy, J.-B. 2002. "Reply to Massimo Mugnai's review of *La Doctrine Leibnizienne de la vérité*". *The Leibniz Review* 12: 65–9.

Read, S. 2000. "Truthmakers and the Disjunction Thesis". *Mind* 109: 67–79.

Reinach, A. 1911. "Zur Theorie des negativen Urteils". In *Münchener Philosophische Abhandlungen*, A. Pfänder (ed.), 196–254. Leipzig: Barth. [Published in English in Smith (1982b), 315–78.]

Reinach, A. 1979. "Kant's Interpretation of Hume's Problem". *Southwestern Journal of Philosophy* 7(2): 161–88.

Reinach, A. 1989. "Kants Auffassung des Humeschen Problems". In his *Sämtliche Werke*, 2 vols, K. Schuhmann & B. Smith (eds), 67–94. Munich: Philosophia.

Restall, G. 1993. "Deviant Logic and the Paradoxes of Self Reference". *Philosophical Studies* 70: 279–303.

Restall, G. 1994. "On Logics Without Contraction". PhD thesis, University of Queensland.

Restall, G. 1995a. "Information Flow and Relevant Logics". In *Logic, Language and Computation: The 1994 Moraga Proceedings*, J. Seligman & D. Westerstahl (eds), 443–56. Stanford, CA: Center for the Study of Language and Information.

Restall, G. 1995b. "What Truthmakers Can Do for You". Automated Reasoning Project, Australian National University, Canberra.

Restall, G. 2000. "Modelling Truthmaking". *Logique et Analyse* **169–70**: 211–30.

Restall, G. 2005. "Łukasiewicz, Supervaluations and the Future". *Logic & Philosophy of Science* 3: 1–10.

Rodriguez-Pereyra, G. 2002. *Resemblance Nominalism: A Solution to the Problem of Universals*. Oxford: Clarendon Press.

Rodriguez-Pereyra, G. 2006a. "Truthmakers". *Philosophy Compass* 1: 186–200.

Rodriguez-Pereyra, G. 2006b. "Truthmaking, Entailment, and the Conjunction Thesis". *Mind* **115**: 957–82.

Rosen, G. 1990. "Modal Fictionalism". *Mind* 99: 327–54.

Rosen, G. & D. Lewis 2003. "Postscript to 'Things qua Truthmakers': Negative Existentials". In *Real Metaphysics*, H. Lillehammer & G. Rodriguez-Pereyra (eds), 39–42. London: Routledge.

Routley, R., V. Plumwood, R. K. Meyer & R. T. Brady (eds) 1982. *Relevant Logics and Their Rivals*. Atascadero, CA: Ridgeview.

Ruben, D.-H. 1990. *Explaining Explanation*. London: Routledge.

Russell, B. 1900. *A Critical Exposition of the Philosophy of Leibniz*. London: Allen & Unwin.

Russell, B. 1903. *The Principles of Mathematics*. Cambridge: Cambridge University Press.

Russell, B. 1910. "The Monistic Theory of Truth". In his *Philosophical Essays*, 131–46. London: Longmans, Green.

Russell, B. 1912. *The Problems of Philosophy*. Oxford: Oxford University Press.

Russell, B. 1918. "The Philosophy of Logical Atomism". *Monist* 28: 495–527.

Russell, B. 1937. *Principles of Mathematics*, 2nd edn. London: Allen & Unwin.

Russell, B. 1940. *An Inquiry into Meaning and Truth*. London: Allen & Unwin.

Russell, B. 1948. *Human Knowledge: Its Scope and Limits*, London: Allen & Unwin.

Russell, B. 1956a. *Logic and Knowledge: Essays 1901–1950*, R. Marsh (ed.). London: Allen & Unwin.

Russell, B. 1956b. *An Inquiry into Meaning and Truth*. London: Allen & Unwin.

Russell, B. 1959a. *My Philosophical Development*. London: Allen & Unwin.

Russell, B. 1959b. *Philosophical Essays*. London: Allen & Unwin.

Russell, B. 1972. *Russell's Logical Atomism*, D. F. Pears (ed.). London: Fontana.

Russell, B. [1918] 1985. *The Philosophy of Logical Atomism*. La Salle, IL: Open Court.

Ryle, G. 1949. *The Concept of Mind*. London: Hutchinson.

Schnieder, B. 2006a. "Troubles with Truth-making: Necessitation and Projection". *Erkenntnis* **64**: 61–74.

Schnieder, B. 2006b. "Truth-making without Truth-makers". *Synthese* 152: 21–46.

Sharvy, R. 1980. "A More General Theory of Definite Descriptions". *Philosophical Review* 89: 607–24.

Simons, P. 1981a. "A Note on Lesniewski and Free Logic". *Logique et Analyse* 24: 415–20.

Simons, P. 1981b. "Unsaturatedness". *Grazer Philosophische Studien* 14: 73–96.

Simons, P. 1981c. "Logical and Ontological Independence in the Tractatus". In *Ethics: Foundations, Problems, and Applications*, proceedings of the 5th International Wittgenstein Symposium, 25–31 August, Vienna, 464–7. Dordrecht: Reidel.

Simons, P. 1982a. "The Formalisation of Husserl's Theory of Wholes and Parts". See Smith (1982b), 113–59.

Simons, P. 1982b. "Number and Manifolds". See Smith (1982b), 160–98.

Simons, P. 1982c. "Plural Reference and Set Theory". See Smith (1982b), 199–256.

Simons, P. 1983. "A Lesniewskian Language for the Nominalistic Theory of Substance and Accident". *Topoi* 2: 99–109.

Simons, P. 1985. "The Old Problem of Complex of Fact". *Teoria* 5: 205–26.

Simons, P. 1987. *Parts: A Study in Ontology*. Oxford: Clarendon Press.

Simons, P. 1992. "Logical Atomism and its Ontological Refinement: A Defense". In *Language, Truth and Ontology*, K. Mulligan (ed.), 157–79. Dordrecht: Kluwer.

Simons, P. 2007. "The Price of Positivity: Mumford and Negatives". See Monnoyer (2007), 331–3.

Smith, B. 1978. "Essay in Formal Ontology". *Grazer Philosophische Studien* 6: 39–62.

Smith, B. 1981. "Logic, Form, and Matter". *Proceedings of the Aristotelian Society Suppl. Vol.* **55**: 47–63.

Smith, B. 1982a. "Some Formal Moments of Truth". In *Language and Ontology*, Proceedings of the 6th International Wittgenstein Symposium, Vienna, 186–90. Dordrecht: Reidel.

Smith, B. (ed.) 1982b. *Parts and Moments: Studies in Logic and Formal Ontology*. Munich: Philosophia.

Smith, B. 1999. "Truthmaker Realism". *Australasian Journal of Philosophy* **77**: 274–91.

Smith, B. & K. Mulligan 1982. "Pieces of a Theory". See Smith (1982b), 15–110.

Smith, B. & K. Mulligan 1983. "Framework for Formal Ontology". *Topoi* **2**: 73–86.

Smith, B. & J. Simon 2007. "Truthmaker Explanations". See Monnoyer (2007), 79–98.

Soames, S. 1999. *Understanding Truth*. Oxford: Oxford University Press.

Stenius, E. 1964. Wittgenstein's Tractatus. Oxford: Blackwell.

Spade, P. (trans. & ed.) 1994. *Five Texts on the Medieval Problem of Universals: Prophyry, Boethius, Abelard, Duns Scotus, Ockham*. Indianapolis, IN: Hackett.

Spinoza 1985. *Ethics*. In *The Collected Writings of Spinoza*, E. Curley (trans.). Princeton, NJ: Princeton University Press.

Sprigge, T. 1979. "Russell and Bradley on Relations". In *Bertrand Russell Memorial Volume*, G. W. Roberts (ed.). London: Allen & Unwin.

Stenius, E. 1964. *Wittgenstein's Tractatus*. Oxford: Blackwell.

Stout, G. F. 1911. "The Object of Thought and Real Being". *Proceedings of the Aristotelian Society* **XI**: 187–205.

Stout, G. F. 1923. "Are the Characteristics of Particular Things Universal or Particular?". *Proceedings of the Aristotelian Society Supp. Vol.* **3**: 95–113.

Stout, G. F. 1930. "Real Being and Being for Thought". In his *Studies in Philosophy and Psychology*, 335–52. London: Macmillan.

Strawson, P. F. 1959. *Individuals: An Essay in Descriptive Metaphysics*. London: Methuen.

Strawson, P. F. 1974. *Subject and Predicate in Logic and Grammar*. London: Methuen.

Stumpf. C. 1873. *Über den psychologischen Ursprung der Raumvorstellung*. Leipzig: Hirzel.

Sundholm, G. 1994. "Existence, Proof and Truth-Making: A Perspective on the Intuitionistic Conception of Truth". *Topoi* **13**: 117–26.

Tarski, A. 1944. "The Semantic Conception of Truth and the Foundations of Semantics". *Philosophy and Phenomenological Research* **4**: 341–75.

Twain, M. [1883] 1962. *Life on the Mississippi*. Oxford: Oxford University Press.

van Fraassen, B. 1969. "Facts and Tautological Entailments". *Journal of Philosophy* **66**: 477–86.

van Inwagen, P. 1986. *An Essay on Free Will*. Oxford: Clarendon Press.

Vendler, Z. 1967. *Linguistics in Philosophy*. Ithaca, NY: Cornell University Press.

Weyl, H. 1918. *Das Kontinuum*. Leipzig: Veit.

Whitehead, A. N. & B. Russell 1950. *Principia Mathematica*, vol. 1, 2nd edn. Cambridge: Cambridge University Press.

Williams, D. C. 1953. "The Elements of Being". *Review of Metaphysics* **6**: 1–18, 172–92.

Williams, M. 2002. "On Some Critics of Deflationism". In *What is Truth?*, R. Schantz (ed.), 146–58. Berlin: de Gruyter.

Williamson, T. 1999. "Truthmakers and the Converse Barcan Formula". *Dialectica* **53**: 253–67.

Wilson, J. C. 1926. *Statement and Inference, With Other Philosophical Papers*, 2 vols. Oxford: Clarendon Press.

Wittgenstein, L. 1922. *Tractatus Logico-Philosophicus*. London: Routledge.

Wittgenstein, L. 1972. *On Certainty*. New York: Harper & Row.

Wittgenstein, L. 1979. *Notebooks 1914–1916*. Chicago, IL: University of Chicago Press.

Wolterstorff, N. 1970. *On Universals*. Chicago, IL: University of Chicago Press.

Wright, C. 1992. *Truth and Objectivity*. Cambridge, MA: Harvard University Press.

Index

apriority 40, 57, 63, 102, 133, 203
Abelard, P. 159, 161, 162, 163, 164–74
aboutness 160, 212–13, 214
absences 15, 78–9, 111, 179–80
abstract entity 12, 72, 105
accidents 62
actual world 104, 128
actuality 88, 94, 124
Adams, R. 114
Alexander, H. G. 83
Allaire, E. 85
Alston, W. P. 31
Anderson, A. R. 86, 95, 96
Angelelli, I. 83
anti-realism 5
anti-reductionism 217, 219–20, 221–3, 225
Aristotle 62, 63, 64–5, 66, 68, 115, 172, 173
Armstrong, D. M. 2, 9, 35, 36, 155, 157, 165, 185, 197, 198, 200, 216, 219, 221
  against behaviourism and phenomenalism 3, 6, 109, 196–7
  and the correspondence theory of truth 137, 142
  and the entailment principle 25–6, 120–25, 127
  and general truths 16, 127–8, 132
  and internal relations 8, 119
  and minimal truth-makers 25, 128–32, 190
  and modal truths 16, 120, 125, 130, 186
  and negative truths 120, 132, 180
  and necessitation 17, 117, 190, 199
  and possible worlds 105, 111
  and properties 126, 162, 203, 210
  and states of affairs 53, 87, 218, 223–4
  and supervenience theories 109, 118
  and truth-bearers 10, 121–5
  and truth-maker arguments 3, 129, 142, 210
  and the truth-maker principle 17, 104, 116, 126, 137, 141, 187, 190
asymmetry 29, 118, 138, 146, 147–8, 152–4, 157, 190, 199, 229, 231, 232, 236, 247–8, 250

Austin, J. L. 39, 155, 156

Beall, J. C. 15
because 21–2, 191–3, 196, 227, 231, 235, 243, 247–8, 250
Beck, M. 52
Beebee, H. 5, 6, 9, 17, 28, 29, 155
behaviourism 6, 114, 185, 197
beliefs, vague 123
Belnap, N. 86, 95, 96
Bergmann, G. 72, 85, 165, 182, 183
Bigelow, J. 35, 87, 119, 155, 157, 198, 240
  and entailment 94–6
  and negative propositions 96, 133
  and supervenience theories 28–30, 110, 112–13, 118, 228
  and the truth-maker principle 16, 118, 141
  and the vacuity objection 32, 199
Bolzano, B. 41, 48, 57, 59
Bradley, F. H. 220, 225, 226
Bradley's regress 161, 211
Brentano, F. 63, 83, 85
bridge principles 144–52
Broad, C. D. 39, 58
Brower, J. E. 173
bundles
  of qualities 168, 175–7
  of tropes 205, 206

Campbell, K. 83, 182, 217, 219–20, 225
Caputo, S. 13, 14, 18, 19, 21, 36
categories, ontological 62–5, 203–7, 210, 212
Champeaux, W. of 167, 169
Chisholm, R. 85, 226
Clanchy, M. 167
Clark, R. 85
coherence *see* theory of truth
combinatorial nature of possibility 111
common nature 169

compresence relation 175
concepts 31, 43, 52, 126
   formal 52
conceptual priority 103
contingency restriction 91, 121
converse Barcan formula 15
correspondence *see* theory of truth
   as congruity 139–40
   as correlation 139
cosmoi 104, 105
counterfactuals 109, 196, 236
counterparts 105, 219

Daly, C. 5, 6
David, M. 8, 10, 122, 156
Davidson, D. 65, 70–71, 84, 96, 167, 183
definition, real 155
deflationism *see* theory of truth
dependence
   essential 207–9, 212
   identity 213
   necessary 208, 213
   ontological 64, 206–8
Descartes, R. 63
Dietrich, R.-A. 86
difference-makers 106
difference-making
   one-way 109–10
   principle 106, 108, 109–10, 112
   two-way 108, 110
disjunctive syllogism 96
distinctive occupant 107
diversity 170–71
Dodd, J. 5, 6, 17, 155, 156, 239, 242
   and the identity theory of truth 156, 238, 240–41
   against necessitarianism 15, 227, 229–30, 232–4
   and negative propositions 15–16, 28
   and supervenience theories 28–30, 229
   and truth-bearers 10
   and truth-maker anti-maximalism 4
   and truth-maker anti-monism 9, 240
   and the truth-maker principle 13, 249–50
Dummett, M. 68, 137, 142, 206
duplicates 219

elements of being 202–5
entailment 13, 88, 89, 94, 99, 116, 117, 199
   "appropriate" 95
   classical 95, 101, 120, 121
   principle of 25–6, 80, 91, 120–21, 127
   relevant 17, 95–6, 104
equivalence schema 125, 188, 189, 198–9
essence 19, 45, 49, 50, 201, 206, 211, 214
events 100, 123, 194, 200
   as truth-makers 10, 65
excluders 15
exemplification 211–12
existence 88, 116–17, 119, 126
explanation 21–2, 190–97, 199, 202, 236, 242
explanatory, fundamental 192, 197–8

expressibility 119

facts 174–5, 179, 191–5
   atomic 142, 158, 176
   funny 151
   negative 15, 98, 132, 180, 195
   relational 217–25
   as truth-makers 10, 65, 70, 80, 101, 125, 138–40, 147–8, 158, 210, 218
   are true propositions 194–5, 199–200, 218
   universal 98
false-makers 119–20
Findlay, J. N. 83, 84
Fine, K. 19, 51, 200, 216
Fox, J. 13, 32, 88, 141, 155, 157, 218, 225
Frege, G. 57, 59, 84, 160, 172
fundaments 64

Geach, P. T. 83
gerundial phrases 66
Goodman, N. 159, 162, 182, 226
Grossman, R. 72, 83, 219, 221
grounded
   in how things are 230, 232–4
   in whether things are 230, 232–34
grounding 43, 48–50, 56, 230–39, 243, 249–50
Guilfoy, K. 173

haecceitism 222–3, 226
Hartmann, N. 42, 57, 58
Heidegger, M. 55
Hempel, C. G. 145
Hill, C. 31
Hochberg, H. 133, 175, 182, 183, 184
Hofmann, F. 28, 30
Horgan, T. 85
Hornsby, J. 7, 241, 242–9
horse race 98–9, 100
Horwich, P. 6, 13, 16, 31, 32, 33, 103, 125, 130, 133, 236, 240
Hume, D. 63
Husserl, E. 40, 42–3, 46, 47, 48, 50, 51, 53, 55, 56, 57, 59, 64, 82, 83, 85

identity 26–7, 50
ideology 131
in virtue of see true
Incompatibility theory 120, 133
infinity 130
Ingarden, R. 47, 48, 58, 82, 84
instantiation 50, 159, 233, 246
intentional objects 122–5
intrinsicality 23, 219, 222, 223

Jackson, F. 87, 90–91, 93, 121, 127
judgements 47, 52, 53
   assertive function 52
   relational 53

Kant, I. 84, 117

Keller, S. 114
Kenny, A. 83, 85
kinds 64, 160
King, P. 173
knowledge 55–6
 metaphysical 189–91
Krikham, R. 121–2
Kripke, S. A. 35, 109
Küng, G. 83
Künne, W. 6, 7, 32, 199

Langtry, B. 219
laws of physics 191
Leibniz, G. W. 39, 41–2, 57, 83, 220, 226
Lewis, D. 98, 129, 216, 226
 against the truth-maker principle 102–5, 227, 230
 against a truth-maker theory of truth 32, 199
 and difference-making 106–9
 and negative propositions 110–11
 and possible worlds 11, 88, 104–5, 106, 111, 128, 222–3, 240
 and properties 35, 120
 and propositions 94, 128–9
 and superveniences theories 28–30, 110–14, 229, 230
liar paradox 153
Liggins, D. 5, 6
Locke, J. 63, 85, 207
logical atomism 4, 60, 177
logical constants, representation 42–3, 60, 155
logical equivalence 133
logical forms 43
Long, D. C. 83
Lowe, E. J. 10, 19, 36
Łukasiewicz, J. 101

MacBride, F. 5, 28, 30, 183
making 48, 55, 116
Marenbon, J. 161, 162, 164, 181
Martin, C. B. 2, 104, 108, 109, 111, 116, 183
Martin, C. J. 173
Marty, A. 53
Mates, B. 220
McDermott, M. 114
McTaggart, J. 39, 53–5, 58
meaning 68, 122–3, 150–51, 203
Meinong, A. 47, 51, 53, 64, 82, 84
Meinongianism 14
Mellor, D. H. 235
mereological fusions 78, 108, 221
mereology 127–8
Merricks, T. 5, 9, 10, 16, 17, 32, 36
metaphysics 115, 122, 131, 185, 218, 222, 224
modes 63, 142, 202, 207, 210, 211–12
Molnar, G. 15–16, 17, 28
moments 61, 63–5, 142
 and causal relations 72
 as objects of perception 71–4
 as truth-makers 66–7, 79

monotonicity principle 218, 221
Moore, G. E. 154, 155, 156, 158, 163, 168, 170, 174, 182, 218
Morris, M. 6
Mugnai, M. 42
Mulligan, K. 2, 36, 83, 85, 86, 116, 155, 157, 198
 and the entailment principle 25, 80
 and essences 51, 57
 and moments 61–74, 218
 and the principle of conjunctive distribution 25, 80
 and states of affairs 16, 35, 218, 219
 and truth-maker anti-monism 9, 66–71, 142
 and the truth-maker principle 104, 141
Mumford, S. 178–81

naturalism 122
necessary connections 30, 111–12, 113, 165
necessitarianism see truth-maker
 conditional 13
necessitation 116, 117, 124, 126, 168, 191, 197, 199, 228
necessity 88, 89, 201
 metaphysical 209–10
negation 178–81
negative existentials see proposition
nominalism 159, 162, 167, 172, 202–3

objection
 circularity 32, 33, 144, 155–6
 from explanatory order 34
 generality 32–3
 vacuity 32, 33, 189, 191
objectives 51
objects
 formal 48
 material 48, 85, 109, 111, 204
 simple 76
 as truth-makers 88, 92, 129
Ockham, W. 172
Ockham's razor 141
Oliver, A. 137, 142
Olson, K. 225
ontological
 "cheater" 3
 commitment 5, 131–2, 143, 160, 204, 244
 pluralism 203
 relativity 204
ontology 3, 63, 64, 82, 84–5, 124, 128, 131, 133, 142, 160, 203, 243
 no-category 205
 one-category 204–5

Parsons, J. 15, 36, 219
Parsons, T. 85
perception
 mental act of 71–2
 veridical 123
Perry, J. 96
Pfänder, A. 39, 40, 42, 44–6, 48, 49, 50–53, 55–7

phenomenalism 6, 114, 185, 196
philosophy of mind 123
Pitcher, G. 139
Plantinga, A. 11
pluralism about truth-makers 100–101
pluriverse 128
polarities 15
Politis, V. 51
population, possible world 112
possibility, mere 125
possible worlds 11–12, 94, 104, 109, 128
  semantics 96
potentiality 160
predicates 131–2
  formal ontological 202, 206
predication 159, 160, 163–6, 168, 170, 175, 203
predications, inessential 14, 228, 234, 239, 240
Priest, G. 15
principle of distinctive occupants 107, 108
Prior, A. N. 83
"proper explication" 247
properties 125, 201, 218, 246
  impure 123
  intrinsic 123, 222
  monadic 53–4
  relational 144, 202, 224, 235
  sparse 126
  uninstantiated 124–5
property of truth 31, 158, 198–9, 201
propositions 10, 49, 94, 102, 103, 116, 122–4, 126,
    138, 186, 194, 202, 214, 217, 227, 248, 250
  atomic 97, 142, 192
  as a class of worlds 106, 128
  contingent 104
  discerning 107
  Fregean 194–5
  general 16, 18, 141, 186, 198
  modal 16, 116, 125
  negative 178-181, 185, 186, 195, 198, 245
  negative existential 15, 110–12, 113
  relational 224, 226
  Russellian 194–5

"quantifying over" 131
Quine, W. V. 5, 85, 131, 133, 159, 160, 162, 181,
    182, 203–7, 231, 237, 240

Ramsey, F. P. 65, 70–71, 83, 84
Rauzy, J.-B. 42
Read, S. 14, 17, 25, 98, 99, 119, 121
realism 5, 116, 231
reductionism 217, 218, 223–5
Reinach, A. 46, 53, 82
relational difference 170
relations 163–7, 176–7, 234–5, 249–50
  asymmetric *see* asymmetry
  complex 147
  cross-categorial 116, 133
  external 220
  genuine 9

holistic 221
  internal 8, 119, 133, 219, 220
  isomorphic 9, 74, 139
  reflexive 146
  symmetric 146
Restall, G. 13, 14, 24, 25, 36, 97, 98, 104, 121, 130,
    190
restrictivism about truth-makers 99
Rodriguez-Pereyra, G. 5, 7, 8, 10, 13, 14, 15, 22,
    25, 26–7, 28, 29, 35, 36
Rosen, G. 105
Ross, G. 121
Routley, R. 96
Ruben, D.-H. 236
Russell, B. 2, 83, 96, 133, 156, 182–4, 198, 226
  and facts 158, 177, 195
  and judgements 249
  and logical-atomism 35, 67, 76, 155
  and negative propositions 178–81
  and particulars 165, 170, 175, 177
  and properties 160–62, 165, 170, 174, 177
  and propositions 59, 116, 158, 194–5
  and relations 162–4, 168–9, 218–22, 225
  and truth-makers 65–6
  and truth-making 39, 59, 116, 141, 150
Ryle, G. 117

Sachverhalt 47, 74–7, 81–2
Scheler, M. 46
Schlick, M. 55
Schnieder, B. 7, 13, 14, 18, 21, 36
Sellars, W. 159
sense-data 67
sentences
  atomic 66, 67, 68, 70
  equivalence classes of 122
  identity 69
  singular existential 69
Sharvy, R. 83
shmor 91–2
similarity 161–2, 163–4, 214, 215
Simons, P. 2, 26, 83, 84, 85, 86, 116, 133, 179, 218,
    221, 226
Smith, B. 2, 14, 17–18, 32, 82, 83, 84, 85, 86, 116
Soames, S. 103
Spade, P. 182
Spinoza, B. 83
Sprigge, T. 221
states of affairs 10, 42, 49, 52, 70, 81, 125, 127,
    130, 131, 158, 165–6, 172, 218, 223, 243, 244–5
  abundant 16
  totality 16, 211
Stenius, E. 85
Stout, G. F. 39, 172
Strawson, P. F. 83
structures, similar 139–40
Stumpf, C. 64, 85
substances 62, 63, 64–5, 202, 210
  complex 160
  essential 159

material 159
  secondary 62, 160
substrata 85, 174, 175, 178, 182–3
Sundholm, G. 55, 57, 58
supervenience *see* truth

Tarski, A. 59
Tarski-bicondtionals 66, 236
Tarski's theory of truth 60
'that'-clauses 102–3, 123–4
theory of truth
  coherence 103
  correspondence 2, 5, 6, 53–4, 59, 70, 87, 103,
    125, 137–54, 185, 217, 240
  deflationary 103, 105, 188–9
  folk 150–51, 153
  grand 103, 105
  identity 238–9
  pragmatic 103
things, as truth-makers 69
trope theory 161, 164, 167, 168, 171, 174, 205,
  207
tropes 164, 167, 168, 172, 202, 205, 218
true, in virtue of 22–3, 116, 126, 129, 189, 202,
  206, 212, 228, 235
truth 30–31, 51–4, 102–3, 215
  basic intuition about 145
  concept vs. property 31
  definition of 144, 149
  and dependence 4, 5, 6–8, 98, 103–4, 201, 231
  essence of 51
  and grounding 4, 5, 6–8, 48–50, 87, 230–39,
    243–50
  judgements aim at 46
  relation 53–4
  relative 10–11
  and semantic ascent or descent 237, 247
  and supervenience 27–30, 114, 118, 228–30
  theory of 30–31, 103, 187
  understanding of 188, 196
  values 106
truth-bearers 10, 42, 59, 121–5, 138, 186, 201,
  227, 231, 247
  primary *or* fundamental 10, 124, 199
truth-conditions 68
truth-maker principle, plural 107
truth-maker
  anti-maximalism 4
  argument 3, 129, 157, 210
  axiom 88, 215
  essentialism 219, 223, 224
  maximalism 3, 15, 27–8, 40, 57, 104, 116, 117,
    118, 208, 248
  monism 9, 89
  necessitarianism 13, 16–17, 78, 116, 117, 124,
    144
  notion of 61, 87, 115
  principle 3, 39, 43–4, 45, 55, 77, 88, 89, 104,
    105, 106, 107, 109, 111, 137–9, 148, 186, 192,
    208, 213, 217, 228

purism 3–4, 148–9
relation 13-24, 70, 77–80, 116–19, 120, 201,
  209, 212, 214
  strong 101
  theory 195, 196, 217, 218
truth-makers 9, 10, 65, 87, 91, 94, 96, 126–7,
  129, 179, 186, 227, 239, 242, 243, 248–9
  conjunctive distribution of 25, 80, 89, 95, 104
  counterintuitive 13, 14, 18, 20, 89–90, 91, 209
  disjunctive 68
  disjunctive distribution of 14, 80, 89, 91–2,
    93, 94, 95, 99, 100
  excluded 13, 15, 18
  genuine 99
  hierarchy of 243–4
  minimal 24, 67, 88–9, 121, 125, 127, 128–33,
    186, 187, 190, 219
  missing 13, 15, 18
  unnecessary 13, 15, 18, 20
truth-making
  supervaluationist 101
  the simple model of 94
truths
  contingent 91, 118, 120–21
  disjunctive 132, 141, 245
  logical 209
  necessary 90, 91, 92-93, 118, 120–21, 133,
    208–10
  purely contingent 27, 91, 121, 127
  synthetic 228, 242
  unexpressed 123

universals 62, 64–5, 159, 162–3, 201, 203, 210
  genuine 131, 142
  immanent 207
  problem of 5
unrestricted mereological composition 127,
  133

vagueness 123
van Fraassen, B. 96
van Inwagen, P. 57
Vendler, Z. 83
verification 55

Weyl, H. 82
Williams, D. C. 83
Williams, M. 133
Williamson, T. 14, 15, 17
Wilson, J. C. 83
Wittgenstein, L. 2, 55, 83, 119, 182, 200
  and the correspondence theory of truth 2
  and logical atomism 35, 42, 60, 67
  and projection 42, 49, 67
  and states of affairs *or* facts 80–82, 85, 211
  and truth-bearers 48
  and the truth-maker theory 39, 57, 59, 74–7,
    116, 121, 155, 198
Wolterstorff, N. 83
Wright, C. 199, 231, 240